Moral Philosophy from Montaigne to Kant

Moral Philosophy from Montaigne to Kant

An Anthology

VOLUME I

Edited and with introductions by

J. B. SCHNEEWIND
The Johns Hopkins University

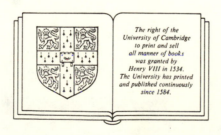

The right of the
University of Cambridge
to print and sell
all manner of books
was granted by
Henry VIII in 1534.
The University has printed
and published continuously
since 1584.

CAMBRIDGE UNIVERSITY PRESS

Cambridge

New York   Port Chester   Melbourne   Sydney

Published by the Press Syndicate of the University of Cambridge
The Pitt Building, Trumpington Street, Cambridge CB2 1RP
40 West 20th Street, New York, NY 10011, USA
10 Stamford Road, Oakleigh, Melbourne 3166, Australia

© Cambridge University Press 1990

First published 1990

Printed in the United States of America

Library of Congress Cataloging-in-Publication Data
Moral philosophy from Montaigne to Kant: an anthology / edited and
with introductions by J.B. Schneewind.
p. cm.
Includes bibliographical references.
ISBN 0-521-35361-0 (v. 1) – ISBN 0-521-35875-2 (pbk.:
v. 1) – ISBN 0-521-35362-9 (v. 2)
(U.S.). – ISBN 0-521-35876-0 (pbk.: v. 2)
1. Ethics, Modern.   I. Schneewind, J. B. (Jerome B.), 1930–
BJ301.M67   1990
170 – dc20   89-48061
CIP

British Library Cataloging in Publication applied for

ISBN 0-521-35361-0 hardback
ISBN 0-521-35875-2 paperback

Contents

PROLEGOMENA: SOME QUESTIONS RAISED

Contents

PART I. REWORKING NATURAL LAW

PART II. INTELLECT AND MORALITY

Preface

This anthology grew out of the frustration I came increasingly to feel because of the unavailability of texts I wanted to use in teaching the history of modern moral philosophy. Of course, the ethical writings of Hobbes, Butler, Hume, Bentham, and Kant are and have been regularly available, and it is easy to fill a term with discussions of their work. From time to time I taught the history of ethics doing just that. But I quickly came to realize that analysis and criticism of the arguments of these five philosophers did not give students a real picture of the development of moral philosophy in the seventeenth and eighteenth centuries. The philosophers' writings alone could not convey a sense of the alternatives already available to each of them, nor could they give the students a sense of what besides technical considerations might have motivated their authors to accept, alter, or go entirely beyond existing views. I came to think that if I did not include some of the less frequently studied writers from the period and did not get beyond critical analysis of the arguments, I could not be sure that I was not using my canonical subjects simply as starting points for discussing problems I happened to find important at the moment. And however valuable such a course might be, it would not be a course in the history of the field.

When I tried to move beyond this way of teaching, however, I was blocked by the difficulty of providing source material. There was the old anthology by L. A. Selby-Bigge, *The British Moralists,* which is sporadically in print, and there was its excellent, more recent successor with the same title, edited by D. D. Raphael, which I used many times. Each has its own drawbacks. Selby-Bigge did not aim to cover the seventeenth century, although he included a little Hobbes and some Locke and Cudworth. Raphael, more comprehensive, likewise made Hobbes his earliest writer. But I was coming to think it a mistake to treat Hobbes as the starting point of modern moral philosophy. And as I learned more about the work of the authors whom these editors included, I came to think also that both anthologists were oversimplifying in treating "the British moralists" as a proper unit of study. The British philosophers were indeed carrying on a lively and interesting conversation among themselves. But they were talking about as much to writers from across the English Channel. Although I had taken for granted the influence of British moral philosophy on France and Germany, it now began to seem to me that

the influence was reciprocal. If so, then the students needed to learn something of the Continental writers in order to understand the British discussion.
But the works of these other participants are even less accessible than those of
the British writers would be without the existing anthologies.

As I came to use more varied material in class – beginning with lengthy
assignments from Montaigne's *Essays* and only gradually getting to actual
scissors-and-paste handouts – I found that my interests were changing. Much
as I was still tempted to linger on the question of the validity of a specific
argument or the soundness of an objection, I found more and more that I
needed to trace patterns of development, the ways in which a thought introduced by one philosopher was taken up and altered by others or was dropped
altogether. I could not, indeed, understand or explain why such changes were
made unless I was clear about the philosophical strengths and weaknesses of
the earlier position, and this, of course, required critical assessment. But I
found equally that many aspects of a later position remained inexplicable until
I knew what the earlier views were from which the philosopher had actually
started his reflections. A satisfactory answer to the question "Why did he say
that?" required a philosophical story, not just a philosophical analysis. And to
be able to tell the story, I had to examine a variety of texts that were generally
ignored.

The "story" part of what I was saying took me, moreover, beyond purely
philosophical considerations into remarks about the philosophers' social, political, economic, and religious situations and about the reasons they might
have had or were known to have had for writing the kinds of things they did.
Historical considerations of this kind shed light on the general orientation of a
theory and helped the students appreciate the cultural importance of a philosopher's work. They did not, however, suffice to explain the structure and inner
workings of what the philosopher was saying. For that, philosophical discussion remained indispensable. It turned out that the different approaches to
the texts could be combined in one course, but it was a different kind of
course from the one I had initially taught.

In trying to learn enough to teach the history of ethics in this new way, I
made another discovery: that there is surprisingly little secondary literature
on many of the moral philosophers of the seventeenth and eighteenth centuries. This is particularly noticeable if one is looking for help in gaining a
historical perspective on them. Among the innumerable studies of the ethics
of Hobbes or Hume or Kant, few indeed make serious attempts to locate
them in the controversies in which they took themselves to be engaging, and
there are not even many critical studies of lesser figures – sometimes none at
all. I came to think, therefore, that an anthology of primary material might
help stimulate interest in a neglected but quite important part of the history of
philosophy. In the bibliographies I give here I have usually omitted German
and French writings; but even had I included them, many lists would have
remained very short.

The present anthology obviously contains much more material than one could teach in a term or even in a year. The excess is deliberate. It makes it possible for the instructor to give the same basic course several times while varying at least some of the readings. It also enables the instructor to assign several of the authors in each main section while lecturing on only one or two and to assign papers or ask examination questions in which the student is expected to show knowledge of more material than has been covered in class. Students will gain as much from finding out how to do a careful comparative study as from learning how to analyze in detail one philosopher's arguments. Finally, the quantity of material allows the instructor to refer to some of the less familiar philosophical works that constitute the intellectual context of the canonical great writings, knowing that the interested student can read selections from them in the course textbook.

Some of the material included here is so simple as hardly to call for assistance from an instructor, and some is quite difficult. The harder excerpts are, however, no more difficult than those we conventionally expect students to master in a survey course in the history of modern epistemology and metaphysics from Descartes to Kant. Like that course, an introductory course on the history of modern ethics would be accessible to students with little or no preparation in philosophy. The material assembled here can also be used for more advanced courses, including graduate seminars. I need hardly say that it is not suitable for intensive study of any of the individual authors represented.

To anthologize is to mutilate. The period as a whole is only partly represented, because I have not been able to include every philosophical writer who is entitled to a place. Pierre Bayle and Christian Thomasius are the omissions I regret most; readers will readily create their own lists of unfortunate absences. The individual writers suffer as well, with the mutilation more apparent in some cases than in others. The lecturer will, therefore, often need to supplement as well as to comment on what I have included, but I have tried to give enough in each case to ensure that the text presents at least the main points of each author's moral philosophy.

I hope the availability of these texts will enable the development of modern moral philosophy to find its place in the curriculum alongside the history of modern epistemology and metaphysics. The subject is at least as important, and it does not presuppose knowledge of the latter. If the biases in my story of the development of moral philosophy, and their consequences for the selections, turn out to provoke the reader to investigate the history of ethics more fully than the anthology itself makes possible, then my second hope for the book will be realized. The anthology was designed as an aid to teaching and learning. If it leads to more research in a neglected field, so much the better.

Acknowledgments

At the end of the job it is a pleasure to thank the people who helped me create this anthology. Jonathan Sinclair-Wilson first encouraged me to present a proposal for it to the Cambridge University Press. Terence Moore made important suggestions about its final form and provided thoughtful comments about many of its details. I am grateful to both of them. I thank the anonymous referee who wrote a thoroughly informed and very valuable report on a draft table of contents. My thanks also go to Knud Haakonssen, who commented on a first attempt to abridge Grotius and Pufendorf, and to Onora O'Neill, who read over the Kant selections. I am particularly indebted to Elborg Forster, who delivered an excellent translation of the selection from Nicole in what seemed like no time at all.

I am deeply indebted to Edna Ford, who transposed into the computer endless amounts of more or less unreadable seventeenth- and eighteenth-century text. Her skill is remarkable, and her willingness to tackle "just one more" – and then another – seems to be inexhaustible. Without her assistance it would have been much more difficult to make accessible many of these texts.

My greatest debt is to the students who have taken the courses out of which the anthology grew, listening patiently to my efforts to construct a sensible narrative and, in more recent years, offering their views of the usefulness of tentative selections.

Much of the work on this anthology was done during a sabbatical leave from Johns Hopkins University, whose administration in this as in many other ways has been understanding and helpful in fostering research.

Acknowledgments to publishers who granted permission to use excerpts to which they hold copyright are given in the introductions to the individual authors.

Introduction

The development of modern science from the sixteenth century onward altered the European culture that was its home, and the philosophies that arose from the effort to comprehend and to aid or halt the growth of scientific understanding have occupied a central place in our thinking and teaching ever since. A second change in European culture during this period, no less momentous, was equally intertwined with philosophy. The view people had of themselves as moral agents changed, and with it their view of their responsibilities and their possibilities. The philosophy involved in this change, resisting it or helping create and understand it, was moral philosophy. Its history has not been as carefully studied and as regularly taught as has the history of epistemology and metaphysics. Yet the problems that engaged moral philosophers during the seventeenth and eighteenth centuries have their own distinctive motivations and are at least as significant as those of epistemology and metaphysics. It is not necessary that our work on the history of modern philosophy be mainly concentrated – as it conventionally has been – on the latter issues. The history of ethics is an equally significant field of study.

Aims of the Anthology

The readings gathered in this anthology were chosen to show what the issues regarding morality were and how philosophical thought about them developed during this period. I have, of course, included the well-known philosophers to whose work we commonly trace the origins of our current problems and options in philosophical ethics: Hobbes, Butler, Hume, Bentham, Kant. I have set their writings amid selections from some of the now lesser-known writers who were their predecessors and contemporaries. The views of those who have become the canonical great thinkers emerged from protracted interchange with these writers, as well as with such writers from classical antiquity as Cicero, Seneca, and Sextus Empiricus. But reading only the famous figures is like hearing only one or two voices in a complex discussion. Unless we catch something of what the others had to say, we will not understand what the philosophical problems were or why the discussions took the turns they did. We will also fail to see just why we now understand the problems of moral philosophy as we do.

1

Many other kinds of writing about morality might have been included. Commentaries on Aristotle's *Nicomachean Ethics,* books of both Roman Catholic and Protestant casuistry,[1] political and moral tracts, polemics against theorists and their theories, exhortations to the virtuous life, demonstrations of the truth of Christianity and its morality, volumes on the way to true happiness, and popular moralizing journals like the *Spectator* and its innumerable imitations – all contributed to public debate about morality and to the changing understanding of it. An ideal anthology showing the growth of thought about morality would represent writings of all these kinds. But the ideal anthology would demand more time for the subject than most readers are likely to have.

In choosing and organizing the selections, I have had to adjust the past. One of the adjustments was necessary because the very subject of this anthology, moral philosophy, was not always understood as we understand it today. We distinguish the subject from both political theory and religious ethics, and we do not think it includes discussion of how to be successful, polite, and happy. The seventeenth- and eighteenth-century writings in which we find the material we think of as part of ethics did not generally have so narrow a focus. Rather, moral philosophy was simply the study of the whole of human action, undertaken with the hope of improving practice. In selecting material for studying the history of thought about morality, I have frequently had to be anachronistic in deciding that some parts of a book were moral philosophy and other parts were not.

I have further adjusted the past in organizing the selections topically rather than chronologically. The organization that I have imposed comes from my own view of the historical development of modern moral philosophy. Other views of its development would naturally result in somewhat different selections and in other ways of grouping them. Indeed, even in the light of my own outlook, my groupings are to some extent arbitrary. Some of the philosophers I have put in one section might have gone into another one. Hobbes, for instance, is placed among the natural lawyers, although he might have gone in with the Epicureans. I hope, however, that there is enough in these excerpts to enable to reader to judge whether my way of organizing the material is helpful and to improve on it or to ignore it where called for.

A full introduction to the readings I have assembled would require a substantial volume interpreting the course of modern moral philosophy. In the comments I prefix to each of the selections, therefore, I try only to relate the specific contribution of the writer to the kind of view he represents and to the issues he addresses. As an introduction to the readings generally, I first outline some of the earlier views of morality that formed the intellectual context within which modern moral philosophy began its course. I then explain the categories into which I have divided the moral philosophy of the period, by discussing briefly some of the themes and problems running through its development.

European Religious Controversies

Modern moral philosophy originated in the need to rethink the inherited ways in which European culture defined proper conduct and good character. There was a certain amount of general agreement about how civilized people were to behave, but there was increasing disarray in the ways in which the accepted demands on action were explained. The new natural science, by its challenge to the authority of received opinion rather than by any direct assault on religion, was slowly beginning to arouse questions. Europeans were also perplexed by the stories that travelers brought back from remote parts of the world – reports about people living peacefully and happily in ways quite different from those that were known at home. Yet neither of these sources of disquiet raised problems as difficult as those that came from within the Christian framework of Western culture.

The reformation of religion begun by Martin Luther in 1517 and carried forward by John Calvin had broken up the seeming agreement of the Western world about the truth of the Christian faith as taught by the Roman Catholic church. Many versions of the Protestants' new theology offered interpretations of the faith, and traditional Catholic teaching was reiterated and developed to answer the Reformers and to resolve new social and political problems. Demands for loyalty and service to one's sovereign were often made in the name of the truth of one or another variety of Christianity, and the savage and brutal wars that devastated Europe during much of the sixteenth and the first half of the seventeenth centuries were usually explained and justified in religious terms. Until the middle of the seventeenth century the warfare must have seemed interminable. The continuing slaughter reinforced the conclusion that the endless controversies of theologians made inescapable: that religion could no longer provide a commonly acceptable account of the ways in which we should live.

Christian visions of the virtuous life and the decent society were not the only ones available. More significant than the travelers' tales were the works of the pagan writers of classical antiquity. New editions and translations were making them more accessible to a wide readership than ever before. Stoicism and Epicureanism had long been known, and the teachings of Pyrrhonic skepticism were rediscovered during the sixteenth century as well. These philosophies were taken as doctrines concerning how to live and were understood to be more or less in competition with Christianity. It was natural for thoughtful people to ask what one was to make of all this and what bearing it had on one's behavior.

There was an evident dilemma. It was dangerous if not impossible to appeal to specifically Christian doctrine to justify proposals for settling disputes about political and social issues, because such appeals rapidly degenerated into the standard unresolvable arguments about religion. Yet for most people a wholly secular morality was not a genuine option. Christian Europe might be divided into warring factions, but it was Christian still. Open doubt about religion was rarely expressed; a declaration of atheism could be dangerous even in the later eighteenth century. For a small elite, a private life lived in terms provided by pagan writers might be acceptable, although even such views were usually "Christianized" to a greater or lesser extent. But the language of statecraft, like the language most people used in thinking of personal relations, was religious. An acceptable public morality thus would have to present itself as a reconstruction of Christian morality, however that might be understood.

A bare minimum of Christian morality would be taken in the seventeenth century as the Decalogue interpreted in the light of the summary Christ gave of the law: Love God above all else and your neighbor as yourself. (Matt. 22:37–40).[2] The teaching of Saint Paul added two dimensions to these precepts. First, he declared that knowledge of God's requirements is not restricted to those who have a written revelation of them. For "when the Gentiles, which have not the law, do by nature the things contained in the law, these, having not the law, are a law unto themselves" (Rom. 2:14).[3] At the same time Paul stressed the sinfulness of fallen man and the general decay of human nature that is its outcome. These biblical texts made it necessary for Christian theologians and moral philosophers to explain the relations between law and love and between natural awareness of what morality requires and sinful temptations to ignore that awareness. Two earlier explanations of how all these things fit together were essential to our period: those proposed by Saint Augustine and by Saint Thomas Aquinas. Augustinianism was a major source of the distinctive views of Luther and Calvin, as well as of the Catholic Jansenist movement in seventeenth-century France; Thomism shaped the positions of numerous Protestants as well as of Catholics. I offer here only the most compressed reminders of the main pertinent aspects of the two positions.

Saint Augustine and Saint Thomas

Augustine (353–430 c.e.) began by interpreting the creation in Neoplatonic terms, as the overflowing of God's infinite being into an ordered hierarchy of entities that exist or possess being in lesser degrees than God does.[4] For Augustine, being and goodness were essentially the same, so that whatever God made is good. What we take to be evil, Augustine held, is only an absence of good, an absence we notice when we see something to be less good than others of its kind or of some other kind. Things of even the least degree of being or goodness have a role and a place in declaring God's glory, and the world would be less perfect without them. Admitting that we see things as ugly, as destructive, or in other ways as suffering from defects, Augustine insisted that all of this is unavoidably part of the infinite variety that expresses God's essence. We, of course, with our limited minds, do not see this. "We cannot observe the whole design, in which these small parts, which are to us so disagreeable, fit together to make an ordered scheme of beauty."[5] And so we think that there is evil.

The one kind of evil whose existence Augustine admitted is the kind that humans do. We were created, he held, loving the good, and we were meant to pursue different things in accordance with the degree of goodness embodied in them. Because we are finite beings, we have needs and desires, and there is nothing wrong with satisfying them, nor is there anything evil about the things and actions needed for our sustenance and enjoyment. Rather, what is evil is the love that loves things more than they deserve. God, being infinitely good, is our true final end. Only in union with him can we find satisfaction and final peace. But our desires tempt us to want things regardless of their true place in the hierarchy of being. We want worldly wealth, for example, as if it were our final good. And because we were created with a free will, which enables us to choose among the various goods that are presented to us, we can choose to act for the sake of a wrong love. When we do so, we are acting evilly. The good person is one who chooses what he or she knows, through reason or faith, to be truly good; the evil person is one who chooses to follow desire even when it leads to the pursuit of overvalued ends.

Adam's decision to follow Eve rather than to obey God – to choose the lesser rather than the greater good – was not only the prototype of all bad willing; it was also the cause of a disaster to the human species. Since Adam's Fall our nature has been spoiled, and the second nature we have acquired is a sinful one. We are no longer able to choose freely between true good and merely apparent good. We are able to choose freely only to do evil, for we can no longer choose freely to do all things for the love of God. We act always for the gratification of our own desires, and even when these are relatively decent, as they were in many of the fabled pagan heroes, they still are sinful because they are the expression of the pride and self-will of their possessors. And pride – reliance on himself rather than on God – was the sin of the chief of the fallen angels, the devil.

The consequence of the Fall was that although God has let us know what he expects us to do, we do not have the moral capacity to do it, at least not as we should. No effort of ours will enable us to be what God commands us to be. We will be lost eternally if he does not aid us. And of course, through the coming of Christ, God told us that he will aid us. Augustine held that God's aid must come to us without any merit on our part. It is "prevenient," or coming before we deserve it. From our point of view, therefore, it looks arbitrary. God saves whom he will, and according to Augustine, he saves very few indeed. To those whom he saves he gives right love; they constitute the members of the City of God, and they will see him after death. The others, members of the earthly city, remain cumbered with wrong love, condemned even after death to exile from God's presence.

In his own time Augustine's position was challenged by an Irish monk named Pelagius (c. 360–431 C.E.), who denied that the Fall had ruined anyone besides Adam himself. God would not be so unjust, Pelagius believed, as to command us to do what he himself had made it impossible for us to do, and he was not so ignorant of our abilities as to misjudge them. Our freedom remains with us and, with it, the sole responsibility for our condition. We can at any time cease to live sinfully and begin to live righteously, and if we do so, we can come to deserve an eternal reward. Augustine was appalled by this view, however: It presumed that humans could make God into their debtor. It seemed to make the coming of Christ superfluous. It offended Augustine's sense of the majesty of God and the littleness of humanity, and he wrote tract after tract to refute it.[6] Augustine was a mighty dialectician and a convincing writer. Pelagianism became a heresy, but the position did not die. Indeed, some see traces of it in the highly orthodox position of Saint Thomas.

Thomas accepted the Augustinian vision of the world as a hierarchy of creatures possessing different degrees of being and goodness. His own explanation of this ordered whole was given in terms of laws and Aristotelian ends or goals natural to each kind of thing. God's eternal wisdom is contained in the eternal law, which leads each kind of thing to work for the common good as it strives to attain its own natural end. We humans are unique among the visible created beings in that we participate in the eternal law through our reason. The natural law is what results from our sharing in the divine reason, and it is what Saint Paul alluded to in his dictum about our being a law unto ourselves. The dictum, Thomas made clear, does not mean that we are independent of God's rule:

Law is present not only in the ruling principle but derivatively as well in the subject ruled. In this last manner each is a law unto himself, in so far as he enters into the plan of the governing authority. So St. Paul goes on to say that people show the work of the law written in their hearts.[7]

In addition to the natural law, which directs our striving for our natural end – earthly happiness – there is another law, the divine law, which shows us how to attain our supernatural end, union with God. The natural law is given to reason, by being imprinted in the special part of conscience that Thomas occasionally called the "synteresis," or repository of principles.[8] The divine law, however, can be known only by revelation.

For Saint Thomas, all knowledge starts with self-evident principles, and practical knowledge is no exception. The Decalogue contains some of the laws of nature but does not itself spell out the most basic axioms. They are contained in it only as its presupposed principles. Of these the first is that good is to be sought and evil avoided. This tells us that the main features of our nature are to be turned to good. Although we can come to know the laws of nature directly from the synteresis, we can explain them by seeing that they instruct beings with our nature about their proper good. Some precepts of natural law pertain to not killing and to honoring parents, for example, because as animals we all desire life and offspring. We are rational as well as animal beings, and the natural law tells us that it is for the good of such beings not only to seek the knowledge of God through which we can be united with him but also to live with others of their kind. Hence we must worship God and do whatever facilitates life in a community of rational beings. The other precepts of the Decalogue, and all the rest of the natural law, can be given similar explanations. Everyone can grasp at least the most basic principles, although only few can see everything they entail. Although all of these laws may be carried out in many different ways – as there are many ways of paying a debt or of honoring God – the basic moral precepts are always valid "because they belong of themselves to the nature of virtue."[9]

Thomas's doctrine of natural law is at heart a doctrine not of natural rights but of natural responsibilities. "The good of the part is for the good of the whole," Thomas asserted, "hence everything, by its natural appetite and love, loves its own proper good because of the common good of the whole universe, which is God."[10] The laws of nature show us what we are to do as our proper work for the common good, and other people should allow us to do those things. In this way we might have rights arising from our responsibilities in the cosmic venture. But the responsibilities come before the rights, and both belong to us only as members of a community. Only the laws of nature, and not rights as such, can place any restraints on the laws that humans can pass.

Within this vision of entities of every kind striving for their natural ends or goods and thereby working to create a common universe that declares God's glory, what place is there for sin and grace? Thomas's doctrine is too complex for adequate summary here but in outline is roughly as follows: Even Adam unfallen had need of God's grace to enable him to win salvation, and we now, damaged by his Fall, need it more. For us it is harder than it was for Adam to know our duty and to do it as we ought, from love. Yet a first grace is offered to all of us, and although it comes without our deserving it, our active participation through our natural power of free choice is required if it is to be effective within us. That power was not destroyed by the Fall, and the grace that is offered to everyone does not remove it. We can and must continue to cooperate in the acceptance of grace in order ultimately to merit salvation; and if we do so, we are cooperating in a work that does not replace our nature but restores and perfects it.[11]

Luther and Calvin

If Thomas is not a Pelagian, he at least sees us as able to contribute voluntarily to our salvation. Martin Luther (1483–1546) revolutionized Christianity as an organized institution and did so in part because he held views of our moral and religious capacities that were considerably grimmer than Thomas's. Luther accepted the belief that God had created an ordered cosmos to express his glory. He agreed that the cosmos was governed by laws, the natural laws for humanity among them. Like all his predecessors, Luther saw God as humanity's final end, and people as mistakenly and fruitlessly seeking for the highest good among earthly possessions and pleasures. But he followed Saint Augustine rather than Thomas in stressing the disorder introduced by human sin, and our inability to address it adequately by institutional actions. It was in part because Luther felt that the Catholic church was underestimating the seriousness of that disorder that he thought reform was needed.

Saint Thomas tried everywhere to remove the mystery of the Christian teaching and to make it as reasonable as possible. Luther insisted that God surpasses human understanding and that consequently his actions must often be incomprehensible. Why does a just and loving God create beings who, as he knows, will inevitably sin and thereby come to deserve eternal punishment? This question, Luther declared,

touches on the secrets of His Majesty. . . . It is not for us to inquire into these mysteries, but to adore them . . . God is He for Whose will no cause or ground may be laid down as its rule or standard; for nothing is on a level with it or above it, but it is itself the rule for all things. . . . What God wills is not right because He ought, or was bound, so to will; on the contrary, what takes place must be right, because he so wills it.[12]

Here Luther is in the company of the voluntarist thinkers who from Duns Scotus (c. 1265–1308) to William of Ockham (1285–1349) and Gabriel Biel (c. 1410–95) opposed the intellectualism of Saint Thomas and his followers. They all denied that God wills things to exist because there are independent and eternal standards of goodness or rightness to which his willing must conform. Any such standards, they thought, would impose a limit to God's omnipotence, and such limits cannot be accepted. Although they allowed that God could not contradict himself, they did not see any problem in supposing that God might have willed laws for human conduct other than those enshrined in the Decalogue. Had he done so, those other laws would now be as binding on us as the Ten Commandments currently are.[13] John Calvin agreed on this matter with Luther: God's will, he said,

is, and rightly ought to be, the cause of all things that are. For if it has any cause, something must precede it, to which it is, as it were, bound; this is unlawful to imagine. For God's will is so much the highest rule of righteousness that whatever he wills, by the very fact that he wills it, must be considered righteous.[14]

The most important way in which the sovereignty of God's will shows itself in our lives is in the distribution of salvation. Both of these Reformers held that we can do nothing to deserve God's saving grace. He chooses – arbitrarily as it must seem to us – some to be saved and most to be cut off forever from the contact with him that is our only enduring good. To ask why just these people are saved and all others damned, why so few are saved and so many lost, is to display the pride characteristic of our fallen condition.

Like Saint Augustine, Luther and Calvin saw unredeemed humanity as utterly selfish. The sinner, Luther observed,

does not seek God. . . . he seeks his own riches, and glory and works, and wisdom, and power, and sovereignty in everything, and wants to enjoy it in peace. If anyone stands in his way . . . he is moved with the same perverted desire that moves him to seek them, and is outraged and furious with his opponent. He can no more restrain his fury than he can stop his self-seeking.[15]

Although Luther takes us to be free on one level – we can control much of our publicly observable behavior such as eating or accepting an offer of help – we are not inwardly free to reject our selfish motives and act from loving ones. Only grace enables us to do that, and grace comes only to the few. The saved must live in society with those who are not saved, and the latter would be like wild savage beasts[16] if they were not restrained by laws and magistrates with power to enforce them. Hence there is justification for earthly power and earthly law, and earthly law must conform to God's laws for humankind. But God's laws have a function more important than that of showing how the wicked must be constrained so that people can live in peaceful societies.

The first function of the law – Luther is thinking of the Ten Command-ments – is to show us that without God's aid we are hopelessly sinful and weak. It shows us what we ought to do, or what it would be good to do, in order to show us first of all that we cannot do what it directs.

Although the commandments teach things that are good, the things taught are not done as soon as they are taught, for the commandments show us what we ought to do but do not give us the power to do it. They are intended to teach man to know himself, that through them he may recognize his inability to do good and may despair of his own ability.[17]

This view of the old or Mosaic law was anticipated by Saint Thomas. The new law, he stated, is the law of grace. It could only function after man had been "left to himself under the state of the Old Law," which taught him to "realize his weakness, and acknowledge his need of grace."[18] Luther was far more emphatic:

The law is . . . to reveal unto a man his sin, his blindness, his misery, his impiety, ignorance, hatred and contempt of God, death, hell, the judgment and deserved wrath of God. . . . This . . . is the proper and principal use of the law . . . and also the most necessary. . . . For as long as the opinion of righteousness abideth in man, so long there abideth also in him incomprehensible pride, presumption, security, hatred of God, contempt of his grace and mercy.[19]

Calvin agreed that the first use of the law was to strike down pride and presumption and to convict us of our sinfulness by increasing our transgres-sions. He, along with Luther, saw the law's second use as restraining the wicked, through threats of punishment. And Calvin added a third use, which Luther did not admit: "The Lord instructs by their reading of [the law] those whom he inwardly instills with a readiness to obey." He took Saint Paul's dictum in Romans 2:14–15 to be saying that we understand the laws needed for sociable living – the precepts of the second table of the Decalogue – better than we do the precepts of the first table ordering our relations with God. Reason alone can hardly grasp the latter, and even with the former, Calvin insisted, we persistently fail to see everything that is required. Without divine assistance we would be not only unable to act in the appropriate loving spirit but also ignorant of much that we should do.[20]

Luther and Calvin divided human concerns into the worldly and the other-worldly.[21] The scope of the former was whatever pertains to peaceable social life on earth; and of the latter, all that affects our attainment of salvation. For the most part our worldly affairs are matters of the way we act and usually not matters of the spirit in which we act. According to the Reformers we are able to develop habits of acting in ways that conform to the requirements of law, but our sinful nature would not permit us, without divine assistance, to go beyond that to genuine loving motives. In all our worldly affairs we need to be ruled by the magistrate; and in all our other-worldly ones, by God. There is no realm in which we govern ourselves both inwardly and outwardly. We do not have the capacity to do so.

Stoicism and Epicureanism

Along with their Christian heritage – however it was to be interpreted – educated Europeans of the seventeenth and eighteenth centuries knew a good deal of the culture of classical antiquity. Aristotle was still a presence, although the acceptance of many of his views by Catholic theologians made him suspect in the minds of some (though not all) Protestants, and the new science had done much to shake his authority generally. Plato, despite the efforts of Renaissance scholars and admirers, was not as widely read or taught as Aristotle was. And in the development of moral thought neither of them was as significant as Cicero and Seneca were.[22] These Roman writers were far more universally read and did more to provide the topics and starting points for discussions of morals in the seventeenth and eighteenth centuries than did either Plato or Aristotle. Not everyone studied Greek, but everyone learned Latin: What Cicero and Seneca had written for grave Roman gentlemen was taught as lessons for schoolchildren and was not forgotten.[23]

Neither Cicero (106–43 B.C.E.) nor Seneca (4 B.C.D.–65 C.E.) was a philosopher of any originality; in all their writings they drew heavily on the work of earlier Greek philosophers. They wrote consolatory or exhortative essays on topics to which a "philosophical attitude" – a vaguely Stoic refusal to feel distressed by the difficulties of life – was appropriate. Among other things they reflected on old age, death, pain, grief, the shortness of life, and the loss of friends. They examined more thoroughly special points of personal life and politics. For example, Cicero's essay on friendship explores not only one's duties to one's friends but also the limits a virtuous man will place on what one friend will do for another. Seneca explained the importance of the virtue of clemency for rulers as a means of remaining loved by their subjects. Seneca also wrote a lengthy treatise, *De beneficiis,* on the importance of generosity or liberality and gratitude in holding society together. He discussed the importance for one's character of a genuine concern for the well-being of one's beneficiary, the proprieties of giving (to whom should one give? from whom may one receive?), the difference between what is truly given and what can be demanded by law, the ways in which everyone in society – slaves as well as free men – must be involved in exchanges of benefits, and many related subjects. In these essays Cicero and Seneca are moralists rather than moral philosophers. They advise and exhort, but although they refer to theories, they do not systematically expound or argue for them.

It was Cicero rather than Seneca who served as the major transmitter of the ancients' philosophical ethics to the modern world. His long philosophical writings (composed in the last two or three years of his life) are devoted to bringing the main Greek theories to the attention of the Romans and to giving Cicero's own assessment of them. In order to summarize the Greek philosophers, Cicero had to invent or assign Latin words to carry the meanings of their technical terms. By doing so he became the originator of much of the Latin vocabulary for moral philosophy which during our period had to be translated into various vernaculars. His *De finibus bonorum et malorum,* concerning our ultimate ends or goods, is a dialogue in which Cicero had a number of figures, drawn from life, debate the merits of different moral theories. In *De officiis,* concerning our duties, Cicero presented a fairly comprehensive outline of what he took to be our main obligations and responsibilities and how they are related to our own good and that of others. Through these works in particular, the systematic ethical theories of pagan antiquity found their way into the thinking of the period that concerns us.

Cicero devoted one of his philosophical works, *De natura deorum,* to a discussion of the gods, arguments for their existence, and an investigation of their connection with human affairs. In his two main treatises on ethics, although he occasionally mentions the deities, there is no thought that their wishes or commands are especially relevant to morality. To those raised in a Christian culture, particularly in a Protestant culture that encouraged intense concern about the individual's daily relations with a single deity, the absence of reference to divine will or divine punishments and rewards would necessarily stand out. But Cicero assumed that reasonable people, with no resources other than their own intelligence, could come up with generally acceptable answers to questions about how to live and what to do. The only sources of authority, for Cicero as for the interlocutors in his dialogues, are men who may be recognized as wiser than the speakers themselves but who are different in no other way. Their claims to wisdom are always open to challenge. The speakers' own experience of life and their reflections on it are all that is available and all that is needed to construct a morally acceptable way of living.

Cicero presented himself and the participants in his discussions as agreeing that the part of philosophy that matters most is ethics, rather than logic or physics, which were the other conventionally accepted divisions of the subject. Ethics is the study of how to attain the good life, and the good life, it is agreed, must be a life with which its possessor is happy or contented, a life that suffices. The principal question, then, is, What sort of life gives us that outcome?

The followers of Epicurus say that the chief good is pleasure. We are urged to seek it by nature, as is shown by the fact that we voluntarily undergo something painful only because we expect a greater pleasure for ourselves as a result. The greatest pleasure comes not from sensuous enjoyment or animal gratification but from the absence of pain. This is itself the most reliable and enduring pleasure and is therefore what the wise man seeks. Wisdom teaches us how to attain it; temperance gives us a pleasing harmony within the soul; courage keeps us free from fear of death and other perturbations; and our own justice not only keeps us from harming others but also assures us of tranquillity because the just man knows that others will have no cause to harm him, whereas the unjust man must always be fearful that his wrong actions will become known and make him subject to reprisal. All the virtues are therefore valuable as means to the tranquil and enjoyable condition that is the highest good.

Stoics, in direct opposition to Epicureans, saw the honorable or virtuous life as itself the good life. The *honestum* they defined as "that which, though devoid of all utility [*utilitatem*] can justly be commended in and for itself, apart from any reward or profit."[24] The life of *honestas* springs not from our desires but from reason, which separates us from the beasts, makes us sociable, and enables us to lift ourselves above the blows of fortune so that we can achieve a good that cannot be taken from us. Reason makes us wish to contemplate truth and so leads us to wisdom; it keeps us truthful in all things and thereby renders us just; it is intrinsically superior to all other things and hence makes us courageous; and in ordering these aspects of virtue – of *honestum* – it generates temperance. The virtues are simply aspects of the life worth living for its own sake, and we need no ulterior motive for striving for them.

Cicero, plainly more sympathetic to the Stoic than to the Epicurean outlook, presented many objections to the latter. But he asked whether the Stoics were not excessive in claiming to be wholly independent of external goods and in holding that there was no intermediate condition between being a perfect sage, indifferent to all feeling, and being a complete fool. Although the later Stoics were prepared to emend the system so as to grant that there are some natural goods that even wise people may enjoy and some proper actions that even those who are not sages can do,[25] Cicero allowed himself to enter the dialogue expounding a different view. It is one that he traced back to the "ancients" – the Peripatetics and the Old Academy – who, admitting that reason is the highest part of man, reminded us that it is not the only part. Hence, although a life of virtue is surely part of our end, it cannot be the whole of it. The satisfaction of the natural desires must be allowed as well if our good is to be the good for the whole person.[26]

Other variations on these themes were pursued, and Cicero ended the dialogues without claiming to have obtained a conclusive result. In the *De officiis* he was more assertive. Adopting an essentially Stoic position, he told his young son, to whom he was writing, that the good offices we must perform if we would be morally worthy fall into the four traditional categories of wisdom, justice, courage, and temperance. The *honestum,* Cicero explained, is concerned either with the full perception and intelligent development of the true; or with the conservation of organized society, with rendering every man his due and with the faithful discharge of obligations assumed [*rerum contractarum*]; or with the greatness and strength of a noble and invincible spirit; or with the orderliness and moderation of everything that is said and done.[27]

In Cicero's elaboration of the various more specific duties that fall under these four traditional headings, two points in particular stand out. One is his insistence that both justice and beneficence or liberality are needed to hold society together and that both are indispensable aspects of individual virtue.[28] Justice involves, first, doing no harm to others and, then, keeping one's promises. Liberality takes one beyond this and aids others. In being generous, however, one must respect the bounds set by justice and also consider whether the objects of one's bounty are deserving of it.[29] The second point is that although Cicero stressed throughout *De officiis* the importance of *honestas,* he held that what is virtuous (*honeste*) must always coincide with what is useful (*utile*). The notion of what is expedient, he explained, had been perverted to such a point that "separating moral rectitude from expediency [*honestatem ab utilitate*], it is accepted that a thing may be morally right without being expedient. No more pernicious doctrine than this could be introduced into human life."[30] Both of these teachings were to have long lives.

Skepticism

One other school of philosophy from classical antiquity came to be of great importance during the sixteenth century and attracted followers well beyond then: the skeptical school.[31] The most influential version of skepticism, which claimed Pyrrho (c. 360–270 B.C.E.) as its founder, became available to Europe when a new edition of Sextus Empiricus's *Outlines of Pyrrhonism* was published in 1562. Sextus was a reporter of the doctrines of others rather than a philosopher himself, but he gave a full report, thereby preserving views that otherwise would have been lost to us. Some skeptics taught that although we cannot attain knowledge, some opinions are more probable than others are, and so we should seek the more probable view and live accordingly. The Pyrrhonic skepticism that Sextus presented was more radical. According to him, these skeptics held that for every way in which things appear to be to one person, there is someone at some time to whom they have appeared to be different. To each person the way things appear is utterly convincing: how are we to choose between differing appearances? In order to do so reasonably, we would need a criterion for telling true appearances from false. But for any proposition that anyone has taken to be the right criterion, there is a different and opposed proposition that has seemed the right criterion to someone else. And to choose between these we would need yet another criterion.

Consistent Pyrrhonic skeptics did not teach that we never know anything, nor did they say that we ought to refuse to believe anything. But each time they found an appearance convincing, they would find another, opposed appearance that was equally so; and because the two canceled out each other, they found themselves with no beliefs. The skeptical writings consisted largely of arguments to show that a belief of any sort could be counterposed with a conflicting belief of the same sort. Reading their work, the skeptical philosophers thought, would induce suspension of belief. And suspension of belief, the reader would find, brought in its wake the kind of tranquillity and satisfaction with life that the Epicurean and the Stoic sought in vain. One would no longer be convinced that what appears good really is so. One could consequently be indifferent to attaining it or failing to attain it. One would still be moved by natural impulses to eat, or to avoid danger, or to propagate. But one would not do so in the belief that these activities brought good. One would simply be the vehicle of one's impulses, maintaining all the while an indifference to the outcome of one's behavior.

Thus skepticism, like its rivals, was a way of life. It was, to be sure, a way of life that could, so to speak, only be backed into. It could not be pursued out of the belief that it was the best way of life. But it had the same kind of appeal as did the more positive approaches of the other classical views, and much of the skeptics' argumentation was directed against the claims to knowledge that both Epicureans and Stoics had to make if their teaching was to be viable.

The Classical Republic

The historians of classical antiquity, as well as its theorists of the good life, provided resources for the thought of the seventeenth and eighteenth centuries and thereby contributed indirectly to the development of modern moral philosophy. Machiavelli,[32] widely feared and condemned as the devilish teacher of a radical amoralism regarding politics, drew on his understanding of Roman history to offer advice about how a political society could best struggle against the adversities that fortune is bound to send its way. He believed that under the right circumstances a republican form of government would give a society the strength it needed to defend itself against external aggression and the ability to become a successful aggressor itself. The key to successful government was the citizens' active participation in the tasks of ruling and their willingness to take turns ruling and being ruled. Machiavelli did not think everyone, not even every adult male, was called on to do the same things. Rather, he accepted a realistic distinction between nobles and populace and assigned different functions to each group.

If the republic is to survive, some people must be willing and able to lead and to fight for their society. Only those could do so who had sufficient wealth to afford the costs of arms, the training to use them, and the time required for governing and fighting. These noblemen would be the natural rulers, chosen in rotation by the populace and submitting their political decisions to the populace for approval. The nobles would naturally tend to try to aggrandize themselves at the expense of the populace and of other nobles not actually in office. The populace, under the right conditions, would be wise enough to prevent all such moves, which would threaten their own liberty. But the populace would not be wise enough to lead in wartime or to devise the various possible strategies the republic might use in coping with its internal difficulties and its external enemies, which the learning and experience of the nobles would, ideally, enable them to do.

For the republic to turn to advantage the inevitable tensions between nobles and populace and to survive despite them and the attacks of enemies, the essential condition, Machiavelli held, was that its citizens possess the proper character. He used the term *virtù* for this, and there has been considerable debate about what he meant by it. He did not mean simply "virtue" in any moralistic sense. On the contrary: he meant roughly the wholehearted willingness as well as the ability to do whatever is needed for the good of the republic. In its leaders this is a readiness to do things most people would think immoral, such as murdering a subordinate who is alienating the populace. To the populace as well as the leaders, it means dedication to the common good. Such dedication usually shows itself in the commonly recognized virtues, but not always. It leads one to care little for material prosperity – Machiavelli admired those Roman heroes who farmed their own small plots when they were not leading great armies to victory – and it means that the populace as well as the nobles find their own well-being in the prosperity and glory of their country rather than in private enjoyments or attainments.

Machiavelli paid no attention to Christianity in his analyses of what is required to set up and maintain a successful political society. If the prince must have someone murdered, so be it: Machiavelli said nothing at all about the possible eternal damnation of his soul. The populace can be molded into the right kind of character only by means of good laws, and it takes an exceptional statesman to know what these are and to seize the fortuitous opportunity to bring them into play. But Machiavelli did not talk of laws of nature as setting the limits to what the statesman may do, nor indeed of any limits except those set by the resources that his country and its inhabitants could provide. Rome had shown, Machiavelli argued, that a republic governed by tenets such as those he was recommending could actually achieve lasting greatness, and he hoped his own Florence would do the same.

Machiavelli made a claim about what men can do without any divine guidance or divine aid. He thought it possible that we could live with one another in a society in which through participation in governing ourselves the liberty of each of us would be assured. Machiavelli's name became a byword for immorality and ruthlessness, and it seems odd to cite him as a precursor of those later theorists of morality who contended that we all are capable of moral self-governance. Yet in fact Machiavelli had followers who, without being moral philosophers themselves, nonetheless influenced those who were. For example, James Harrington (1611–77)[33] tried to show what a classical republic would look like if established in England, and the model of an ideal state sketched by Jean-Jacques Rousseau (1712–78) owed debts not only to his recollections of the Geneva of his childhood but to his knowledge of the classical republican tradition as well. Harrington and those influenced by him – among them, Shaftesbury and Hutcheson – were important to the development of the opposition of Hobbes's political and moral views in England. Rousseau was responsible for some radical changes in Kant's thought. Machiavelli would have been quite surprised at the directions in which his ideas were taken.

Montaigne's Two Attitudes

I have used selections from the *Essais* of Michel de Montaigne (1533–92) as the "Prolegomena," or preliminary readings, for this anthology because his work seems to me to be the first self-conscious and comprehensive attempt to ask the entire European heritage, What can you tell me about how to live? Montaigne is usually classified as a skeptic, and although he is much more than that, the skeptical aspect of his thought is certainly important. He declared himself a devout Catholic and submitted his judgment in matters of faith to the church, but there was nothing in the human realm, including the practices of Christians, that he did not look at afresh. Montaigne's skepticism was not skepticism of the kind Descartes invented half a century later. It was not derived from a few sweeping arguments denying foundations to all knowledge, and it could not be cured by finding a new and unshakable foundation. Rather, Montaigne's skepticism was much more Pyrrhonic. It arose from the contrarieties that Montaigne found – and delighted in – between one opinion and another, between customs in one country and those in another, between his own opinions when young and his opinions when old, and, not least, between firm declarations on the subject of how to live and vacillating practice by those who made them. If things appeared at one time or place in one way, then they appeared differently at other times and places, and who was in a position to judge which was right? Not Montaigne. He took as his motto the question, What do I know?

No theories, not even any general attitudes survived Montaigne's scrutiny, but he was not without convictions. He found no plausible opinion to counterbalance his hatred of cruelty and deceit, or his abhorrence of torture and the burning of witches. About the hideousness of these things he had no doubts. Eventually he arrived also at some firm convictions about what was, at least for him, the best way to live. He could recommend it to others as a cupbearer can recommend the wine. He had tried it, and it tasted good to him. Beyond that, however, he would not go. In public matters, Montaigne held, there is only this to be said: obey the laws of your country. They may not be good, but they are the nearest thing to stability you will ever find in this shaky world. You will try to improve on them only at the great risk of making everything worse. And if the laws bid you act in ways your private convictions make abhorrent to you? On this Montaigne was silent.

Everyone read Montaigne, and if few could fail to feel the charm of his writing, few could be content with the limited answers he gave to the questions he raised. The life of skeptical tranquillity could be available, at most, to the privileged few, and it is not clear how many of them tried to live it. Skepticism could not make much sense of the lives of those involved in the turmoil of daily life, commercial rivalry, legal struggles, the tensions of married life, international diplomacy, and trade. It was more likely to seem a threat to everything they most deeply believed than a relief from anxiety.

There was also a general fear about the effects of skepticism. Montaigne was not the only serious writer spreading such views,[34] and there was in addition a notorious literature by so-called libertines – poets and others who were freethinkers concerning God and who earned thereby a reputation (sometimes deserved) for loose living. Their prose as well as their verse was witty and readable; it won a large audience and drew a number of earnest and weighty attacks.[35] Many people regarded their work as a sign that skepticism was endangering society. If nothing but custom and the laws of the state existed to restrain us, if we could know nothing of eternal laws, would we not begin to live sensuously and selfishly, if we thought we could get away with it? If we could know of nothing outside ourselves to check us, and if we were as weak and as easily swayed by passion as the Christian tradition said we were, then there would seem to be no prop for personal virtue and nothing we could count on to enable us to sustain social order.

Although Montaigne eloquently expressed his doubt about our ability to discover how God intended us all to live, or to find in external nature a common guide to the good life, he also offered another point of view. In his late writings he revealed his confidence that we have within ourselves the capacity to develop an orderly life in accordance with demands arising from our own inner nature. Socrates showed us, Montaigne said, how much human nature can do without divine aid – how much it can do by itself. In this mood Montaigne held that we are stronger than the wretched beings he himself portrayed in his earlier, despairing essays. He suggested that we all may have the potential he saw realized in Socrates, because he eventually discovered some of it within himself. And if this is so, then we may not need to look beyond ourselves to find a source of order that would enable us to live virtuously and to form a decent and honorable society.

Montaigne thus gave voice, in varying degrees, to two attitudes toward human moral capacity. One leads us to think that we are so constituted that we can be gotten to live together decently only if there is something outside us, whether it be God or nature, that both shows us what we are to do and induces or requires us to do it. The other suggests that we are so constituted that the expression of our own nature, without external directives, will lead us to live decent private lives; and this opens the possibility, which Montaigne did not broach, that the same self-expression would enable us to constitute a morally satisfactory society.

General Problems for Moral Philosophy

Both of Montaigne's outlooks found exponents as moral philosophy developed through the seventeenth and eighteenth centuries. At one extreme it was held that we cannot learn the laws to which we must conform except through God's revelation, that only some of us are capable of knowing what those laws direct, so that the many must be instructed by the few, and that we must be brought to obey them by threats of punishment for failing to do so. At the other extreme there emerged the view that morality is itself a creation or projection of our inmost nature and that consequently we are naturally both aware of what it tells us to do and motivated to do it. Modern moral philosophy in the two formative centuries covered by this anthology was the attempt to show where human moral capacities should be located on the scale marked out by these extremes.

We can make clearer the general issues of moral philosophy in the seventeenth and eighteenth centuries by keeping in mind three questions. First, is the moral order that is required in our behavior and our character patterned after some external source, or does it come from within us, expressing ourselves rather than requiring us to conform to a model that is authoritative for us? Second, is the knowledge or awareness of how we should behave directly available only to some among us, or is it equally available to everyone? Third, must we be induced or compelled to bring ourselves and our actions into line with the requirements of morality by some motivation arranged to bring us into compliance, or are we so constituted that we have within ourselves motives that lead us to morality without regard for external inducements?

These three questions lead to epistemological issues; yet an epistemology suitable for understanding claims to theoretical knowledge cannot alone provide the answers. Those who held that we can have virtue in our lives only by being brought into conformity with a moral order existing independently of us had, of course, to explain how we can know the values by which we are meant to live. Although they did not need to take on the whole of the skeptical challenge to human claims to knowledge, they had to remove any doubt about whether we can, even in principle, know what morality in particular requires. Moral knowledge presumably matters because people must have it in order to act decently, but everyone (or almost everyone) must act decently if social life is to be possible. So there is a problem for the epistemology of morals that does not arise in the same way for the epistemology of theoretical knowledge. If even one person at one time knows some truth, Cartesian skepticism is mistaken. Of course, if one person at one time knows a practical principle, moral skepticism is also mistaken, but that by itself would hardly allay the fears of those who thought that if skepticism spread, libertinism would be rampant and society would disintegrate. A response to skepticism about morality needed to specify, therefore, whether everyone is able to know the requirements of morality and, if not, then to indicate how the moral knowledge that some people can possess could be made effective among the others.

This leads to another matter on which theorists of morality had to move beyond epistemology as such. They had to consider the connection between the knowledge of what one ought to do and one's willingness to do it. Moral knowledge is important because it answers practical questions by showing us what to do. Theoretical knowledge may or may not move us to action, but no one ever doubted that moral knowledge is somehow supposed to influence our behavior. A full reply to the moral skeptic would have to show what it is about moral knowledge, or about us, that moves us to act at its behest. The problem of moral motivation was at least as important to the development of modern moral philosophy as was the problem of moral knowledge.

Philosophical argument was not the only determinant of answers to these questions. Luther and Calvin, following Saint Augustine, had religious reasons for attributing to us a very low degree of moral capacity. There were many who accepted something like their view and worked out a moral philosophy to accord with it. Roman Catholicism, however, did not give so negative an estimate of our ability to follow the laws written in our consciences, though it found ample room for the guidance of one's confessor. And many Protestants thought that Calvinism's low estimate of human potential, and its portrayal of God as harsh and arbitrary, was not an acceptable interpretation of their faith.

Political as well as religious concerns were duly pondered. Those who supported a strong central government would not be apt to portray everyone as having a considerable capacity for self-governance. But if they opposed the theory of the divine right of kings, they might be forced to grant to individuals sufficient moral capacity at least to make a binding contract to obey the magistrate. And if our capacity for self-mastery could take us that far, why not farther? When overtly antireligious writers eventually tried to show how a wholly secular morality is possible, their differences among themselves about how far up or down on the scale of autonomy our capacities would entitle us to be placed were due in part to their different views about what kind of politics their secular ethics should warrant.

Moral philosophy owed much of its vitality and its public recognition to the social, political, and religious forces pulling toward or away from these opposed views of the extent to which we are able to govern ourselves. Those who disagreed on these issues held remarkably similar views on many of the details of morality. No one doubted that both law and love, both justice and beneficence, had to be incorporated into any acceptable system of morality. No one thought that ruthless and overt self-seeking could be allowed, or defiance of the laws of the land encouraged. There were indeed disagreements about more specific important issues, such as whether or not slavery is permissible or whether there are limits to the sanctity of private property. But these differences were small in comparison with the extent of agreement. No one doubted that there ought to be general respect for property, fidelity to promises, truthfulness, honoring of contracts, supremacy of the husband within the family, obedience to parents, avoidance of offensive and arrogant behavior, and charity to those needier than oneself. Moral philosophers tried to connect these undoubted requirements with their understanding of morality as a whole and of ourselves as moral agents. In so doing they sometimes proposed revisions of accepted morality, but it was not these suggested alterations that gave their work its importance.

The importance of moral philosophy, furthermore, was not dependent on its ability to provide epistemologically indubitable foundations for moral principles. The philosophers often promised such foundations, but although some were more convincing than others, no one came up with an uncontestable theory. If their work nonetheless attracted attention, it was, I suggest, because it served another purpose, which, briefly, is as follows:

Human beings may not be swayed a great deal by purely rational argument, but human identity requires a vocabulary, and a coherent vocabulary involves a coherent outlook. In everything beyond the most elementary physical and biological life, we can be only what we can think and say we are. If we are to think of ourselves in more than sectarian or local terms, we need a view that enables us to explain who and what we are in addition to being members of some special group, and how this aspect of our identity enables and requires us to act. Every culture provides such modes of understanding and explaining ourselves. But when circumstances change drastically, old modes of self-understanding may become too cumbersome, too much weighed down by outmoded assumptions, too much out of kilter with the problems people face. Then a new way of looking at things may simply strike people as better, even if it has not been "proved" in any strong sense. The moral philosophy of the seventeenth and eighteenth centuries was that culture's attempt to articulate the merits and drawbacks of old modes of self-understanding and to invent and assess possible new ones.

For centuries the theologians of Christianity had been expected to perform the cultural task of restating and improving the comprehensive doctrine from which a common moral vocabulary was drawn to provide a shared self-understanding. In the seventeenth and eighteenth centuries clerical thinkers were joined, usually to their dismay, by nonclerical philosophers who took it upon themselves to provide comprehensive views that would improve on the ideas of the theologians – or that even would replace them. Religious, political, social, and economic changes increasingly forced philosophers to face the question of the extent to which human beings are capable of moral self-governance. The development of moral philosophy in our period is best understood by seeing the complex problem of autonomy at its core. This, at least, is the assumption on which I have assembled the readings in this anthology.

I have divided the moral philosophers of the seventeenth and eighteenth centuries into four categories: those who reworked ideas of natural law, those who appealed basically to knowledge of the good to structure morality, those who saw self-interested motivation as the key to moral order, and those who with increasing clarity argued for moral autonomy. The categories are built around philosophical differences of view that I shall explain briefly. Chronology is not, however, wholly ignored. Within each of the four categories it is respected, and the order of the categories reflects chronology as well. All of the natural law writers presented here immediately after Montaigne are seventeenth-century thinkers. Those whom I have placed in the next two divisions, the rationalists and the egoists, come from the eighteenth as well as the seventeenth century, and the section on the egoists ends with the most influential of late eighteenth-century representatives of this line of thought, Jeremy Bentham. All of the writers in the fourth division are eighteenth-century philosophers, and the section ends with two – Thomas Reid and Immanuel Kant – from the latter part of the century whose work profoundly influenced the following century. The actual sequence of philosophical change is thus roughly mirrored in the topical divisions.

Any attempt to divide into tidy groupings as diverse an assemblage of philosophers as I have collected here is bound to involve some simplification. But if there is some artifice in the divisions I use, there are also some grounds for them in the writings that they include. I shall explain these in the following four sections.

Reworking Natural Law

In Part I, "Reworking Natural Law," I have brought together writers who have a common ancestry in the Stoic and Christian traditions synthesized by Saint Thomas. Although their differences from one another are considerable, there are two reasons for considering them as a group. One is historical. During the later seventeenth century and the eighteenth century, these writers were usually considered to constitute a group. Pufendorf, the most widely read of these theorists, and undoubtedly the most widely read of anyone who wrote on moral philosophy during the entire period, claimed that he was Grotius's successor and that Hobbes was the great intervening figure. This self-portrayal was accepted by a number of historians of natural law theory and became the prevailing view of the past.[36]

The second reason is more systematic. All the natural law writers stressed our need to cooperate with one another in creating and preserving a decent society that will provide us with the things we need and the security to enjoy them. They also held that we are by nature strongly and unalterably moved to seek our own good. Competition and controversy are therefore inevitable and cannot be eliminated even in a well-organized society. Our unsocial sociability therefore requires the control of laws imposing obligations. And such laws, so the thinkers of this school held, are in place in the "state of nature," the condition in which people must be considered to live prior to the formation of the actual governments that are now in place. The laws of nature can therefore serve as the framework within which people can construct and evaluate various forms of social organization.

The natural law philosopher Richard Cumberland used an image that clearly reveals the problem that people have in understanding how morality functions. He attempted to explain why political authority is needed, by reminding us of

the common experience of all in those things which respect the care of a family or the building a house or the production of any other effect, to which the different services of several persons are required; where we perceive that all our labor is bestowed in vain except some command and others obey. For it is evident that the procuring the greatest good the whole society of rational beings is capable of is an effect more complicated and intricate than any of these now mentioned, and that it depends necessarily upon the concurrent assistance of everyone, by mutual services of very different kinds; and that it is therefore impossible to obtain such effect, though foreseen and designed, with certainty and steadiness, except a subordination of rational beings be established, and all obey God as the supreme and most rational agent by observing those natural laws, common to all nations, which I have explained.[37]

The natural lawyers saw the laws of nature as providing the only viable solution to an unavoidable problem: how beings with natures like ours are to succeed in living together, as we must, in ways that we all will find acceptable. They believed – the reader will see that they offered many different theories about this – that compliance with those laws would always be for the good of the individual as well as the good of society. But they did not suppose that most people most of the time could fully see that both of these goods would be achieved by means of obedience. The solution given by the laws of nature to the problem of common life is simply too complex for most people to grasp. And even if all of us equally could understand it, our primary concern with our own individual good would always tempt us to disobedience. There is only one way to obtain compliance from us: by offering sanctions. If there is a reliable threat of punishment or a promise of reward backing up the requirement that we obey the laws of nature, anyone will be able to understand it and so will be moved to act appropriately.

Through the notion of sanctions the natural lawyers explained the concept of obligation, which they took to be the most salient feature of morality. To be obligated, according to most of them, was to be given a powerful motive by someone to do something. As the civil sovereign obligates us to obey his laws through threats of punishment for disobedience, so God obligates us in a similar way to obey the laws of nature. Unlike our earthly rulers, God always aims at the common good and obligates us to act in ways that will in fact bring it about. The obligation of morality arises, then, not simply from the good that compliance will bring for humankind at large but from the good it will bring to the dutiful agent. Thus the natural lawyers agreed in seeing us as needing to be ruled by some intelligence or power external to and greater than that of the individual. Although morality suits our nature, it must nonetheless be imposed on us.

Intellect and Morality

The natural lawyers used a law-enforcement model of morality. Some of them, as the reader will see, began to attenuate it, but it remained as the animating spirit or metaphor of their thinking. Powerful opposition to this model arose among thinkers who held that its religious implications were untenable. The model allowed too little to humanity and made God too much a distant ruler rather than a loving father. The natural lawyers thereby underestimated our ability to recognize what we ought to do to bring about the common good, as well as our inner motivation to act accordingly. In Part II, "Intellect and Morality," I have assembled philosophers who tried, in different ways, to break with the law-enforcement model of the natural lawyers and to find other accounts of the laws of morality.

The natural lawyers held that we must study human nature empirically in order to learn from it the ways in which God commands us to behave. In opposition to them, the view developed that the knowledge we need is not empirical knowledge at all. Rather, it is knowledge of the eternal relations of things in the universe. It may be knowledge enabling us to compare degrees of the essential perfections of things, or knowledge of laws stating relations of fitness between things, comparable to mathematical relations, or knowledge of the necessary connections of things. The mind thus has the power to see that one kind of action is better than another, or more perfect than another, or more appropriate than another, and through these insights we learn what morality requires.

We are, moreover, capable of being moved as a result of our insights, because what we pursue when we act voluntarily is what we take to be good. It is only ignorance or error that leads us astray. When our knowledge is clear we do not need sanctions, appealing to self-interest, to move us to act virtuously. We can display the kind of love that Christ urged upon us. Knowledge of the eternal fitnesses of things, if only it is clear enough, can in effect transform us from shortsighted seekers of our own good into wise seekers of the common good.

According to this view, is there then no place for obligation? Obligation of the sort that the natural lawyers explained would always be needed for at least some people – the sinful, who willfully refuse to see where the good lies and who therefore must be controlled by sanctions – but the rudiments of a distinction began to be drawn. Perhaps the kind of obligation arising from sanctions is not really the kind that is central to morality. It is, after all, merely an external sort of obligation, and morality is an inner matter. And of the inner obligation, a definite account emerged. We are obliged, these philosophers held, to do what we believe will bring about more good or more perfection than will any other action open to us. The essential nature of things entails that different degrees of perfections are attained through different actions, and we can learn what these are. It is thus the very nature of things that obliges us morally to act in some ways and not in others. The model of laws of nature that the lawyers used is thus misleading. We are not ruled by some conscious external power who needs to induce us to obey by deliberately attaching sanctions to edicts. Instead, our innate ability to know and respond with love to the perfections inherent in the nature of things explains moral obligation quite satisfactorily. And does this kind of view not show that we are a law unto ourselves, as Saint Paul had said, in a fuller sense than the natural lawyers could allow?

According to this view, perhaps some of us approach autonomy, but not all. The rationalists did not hold that the knowledge essential to virtue is equally available to everyone. I shall quote here a passage I have included in the selections, simply to emphasize how untroubled such philosophers were about the implication of their doctrine that only an elite could possess firsthand moral knowledge. Christian Wolff, after summarizing the difficult thinking needed in order to know how to act, raised the following question:

Perhaps someone will wonder how it will go with the pursuit of good if so much is required in order to distinguish good from bad. Here it will do to respond that we are now speaking only of those who are to generate from their own reflections the rules . . . that belong to a doctrine of morals. But it is not necessary that all men be discoverers. It is enough if some among the learned devote themselves to discovery, whose findings the others can afterwards learn, which is much easier.[38]

Epicureans and Egoists

The psychology of the rationalists offered a major target for criticism. In Part III, "Epicureans and Egoists," I have assembled philosophers who worked from a different psychological view. It might have been true of humans as God first created them that they pursued whatever they took to be good, for no matter whom. But fallen humans – and surely the evidence for this is overwhelming? – look out for themselves not merely at first, as many of the rationalists would have admitted, but always. The similarity between the visions of humanity given by Augustine, Luther, Calvin, and the atheist (as he was thought to be) Hobbes suggested that this was a point on which believer and unbeliever would agree.[39] If so, the basic point about morality is quite straightforward. Each of us knows or has beliefs about what we ourselves want, and it is easy enough to let others know what that is. Our actions will be steered, of course, always and only by our knowledge or belief about what enables us to attain our aim. So the moralist who wishes to show us that we are obligated to act justly or generously to others will have to show us that such action pays. And surely it does! For we need the help of others, and we will obtain it only if we show ourselves prepared to help them; and besides (some added), it is simply enjoyable to help others. If only we each knew where our own true good was, everyone would act, out of self-interest, in ways that would in fact bring about the general good.

It is important to see that the egoists were not simply selfish thinkers seeking to excuse their unpleasant proclivities by appealing to an implausible theory. Rather, the egoists were saying that morality must accommodate our essential nature as agents. Because we are by nature unalterably self-seeking, only a morality that pays will be effective in guiding us. Theories of this kind could spring from the belief that our nature is fundamentally flawed, but they could be – and they became – affirmations of the self as it is. For the later, secular, theorists of self-interest, we are not required to repent for being what we are and to try to become something fundamentally different. Consciously or not, they repeat the burden of one of Montaigne's greatest essays.

Some of the egoists were in many ways more conventional than Montaigne was. They accepted the main commonplaces of morality. They argued, rather complacently, that with God in his heaven, all is well, because God has so arranged things that when we each act for our own (enlightened) self-interest, we are doing as much as we can for others. But some philosophers, less at ease in the world, took a different view. An unprejudiced look at society might convince one that it was not in fact in each person's own interest to act in morally acceptable ways. Society might be so structured that some were exploited by others, kept in ignorance and superstition, and thereby led to believe that nonetheless all was well. In a corrupt society, immorality and crime might be the result of accurate knowledge of one's interests. Hence some thinkers were led to conclude that if God or nature failed to arrange things so that we could find our own good in bringing about the good of others, we ourselves would have to construct a society in which this was possible.

It was no accident that Bentham's version of utilitarianism developed out of a line of thought dominated by egoistic psychology. Nor was there any incongruity in his combining an egoistic psychology with the thesis that right action always is action that aims at the greatest good for the greatest number. To enable us to do what we ought to do, Bentham held, we need to reform society. The theory that led him to this conclusion did more, he thought, than simply explain morality. It gave him a criterion by which to judge the existing situation and to make decisions about where it needed to be changed.

Psychological egoism put its exponents in a position to claim that moral order must be something we create, not something to which we merely conform, and to argue that we possess within ourselves the resources needed for this task. Even so, the egoists could not say that our moral capacities make us all completely autonomous. They were, for one thing, blocked from making this claim by the problem of access to relevant knowledge. Only enlightened self-interest can lead one to act in ways that benefit others as well as oneself, and the amount of knowledge needed for this enlightenment – an understanding of the social system so complete that we can see that each of our possible actions benefiting others will benefit us as well – is so considerable that it is hard to suppose realistically that everyone could have it. Nor, indeed, did most egoists think everyone could: they tended to share Christian Wolff's attitude. There is, moreover, another way in which psychological egoism blocks autonomy. Even an enlightened agent can be virtuous only in a well-ordered society. Otherwise, as I have noted, enlightenment must necessarily lead to vice. Virtue as the psychological egoists can understand it – action that in fact benefits others, regardless of its self-interested motive – is not ours to command; it emerges only when society evokes it.

Autonomy and Responsibility

Two kinds of interests led some philosophers to argue that we are capable of fuller or more deeply rooted autonomy than had been allowed by any of the thinkers considered thus far.

One interest was political. The idea of a classical republic, reinvigorated by Machiavelli, was the idea of a society governed by its citizens, who are able to govern themselves and others because of their dedication to the common good. The citizens are free under their laws because they themselves make the laws. What must we be like as individuals if we can have such a political system, opposed to rule by interest-driven majorities no less than to monarchical governance? The effort to answer this question initiated lines of thought that moved toward the conclusion that we must be morally autonomous.

The second interest was religious. The thought behind it was expressed as early as 1706 by Jean Barbeyrac, the scholar who translated into French Grotius, Pufendorf, and Cumberland. In the history of moral philosophy that he prefixed to his translation of Pufendorf, Barbeyrac remarked that because God had made us capable of understanding a "vast number of mathematical truths," he must surely have made us even more capable of "knowing and establishing with the same evidence the maxims of morality, in which are contained those duties he indispensably requires of us." God's goodness "will not permit us to doubt" the point, Barbeyrac stated, for how could a good deity hold us responsible for obeying laws we cannot know?[40] Implicit in the question is the assumption that we can do what we know we ought to do, and so again there was a reason for taking a less restricted view of human moral capacities than earlier thinkers had taken.

In Part IV, "Autonomy and Responsibility," I have assembled selections from the diverse group of philosophers who contributed to this rehabilitation of human nature. They were very much at odds with one another. Yet their controversies can perhaps be organized usefully around two now-familiar themes: the problem of motivation and the problem of the accessibility of awareness of what morality requires.

Two main ways of coping with the latter issue emerged during the eighteenth century. One was to deny that awareness of the requirements of morality is primarily a matter of knowing something. Instead, it was taken to be a matter of feeling. Not everyone can grasp complicated sets of rules, or the endless unfolding of the consequences of actions throughout all of society. But everyone has feelings. Feelings respond much more quickly to situations calling for action than calculation does; feelings move us to action, whereas we often are indifferent to rules or results; and through feelings we can be associated with our fellows, whereas we tend to disagree with them when we must reason and dispute. Suppose, then, that moral judgments express not knowledge of eternal laws or ontological perfections or calculable consequences but feelings of approval and disapproval that spring forth spontaneously from a special moral faculty, a moral sense existing within every human being. Will this not enable us to explain at one stroke how it is that awareness of what morality requires is equally accessible to everyone alike? The sentimentalists – as these thinkers were known to their contemporaries[41] – believed that it would, and they contended, moreover, that the feelings arising from a moral sense alone could explain the very meanings of moral terms.

In opposition to the sentimentalists, there developed a new effort to show exactly why awareness of the requirements of morality had to be understaood as a matter of knowing what one ought to do. The arguments between these two groups are still of interest, but what we should notice in particular here is that the champions of moral knowledge went out of their way to offer accounts of how that knowledge could be available to everyone alike.

Most of them claimed, in one way or another, that moral truths are simply self-evident and that they are known by "intuition" – the ability to grasp truths that cannot themselves be proved but that are the sources of any truths that can be. Everyone alike, it was assumed, has the ability to intuit; and if there are some situations in which it is difficult to see how the intuitively evident truths of morality apply, such difficulties will similarly arise for everyone. Those taking this line of thought sometimes reinterpreted conscience as the ability to grasp immediately what morality requires in each case. Others believed that intuitions are required in all knowledge and that morality is no different in this respect from geometry or the sciences or even a commonsense knowledge of physical objects.

The appeal to intuition, however, had its drawbacks, as Bentham pointed out in a scathing footnote.[42] Like the sentimentalist doctrine of the moral sense, the appeal to intuition cut off debate and served as an authoritative way to impose one's will on others. It did not – unlike the utilitarian calculus that Bentham proposed – permit rational discussion of basic moral issues. One version of the belief that morality involves distinctive moral knowledge tried to avoid this kind of objection. Immanuel Kant argued that there is a rational formula for morality capable of showing us what we ought to do and that it is so simple that anyone, even an uneducated worker, could use it. Hence he held that even without intuition there could be equal access to awareness of the requirements of morality. Wolff's instructions would not be needed.

The new views of the accessibility of awareness of morality's requirements, in turn, called for new views of motivation. All of the thinkers in Part IV were opposed to the egoistic position, with some of them, particularly Butler, mounting effective attacks on it. Human motivation is simply more complex, they held, than the egoists had realized. We have both self-interested and disinterested motives. On this basis the sentimentalists, beginning with Shaftesbury, took another important step. They held that the immediate objects of the feelings of moral approval and disapproval are themselves human motives. Assuming that it is not difficult to know either our own motives or those of others, they believed that moral feeling responds not to mere bodily motion but to whatever in the agent gives human meaning to such motions – to the passions and desires from which the agent acts. When we find ourselves or others acting from desires for the good of others, we also find ourselves approving them. To have strong and firm dispositions to act for the sake of the good of others is in fact to be virtuous. And it is happily true that having such dispositions is the surest route to enjoying life oneself. Thus virtue and interest coincide, but only if the good of others is disinterestedly pursued.

The claim that the possession of reliable benevolent motives is the core of virtue raised a number of problems. Butler argued tellingly that we have obligations other than to act benevolently in this life, such as the obligation to act justly. Hume replied by contending that even the claims of justice move us because they appeal to our concern for the good of all alike. What was at stake in this debate went beyond the important matter of the correct analysis of justice; it involved the most basic understanding of the psychology of action.

The standard view of human motivation, going back to Plato, was that insofar as we act voluntarily and rationally, we act to obtain what we believe to be the greatest good we can get. If we act otherwise, we are ignorant, or irrational, or acting out of deliberate wickedness. Locke voiced his dissent from this accepted view, asserting that we are moved not by the greatest good in prospect but by the greatest uneasiness felt at the moment of action. He did not say what this uneasiness might be. Later thinkers, Richard Price among them, argued that among the many motives capable of affecting us, one is a concern to do what we see to be right or obligatory, simply because it is so.

In one way this was not a new idea. The Stoics had held that the wise man chooses virtue for its own sake. But now the idea was disconnected from the Stoic belief that living in accordance with virtue – acting as duty requires – for its own sake constitutes the whole of the good life. Doing what we see to be right, just because we see it to be so, could be considered rational because the principles of duty are themselves rational. We might know that in doing our duty we are not bringing about the greatest good that we might, and nonetheless be acting as reason requires. And given that we have an inner motive to respond to what we see to be our duty, we can be fully autonomous in our moral lives.

Sentimentalists and cognitivists alike, then, were contending that we all are capable of being aware of what morality asks of us and that we all possess our own inner motivation to accede. They were arguing, in short, that morality comes from and expresses our own nature and is not imposed on us from without. Rationalists like Price and Reid, however – rejecting the sentimentalist claim that it is our feelings that project moral distinctions into the world – still left us complying with eternal truths whose nature and origin had not been explained. And in this compliance, they held in the end, we were still obeying God.

Jean-Jacques Rousseau was led to a bold move beyond this view, by his desire to subvert the theories of Grotius and Pufendorf. Their understanding of natural law, he believed, justified political tyranny as well as personal slavery, both of which Rousseau abhorred. He admired the classical republic, a version of which he thought he saw realized in the city of Geneva, where he had been raised. And he asked what we must be like if such a republic is to be possible. We must be fully capable of self-governance, and our lives must be self-governed at all times. Yet this need not exclude our submission to law – if the law is one we make ourselves. In a famous sentence, Rousseau asserted that "the impulse of appetite alone is slavery, and obedience to the law one has prescribed for oneself is freedom."[43] Could this view be used to understand not only politics but also individual morality, treating morality as at its core a matter of self-legislation? Rousseau did not try to work out a detailed answer. Immanuel Kant did.

Although Kant sided with the rationalists in claiming that morality must be a matter of reason, he nonetheless agreed with the sentimentalists in two respects. Like them he held that morality comes into the physical world as an expression of ourselves, but, he argued, it is constructed not by our sentiments but by our own imposition of a requirement of the rational will on our action. The law that we impose requires us to examine not the consequences of our action or the eternal perfections of things but, in line with the sentimentalists' view, our own plans of action. If our intentions pass the test the moral law requires them to pass, we may act on them; if they do not, we may not. And we can always be sure that we can do as morality requires, Kant believed, because even if we must reject intentions springing from our natural motives, the moral law will create in us a special moral motive – respect for the law – which is as universal in humankind as is awareness of the law itself.

Whether Kant succeeded in making this theory of morality coherent and plausible has been a matter of debate ever since he first published it. In any event, it is clear that his position offers an astonishingly high estimate of the extent of human moral autonomy. Kant is as far as one can get from the belief that only a few people can truly know what morality imposes on us and that all or most people must be brought to comply with it by means of sanctions.

Conclusion

At the beginning of the period covered by this anthology, the general question underlying thought about morality was something like this: how can people be taught and brought to act in ways that will make virtue and a decent society possible? By the end of the period, the question was more nearly something like this: what enables us all to be aware of what morality requires and to move ourselves to act accordingly? The second question and its assumptions are today still at the root of our inquiries concerning morals. The history of moral philosophy in the seventeenth and eighteenth centuries is the history of the transformation of the basic question of moral philosophy. It is at the same time the history of the transformation of our basic understanding of ourselves as moral agents.

Notes

1. See Albert R. Jonsen and Stephen Toulmin, *The Abuse of Casuistry* (Berkeley and Los Angeles: University of California Press, 1988).
2. From Christ's summary of the law, moral philosophers derived the widely used division of morality into duties to God, duties to self, and duties to neighbor. Another text frequently used to justify this division was Titus 2:12: "Teaching us that, denying ungodliness and worldly lusts, we should live soberly [duties to self], righteously [duties to neighbor], and godly, in this present world." Innumerable treatises and textbooks were organized along these lines, well into the nineteenth century.
3. Saint Paul's dictum was the great text authorizing and supporting the belief that there is a natural law discoverable by reason. And because in the next verse Paul explained his dictum by saying that the Gentiles "show the work of the law in their hearts, their conscience also bearing witness" (Rom. 2:15), it was generally accepted that the natural law was taught to all through the conscience. The reader will see how differently rationalists and empiricists interpreted conscience and the ability of all people to know the law.
4. Saint Augustine, *The City of God*, trans. Henry Bettenson (London: Penguin, 1972), bk. XII.2, p. 473.
5. Ibid., bk. XII.4, p. 475.
6. For a useful brief selection of texts from both Pelagius and Augustine, see Henry Bettenson, *Documents of the Christian Church* (Oxford: Oxford University Press, 1947), pp. 74–87. There is a good discussion in Peter Brown, *Augustine of Hippo* (Berkeley and Los Angeles: University of California Press, 1967), chaps. 29–31.
7. *Summa Theologiae*, Ia IIae 90.3; abbreviated hereafter as *ST*. I use the translation given in Anton Pegis, ed., *Basic Writings of St. Thomas Aquinas*, 2 vols. (New York: Random House, 1945).
8. The term is also spelled "synderesis." For a good discussion, see M. B. Crowe, *The Changing Profile of Natural Law* (The Hague: Nijhoff, 1972), pp. 123–41. Conscience involves, in addition, the ability to apply principles to cases.
9. *ST*, Ia IIae 108.3 r3.
10. *ST*, Ia IIae 109.3.
11. *ST*, Ia IIa 109–14.
12. Martin Luther, *The Bondage of the Will*, 1525, in John Dillenberger, ed., *Martin Luther* (New York: Doubleday, 1961), pp. 195–6.
13. Scotus thought God could not will that he himself not be loved, and concluded that therefore the first table of the Decalogue contained natural law in a strong sense, whereas the second table contained what is now natural law but might be otherwise. See Allan B. Wolter, *Duns Scotus on the Will and Morality* (Washington, D.C.: Catholic University of America Press, 1986), p. 277. For Biel's similar view, see Heiko A. Oberman, *The Harvest of Late Mediaeval Theology* (Cambridge, Mass.: Harvard University Press, 1963), pp. 100–2.
14. John Calvin, *Institutes of the Christian Religion*, trans. Ford Lewis Battles (London: SCM Press, 1961), III.xxiii.2, p. 949.
15. Luther, *The Bondage of the Will*, in Dillenberger, *Martin Luther*, p. 192.
16. Luther, *Secular Authority: To What Extent It Ought to Be Obeyed*, in Dillenberger, *Martin Luther*, p. 370.
17. Luther, *The Freedom of a Christian* (1520), in Dillenberger, *Martin Luther*, p. 57.
18. *ST*, Ia IIae 106.3.

19. Luther, *A Commentary on St. Paul's Epistle to the Galatians* (1531), in Dillenberger, *Martin Luther,* pp. 140–1.
20. *Institutes,* II.ii.22, pp. 280–2, and II. ii.24, pp. 283–4.
21. See Luther, *Secular Authority,* in Dillenberger, *Martin Luther,* pp. 370 ff.; Calvin, *Institutes,* II.ii.13, p. 272, and III.xix.15, p. 847.
22. For an excellent collection of philosophically relevant texts, not only from Cicero and Seneca but also from other important sources of the philosophical thought of late antiquity, see A. A. Long and D. N. Sedly, *The Hellenistic Philosophers,* vol. 1: *Translations of the Principal Sources* (Cambridge, England: Cambridge University Press, 1987). This is the best place to begin studying the ethics of the Stoics, the Epicureans, and the Skeptics.
23. Plutarch's *Moralia* was also widely read, especially after its translation into French by Amyot in 1572 and into English by Holland in 1603.
24. *De finibus,* trans. H. Rackham (Cambridge, Mass.: Harvard University Press, 1914), II.xiv, p. 133.
25. See *De finibus,* III. xv–xviii.
26. *De finibus,* IV.xiv–xv.
27. *De officiis,* trans. Walter Miller (Cambridge, Mass.: Harvard University Press, 1913), I.v, p. 16.
28. *De officiis,* I.vii, pp. 21ff.
29. *De officiis,* I.xiv–xv; see also II.xvff.
30. *De officiis,* II. iii, p. 177; also cf. III.iii, p. 279: "It is beyond question that expediency can never conflict with moral rectitude."
31. For this development, see Julia Annas and Jonathan Barnes, *The Modes of Scepticism* (Cambridge, England: Cambridge University Press, 1985); Myles Burnyeat, ed., *The Skeptical Tradition* (Berkeley and Los Angeles: University of California, 1983); and Richard Popkin, *The History of Scepticism from Erasmus to Spinoza* (Berkeley and Los Angeles: University of California Press, 1979).
32. For the best short introduction to Machiavelli, see Quentin Skinner, *Machiavelli* (Oxford: Oxford University Press, 1981). Isaiah Berlin, "The Originality of Machiavelli," in Isaiah Berlin, *Against the Current* (New York: Viking, 1980), is a brilliant essay with an extensive discussion of the literature. For classical republicanism as a historical movement, see J. G. A. Pocock, *The Machiavellian Moment* (Princeton, N.J.: Princeton University Press, 1975).
33. See J. G. A. Pocock, ed., *The Political Works of James Harrington* (Cambridge, England: Cambridge University Press, 1977).
34. Pierre Charron, author of *De la sagesse* (1601, translated into English before 1612 as *Of Wisdome*) was one of the most widely read of the others.
35. On the libertines see J. S. Spink, *French Free Thought from Gassendi to Voltaire* (London: Athlone, 1960); Leroy E. Loemker, *Struggle for Synthesis: The Seventeenth Century Background of Leibniz's Synthesis of Order and Freedom* (Cambridge, Mass.: Harvard University Press, 1972); and for a good selection of texts, Antoine Adam, *Les libertins au XVIIe siècle* (Paris: Editions Buchet/Chastel, 1964).
36. For an excellent brief discussion of this, see Richard Tuck, *Hobbes* (Oxford: Oxford University Press, 1989), pp. 92–100, which gives further references.
37. Richard Cumberland, *Treatise of the Laws of Nature,* 1672, chap. 9, §V, p. 348.
38. Wolff, *Reasonable Thoughts About the Actions of Men,* §150; see the selections in Part II of this anthology.
39. Of course the Christian thinkers held that our selfishness was a sinful result of sin, and Hobbes was careful to point out that he held no such opinion of our inevitable self-interest.
40. Jean Barbeyrac, *Prefatory Discourse,* in S. Pufendorf, *Of the Law of Nature and of Nations,* trans. B. Kennett, London, 4th ed., 1729, sec. II, p. 3.

41. Some scholars believe that Hutcheson was not a "sentimentalist" in morals but a "moral realist" and that Hume, influenced by him, resembled him in this respect. I give references to the literature on this issue in the Further Reading section for Hutcheson, in Part IV of Volume II. Historically, readers have assumed that these writers were sentimentalists. I agree with that assumption and find it appropriate to present them as such in a historical anthology.
42. See the Bentham selections in Part III of Volume II.
43. *Social Contract,* I.viii §4, in the Rousseau selections in Part IV of Volume II.

Bibliography

What follows is not intended as a full bibliography of the history of ethics. Rather, it is a list of some of the standard works on the subject, together with other books I have found useful in preparing the Introduction to this anthology. The "Further Reading" section for each philosopher is an additional bibliography.

Adam, Antoine. *Les libertins au XVIIe siècle.* Paris: Editions Buchet/Chastel, 1964.

Albee, Ernest. *A History of English Utilitarianism.* London: Allen & Unwin, 1901.

Annas, Julia, and Jonathan Barnes. *The Modes of Scepticism.* Cambridge, England: Cambridge University Press, 1985.

Berlin, Isaiah. *Against the Current.* New York: Viking, 1980.

Bettenson, Henry. *Documents of the Christian Church.* Oxford: Oxford University Press, 1947.

Bourke, V. J. *History of Ethics.* 2 vols. New York: Image Books, 1968.

Brown, Peter. *Augustine of Hippo.* Berkeley and Los Angeles: University of California Press, 1967.

Burnyeat, Myles, ed. *The Skeptical Tradition.* Berkeley and Los Angeles: University of California Press, 1983.

Cassirer, E. *The Platonic Renaissance in England.* Translated by James Pettegrove. Austin: University of Texas Press, 1953.

Crocker, Lester. *Nature and Culture: Ethical Thought in the French Enlightenment.* Baltimore: Johns Hopkins University Press, 1963.

Crowe, M. B. *The Changing Profile of Natural Law.* The Hague: Nijhoff, 1972.

Deane, Herbert A. *The Political and Social Ideas of St. Augustine.* New York: Columbia University Press, 1963.

Douglas, A. E. "Cicero the Philosopher." In T. A. Dorey, ed., *Cicero.* London: Routledge & Kegan Paul, 1965.

Forbes, Duncan. *Hume's Philosophical Politics.* Cambridge, England: Cambridge University Press, 1975.

Gierke, Otto. *Natural Law and the Theory of Society 1500 to 1800.* 2 vols. Translated by Ernest Barker. Cambridge, England: Cambridge University Press, 1934.

Haakonssen, Knud. "Natural Law and Moral Realism: The Scottish Synthesis." In M. A. Stewart, ed., *The Philosophy of the Scottish Enlightenment.* Oxford: Oxford University Press, 1989.

Hirschman, Albert O. *The Passions and the Interests.* Princeton, N.J.: Princeton University Press, 1977.

Hope, Vincent, ed. *Philosophers of the Scottish Enlightenment.* Edinburgh: Edinburgh University Press, 1984.

Ilting, Karl-Heinz. *Naturrecht und Sittlichkeit.* Stuttgart: Klett-Cotta, 1983.

Jobl, Friedrich. *Geschichte der Ethik.* 2 vols. 2nd. ed. Stuttgart, 1906.

Jonsen, Albert R., and Stephen Toulmin. *The Abuse of Casuistry.* Berkeley and Los Angeles: University of California Press, 1988.

Keohane, Nannerl O. *Philosophy and the State in France.* Princeton, N.J.: Princeton University Press, 1980.

Kirk, Kenneth E. *The Vision of God.* London: Longmans Green, 1932.

Knox, Ronald. *Enthusiasm.* Oxford: Oxford University Press, 1950.

Kors, Alan C. *D'Holbach's Coterie.* Princeton, N.J.: Princeton University Press, 1976.

Leites, Edmund, ed. *Conscience and Casuistry in Early Modern Europe.* Cambridge, England: Cambridge University Press, 1988.

Levi, Anthony. *French Moralists: The Theory of the Passions 1585–1659.* Oxford: Oxford University Press, 1964.

Loemker, Leroy E. *Struggle for Synthesis: The Seventeenth Century Background of Leibniz's Synthesis of Order and Freedom.* Cambridge, Mass.: Harvard University Press, 1972.

Long, A. A. *Hellenistic Philosophy.* 2nd ed. Berkeley and Los Angeles: University of California Press, 1986.

Long, A. A., and D. N. Sedley. *The Hellenistic Philosophers.* Vol. 1: *Translations of the Principal Sources.* Cambridge, England: Cambridge University Press, 1987.

Lovejoy, Arthur O. *Reflections on Human Nature.* Baltimore: Johns Hopkins University Press, 1961.

MacIntyre, Alasdair. *A Short History of Ethics.* New York: Macmillan, 1966.

Norton, David Fate. *David Hume, Common-Sense Moralist, Sceptical Metaphysician.* Princeton, N.J.: Princeton University Press, 1982.

Oberman, Heiko A. *The Harvest of Late Mediaeval Theology.* Cambridge, Mass.: Harvard University Press, 1963.

Passerin d'Entreves, A. *Natural Law.* London: Hutchinson, 1951.

Passmore, J. A. *Ralph Cudworth.* Cambridge, England: Cambridge University Press, 1951.

Perelman, Chaim. *Introduction historique à la philosophie morale.* Brussels: Editions de l 'Université de Bruxelles, 1980.

Pocock, J. G. A. *The Machiavellian Moment.* Princeton, N.J.: Princeton University Press, 1975.

   ed. *The Political Works of James Harrington.* Cambridge, England: Cambridge University Press, 1977.

Popkin, Richard. *The History of Scepticism from Erasmus to Spinoza.* Berkeley and Los Angeles: University of California Press, 1979.

Rommen, H. A. *The Natural Law.* Translated by Thomas R. Hanley. St. Louis: Herder, 1947.

Rupp, Gordon. *The Righteousness of God: Luther Studies.* London: Hodder & Stoughton, 1953.

Schmucker, Josef. *Die Ursprünge der Ethik Kants.* Meisenheim, West Germany: Verlag Anton Hain KG, 1961.

Schneiders, Werner. *Naturrech und Liebesethik.* Hildesheim, West Germany: Olms Verlag, 1971.

Shklar, Judith. *Montesquieu.* Oxford: Oxford University Press, 1987.

Sidgwick, Henry. *Outlines of the History of Ethics.* London: Macmillan, 1896.

Skinner, Quentin. *The Foundations of Modern Political Thought.* 2 vols. Cambridge, England: Cambridge University Press, 1978.

  Machiavelli. Oxford: Oxford University Press, 1981.

Spink, J. S. *French Free Thought from Gassendi to Voltaire.* London: Athlone, 1960.

Stephen, Sir Leslie. *History of English Thought in the Eighteenth Century.* 2 vols. London, 1876.

Tuck, Richard. *Natural Rights Theories.* Cambridge, England: Cambridge University Press, 1979.

Viner, Jacob. *The Role of Providence in the Social Order.* Princeton, N.J.: Princeton University Press, 1972.

Wendel, François. *Calvin.* Translated by Philip Mairet. London: Collins, 1963.

Wolter, Allan B. *Duns Scotus on the Will and Morality.* Washington, D.C.: Catholic University of America Press, 1986.

Wood, Neal. *Cicero's Social and Political Thought.* Berkeley and Los Angeles: University of California Press, 1988.

Wundt, Max. *Die Deutsche Schulphilosophie im Zeitalter der Aufklärung.* Hildesheim, West Germany: Olms Verlag, 1964.

Prolegomena:
Some Questions Raised

Michel de Montaigne

Introduction

Michel de Montaigne is discussed in a section of the Introduction to this anthology, and little need be added here.

He was born in 1533, in a family mansion near Bordeaux, France. His father had him educated at home, where he spoke only Latin until he was six, learning French thereafter. His family was noble and well connected. For thirteen years, from 1557 on, Montaigne served in the local parliament. He married in 1565 and a few years later, on the death of his father, became the owner of an ample estate. With leisure at his command, Montaigne left politics and devoted himself to writing, completing the first edition of his *Essais* for publication in 1580. After extensive travels he returned to become the mayor of Bordeaux, in reluctant but dutiful obedience to the king. Although Montaigne spent four years in office, he continued to work on his book, adding new essays and revising – without omitting what was already written – the earlier ones. An enlarged edition was published in 1588, but Montaigne continued revising until his death, in 1592. In good editions of Montaigne's works, the writings from the different periods are marked accordingly, with "A" indicating the earliest material, "B" the additions made in the 1588 version, and "C" the insertions made during Montaigne's last years.

The *Essais* are anything but systematic philosophy, and moral concerns are not their sole focus. If they have any central theme, it is Montaigne's project of writing his life as he lived and perceived it, suppressing nothing, altering nothing, leaving nothing untouched by his own way of articulating it. Questions about how to live and what to live for were among his interests. So was almost everything else. In the following selections I have had to ignore most of the variety of the *Essais* in order to give the reader some sense of Montaigne's way of thinking about the ethical questions that had engaged the classical moralists, which were to be dealt with in very different ways by later writers.

Montaigne adorned his writings with so many references to and quotations (or misquotations) from classical authors that he suspected, he said, that others might think he was doing no more than collecting other men's flowers. But even if his quotations add grace to his prose and indicate something of the range of his learning, they are not used to give authority to his views. In the end Montaigne tested every view against his own experience, his own reactions, and his own capacity to absorb what is said and make it truly a part of his life. He did not proselytize, but his manner of thought is contagious. Careful reading of Montaigne will not leave the reader untouched.

I have included five selections: "Of Repentance" (Book III.2) is given in its entirety.

It is preceded by parts of the longest and most skeptical of the essays, the "Apology for Raymond Sebond" (Book II.12), and followed by shorter excerpts from "Of Vanity" (Book III.9), "Of Physiognomy" (Book III.12), and "Of Experience" (Book III.13), the last of the essays. In the notes I have indicated the sources of a few of the quotations and identified some of the people to whom he referred. Because the significance of most of Montaigne's references is clear from their use in the text, it did not seem necessary to annotate each one.

The translation is by Donald Frame, reprinted from *The Complete Essays of Montaigne*, with permission of the publishers, Stanford University Press, © 1958. The translator has kept the marks indicating the edition from which the passages come and has identified the sources of quotations. He has also broken the text into paragraphs, which were not used in the original.

Apology for Raymond Sebond

. . . Yet must I see at last whether it is in the power of man to find what he seeks, and whether that quest that he has been making for so many centuries has enriched him with any new power and any solid truth.

I think he will confess to me, if he speaks in all conscience, that all the profit he has gained from so long a pursuit is to have learned to acknowledge his weakness. The ignorance that was naturally in us we have by long study confirmed and verified.

To really learned men has happened what happens to ears of wheat: they rise high and lofty, heads erect and proud, as long as they are empty; but when they are full and swollen with grain in their ripeness, they begin to grow humble and lower their horns. Similarly, men who have tried everything and sounded everything, having found in that pile of knowledge and store of so many various things nothing solid and firm, and nothing but vanity, have renounced their presumption and recognized their natural condition.

ᶜIt is what Velleius reproaches Cotta and Cicero for, that they learned from Philo that they had learned nothing.[1]

Pherecydes, one of the Seven Sages, writing to Thales as he was dying, said: "I have ordered my friends, after they have buried me, to bring you my writings. If they satisfy you and the other sages, publish them; if not, suppress them: they contain no certainty that satisfies myself. Nor do I profess to know the truth and to attain it. I uncover things more than I discover them."[2]

ᴬThe wisest man that ever was, when they asked him what he knew, answered that he knew this much, that he knew nothing.[3] He was verifying what they say, that the greatest part of what we know is the least of those parts that we do not know; that is to say that the very thing we think we know is a part, and a very small part, of our ignorance. . . .

I wish to take man in his highest estate. Let us consider him in that small number of excellent and select men who, having been endowed with fine and particular natural ability, have further strengthened and sharpened it by care, by study, and by art, and have raised it to the highest pitch ᶜof wisdom ᴬthat it can attain. They have fashioned their soul to all directions and all angles, supported and propped it with all the outside assistance that was fit for it, and enriched and adorned it with all they could borrow, for its advantage, from the inside and the outside of the world; it is in them that the utmost height of human nature is found. They have regulated the world with governments and laws; they have instructed it with arts and sciences, and instructed it further by the example of their admirable conduct.

I shall take into account only these people, their testimony, and their experience. Let us see how far they have gone and where they have halted. The infirmities and defects that we shall find in this assembly the world may well boldly acknowledge as its own.

Whoever seeks anything comes to this point: he says either that he has found it, or that it cannot be found, or that he is still in quest of it. All philosophy is divided into these three types. Its purpose is to seek out truth, knowledge, and certainty.

The Peripatetics, Epicureans, Stoics, and others thought they had found it. These established the sciences that we have, and treated them as certain knowledge.

Clitomachus, Carneades, and the Academics despaired of their quest, and judged that truth could not be conceived by our powers. The conclusion of these men was man's weakness and ignorance. This school had the greatest following and the noblest adherents.[4]

Pyrrho and other Skeptics or Epechists[5] ᶜwhose doctrines, many of the ancients maintained, were derived from Homer, the Seven Sages, Archilochus, and Euripides, and were held by Zeno, Democritus, Xenophanes – ᴬsay that they are still in search of the truth. These men judge that those who think they have found it are infinitely mistaken; and that there is also an overbold vanity in that second class that assures us that human powers are not capable of attaining it. For this matter of establishing the measure of our power, of knowing and judging the difficulty of things, is a great and supreme knowledge, of which they doubt that man is capable:

> Whoever thinks that we know nothing does not know
> Whether we know enough to say that this is so.
> Lucretius

Ignorance that knows itself, that judges itself and condemns itself, is not complete ignorance: to be that, it must be ignorant of itself. So that the profession of the Pyrrhonians is to waver, doubt, and inquire, to be sure of nothing, to answer for nothing. Of the three functions of the soul, the imaginative, the appetitive, and the consenting, they accept the first two; the last they suspend and keep it ambiguous, without inclination or approbation, however slight, in one direction or the other.

ᶜZeno pictured in a gesture his conception of this division of the faculties of the soul: the hand spread and open was appearance; the hand half shut and the fingers a little hooked, consent; the closed fist, comprehension; when with his left hand he closed his fist still tighter, knowledge.

ᴬNow this attitude of their judgment, straight and inflexible, taking all things in without adherence or consent, leads them to their Ataraxy,[6] which is a peaceful and sedate condition of life, exempt from the agitations we receive through the impression of the opinion and knowledge we think we have of things. Whence are born fear, avarice, envy, immoderate desires, ambition, pride, superstition, love of novelty, rebellion, disobedience, obstinacy, and most bodily ills. Indeed, they free themselves thereby from jealousy on behalf of their doctrine. For they dispute in a very mild manner. They do not fear contradiction in their discussion. When they say that heavy things go down, they would be very sorry to have anyone take their word for it; and they seek to be contradicted, so as to create doubt and suspension of judgment, which is their goal. They advance their propositions only to combat those they think we believe in. . . .

The Pyrrhonians have kept themselves a wonderful advantage in combat, having rid themselves of the need to cover up. It does not matter to them that they are struck, provided they strike; and they do their work with everything. If they win, your proposition is lame; if you win, theirs is. If they lose, they confirm ignorance; if you lose, you confirm it. If they prove that nothing is known, well and good; if they do not know how to prove it, just as good. ᶜ*So that, since equal reasons are found on both sides of the same subject, it may be the easier to suspend judgment on each side* [Cicero].

And they set store by the fact that they can find much more easily why a thing is false than that it is true; and what is not than what its; and what they do not believe than what they believe.

ᴬTheir expressions are: "I establish nothing; it is no more thus than thus, or than neither way; I do not understand it; the appearances are equal on all sides; it is equally legitimate to speak for and against. ᶜNothing seems true, which may not seem false." ᴬTheir sacramental word is ἐπέχω,[7] that is to say, "I hold back, I do not budge." Those are their refrains, and others of similar substance. Their effect is a pure, complete and very perfect postponement and suspension of judgment. They use their reason to inquire and debate, but not to conclude and choose. Whoever will imagine a perpetual confession of ignorance, a judgment without leaning or inclination, on any occasion whatever, he has a conception of Pyrrhonism.

I express this point of view as well as I can, because many find it difficult to conceive; and its authors themselves represent it rather obscurely and diversely. . . .

ᴬThere is nothing in man's invention that has so much verisimilitude and usefulness.[8] It presents man naked and empty, acknowledging his natural weakness, fit to receive from above some outside power; stripped of human knowledge, and all the more apt to lodge divine knowledge in himself, ᴮannihilating his judgment to make more room for faith; ᶜneither disbelieving ᴬnor setting up any doctrine ᴮagainst the common observances; humble, obedient, teachable, zealous; a sworn enemy of heresy, ᴬand consequently free from the vain and irreligious opinions introduced by the false sects. ᴮHe is a blank tablet prepared to take from the finger of God such forms as he shall be pleased to engrave on it. The more we cast ourselves back on God and commit ourselves to him, and renounce ourselves, the better we are. ᴬ"Receive things thankfully," says the Preacher, "in the aspect and taste that they are offered to thee, from day to day; the rest is beyond thy knowledge." ᶜ*The Lord knoweth the thoughts of man, that they are vanity* [Psalms].

ᴬThat is how, of three general sects of philosophy, two make express profession of doubt and ignorance; and in that of the dogmatists, which is the third, it is easy to discover that most of them have put on the mask of assurance only to look better. They have not thought so much of establishing any certainty for us as of showing us how far they had gone in this pursuit of the truth: ᶜ*which the learned suppose rather than know* [Livy]. . . .

ᴬIf nature enfolds within the bounds of her ordinary progress, like all other things, also the beliefs, judgments, and opinions of men; if they have their rotation, their season, their birth, their death, like cabbages; if heaven moves and rolls them at its will, what magisterial and permanent authority are we attributing to them? ᴮIf we feel palpably by experience that the form of our being depends on the air, the climate, and the soil where we are born – not only the complexion, the stature, the constitution and countenance, but also the faculties of the soul: ᶜ*the climate affects not only the vigor of the body, but also that of the soul,* says Vegetius – and if the goddess who founded the city of Athens chose for its situation a climate which made men prudent, as the priests of Egypt taught Solon: *the air of Athens is thin, whereby the Atticans are reputed more acute; that of Thebes is thick, wherefore the Thebans are reputed gross and solid* [Cicero]; ᴮso that just as fruits are born different, and animals, men too are born more or less bellicose, just, temperate, and docile – here subject to wine, elsewhere to theft or lechery; here inclined to superstition, elsewhere to unbelief; ᶜhere to freedom, here to servitude; ᴮcapable of one science or of one art, dull or ingenious, obedient or rebellious, good or bad, according to the influence of the place where they are situated – and take on a new disposition if you change their place, like trees; which was the reason why Cyrus would not allow the Persians to abandon their rugged and hilly country to move into another that was mild and flat, ᶜsaying that fat, soft lands make men soft, and fertile lands infertile minds; ᴮif we see flourishing now one art, one opinion, now another, by some celestial influence; such-and-such a century produce such-and-such natures, and incline the human race to such-and-such a bent; the minds of men now lusty, now lean, like our fields; what becomes of all those fine prerogatives on which we flatter ourselves? Since a wise man can be mistaken, and a hundred men, and many nations, yes, and human nature according to us is mistaken for many centuries about this or that, what assurance have we that sometimes it stops being mistaken, ᶜand that in this century it is not making a mistake?

ᴬAmong other tokens of our imbecility, it seems to me that this does not deserve to be forgotten: that even through desire, man does not know how to find what he needs; that not by enjoyment, not even by imagination and wish, can we agree about what we need for our contentment. Let our thought cut out and sew at its pleasure, it will not even be able to desire what is fit for it, Cand satisfy itself:

> BFor what by reason do we want or fear?
> What plan so happily do you conceive
> But its successful trial makes you grieve?
> 　　　　　　　　　　　　　　　　Juvenal

. . . AThere is no combat so violent among the philosophers, and so bitter, as that which arises over the question of the sovereign good of man, Cout of which, by Varro's reckoning, two hundred and eighty-eight sects were born.[9] *But he who disagrees about the supreme good, disagrees about the whole principle of philosophy* [Cicero].

> AThree guests of mine differ on what is good;
> 　Their various palates call for various food.
> What shall I serve? What not? What makes one glad,
> You don't enjoy; what you like, they find bad.
> 　　　　　　　　　　　　　　　　Horace

Nature should reply thus to their arguments and disputes.

Some say that our good lies in virtue, others in sensual pleasure, others in conforming to nature; one man in knowledge, Cone in having no pain, Aone in not letting ourselves be carried away by appearances. And this notion seems to resemble this other, Bof the ancient Pythagoras:

> AWonder at nothing: that is all I know
> To make men happy and to keep them so;
> 　　　　　　　　　　　　　　　　Horace

which is the goal of the Pyrrhonian school.

CAristotle attributes wondering at nothing to greatness of soul.[10] AAnd Arcesilaus used to say that to suspend the judgment and keep it upright and inflexible is a good thing, but to consent and incline it is a vice and a bad thing. It is true that by establishing this by a certain axiom, he was departing from Pyrrhonism. The Pyrrhonians, when they say that the sovereign good is Ataraxy, which is the immobility of the judgment, do not mean to say it in an affirmative way; but the same impulse of their soul that makes them avoid precipices and take cover in the cool of the evening, itself offers them this fancy and makes them refuse any other. . . .

AMoreover, if it is from ourselves that we derive the ruling of our conduct, into what confusion do we cast ourselves! For the most plausible advice that our reason gives us in the matter is generally for each man to obey the laws of his country, Bwhich is the advice of Socrates, inspired, he says, by divine counsel. AAnd what does reason mean by that, unless that our duty has no rule but an accidental one?

Truth must have one face, the same and universal. If man knew any rectitude and justice that had body and real existence, he would not tie it down to the condition of the customs of this country or that. It would not be from the fancy of the Persians or the Indians that virtue would take its form.

There is nothing subject to more continual agitation than the laws. Since I was born I have seen those of our neighbors the English change three or four times; not only in political matters, in which people want to dispense with constancy, but in the most important subject that can be, to wit, religion. At which I am shamed and vexed, the more so because that is a nation with which the people of my region formerly had such intimate acquaintance that there still remain in my house some traces of our old cousinship.

CAnd here at home I have seen things which were capital offenses among us become legitimate; and we who consider other things legitimate are liable, according to the uncertainty of the fortunes of war, to be one day guilty of human and divine high treason, when our justice falls into the mercy of injustice, and, after a few years of captivity, assumes a contrary character.

How could that ancient god[11] more clearly accuse human knowledge of ignorance of the divine being, and teach men that religion was only a creature of their own invention, suitable to bind their society together, than by declaring, as he did, to those who sought instruction therein at his tripod, that the true cult for each man was that which he found observed according to the practice of the place he was in?

O God, what an obligation do we not have to the benignity of our sovereign creator for having freed our belief from the folly of those vagabond and arbitrary devotions, and having based it on the eternal foundation of his holy word?

AWhat then will philosophy tell us in this our need? To follow the laws of our country – that is to say, the undulating sea of the opinions of a people or a prince, which will paint me justice in as many colors, and refashion it into as many faces, as there are changes of passion in those men? I cannot have my judgment so flexible.

What am I to make of a virtue that I saw in credit yesterday, that will be discredited tomorrow, Cand that becomes a crime on the other side of the river? What of a truth that is bounded by these mountains and is falsehood to the world that lives beyond?

ABut they are funny when, to give some certainty to the laws, they say that there are some which are firm, perpetual, and immutable, which they call natural, which are imprinted on the human race by the condition of their very being. And of those one man says the number is three, one man four, one more, one less: a sign that the mark of them is as doubtful as the rest. Now they are so unfortunate (for what else can I call it but misfortune, that out of such an infinite number of laws not even one is found that fortune Cand the heedlessness of chance Ahave allowed to be universally accepted by the consent of all nations?), they are, I say, so wretched that of these three or four selected laws there is not a single one that is not contradicted and disavowed, not by one nation but by many. Now the only likely sign by which they can argue certain laws to be natural is universality of approval. For what nature had truly ordered for us we would without doubt follow by common consent. And not only every nation, but every individual, would resent the force and violence used on him by anyone who tried to impel him to oppose that law. Let them show me just one law of that sort – I'd like to see it.

Protagoras and Aristo assigned no other essence to the justice of the laws than the authority and judgment of the lawgiver; and said that apart from that, the good and the honest lost their qualities and remained empty names of indifferent things. Thrasymachus, in Plato,[12] thinks that there is no other right than the advantage of the superior.

There is nothing in which the world is so varied as in customs and laws. A given thing is abominable here, which bring commendation elsewhere: as in Lacedaemon cleverness in stealing. Marriages between close relatives are capital offenses among us, elsewhere they are in honor:

> There are some nations, it is said,
> Where mothers sons, and fathers daughters wed;
> And thus affection grows, doubled by love.
> Ovid

The murder of infants, the murder of fathers, sharing of wives, traffic in robberies, license for all sorts of sensual pleasures, nothing in short is so extreme that it is not accepted by the usage of some nation.

ᴮIt is credible that there are natural laws, as may be seen in other creatures; but in us they are lost; that fine human reason butts in everywhere, domineering and commanding, muddling and confusing the face of things in accordance with its vanity and inconsistency. ᶜ*Nothing is ours any more; what I call ours is a product of art* [Cicero]. . . .

Finally, there is no existence that is constant, either of our being or of that of objects. And we, and our judgment, and all mortal things go on flowing and rolling unceasingly. Thus nothing certain can be established about one thing by another, both the judging and the judged being in continual change and motion.

We have no communication with being,[13] because every human nature is always midway between birth and death, offering only a dim semblance and shadow of itself, and an uncertain and feeble opinion. And if by chance you fix your thought on trying to grasp its essence, it will be neither more nor less than if someone tried to grasp water: for the more he squeezes and presses what by its nature flows all over, the more he will lose what he was trying to hold and grasp. Thus, all things being subject to pass from one change to another, reason, seeking a real stability in them, is baffled, being unable to apprehend anything stable and permanent; because everything is either coming into being and not yet fully existent, or beginning to die before it is born. . . . we must conclude that God alone *is* – not at all according to any measure of time, but according to an eternity immutable and immobile, not measured by time or subject to any decline; before whom there is nothing, nor will there be after, nor is there anything more new or more recent; but one who really is – who by one single *now* fills the *ever;* and there is nothing that really is but he alone – nor can we say "He has been," or "He will be" – without beginning and without end.

To this most religious conclusion of a pagan I want to add only this remark of a witness of the same condition,[14] for an ending to this long and boring discourse, which would give me material without end: "O what a vile and abject thing is man," he says, "if he does not raise himself above humanity!"

^CThat is a good statement and a useful desire, but equally absurd. For ^Ato make the handful bigger than the hand, the armful bigger than the arm, and to hope to straddle more than the reach of our legs; is impossible and unnatural. Nor can man raise himself above himself and humanity; for he can see only with his own eyes, and seize only with his own grasp.

He will rise, if God by exception lends him a hand; he will rise by abandoning and renouncing his own means, and letting himself be raised and uplifted by purely celestial means.

^CIt is for our Christian faith, not for his Stoical virtue, to aspire to that divine and miraculous metamorphosis.

Of Repentance

^BOthers form man; I tell of him, and portray a particular one, very ill-formed, whom I should really make very different from what he is if I had to fashion him over again. But now it is done.

Now the lines of my painting do not go astray, though they change and vary. The world is but a perennial movement. All things in it are in constant motion – the earth, the rocks of the Caucasus, the pyramids of Egypt – both with the common motion and with their own. Stability itself is nothing but a more languid motion.

I cannot keep my subject still. It goes along befuddled and staggering, with a natural drunkenness. I take it in this condition, just as it is at the moment I gave my attention to it. I do not portray being: I portray passing. Not the passing from one age to another, or, as the people say, from seven years to seven years, but from day to day, from minute to minute. My history needs to be adapted to the moment. I may presently change, not only by chance, but also by intention. This is a record of various and changeable occurrences, and of irresolute and, when it so befalls, contradictory ideas: whether I am different myself, or whether I take hold of my subjects in different circumstances and aspects. So, all in all, I may indeed contradict myself now and then; but truth, as Demades said, I do not contradict. If my mind could gain a firm footing, I would not make essays, I would make decisions; but it is always in apprenticeship and on trial.

I set forth a humble and inglorious life; that does not matter. You can tie up all moral philosophy with a common and private life just as well as with a life of richer stuff. Each man bears the entire form of man's estate.

ᶜAuthors communicate with the people by some special extrinsic mark; I am the first to do so by my entire being, as Michel de Montaigne, not as a grammarian or a poet or a jurist. If the world complains that I speak too much of myself, I complain that it does not even think of itself.

ᴮBut is it reasonable that I, so fond of privacy in actual life, should aspire to publicity in the knowledge of me? Is it reasonable too that I should set forth to the world, where fashioning and art have so much credit and authority, some crude and simple products of nature, and of a very feeble nature at that? Is it not making a wall without stone, or something like that, to construct books without knowledge and without art? Musical fancies are guided by art, mine by chance.

At least I have one thing according to the rules: that no man ever treated a subject he knew and understood better than I do the subject I have undertaken; and that in this I am the most learned man alive. Secondly, that no man ever ᶜpenetrated more deeply into his material, or plucked its limbs and consequences cleaner, or ᴮreached more accurately and fully the goal he had set for his work. To accomplish it, I need only bring it to fidelity; and that is in it, as sincere and pure as can be found. I speak the truth, not my fill of it, but as much as I dare speak; and I dare to do so a little more as I grow old, for it seems that custom allows old age more freedom to prate and more indiscretion in talking about oneself. It cannot happen here as I see it happening often, that the craftsman and his work contradict each other: "Has a man whose conversation is so good written such a stupid book?" or "Have such learned writings come from a man whose conversation is so feeble?"

ᶜIf a man is commonplace in conversation and rare in writing, that means that his capacity is in the place from which he borrows it, and not in himself. A learned man is not learned in all matters; but the capable man is capable in all matters, even in ignorance.

ᴮIn this case we go hand in hand and at the same pace, my book and I. In other cases one may commend or blame the work apart from the workman; not so here; he who touches the one, touches the other. He who judges it without knowing it will injure himself more than me; he who has known it will completely satisfy me. Happy beyond my deserts if I have just this share of public approval, that I make men of understanding feel that I was capable of profiting by knowledge, if I had had any, and that I deserved better assistance from my memory.

Let me here excuse what I often say, that I rarely repent ᶜand that my conscience is content with itself – not as the conscience of an angel or a horse, but as the conscience of a man; ᴮalways adding this refrain, not perfunctorily but in sincere and complete submission: that I speak as an ignorant inquirer, referring the decision purely and simply to the common and authorized beliefs. I do not teach, I tell.

There is no vice truly a vice which is not offensive, and which a sound judgment does not condemn; for its ugliness and painfulness is so apparent that perhaps the people are right who say it is chiefly produced by stupidity and ignorance. So hard it is to imagine anyone knowing it without hating it.

^CMalice sucks up the greater part of its own venom, and poisons itself with it. ^BVice leaves repentance in the soul, like an ulcer in the flesh, which is always scratching itself and drawing blood. For reason effaces other griefs and sorrows; but it engenders that of repentance, which is all the more grievous because it springs from within, as the cold and heat of fevers is sharper than that which comes from outside. I consider as vices (but each one according to its measure) not only those that reason and nature condemn, but also those that man's opinion has created, even false and erroneous opinion, if it is authorized by laws and customs.

There is likewise no good deed that does not rejoice a wellborn nature. Indeed there is a sort of gratification in doing good which makes us rejoice in ourselves, and a generous pride that accompanies a good conscience. A boldly vicious soul may perhaps arm itself with security, but with this complacency and satisfaction it cannot provide itself. It is no slight pleasure to feel oneself preserved from the contagion of so depraved an age, and to say to oneself: "If anyone should see right into my soul, still he would not find me guilty either of anyone's affliction or ruin, or of vengeance or envy, or of public offense against the laws, or of innovation and disturbance, or of failing in my word; and in spite of what the license of the times allows and teaches each man, still I have not put my hand either upon the property or into the purse of any Frenchman, and have lived only on my own, both in war and peace; nor have I used any man's work without paying his wages." These testimonies of conscience give us pleasure; and this natural rejoicing is a great boon to us, and the only payment that never fails us.

To found the reward for virtuous actions on the approval of others is to choose too uncertain and shaky a foundation. ^CEspecially in an age as corrupt and ignorant as this, the good opinion of the people is a dishonor. Whom can you trust to see what is praiseworthy? God keep me from being a worthy man according to the descriptions I see people every day giving of themselves in their own honor. *What were vices now are moral acts* [Seneca].

Certain of my friends have sometimes undertaken to call me on the carpet and lecture me unreservedly, either of their own accord or at my invitation, as a service which, to a well-formed soul, surpasses all the services of friendship, not only in usefulness, but also in pleasantness. I have always welcomed it with the wide-open arms of courtesy and gratitude. But to speak of it now in all conscience, I have often found in their reproach or praise such false measure that I would hardly have erred to err rather than to do good in their fashion.

^BThose of us especially who live a private life that is on display only to ourselves must have a pattern established within us by which to test our actions, and, according to this pattern, now pat ourselves on the back, now punish ourselves. I have my own laws and court to judge me, and I address myself to them more than anywhere else. To be sure, I restrain my actions

according to others, but I extend them only according to myself. There is no one but yourself who knows whether you are cowardly and cruel, or loyal and devout. Others do not see you, they guess at you by uncertain conjectures; they see not so much your nature as your art. Therefore do not cling to their judgment; cling to your own. ᶜ*You must use your own judgment. . . . With regard to virtues and vices, your own conscience has great weight: take that away, and everything falls* [Cicero].

ᴮBut the saying that repentance follows close upon sin does not seem to consider the sin that is in robes of state, that dwells in us as in its own home. We can disown and retract the vices that take us by surprise, and toward which we are swept by passion; but those which by long habit are rooted and anchored in a strong and vigorous will cannot be denied. Repentance is nothing but a disavowal of our will and an opposition to our fancies, which leads us about in all directions. It makes this man disown his past virtue and his continence:

> Why had I not in youth the mind I have today?
> Or why, with old desires, have red cheeks flown away?
> Horace

It is a rare life that remains well ordered even in private. Any man can play his part in the side show and represent a worthy man on the boards; but to be disciplined within, in his own bosom, where all is permissible, where all is concealed – that's the point. The next step to that is to be so in our own house, in our ordinary actions, for which we need render account to no one, where nothing is studied or artificial. And therefore Bias, depicting an excellent state of family life, says it is one in which the master is the same within, by his own volition, as he is outside for fear of the law and of what people will say. And it was a worthy remark of Julius Drusus to the workmen who offered, for three thousand crowns, to arrange his house so that his neighbors would no longer be able to look into it as they could before. "I will give you six thousand," he said; "make it so that everyone can see in from all sides." The practice of Agesilaus is noted with honor, of taking lodging in the churches when traveling, so that the people and the gods themselves might see into his private actions. Men have seemed miraculous to the world, in whom their wives and valets have never seen anything even worth noticing. Few men have been admired by their own households.

ᶜNo man has been a prophet, not merely in his own house, but in his own country, says the experience of history. Likewise in things of no importance. And in this humble example you may see an image of greater ones. In my region of Gascony they think it a joke to see me in print. The farther from my lair the knowledge of me spreads, the more I am valued. I buy printers in Guienne, elsewhere they buy me. On this phenomenon those people base their hopes who hide themselves while alive and present, to gain favor when dead and gone. I would rather have less of it. And I cast myself on the world only for the share of favor I get now. When I leave it, I shall hold it quits.

[B]The people escort this man back to his door, with awe, from a public function. He drops his part with his gown; the higher he has hoisted himself, the lower he falls back; inside, in his home, everything is tumultuous and vile. Even if there is order there, it takes a keen and select judgment to perceive it in these humble private actions. Besides, order is a dull and somber virtue. To win through a breach, to conduct an embassy, to govern a people, these are dazzling actions. To scold, to laugh, to sell, to pay, to love, to hate, and to deal pleasantly and justly with our household and ourselves, not to let ourselves go, not to be false to ourselves, that is a rarer matter, more difficult and less noticeable.

Therefore retired lives, whatever people may say, accomplish duties as harsh and strenuous as other lives, or more so. [C]And private persons, says Aristotle, render higher and more difficult service to virtue than those who are in authority. [B]We prepare ourselves for eminent occasions more for glory than for conscience. [C]The shortest way to attain glory would be to do for conscience what we do for glory. [B]And Alexander's virtue seems to me to represent much less vigor in his theater than does that of Socrates in his lowly and obscure activity. I can easily imagine Socrates in Alexander's place; Alexander in that of Socrates, I cannot. If you ask the former what he knows how to do, he will answer, "Subdue the world"; if you ask the latter, he will say, "Lead the life of man in conformity with its natural condition"; a knowledge much more general, more weighty, and more legitimate.

The value of the soul consists not in flying high, but in an orderly pace. [C]Its greatness is exercised not in greatness, but in mediocrity.[15] As those who judge and touch us inwardly make little account of the brilliance of our public acts, and see that these are only thin streams and jets of water spurting from a bottom otherwise muddy and thick; so likewise those who judge us by this brave outward appearance draw similar conclusions about our inner constitution, and cannot associate common faculties, just like their own, with these other faculties that astonish them and are so far beyond their scope. So we give demons wild shapes. And who does not give Tamerlane[16] raised eyebrows, open nostrils, a dreadful face, and immense size, like the size of the imaginary picture of him we have formed from the renown of his name? If I had been able to see Erasmus[17] in other days, it would have been hard for me not to take for adages and apophthegms everything he said to his valet and his hostess. We imagine much more appropriately an artisan on the toilet seat or on his wife than a great president, venerable by his demeanor and his ability. It seems to us that they do not stoop from their lofty thrones even to live.

[B]As vicious souls are often incited to do good by some extraneous impulse, so are virtuous souls to do evil. Thus we must judge them by their settled state, when they are at home, if ever they are; or at least when they are closest to repose and their natural position.

Natural inclinations gain assistance and strength from education; but they are scarcely to be changed and overcome. A thousand natures, in my time, have escaped toward virtue or toward vice through the lines of a contrary training:

> As when wild beasts grow tame, shut in a cage,
> Forget the woods, and lose their look of rage,
> And learn to suffer man; but if they taste
> Hot blood, their rage and fury is replaced,
> Their reminiscent jaws distend, they burn,
> And for their trembling keeper's blood they yearn.
>
> Lucan

We do not root out these original qualities, we cover them up, we conceal them. Latin is like a native tongue to me; I understand it better than French; but for forty years I have not used it at all for speaking or writing. Yet in sudden and extreme emotions, into which I have fallen two or three times in my life – one of them when I saw my father, in perfect health, fall back into my arms in a faint – I have always poured out my first words from the depths of my entrails in Latin; ᶜNature surging forth and expressing herself by force, in the face of long habit. ᴮAnd this experience is told of many others.

Those who in my time have tried to correct the world's morals by new ideas, reform the superficial vices; the essential ones they leave as they were, if they do not increase them; and increase is to be feared. People are as likely to rest from all other well-doing on the strength of these external, arbitrary reforms, which cost us less and bring greater acclaim; and thereby they satisfy at little expense the other natural, consubstantial, and internal vices.

Just consider the evidence of this in our own experience. There is no one who, if he listens to himself, does not discover in himself a pattern all his own, a ruling pattern, which struggles against education and against the tempest of the passions that oppose it. For my part, I do not feel much sudden agitation; I am nearly always in place, like heavy and inert bodies. If I am not at home, I am always very near it. My excesses do not carry me very far away. There is nothing extreme or strange about them. And besides I have periods of vigorous and healthy reaction.

The real condemnation, which applies to the common run of men of today, is that even their retirement is full of corruption and filth; their idea of reformation, blurred; their penitence, diseased and guilty, almost as much as their sin. Some, either from being glued to vice by a natural attachment, or from long habit, no longer recognize its ugliness. On others (in whose regiment I belong) vice weighs heavily, but they counterbalance it with pleasure or some other consideration, and endure it and lend themselves to it for a certain price; viciously, however, and basely. Yet it might be possible to imagine a disproportion so extreme that the pleasure might justly excuse the sin, as we say utility does; not only if the pleasure was incidental and not a part of the sin, as in theft, but if it was in the very exercise of the sin, as in intercourse with women, where the impulse is violent, and, they say, sometimes invincible.

The other day when I was at Armagnac, on the estate of a kinsman of mine, I saw a country fellow whom everyone nicknames the Thief. He gave this account of his life: that born a beggar, and finding that by earning is bread by the toil of his hands he would never protect himself enough against want, he had decided to become a thief; and he had spent all his youth at this trade in security, by virtue of his bodily strength. For he reaped his harvest and vintage from other people's lands, but so far away and in such great loads that it was inconceivable that one man could have carried off so much on his shoulders in one night. And he was careful besides to equalize and spread out the damage he did, so that the loss was less insupportable for each individual. He is now, in his old age, rich for a man in his station, thanks to this traffic, which he openly confesses. And to make his peace with God for his acquisitions, he says that he spends his days compensating, by good deeds, the successors of the people he robbed; and that if he does not finish this task (for he cannot do it all at once), he will charge his heirs with it, according to the knowledge, which he alone has, of the amount of wrong he did to each. Judging by this description, whether it is true or false, this man regards theft as a dishonorable action and hates it, but hates it less than poverty; he indeed repents of it in itself, but in so far as it was thus counterbalanced and compensated, he does not repent of it. This is not that habit that incorporates us with vice and brings even our understanding into conformity with it; nor is it that impetuous wind that comes in gusts to confuse and blind our soul, and hurls us for the moment headlong, judgment and all, into the power of vice.

I customarily do wholeheartedly whatever I do, and go my way all in one piece. I scarcely make a motion that is hidden and out of sight of my reason, and that is not guided by the consent of nearly all parts of me, without division, without internal sedition. My judgment takes all the blame or all the praise for it; and the blame it once takes, it always keeps, for virtually since its birth it has been one; the same inclination, the same road, the same strength. And in the matter of general opinions, in childhood I established myself in the position where I was to remain.

There are some impetuous, prompt, and sudden sins: let us leave them aside. But as for these other sins so many times repeated, planned, and premeditated, constitutional sins, ᶜor even professional or vocational sins, ᴮI cannot imagine that they can be implanted so long in one and the same heart, without the reason and conscience of their possessor constantly willing and intending it to be so. And the repentance which he claims comes to him at a certain prescribed moment is a little hard for me to imagine and conceive.

ᶜI do not follow the belief of the sect of Pythagoras, that man take on a new soul when they approach the images of the gods to receive their oracles. Unless he meant just this, that the soul must indeed be foreign, new, and loaned for the occasion, since their own showed so little sign of any purification and cleanness worthy of this office.

ᴮThey do just the opposite of the Stoic precepts, which indeed order us to correct the imperfections and vices that we recognize in us, but forbid us to be repentant and glum about them. These men make us believe that they feel great regret and remorse within; but of amendment and correction, ᶜor interruption, ᴮthey show us no sign. Yet it is no cure if the disease is not thrown off. If repentance were weighing in the scale of the balance, it would outweigh the sin. I know of no quality so easy to counterfeit as piety, if conduct and life are not made to conform with it. Its essence is abstruse and occult; its semblance, easy and showy.

As for me, I may desire in a general way to be different; I may condemn and dislike my nature as a whole, and implore God to reform me completely and to pardon my natural weakness. But this I ought not to call repentance, it seems to me, any more than my displeasure at being neither an angel nor Cato.[18] My actions are in order and conformity with what I am and with my condition. I can do no better. And repentance does not properly apply to the things that are not in our power; rather does regret. I imagine numberless natures loftier and better regulated than mine, but for all that, I do not amend by faculties; just as neither my arm nor my mind becomes more vigorous by imagining another that is so. If imagining and desiring a nobler conduct than ours produced repentance of our own, we should have to repent of our most innocent actions, inasmuch as we rightly judge that in a more excellent nature they would have been performed with greater perfection and dignity, and we should wish to do likewise.

When I consider the behavior of my youth in comparison with that of my old age, I find that I have generally conducted myself in orderly fashion, according to my lights; that is all my resistance can accomplish. I do not flatter myself; in similar circumstances I should always be the same. It is not a spot, it is rather a tincture with which I am stained all over. I know no superficial, halfway, and perfunctory repentance. It must affect me in every part before I will call it so, and must grip me by the vitals and afflict them as deeply and as completely as God sees into me.

In business matters, several good opportunities have escaped me for want of successful management. However, my counsels have been good, according to the circumstances they were faced with; their way is always to take the easiest and surest course. I find that in my past deliberations, according to my rule, I have proceeded wisely, considering the state of the matter proposed to me, and I should do the same a thousand years from now in similar situations. I am not considering what it is at this moment, but what it was when I was deliberating about it.

ᶜThe soundness of any plan depends on the time; circumstances and things roll about and change incessantly. I have fallen into some serious and important mistakes in my life, not for lack of good counsel but for lack of good luck. There are secret parts in the matters we handle which cannot be guessed, especially in human nature – mute factors that do not show, factors sometimes unknown to their possessor himself, which are brought forth and aroused by unexpected occasions. If my prudence has been unable to see into them and predict them, I bear it no ill will; its responsibility is restricted within its limitations. It is the outcome that beats me; and ᴮif it favors the course I have refused, there is no help for it; I do not blame myself; I accuse my luck, not my work. That is not to be called repentance.

Phocion had given the Athenians some advice that was not followed. When however the affair came out prosperously against his opinion, someone said to him: "Well, Phocion, are you glad that the thing is going so well?" "Indeed I am glad," he said, "that it has turned out this way, but I do not repent of having advised that way."

When my friends apply to me for advice, I give it freely and clearly, and without hesitating as nearly everyone else does because, the affair being hazardous, it may come out contrary to my expectations, wherefore they may have cause to reproach me for my advice; that does not worry me. For they will be wrong, and I should not have refused them this service.

CI have scarcely any occasion to blame my mistakes or mishaps on anyone but myself. For in practice I rarely ask other people's advice, unless as a compliment and out of politeness, except when I need scientific information or knowledge of the facts. But in things where I have only my judgment to employ, other people's reasons can serve to support me, but seldom to change my course. I listen to them all favorably and decently; but so far as I can remember, I have never up to this moment followed any but my own. If you ask me, they are nothing but flies and atoms that distract my will. I set little value on my own opinions, but I set just as little on those of others. Fortune pays me properly. If I do not take advice, I give still less. Mine is seldom asked, but it is followed even less; and I know of no public or private enterprise that my advice restored to its feet and to the right path. Even the people whom fortune has made somewhat dependent on it have let themselves be managed more readily by anyone else's brains. Being a man who is quite as jealous of the rights of my repose as of the rights of my authority, I prefer it so; by leaving me alone, they treat me according to my professed principle, which is to be wholly contained and established within myself. To me it is a pleasure not to be concerned in other people's affairs and to be free of responsibility for them.

BIn all affairs, when they are past, however they have turned out, I have little regret. For this idea takes away the pain: that they were bound to happen thus, and now they are in the great stream of the universe and in the chain of Stoical causes. Your fancy, by wish or imagination, cannot change a single point without overturning the whole order of things, and the past and the future.

For the rest, I hate that accidental repentance that age brings. The man[19] who said of old that he was obliged to the years for having rid him of sensuality had a different viewpoint from mine; I shall never be grateful to impotence for any good it may do me. C*Nor will Providence ever be so hostile to her own work that debility should be ranked among the best things* [Quintilian]. BOur appetites are few in old age; a profound satiety seizes us after the act. In that I see nothing of conscience; sourness and weakness imprint on us a sluggish and rheumatic virtue. We must not let ourselves be so carried away by natural changes as to let our judgment degenerate. Youth and pleasure in other ways did not make me fail to recognize the face of vice in voluptuousness; nor does the distaste that the years bring me make me fail to recognize the face of voluptuousness in vice. Now that I am no longer in that state, I judge it as though I were in it.

CI who shake up my reason sharply and attentively, find that Bit is the very same I had in my more licentious years, except perhaps in so far as it has grown weaker and worse as it has grown old. CAnd I find that even if it refuses, out of consideration for the interests of my bodily health, to put me in the furnace of this pleasure, it would not refuse to do so, any more than formerly, for my spiritual health. BI do not consider it any more valiant for seeing it *hors de combat*. My temptations are so broken and mortified that they are not worth its opposition. By merely stretching out my hands to them, I exorcise them. If my reason were confronted with my former lust, I fear that it would have less strength to resist than it used to have. I do not see that of itself it judges anything differently than it did then, nor that it has gained any new light. Wherefore, if there is any convalescence, it is a deformed convalescence.

CMiserable sort of remedy, to owe our health to disease! It is not for our misfortune to do us this service, it is for the good fortune of our judgment. You cannot make me do anything by ills and afflictions except curse them. They are for people who are only awakened by whipping. My reason runs a much freer course in prosperity. It is much more distracted and busy digesting pains than pleasures. I see much more clearly in fair weather. Health admonishes me more cheerfully and so more usefully than sickness. I advanced as far as I could toward reform and a regulated life when I had health to enjoy. I should be ashamed and resentful if the misery and misfortune of my decrepitude were to be thought better than my good, healthy, lively, vigorous years, and if people were to esteem me not for what I have been, but for ceasing to be that.

In my opinion it is living happily, not, as Antisthenes said, dying happily, that constitutes human felicity. I have made no effort to attach, monstrously, the tail of a philosopher to the head and body of a dissipated man: or that this sickly remainder of my life should disavow and belie its fairest, longest, and most complete part. I want to present and show myself uniformly throughout. If I had to live over again, I would live as I have lived. I have neither tears for the past nor fears for the future. And unless I am fooling myself, it has gone about the same way within me as without. It is one of the chief obligations I have to my fortune that my bodily state has run its course with each thing in due season. I have seen the grass, the flower, and the fruit; now I see the dryness – happily, since it is naturally. I bear the ills I have much more easily because they are properly timed, and also because they make me remember more pleasantly the long felicity of my past life.

Likewise my wisdom may well have been of the same proportions in one age as in the other; but it was much more potent and graceful when green, gay, and natural, than it is now, being broken down, peevish, and labored. Therefore I renounce these casual and painful reformations.

ᴮGod must touch our hearts. Our conscience must reform by itself through the strengthening of our reason, not through the weakening of our appetites. Sensual pleasure is neither pale nor colorless in itself for being seen through dim and bleary eyes. We should love temperance for itself and out of reverence toward God, who has commanded it, and also chastity; what catarrh lends us, and what I owe to the favor of my colic, is neither chastity nor temperance. We cannot boast of despising and fighting sensual pleasure, if we do not see or know it, and its charms, its powers, and its most alluring beauty.

I know them both; I have a right to speak; but it seems to me that in old age our souls are subject to more troublesome ailments and imperfections than in our youth. I used to say so when I was young; then they taunted me with my beardless chin. I still say so now that my ᶜgray ᴮhair gives me authority to speak. We call "wisdom" the difficulty of our humors, our distaste for present things. But in truth we do not so much abandon our vices as change them, and, in my opinion, for the worse. Besides a silly and decrepit pride, a tedious prattle, prickly and unsociable humors, superstition, and a ridiculous concern for riches when we have lost the use of them, I find there more envy, injustice, and malice. Old age puts more wrinkles in our minds than on our faces; and we never, or rarely, see a soul that in growing old does not come to smell sour and musty. Man grows and dwindles in his entirety.

ᶜSeeing the wisdom of Socrates and several circumstances of his condemnation, I should venture to believe that he lent himself to it to some extent, purposely, by prevarication, being seventy, and having so soon to suffer an increasing torpor of the rich activity of his mind, and the dimming of its accustomed brightness.

ᴮWhat metamorphoses I see old age producing every day in many of my acquaintances! It is a powerful malady, and it creeps up on us naturally and imperceptibly. We need a great provision of study, and great precaution, to avoid the imperfections it loads upon us, or at least to slow up their progress. I feel that, notwithstanding all my retrenchments, it gains on me foot by foot. I stand fast as well as I can. But I do not know where it will lead even me in the end. In any event, I am glad to have people know whence I shall have fallen.

Of Vanity

. . . human society holds and is knit together at any cost whatever. Whatever position you set men in, they pile up and arrange themselves by moving and crowding together, just as ill-matched objects, put in a bag without order, find of themselves a way to unite and fall into place together, often better than they could have been arranged by art. King Philip collected the most wicked and incorrigible men he could find, and settled them all in a city he had built for them, which bore their name. I judge that from their very vices they set up a political system among themselves and a workable and regular society.

I see not one action, or three, or a hundred, but morals in common and accepted practice, so monstrous, especially in inhumanity and treachery, that I have not the heart to think of them without horror; and I marvel at them almost as much as I detest them. The practice of these arrant villainies bears the mark of vigor and strength of soul as much as of error and disorder.

Necessity reconciles men and brings them together. This accidental link afterward takes the form of laws; for there have been some as savage as any human opinion can produce, which have nevertheless maintained their bodily health and long life as well as those of Plato and Aristotle could do.

And indeed all those imaginary, artificial descriptions of a government prove ridiculous and unfit to put into practice. These great, lengthy altercations about the best form of society and the rules most suitable to bind us, are altercations fit only for the exercise of our minds; as in the liberal arts there are several subjects whose essence is controversy and dispute, and which have no life apart from that. Such a description of a government would be applicable in a new world, but we take men already bound and formed to certain customs; we do not create them, like Pyrrha or Cadmus.[20] By whatever means we may have power to correct and reform them, we can hardly twist them out of their accustomed bent without breaking up everything. Solon was asked whether he had established the best laws he could for the Athenians. "Yes indeed," he answered, "the best they would have accepted."

CVarro excuses himself in the same way, saying that if he had to write about religion as something new, he would say what he thinks of it; but since it is already formed and accepted, he will speak of it more according to custom than according to nature.

BNot in theory, but in truth, the best and most excellent government for each nation is the one under which it has preserved its existence. Its form and essential fitness depend on habit. We are prone to be discontented with the present state of things. But I maintain, nevertheless, that to wish for the government of a few in a democratic state, or another type of government in a monarchy, is foolish and wrong.

Of Physiognomy

BAlmost all of the opinions we have are taken on authority and on credit. There is no harm in this: we could not make a worse choice than our own in so feeble an age. The version of the sayings of Socrates that his friends have left us we approve only out of respect for the universal approval these sayings enjoy, not by our own knowledge. They are beyond our experience. If anything of the kind were brought forth at this time, there are few men who would prize it.

We perceive no charms that are not sharpened, puffed out, and inflated by artifice. Those which glide along naturally and simply easily escape a sight so gross as ours. They have a delicate and hidden beauty; we need a clear and well-purged sight to discover their secret light. Is not naturalness, according to us, akin to stupidity and a matter for reproach?

Socrates makes his soul move with a natural and common motion. So says a peasant, so says a woman. ᶜHis mouth is full of nothing but carters, joiners, cobblers, and masons. ᴮHis are inductions and similes drawn from the commonest and best-known actions of men; everyone understands him. Under so mean a form we should never have picked out the nobility and splendor of his admirable ideas, we ᶜwho consider flat and low all ideas that are not raised up by learning, and ᴮwho perceive richness only in pomp and show. Our world is formed only for ostentation; men inflate themselves only with wind, and go bouncing around like balls. This man did not propose to himself any idle fancies: his aim was to furnish us with things and precepts that serve life really and more closely:

> To keep the mean, to hold our aim in view,
> And follow nature.
>
> Lucan

He was also always one and the same, and raised himself not by sallies but by disposition, to the utmost point of vigor. Or, to speak more exactly, he raised nothing, but rather brought vigor, hardships, and difficulties down and back to his own natural and original level, and subjected them to it. For in Cato we see very clearly that his is a pace strained far above the ordinary; in the brave exploits of his life and in his death we feel that he is always mounted on his high horse. The other walks close to the ground, and at a gentle and ordinary pace treats the most useful subjects; and behaves, both in the face of death and in the thorniest trials that can confront us, in the ordinary way of human life.

It happened fortunately that the man most worthy to be known and to be presented to the world as an example should be the one of whom we have most certain knowledge. We have light on him from the most clear-sighted men who ever lived; the witnesses we have of him are wonderful in fidelity and competence.

It is a great thing to have been able to impart such order to the pure and simple notions of a child that, without altering or stretching them, he produced from them the most beautiful achievements of our soul. He shows it as neither elevated nor rich; he shows it only as healthy, but assuredly with a very blithe and clear health. By these vulgar and natural motives, by these ordinary and common ideas, without excitement or fuss, he constructed not only the best regulated but the loftiest and most vigorous beliefs, actions, and morals that ever were. ᶜIt is he who brought human wisdom back down from heaven, where she was wasting her time, and restored her to man, with whom lies her most proper and laborious and useful business. ᴮSee him plead before his judges, see by what reasonings he rouses his courage in the hazards of war, what arguments fortify his patience against calumny, tyranny, death, and his wife's bad temper. There is nothing borrowed from art and the sciences; even

the simplest can recognize in him their means and their strength; it is impossible to go back further and lower. He did a great favor to human nature by
showing how much it can do by itself.

We are each richer than we think, but we are trained to borrow and beg; we
are taught to use the resources of others more than our own. In nothing does
man know how to stop at the limit of his need; of pleasure, riches, power, he
embraces more than he can hold; his greed is incapable of moderation. I find
that it is the same with the curiosity for knowledge. Man cuts out for himself
much more work than he can do or has any reason to do, ^Ctrying to stretch the
usefulness of knowledge as wide as its matter. *In learning, as in all other
things, we suffer from intemperance* [Seneca]. And Tacitus is right to praise
Agricola's mother for having curbed in her son too boiling an appetite for
learning. Looked at steadily, it is like men's other goods; it has in it much
intrinsic and natural vanity and weakness, and it costs dear.

It is far more hazardous to acquire than any other food or drink. For with
other things, what we have bought we carry home in some vessel, and there
we have a chance to examine its value and how much we shall take of it and
when. But learning we can at the outset put into no other vessel than our
mind; we swallow it as we buy it, and leave the market place already either
infected or improved. There is some of it that only hampers and burdens us
instead of feeding us, and also some which, under color of curing us, poisons us.

^BI once took pleasure in seeing men in some place, through piety, take a
vow of ignorance, as one might of chastity, poverty, penitence. It is also
castrating our disorderly appetites, to blunt that cupidity that pricks us on to
the study of books, and to deprive the soul of that voluptuous complacency
which tickles us with the notion of being learned. ^CAnd it is accomplishing
richly the vow of poverty to add to it also that of the mind.

^BWe need hardly any learning to live at ease. And Socrates teaches us that it
is in us, and the way to find it and help ourselves with it. All this ability of ours
that is beyond the natural is as good as vain and superfluous. It is a lot if it
does not load us down and bother us more than it serves us. ^C*Little learning is
needed for a good mind* [Seneca]. ^BThese are feverish excesses of our mind, a
meddlesome and restless instrument. . . .

They may boast about it all they please. *The whole life of a philosopher is a
meditation on death* [Cicero]. But it seems to me that death is indeed the end,
but not therefore the goal, of life; it is its finish, its extremity, but not therefore its object. Life should be an aim unto itself, a purpose unto itself; its
rightful study is to regulate, conduct, and suffer itself. Among the many other
duties comprised in this general and principal chapter on knowing how to live
is this article on knowing how to die; and it is one of the lightest, if our fear did
not give it weight.

^BTo judge by utility and natural truth, the lessons of simplicity yield little
to those which learning preaches to us to the contrary. Men are diverse in
inclination and strength; they must be led to their own good according to

their nature and by diverse routes. ^C*Wherever the tempest drives me, there I land* [Horace]. . . .

As I have said elsewhere, I have very simply and crudely adopted for my own sake this ancient precept: that we cannot go wrong by following Nature, that the sovereign precept is to conform to her. I have not, like Socrates, corrected my natural disposition by force of reason, and have not troubled my inclination at all by art. I let myself go as I have come. I combat nothing. My two ruling parts, of their own volition, live in peace and good accord. But my nurse's milk, thank God, was moderately healthy and temperate.

^CShall I say this in passing: that I see held in greater price than it is worth a certain idea of scholastic probity, almost the only one practiced among us, a slave to precepts, held down beneath fear and hope? What I like is the virtue that laws and religions do not make but perfect and authorize, that feels in itself enough to sustain itself without help, born in us from its own roots, from the seed of universal reason that is implanted in every man who is not denatured. This reason, which straightens Socrates from his inclination to vice, makes him obedient to the men and gods who command in his city, courageous in death not because his soul is immortal but because he is mortal. It is a ruinous teaching for any society, and much more harmful than ingenious and subtle, which persuades the people that religious belief is enough, by itself and without morals, to satisfy divine justice. Practice makes us see an enormous distinction between devoutness and conscience.

Of Experience

. . . As for me, then, I love life and cultivate it just as God has been pleased to grant it to us. I do not go about wishing that it should lack the need to eat and drink, ^Cand it would seem to me no less excusable a failing to wish that need to be doubled. *The wise man is the keenest searcher for natural treasures* [Seneca]. Nor do I wish ^Bthat we should sustain ourselves by merely putting into our mouths a little of that drug by which Epimenides took away his appetite and kept himself alive; nor that we should beget children insensibly with our fingers or our heels, ^Cbut rather, with due respect, that we could also beget them voluptuously with our fingers and heels; nor ^Bthat the body should be without desire and without titillation. Those are ungrateful ^Cand unfair ^Bcomplaints. I accept with all my heart ^C and with gratitude ^Bwhat nature has done for me, and I am pleased with myself and proud of myself that I do. We wrong that great and all-powerful Giver by refusing his gift, nullifying it, and disfiguring it. ^C*Himself all good, he has made all things good. All things that are according to nature are worthy of esteem* [Cicero].

^BOf opinions of philosophy I most gladly embrace those that are most solid, that is to say, most human and most our own; my opinions, in conformity with my conduct, are low and humble. ^CPhilosophy is very childish, to my mind, when she gets up on her hind legs and preaches to us that it is a barbarous alliance to marry the divine with the earthly, the reasonable with the unreason-

able, the severe with the indulgent, the honorable with the dishonorable; that
sensual pleasure is a brutish thing unworthy of being enjoyed by the wise man;
that the only pleasure he derives from the enjoyment of a beautiful young wife
is the pleasure of his consciousness of doing the right thing, like putting on his
boots for a useful ride. May her followers have no more right and sinews and
sap in deflowering their wives than her lessons have!

That is not what Socrates says, her tutor and ours. He prizes bodily pleasure
as he should, but he prefers that of the mind, as having more power, constancy, ease, variety, and dignity. The latter by no means goes alone, according to him – he is not so fanciful – but only comes first. For him temperance is
the moderator, not the adversary, of pleasures.

ᴮNature is a gentle guide, but no more gentle than wise and just. ᶜ*We must
penetrate into the nature of things and clearly see exactly what it demands*
[Cicero]. ᴮI seek her footprints everywhere. We have confused them with
artificial tracks, ᶜand for that reason the sovereign good of the Academics and
the Peripatetics, which is "to live according to nature," becomes hard to limit
and express; also that of the Stoics, a neighbor to the other, which is "to
consent to nature."

ᴮIs it not an error to consider some actions less worthy because they are
necessary? No, they will not knock it out of my head that the marriage of
pleasure with necessity, ᶜwith whom, says an ancient, the gods always conspire, ᴮis a very suitable one. To what purpose do we dismember by divorce a
structure made up of such close and brotherly correspondence? On the contrary, let us bind it together again by mutual services. Let the mind arouse and
quicken the heaviness of the body, and the body check and make fast the
lightness of the mind. ᶜ*He who praises the nature of the soul as the sovereign
good and condemns the nature of the flesh as evil, truly both carnally desires the
soul and carnally shuns the flesh; for his feeling is inspired by human vanity,
not by divine truth* [Saint Augustine].

ᴮThere is no part unworthy of our care in this gift that God has given us; we
are accountable for it even to a single hair. And it is not a perfunctory charge
to man to guide man according to his nature; it is express, simple, ᶜand of
prime importance, ᴮand the creator has given it to us seriously and sternly.
ᶜAuthority alone has power over common intelligences, and has more weight
in a foreign language. Let us renew the charge here. *Who would not say that it
is the essence of folly to do lazily and rebelliously what has to be done, to impel
the body one way and the soul another, to be split between the most conflicting
motions?* [Seneca].

ᴮCome on now, just to see, some day get some man to tell you the absorbing
thoughts and fancies that he takes into his head, and for the sake of which he
turns his mind from a good meal and laments the time he spends on feeding
himself. You will find there is nothing so insipid in all the dishes on your table
as this fine entertainment of his mind (most of the time we should do better to
go to sleep completely than to stay awake for what we do stay awake for); and
you will find that his ideas and aspirations are not worth your stew. Even if

they were the transports of Archimedes himself, what of it? I am not here touching on, or mixing up with that brattish rabble of men that we are, or with the vanity of the desires and musings that distract us, those venerable souls, exalted by ardent piety and religion to constant and conscientious meditation on divine things, ^Cwho, anticipating, by dint of keen and vehement hope, the enjoyment of eternal food, final goal and ultimate limit of Christian desires, sole constant and incorruptible pleasure, scorn to give their attention to our beggarly, waterly, and ambiguous comforts, and readily resign to the body the concern and enjoyment of sensual and temporal fodder. ^BThat is a privileged study. ^CBetween ourselves, these are two things that I have always observed to be in singular accord: supercelestial thoughts and subterranean conduct.

^BAesop, ^Cthat great man, ^Bsaw his master pissing as he walked. "What next?" he said. "Shall we have to shit as we run?" Let us manage our time; we shall still have a lot left idle and ill spent. Our mind likes to think it has not enough leisure hours to do its own business unless it dissociates itself from the body for the little time that the body really needs it.

They want to get out of themselves and escape from the man. That is madness: instead of changing into angels, they change into beasts; instead of raising themselves, they lower themselves. ^CThese transcendental humors frighten me, like lofty and inaccessible places; and nothing is so hard for me to stomach in the life of Socrates as his ecstasies and possessions by his daemon, nothing is so human in Plato as the qualities for which they say he is called divine. ^BAnd of our sciences, those seem to me most terrestrial and low which have risen the highest. And I find nothing so humble and so mortal in the life of Alexander as his fancies about his immortalization. Philotas stung him wittily by his answer. He congratulated him by letter on the oracle of Jupiter Ammon which had lodged him among the gods: "As far as you are concerned, I am very glad of it; but there is reason to pity the men who will have to live with and obey a man who exceeds ^Cand is not content with ^Ba man's proportions."

> ^CSince you obey the gods, you rule the world.
> Horace

^BThe nice inscription with which the Athenians honored the entry of Pompey into their city is in accord with my meaning.

> You are as much a god as you will own
> That you are nothing but a man alone.
> Amyot's Plutarch

It is an absolute perfection and virtually divine to know how to enjoy our being rightfully. We seek other conditions because we do not understand the use of our own, and go outside of ourselves because we do not know what it is like inside. ^CYet there is no use our mounting on stilts, for on stilts we must still walk on our own legs. And on the loftiest throne in the world we are still sitting only on our own rump.

^BThe most beautiful lives, to my mind, are those that conform to the com-

mon ^Chuman ^Bpattern, ^Cwith order, but ^Bwithout miracle and without eccentricity. Now old age needs to be treated a little more tenderly. Let us commend it to that god who is the protector of health and wisdom, but gay and sociable wisdom:

> Grant me but health, Latona's son,
> And to enjoy the wealth I've won,
> And honored age, with mind entire
> And not unsolaced by the lyre.
>
> Horace

Editor's Notes

1. Montaigne is reporting part of a discussion in Cicero, *De natura deorum*, I.vii.
2. Thales (flourished around 580 B.C.E.) is traditionally considered to have been the first Greek philosopher.
3. Socrates.
4. Montaigne drew from Sextus Empiricus this analysis of the aims and schools of ancient philosophy.
5. The "Epechists" are those who suspend judgment – the Pyrrhonic skeptics.
6. A Stoic technical term for the condition more usually called "apathy," the detachment from feeling that gives one tranquility.
7. Greek for "I suspend my judgment."
8. As Pyrrhonic skepticism.
9. Saint Augustine reported that Varro gave this figure, and Augustine began his own discussion of the topic in *The City of God*, XIX.ii.
10. *Nicomachean Ethics*, IV.iii.
11. Apollo.
12. In *Republic*, bk. I.
13. The translator notes that what follows, up to the fourth paragraph from the end, starting with "To this most religious conclusion of a pagan," was copied from an essay by Plutarch. But although Montaigne copied Plutarch's words, the sentiments are his own.
14. Seneca.
15. Montaigne was thinking of mediocrity as the mean or middle between extremes, which Aristotle identified with virtue.
16. The fourteenth-century Turkic conqueror of vast tracts of Asia, traditionally viewed as very fierce.
17. The great Dutch humanistic scholar and theologian, c. 1466–1536.
18. Marcus Portius Cato, 95–46 B.C.E., a Roman statesman who opposed Caesar often cited by Montaigne as a nearly superhuman model of Stoic virtue.
19. According to Cicero, Sophocles had this attitude toward old age.
20. Pyrrha and Deucalion repeopled the earth after a flood, by flinging over their shoulders stones, which turned into humans. Cadmus grew soldiers by planting the teeth of a dragon he had slain.

Further Reading

The most convenient complete French text of Montaigne is Albert Thibaudet and Maurice Rat, eds., *Oeuvres Complètes* (Paris: Gallimard, 1962), with a valuable introduction and copious annotations. Donald Frame, *Montaigne, a Biography* (New York:

Harcourt Brace & World, 1965), is a good brief life. Frame's translation, from which the preceding readings were taken, is the most reliable, but the reader may wish to look at the first English translation, by John Florio, 1603, to see one of the ways in which Montaigne was presented to the seventeenth century.

Peter Burke, *Montaigne* (Oxford: Oxford University Press, 1987), provides a short introduction. R. M. Sayce, *The Essays of Montaigne: A Critical Exploration* (London: Weidenfeld & Nicolson, 1972), is an excellent study of the essays as a whole, with much detailed comment. Dorothy Gabe Coleman, *Montaigne's "Essais"* (London: Allen & Unwin, 1987), gives a sophisticated and useful overview of Montaigne's life, way of writing, background, and general positions. M. A. Screech, *Montaigne and Melancholy* (London: Duckworth, 1983), is a lively and erudite book covering far more than its title suggests and providing a useful review of the philosophical background of Montaigne's thought. Jean Starobinski, *Montaigne in Motion*, trans. Arthur Goldhammer (Chicago: University of Chicago Press, 1985), is a more speculative and imaginative study of its subject. The best discussions of Montaigne's moral outlook are in Hugo Friedrich, *Montaigne*, published in German (Bern: Francke, 1949) and in French (Paris: Gallimard, 1968) but not in English.

Part I.
Reworking Natural Law

Francisco Suarez

Introduction

Francisco Suarez (1548–1617) was one of a number of Spanish scholastic thinkers who transmitted and elaborated the views of Saint Thomas Aquinas (1224–74). Unpromising as a student, he was eventually accepted into the Jesuit order and became a priest. Suarez taught at a number of Spanish universities and in Rome, attaining great fame and wide influence. He was very prolific, writing on many metaphysical and theological topics and on the political problems of his time, such as the treatment of Catholics in England, as well as on natural law. His works tend to be lengthy. He generally gives careful consideration of the views of many others who have written on his subject, discussing their arguments and their biblical and other citations in detail, and only slowly coming to the presentation of his own final position. Drastic cutting was needed to obtain selections that might convey some of the main points of Suarez's theory within a reasonable number of pages. But even in abridged form there are a bewildering number of distinctions and claims to keep in mind if Suarez's theory is to be seen as a coherent whole.

Suarez accepted the general theses of classical natural law theory as it was developed by Saint Thomas Aquinas. Like Saint Thomas he presented a universe created and governed by God in ways designed to benefit each thing in it and to work for the common good of the whole creation. The pattern of governance is set by the eternal law, which is timeless and expresses God's nature; natural law is the special way in which humans "participate in" the eternal law. God directs the movements of stones and animals, but he does not do so, Suarez believed, by law properly so called. Law in the full sense pertains only to free and rational beings. We differ from the lower creatures because we can guide our actions by knowledge of the ways in which God means us to act. The natural law, unlike the law revealed in the Scriptures, can be discovered by reason, without the aid of special grace or revelation. Its first principles are self-evident; its other precepts can be derived from them – some with ease, others only with difficulty.

Suarez did not elaborate on how the laws are to be derived from the basic principles, nor did he give an exhaustive and careful list of the laws, divided according to degrees of evidence. Nonetheless, his general view is reasonably clear. He followed Saint Thomas in holding that one of the basic self-evident laws is that good is to be pursued and evil is to be avoided. Suarez did not suppose that other laws – such as those contained in the Decalogue – are simply deduced from this empty-sounding premise alone. Rather, we are to look at human nature and to apply the basic principle by seeing how each of the main characteristics that all of us have in common as humans can be used for good instead of for evil. God means all things, including the distinguishing features of our nature, to work for good, and the laws of nature spell out the ways in which this is to be done. Suarez did not seem to think there can be any controversy about what constitutes the good we are to work for – the special kind of happiness appropriate to us – nor did he treat as doubtful the content of the law of nature. His aim was not so much to instruct his reader about what kinds of actions are appropriate or required as it was to lay out the structure of natural law and to explain the main concepts involved in understanding it.

In some of his explanations Suarez went into considerably more detail than Saint Thomas did. One of the most important of his elaborations concerns the concept of obligation. Suarez tried to accommodate within a basically Thomistic framework the voluntarist theologians Scotus and Ockham (discussed briefly in the section "Luther and Calvin" in the Introduction to this anthology), who argued that morality arises solely from God's will. The voluntarists were strongly opposed by those who, following Thomas, held that God's legislation reflects or expresses his intellectual nature and therefore complies with the eternal truths of logic and morality. Suarez developed a position that would take account of both of these views. He argued, on the one hand, that God's legislative activity is guided by the goods and evils that are connected to the unalterable natures of created things, but he insisted also that moral obligation arises solely from God's command and that without command there is no law. His theory raised, more acutely than Thomas's did, a number of questions about how moral obligation binds the will, how human freedom is compatible with the will's being bound, and the relation between goodness and rightness as sources of human action generally.

Voluntarism was not merely an issue from the past or for Catholics. The Reformers Luther and Calvin, as I indicated in the Introduction, subscribed to versions of it; Descartes proposed his own variety of it; and the great natural lawyer Pufendorf opened his major work with a restatement of it. Conversely, innumerable writers during the period tried to refute voluntarism and to present alternatives to it. Suarez's mediating position was influential among philosophers and clergymen, including Protestants as well as Catholics. His work, therefore, not only shows one way in which classical natural law doctrine was carried forward into a new era; it also represents an early phase in the development of some of the issues that would become central to modern moral philosophy.

All of the following selections are taken from Suarez's treatise *On Law and God the Lawgiver,* as translated from *De legibus ac Deo legislatore* (1612) by Gwladys Williams, Ammi Brown, and John Waldron (Oxford: Oxford University Press, 1944), reprinted by permission of the Carnegie Endowment for International Peace. I have included the book, chapter, and section numbers, which are useful for giving references.

On Law and God the Lawgiver

Preface

It need not surprise anyone that it should occur to a professional theologian to take up the discussion of laws. For the eminence of theology, derived as it is from its most eminent subject-matter, precludes all reason for wonder. Surely, if the question is rightly examined, it will be evident that a treatise on laws is so included within the range of theology, that the theologian cannot exhaust his subject unless he tarries for a time in the study of laws. For just as theologians should contemplate God on many other grounds, so also should they contemplate Him on this ground: that He is the last end towards Whom rational creatures tend and in Whom their sole felicity consists. It follows, then, that the sacred science has this last end in view, and that it also sets forth the way to attain that end; since God is not only the end, and (as it were) the goal, towards which all intellectual creatures tend, but also the cause of that goal's attainment. For He directs His creatures, and, having shown the way, leads them to Himself. Moreover, He checks them with admonitions, that they may not stray from the path of righteousness, and when they do stray from it, by His ineffable providence He recalls them and shepherds them back, enlightening them by His teaching, admonishing them with His counsels, impelling them by His laws and, above all, succoring them with the aid of His grace. . . .

Since, then, the way of this salvation lies in free actions and in moral rectitude – which rectitude depends to a great extent upon law as the rule of human actions – it follows thence that the study of laws becomes a large division of theology; and when the sacred science treats of law, that science surely regards no other object than God Himself as Lawgiver. . . .

BOOK I: CONCERNING LAW IN GENERAL; AND CONCERNING ITS NATURE, CAUSES, AND EFFECTS

Chapter I: The Meaning of the Term "Law" (Lex)

1. St. Thomas defines the term "law" (*lex*) as follows: "Law is a certain rule and measure in accordance with which one is induced to act or is restrained from acting."[1] This definition would appear to be too broad and general. For law would in that case be applicable not only to men, or rational creatures, since everything has its own rule and measure. . . .

5. . . . accordingly, we should narrow the description given by St. Thomas, so that it runs as follows: law is a certain measure of moral acts, in the sense that such acts are characterized by moral rectitude through their conformity to law, and by perversity, if they are out of harmony with law.

6. Hence, although unrighteous precepts or rules are frequently designated by the term "law" . . . nevertheless, strictly and absolutely speaking, only that which is a measure of rectitude, viewed absolutely, and consequently that which is a right and virtuous rule, can be called law.

Chapter II: What Ius means and How It Is to Be compared with Lex

4. . . . the word *ius* has two principal meanings. . . . *ius* has the same meaning as *iustum* (that which is just), and *aequum* (that which is equitable),

these being the objects of *iustitia* (justice). Yet one must take into consideration the fact that the word *iustitia* has [also] two acceptations. In the first place, this word may stand for every virtue, since every virtue in some wise is directed toward and brings about equity. In the second place, it may signify a special virtue which renders to another that which is his due.[2] Accordingly, the word *ius* conforms, in due proportion, to each of these two meanings [of *iustitia*]. For, in the first sense, *ius* may refer to whatever is fair and in harmony with reason, this being, as it were, the general objective of virtue in the abstract. In the second sense, *ius* may refer to the equity which is due to each individual as a matter of justice. This latter acceptation is more common, since *ius* so taken is most particularly wont to be related to justice in the strict sense. Thus St. Thomas has said[3] that such justice constitutes the primary basis and significance of *ius*. And in consequence he well concludes that *ius* is not *lex*, but is rather that which is prescribed or measured by *lex*. . . .

5. According to the latter and strict acceptation of *ius*, this name is properly wont to be bestowed upon a certain moral power which every man has, either over his own property or with respect to that which is due to him. For it is thus that the owner of a thing is said to have a right (*ius*) in that thing, and the labourer is said to have that right to his wages by reason of which he is declared worthy of his hire. . . . Accordingly, this right to claim (*actio*), or moral power, which every man possesses with respect to his own property or with respect to a thing which in some way pertains to him, is called *ius*, and appears to be the true object of justice. . . .

Chapter III: The Extent of the Necessity for Laws, and of Their Variety

1. Having treated of the terms *ius* and *lex*, we must first demonstrate, before we inquire into the nature of *lex*, that it actually exists.

This demonstration will best be effected by explaining the necessity for *lex*. . . . Necessity, however, is usually divided into two kinds. One is the absolute necessity in accordance with which a given thing is said to be necessary of itself and for itself, in an absolute sense. Thus, there is attributed to God a necessity for His existence in accordance with His actual existence; and it is of this necessity that we are now speaking. The second kind is a relative necessity, having respect to some particular end or effect. This kind is subdivided into two phases: one phase is that of simple necessity; the other, that of necessity for the attainment of the better state, this latter phase being, in stricter parlance, utility.

2. Accordingly, two points seem, generally speaking, to be certain.

The first point is this: absolute necessity does not pertain to law as such. The proof of this assertion is as follows: such necessity is an attribute proper to God, Who alone is a Being existent *per se* and necessary in an absolute sense; whereas every law is either a created thing or at least one which presupposes the existence of some creature on whose account it is estab-

lished; for God cannot be subjected to law; and therefore, inasmuch as a
created thing is not absolutely necessary, law in like manner lacks the attribute of absolute necessity. In addition, I shall state that, if one is speaking of
law in the strict sense of the term (as we are now doing) it can [be considered to] exist only in view of some rational creature; for law is imposed only
upon a nature that is free, and has for its subject-matter free acts alone . . . ;
accordingly law cannot be more necessary than a rational or intellectual
creature; and rational creatures are not characterized by an absolute necessity for their existence; therefore, neither is law itself characterized by this
necessity. . . .

3. Secondly, I make the following assertion: if the creation of rational
creatures is assumed to have taken place, law, both absolutely and with a view
to attaining the better state, has become necessary in the necessity of its
purpose. This truth is (so to speak) . . . a self-evident principle.

Moreover, in so far as concerns the first part [of the assertion] – the part
relating to absolute necessity – one may adduce the argument that an intellectual creature, by virtue of the very fact that he is a created being, has a
superior to whose providence and control he is subject; while, for the very
reason that he is intellectual, he is capable of being subjected to moral government, which is effected through command; and therefore, it is connatural[4] to
such a creature, and necessary to him, that he be made subject to some
superior who will govern him through command, that is, through law.

Furthermore, this creature, because of the very fact that he has been made
out of nothing, may be bent to good or to evil. . . . Consequently, not only is
he capable of being subjected to law, whereby he may be directed towards the
good and held back from the evil, but furthermore, some such law is absolutely necessary for him, that he may live as becomes his nature. . . .

The second part of our assertion – that which relates to utility – is clearly
proved on the basis of the first part. For necessity pertaining to an end must
include utility. . . .

6. . . . a rational principle existing in the mind of God [is] recognized by the
theologians, who . . . call it the eternal law. . . . it as certainly exists in God,
as does His providence over the universe; for the term refers simply to the
essential principle of this providence, a principle dwelling in God, or to some
element of that providence. . . . just as it would be impossible for the universe
to continue in existence apart from divine providence, so would it be impossible apart from this divine and eternal law; and furthermore, all utility and
benefit flowing forth to this universe from divine providence should also be
ascribed to this same divine law.

8. . . . "law" is to be attributed to insensate things, not in its strict sense,
but metaphorically. . . . Not even brute animals are capable of [participating
in] law in a strict sense, since they have the use neither of reason nor of
liberty. . . .

9. Natural law, then, in the proper sense of the term – the natural law which
pertains to moral doctrine and to theology – is that form of law which dwells

within the human mind, in order that the righteous may be distinguished from the evil. . . .

17. It remains to discuss positive human law, which is so named because of the proximate source from which it flows . . . it was devised and established proximately by men . . . because the original derivation of every human law is in a certain sense traced back to the eternal law. . . .

18. . . . the necessity, or the utility, of this human law is also readily to be seen. For as St Thomas has noted,[5] its necessity springs from the fact that the natural, or the divine law, is of a general nature, and includes only certain self-evident principles of conduct, extending, at most, to those points which follow necessarily and by a process of obvious inference from the said principles; whereas, in addition to such points, many others are necessarily involved in the case of a human commonwealth in order that it may be preserved and rightly governed. . . .

19. . . . man is a social animal, requiring by his very nature a civil life and intercourse with other men; therefore, it is necessary that he should live rightly, not only as a private person, but also as a part of a community; and this is a matter which depends to a large extent upon the laws of the individual community. . . . Again, it is necessary that those points which relate to the common good of men, or of the state, should be accorded particular care and observance; yet, men as individuals have difficulty in ascertaining what is expedient for the common good, and moreover, rarely strive for that good as a primary object; so that, in consequence, there was a necessity for human laws. . . .

Chapter IV: What Acts in the Mind of the Lawmaker Are Necessary for the Making of a Law?

2. . . . law is a thing which pertains to the intellectual nature as such, and accordingly, to the mind thereof; both intellect and will being included. . . .

3. Secondly, I assume that law . . . is based upon a concrete act, and not upon a habit or power. This is clearly true, because that which is called law has the virtue of proximately moving its subjects and imposing an obligation upon them; but this virtue does not exist in potency or habit. . . .

6. In the first place, law, in so far as it is externally imposed upon the subjects, is a species of means for securing their welfare and peace or happiness. And therefore, one may assume first of all that the will of the lawmaker includes the purpose of promoting the common welfare. . . . From this purpose there follows forthwith in the intellect a consideration of this or that [possible] law, as to which of them is just, or suitable for the commonwealth. . . .

7. Secondly, it is certain that there is required, in addition to this act of judgment, an act on the part of the will, by which the prince agrees, chooses, and wills that his subjects shall be obedient to that which his intellect has judged expedient.[6] . . . the reason . . . is, briefly, this: law does not merely

enlighten, but also provides motive force and impels; and, in intellectual processes, the primary faculty for moving to action is the will. . . .

Chapter VI: Is it Inherent in the Nature of Law That It Should Be Instituted for Some Community?

8. . . . it is inherent in the nature of law, as signified by this name, that it be a common precept; that is to say, a precept imposed upon the community, or upon a multitude of men. . . .

Chapter VII: Is It Inherent in the Nature of Law That It Be Enacted for the Sake of the Common Good?

1. . . . With respect, then, to the question above set forth, there is no dispute among the various authorities; on the contrary, this axiom is common to them all: it is inherent in the nature and essence of law, that it shall be enacted for the sake of the common good; that is to say, that it shall be formulated particularly with reference to that good. . . .

3. This truth is indeed self-evident in the case of divine laws; so that it does not call for demonstration. For though the said laws are necessarily directed to the honouring of God (since He cannot will anything apart from Himself, or act save for His own sake), nevertheless in those laws He seeks not His own profit, but the good and happiness of humanity. Wherefore, since the divine works are superlatively perfect, and of a finely proportioned suitability, divine laws, in so far as they are given to a particular community, are accordingly given with a view to the common good and felicity of that community; a fact which becomes easily evident through a process of induction, with respect both to natural law and to the positive divine laws.[7]

Chapter IX: Is It Inherent in the Nature of Law That It Be Just?

2. . . . it is inherent in the nature and essence of law that it shall prescribe just things.

This assertion is not only indubitably true by the light of faith, but is also manifest by the light of natural reason.

. . . "justice" sometimes signifies a special virtue; while at other times it refers to all the virtues. But in the present case, our assertion that law should be just must be taken in a general sense, as meaning that whatever the law prescribes should be such that it may be executed justly and virtuously, that is, righteously. . . .

4. . . . a human legislator does not have a perfect will, as God has; and therefore, of himself and with respect to the deed [prescribed], such a legislator may sometimes prescribe unjust things, a fact which is manifestly true; but he has not the power to bind through unjust laws, and consequently, even though he may indeed prescribe that which is unjust, such a precept is not law,

inasmuch as it lacks the force or validity to impose a binding obligation. To be sure, I am speaking of unjust deeds which are opposed to natural or divine law. . . . no inferior can impose an obligation that is contrary to the law and the will of his superior; but a law prescribing a wrongful act is contrary to the law of God, Who prohibits that act; therefore [the former law] cannot be binding, for it is not possible that men should be bound, at one and the same time, to do and to abstain from doing a given thing. . . .

11. . . . However, all the Doctors indicate that the evidence of injustice in the law must be such as to constitute a moral certainty. For if the matter is doubtful, a presumption must be made in favour of the lawgiver. . . . the subjects, if this presumption in his favour did not exist, would assume an excessive licence to disregard the laws. . . .

17. . . . it is inherent in the nature of the law that it shall be practicable. This assertion, interpreted in a general sense, is applicable to every law.

However, in order that it may be proved and expounded, we should note that the term *possibilis* [practicable] admits of two distinct interpretations: first, as opposed, absolutely, to *impossibilis;* secondly, as opposed to what is difficult, oppressive, and burdensome.

Taken in the first sense, this property of practicability is a self-evident [requirement of law], whatsoever the evasive arguments heretics may employ.[8] For that which does not fall within the realm of freedom does not fall within that of law; but what is absolutely impossible does not come within the realm of freedom, since the latter of its very nature demands power to choose either of two alternatives; and therefore [what is impossible] cannot be the subject-matter of law. Similarly, in cases of transgression or omission which cannot be reckoned as involving guilt or calling for punishment, it is impossible for law to intervene. For it is a part of the intrinsic nature of law that it shall contain some intrinsic element of obligation; but the omission to perform impossible deeds cannot be accounted guilt . . . and therefore laws cannot be concerned with matters of this sort.

Chapter XII: What Definition of Law [lex] Is Derived from the Conditions of Law Above Set Forth?

3. . . . that deduced by St. Thomas[9] has more frequently been adopted, namely: "Law is an ordinace of reason for the common good, promulgated by one who is charged with the care of the community." . . .

4. A question indeed may arise owing to the fact that the said definition contains no limitation whereby counsel is excluded from law.

I therefore reply that counsel is excluded in a twofold manner. . . . For counsel, as such, is not of its very nature derived from a superior in so far as he possesses power over and charge of his subjects. . . . Counsel . . . passes essentially between equals. . . . Furthermore, the kind of ordinance in question should be interpreted as being an efficacious ordinance that has compulsory force. . . . For the word promulgation implies an order for the purpose of creating an obligation, and it is in this respect most of all that counsel differs from law.

5. . . . Therefore, law may perhaps be more briefly defined as follows: law is "a common, just, and stable precept which has been sufficiently promulgated."

BOOK II: ON THE ETERNAL LAW, THE NATURAL LAW, AND THE *IUS GENTIUM*

Chapter IV: Is the Eternal Law the Cause of All Laws?

2. . . . the eternal law . . . contains in itself a binding force, if it is sufficiently promulgated and applied.

The proof is that otherwise it would not be law in the true and proper sense, since it is of the essence of law to have binding force. . . .

4. . . . in some way, every law is derived from the eternal law, and receives binding force from the same.

Chapter V: Is the Natural Law Natural Right Reason?

9. . . . two aspects of rational nature are distinguishable: one being that nature itself, in so far as it is (so to speak) the basis of the conformity or non-conformity of human acts with itself; the other consisting in a certain power which this nature possesses, to discriminate between the actions in harmony with it and those discordant with it, a power to which we give the name of natural reason.

With regard to the first aspect, rational nature is said to be the basis of natural rectitude; but with regard to the second, it is said to be the very precept [*lex*] of nature which lays commands or prohibitions upon the human will regarding what must be done [or left undone], as a matter of natural law [*ius*]. . . .

10. The opinion in question may also find a basis in the words of Paul (Rom. 2: [14–15]), who, after saying: "For when the Gentiles who have not the law, do by nature those things that are of the law, these having not the law, are a law to themselves," adds, as if to indicate the way in which the Gentiles are a law unto themselves and the nature of that law: "Who show the work of the law written in their hearts, their conscience bearing witness to them." For conscience is an exercise of the reason, as is evident; and conscience bears witness to and reveals the work of the law written in the hearts of men, since it testifies that a man does ill or well, when he resists or obeys the natural dictates of right reason, revealing also, in consequence, the fact that such dictates have the force of law over man, even though, they may not be externally clothed in the form of written law. Therefore, these dictates constitute natural law; and, accordingly, the man who is guided by them, is said to be a law unto himself, since he bears law written within himself through the medium of the dictates of natural reason. St.

Thomas confirms this view[10] in his comment on the passage from Psalms 4: 6–7: "[Many say,] Who sheweth us good things? The light of thy countenance O Lord, is signed upon us"; for these words, [according to St. Thomas], mean that man participates by the light of reason in the eternal law, which dictates what must be done or left undone. This [rational illumination], then, is the natural law; for the latter is nothing other than a natural participation (so to speak) in the eternal law.

12. The opinion above set forth may be briefly supported by reasoning, in accordance with what has been said.

First, [we may argue] by means of an adequate discrimination: for natural law resides in man, since it does not reside in God, being temporal and created, nor is it external to man, since it is written not upon tablets but in the heart; neither does it dwell immediately within human nature itself, since we have proved that it does not do so; nor is it in the will, since it does not depend upon the will of man, but, on the contrary, binds and (as it were) coerces his will; hence, this natural law must necessarily reside in the reason.

Secondly, one may adduce the argument that the legal effects which may be thought of in the case of natural law, proceed immediately from a dictate of the reason, for that dictate directs and binds and is a rule of conscience which censures or approves what is done, so that law of the kind in question consists in the said dictate.

Thirdly, the exercise of dominion and the function of ruling are characteristic of law; and in man, these functions are to be attributed to right reason, that he may be rightly governed in accordance with nature; therefore, the natural law must be constituted in the reason, as in the immediate and intrinsic rule of human actions.

15. . . . "conscience" is a broader term than "natural law" since it puts into application, not only the law of nature, but also every other law, whether divine or human. Indeed, conscience is wont to apply not merely true law, but even reputed law, in which sense it sometimes occurs that conscience is in error. [True] law, on the other hand, can never be in error, for, by the very fact that it was erroneous, it would fail to be law, an assertion which is especially true with respect to the natural law, of which God is the Author.

Finally, law is properly concerned with acts which are to be performed; while conscience deals also with things which have already been done, and consequently is endowed not only with the attribute of imposing obligations, but also with those of accusing, bearing witness, and defending. . . .

Chapter VI: Is Natural Law in Truth Preceptive Divine Law?

5. . . . My first proposition, then, is as follows: Not only does the natural law indicate what is good or evil, but furthermore, it contains its own prohibition of evil and command of good.

6. This proposition may be proved, first, on the basis of the peculiar nature of law. For the natural law is truly law, inasmuch as all the Fathers, theolo-

gians, and philosophers so speak and think of it; but the mere knowledge or conception of anything existing in the mind cannot be called law, a fact which is self-evident and which follows also from the definition of law given above; therefore, . . .

A second argument may be drawn from those actions which are evil, in that they are prohibited by human law. For in the case of such acts, also, if a man is to be guilty of sin, it is necessary that there be a preceding mental judgment indicating that the thing in question is evil; yet that judgment has not the nature of a law or prohibition, since it merely indicates [a quality] existing within that thing, whatever the source of the quality may be; hence, by the same reasoning, although in those matters which fall within the province of the natural law as it relates to good or evil actions, a judgment pointing out the good or evil involved in a particular thing or act must necessarily precede [that act]; nevertheless, such a judgment has not the character of a law or of a prohibition, but is merely a recognition of some fact already assumed to be true. Accordingly, the act which is recognized as evil by the said judgment, is not evil for the reason that it is thus considered, but because it actually is evil, and is, in consequence, truly adjudged to be so; therefore, that judgment is not a rule of evil or of good; and consequently, neither is it a law nor a prohibition.

Thirdly, if the assertion in question were not true, God Himself would be subject to a natural law relating to His will; since even in God, an intellectual act of judgment logically precedes an act of His will, a judgment indicating that lying is wicked, that to keep one's promises is wholly right and necessary [and so forth]; and therefore, if such an act of the intellect is sufficient to constitute the essence of law, then there will be a true natural law, even with respect to God Himself.

Finally, a judgment showing the nature of a given action is not the act of a superior, but may, on the contrary, be that of an equal or of an inferior who has no binding power; and consequently, it is impossible for that judgment to have the nature of a law or of a prohibition. Otherwise, a teacher when he points out what is good and what is evil, would be imposing a law, an assertion which cannot [truthfully] be made. Law, then, is that sort of authority which can impose a binding obligation; whereas the judgment in question does not impose an obligation, but [simply] points out what obligation should be assumed to exist. Therefore, if this judgment is to have the nature of law, it must indicate some sort of authority as the source of such obligation.

11. My second assertion is as follows: this divine volition, in the form of a prohibition or in that of an [affirmative] command, is not the whole reason for the good or evil involved in the observance of transgression of the natural law; on the contrary, it necessarily presupposes the existence of a certain righteousness or turpitude in these actions, and attaches to them a special obligation derived from divine law. This second assertion is drawn from the words of St. Thomas, in the passages above cited.

The first part of the proposition may be deduced from an axiom common to the theologians, that certain evils are prohibited, because they are evil. For if they are forbidden on that very ground, they cannot derive the primary reason for their evil quality from the fact that they are prohibited, since an effect is not the reason for its cause. . . .

12. As for the latter half of this second proposition, its truth may be inferred from what we have already said in connection with the former conclusion. For the natural law prohibits those things which are bad in themselves; and this law is true divine law and a true prohibition; hence it must necessarily result in some sort of additional obligation to avoid an evil which is already evil of itself and by its very nature. Neither is it irrational to suppose that one may add to an act which is of itself righteous, the obligation to perform it; or that one may add to an act of itself evil, the obligation to avoid it. In fact, even when one obligation already exists, another may be added thereto, especially if it be of a different character, as is clearly true of a vow, a human law, and similar matters. Therefore, the law of nature, as it is true divine law, may also superimpose its own moral obligation, derived from a precept, over and above what may be called the natural evil or virtue inherent in the subject-matter in regard to which such a precept is imposed. This point will presently be more fully expounded, when we reply to the contrary argument.

13. From the foregoing, then, I conclude and state as my third proposition that the natural law is truly and properly divine law, of which God is the Author. . . .

23. Therefore, I hold with Cajetan (on I.–II, q. 100, art. 8),[11] that although the divine will is absolutely free in its external actions, nevertheless, if it be assumed that this will elicit one free act, then it may be necessarily bound, in consequence, to the performance of another action. For example, if through the divine will an unconditional promise is made, that will is obliged to fulfil the promise; and if it be the divine will to speak, or to make a revelation, that will must of necessity reveal what is true. In like manner, if it is the divine will to create the world, and to preserve the same in such a way as to fulfil a certain end, then there cannot fail to exist a providential care over that world; and assuming the existence of the will to exercise such providential care, there cannot but be a perfect providence, in harmony with the goodness and wisdom of the divine will. Accordingly, assuming the existence of the will to create rational nature [in such fashion that it shall be endowed] with sufficient knowledge for the doing of good and evil, and with sufficient divine co-operation for the performance of both, God could not have refrained from willing to forbid that a creature so endowed should commit acts intrinsically evil, nor could He have willed not to prescribe [for performance by the creature] the necessary righteous acts. For just as God cannot lie, neither can He govern unwisely or unjustly; and it would be a form of providence in the highest degree foreign to the divine wisdom and goodness, to refrain from forbidding or prescribing to those who were subject to that providence, such things as are [respectively] intrinsically evil, or necessary and righteous.

Therefore, in the [alleged] argument, we must make a distinction as to the minor premiss. For, absolutely speaking, God could have refrained from laying down any command or prohibition; yet, assuming that He has willed to have subjects endowed with the use of reason, He could not have failed to be their lawgiver – in those matters, at least, which are necessary to natural moral rectitude. In like manner, the arguments suggested above are sufficiently cogent, since God cannot fail to hate that evil which is opposed to right reason, and since, moreover, He entertains this hatred, not merely as a private individual, but also as Supreme Governor; therefore, because of this hatred, He wills to bind His subjects lest they commit such evil.

24. Secondly, however, the objection is raised, that the will of the lawgiver does not suffice for the completeness of law, unless a publication, or declaration, of that will also takes place; and there is no reason which makes it obligatory that God should declare His will; hence, it is possible that He may refrain from making such a declaration, since He is free to refrain; and, therefore, it is possible that He may not establish the law in question, nor create any binding obligation through it, inasmuch as no obligation exists, independently of the declaration.

To this second objection I shall reply, in the first place, that if that volition on the part of God is essential to a fitting and prudent providence and government over mankind, it is in consequence necessary that, by virtue of this same providence, that divine volition shall be capable of being made known to men; and this process is sufficient for the nature of a precept and of law, nor is any other form of declaration necessary. Wherefore, it may further be stated that this very faculty of judgment which is contained in right reason and bestowed by nature upon men, is of itself a sufficient sign of such divine volition, no other notification being necessary. The proof of the foregoing is as follows: the faculty of judgment contained in reason, of itself indicates the existence of a divine providence befitting God, and morally necessary for His complete dominion and for the due subjection of mankind to Him, within which providence the legislation in question is comprehended. Moreover, for this same cause, it is revealed by the light of natural understanding, that God is offended by sins committed in contravention of the natural law, and that the judgment and the punishment of those sins pertain to Him. Hence, this natural light is of itself a sufficient promulgation of the natural law, not only because it makes clearly manifest the intrinsic conformity or non-conformity of actions [with respect to that law] a conformity and non-conformity which are indicated by the increate light of God; but also because it makes known to man the fact that actions contrary [to the law so revealed] are displeasing to the Author of nature, as Supreme Lord, Guardian and Governor of that same nature. This, then, suffices for the promulgation of the law under discussion. . . .

Chapter VII: What Is the Subject-Matter Dealt with by Natural Law; or, What Are the Precepts of That Law?

1. We assume from the foregoing discussion that the subject-matter of natural law consists in the good which is essentially righteous, or necessary to

righteousness, and the evil which is opposed to that good; in the one, as something to be prescribed, in the other, as something to be forbidden.

The proof of this assumption is as follows: since the law in question is true law and God is its Author, it cannot be other than righteous; and, therefore, it cannot prescribe anything save that which is righteous, neither can it prohibit anything which is not opposed to righteousness. Morover, this law prescribes that which is in harmony with rational nature as such, and prohibits the contrary; and it is evident that the former is not otherwise than righteous.

Indeed, the natural law differs from other laws in this very respect, namely, that the latter render evil what they prohibit, while they render necessary, or righteous, what they prescribe; whereas the natural law assumes the existence in a given act or object, of the rectitude which it prescribes, or the depravity which it prohibits. Accordingly, it is usual to say that this law forbids a thing because that thing is evil, or prescribes a thing because it is good. We have already touched on this point, in the preceding Chapter.

4. Nevertheless, we must assert that the natural law embraces all precepts or moral principles which are plainly characterized by the goodness necessary to rectitude of conduct, just as the opposite precepts clearly involve moral irregularity or wickedness.

5. The assertion in question may also be demonstrated by reasoning. For those things which are recognized by means of natural reason, may be divided into three classes. First, some of them are primary and general principles of morality, such principles as: "one must do good, and shun evil," "do not to another that which you would not wish done to yourself," and the like. There is no doubt but that these principles pertain to the natural law. Again, there are certain others, more definite and specific, which, nevertheless, are also self-evident truths by their very terminology. Examples [of the second group] are these principles: "justice must be observed"; "God must be worshipped"; "one must live temperately"; and so forth. Neither is there any doubt concerning [the fact that] this group [comes under the natural law], a point which will become evident, *a fortiori*, as a result of the discussion that is to follow. In the third class, we place those conclusions which are deduced from natural principles by an evident inference, and which cannot become known save through rational reflection. Of these conclusions, some are recognized more easily than others, and by a greater number of persons; as, for example, the inferences that adultery, theft, and similar acts are wrong. Other conclusions require more reflection, of a sort not easily within the capacity of all, as is the case with the inferences that fornication is intrinsically evil, that usury is unjust, that lying can never be justified, and the like.

The assertion set forth above may, then, be understood as applicable to all these [principles and conclusions]; for all of them pertain to the natural law. And if this truth is established with regard even to the conclusions of any one of these classes, then, the same truth will, *a fortiori*, be established with regard to the other conclusions mentioned, provided only that a degree of evidence involving certainty is reached.

6. Therefore, the proof follows; first, by a process of induction. For the precepts of the Decalogue are precepts of natural law, a fact accepted by all. Yet they do not all embody self-evident principles. On the contrary, some of them require reflection, as is also evident. This point is still more clear with regard to many natural precepts which are included within those of the Decalogue; as, for example, the prohibitions against simple fornication, against usury and against vengeance inflicted upon an enemy by one's own authority, all of which according to Catholic doctrine, indubitably pertain to natural law. In like manner, the affirmative commands to keep vows and promises, to give alms out of one's superfluous possessions, to honour one's parents, are natural precepts, not only according to the faith, but also according to the philosophers and all right-thinking persons. Yet the conclusions [leading to these precepts] are not reached without reflection and, in some cases, a great deal of elaborate reasoning.

7. Thirdly, no one is doubtful as to the primary and general principles; hence, neither can there be doubt as to the specific principles, since these, also, in themselves and by virtue of their very terminology, harmonize with rational nature as such; and, therefore, there should be no doubt with respect to the conclusions clearly derived from these principles, inasmuch as the truth of the principle is contained in the conclusion, and he who prescribes or forbids the one, necessarily prescribes or forbids that which is bound up in it, or without which it could not exist. Indeed, strictly speaking, the natural law works more through these proximate principles or conclusions than through universal principles; for a law is a proximate rule of operation, and the general principles mentioned above are not rules save in so far as they are definitely applied by specific rules to the individual sorts of acts or virtues.

Finally, all these precepts proceed, by a certain necessity, from nature, and from God as the Author of nature, and all tend to the same end, which is undoubtedly the due preservation and natural perfection or felicity of human nature; therefore, they all pertain to the natural law.

12. A difficulty arises, however, with regard to the first part of the explanation, a difficulty as to whether there exists in connection with every virtue, a natural precept requiring the exercise of that virtue at one time or another. For, as a general rule, it is a sufficiently self-evident fact that this is the case; but the rule does not seem to hold with regard to certain virtues, such as liberality, which by its very nature would seem to exclude an attendant obligation, or *eutrapelia* (urbanity),[12] which also appears to be in large measure a matter of choice.

An exact treatment of this difficulty, indeed, would necessitate an examination of all the virtues. Consequently, I shall state briefly that if the term "precept" is taken in its rigorous meaning, as involving obligation under pain of mortal guilt, then precepts are to be applied not to every sort of virtue, but only to the more important ones, a fact which is proved by the argument set forth above. With regard to truth [for example], many persons hold that this virtue is never in itself obligatory under pain of mortal guilt, unless there is attached to it an obligation of justice or of some other similar virtue which is involved in it; [otherwise, truth] is not prescribed under penalty of mortal guilt. If, however, we are speaking more broadly, so as to include obligations under pain of venial guilt, there is probably, in that sense, no virtue the practice of which is not at one time or another obligatory. For, in view of the fact that the perfect rectitude of an individual man, his proper behaviour, both relatively to himself and in his relations with others, results from the possession of all the virtues collectively, it is probable that there are for each of the virtues respectively occasions on which it ought to be practised, owing to a special obligation attaching to each, with respect to which neither liberality nor any other virtue is an exception.

Chapter VIII: Is the Natural Law One Unified Whole?

1. Three questions may be asked at this point. First, with respect to a single individual, is the natural law one unified whole? Secondly, with respect to all men and in all places, is it one unified whole? Thirdly, is it also such a unified whole with respect to all time and every condition of human nature?

2. Turning to the first question, then, we must state that with respect to any one individual, there are many natural precepts; but that from all of these there is formed one unified body of natural law. . . . The basis of this unity, apart from the common manner of speaking, consists, according to St. Thomas, in the fact that all natural precepts may be reduced to one first principle in which these precepts are (as it were) united; for where there is union, there is also a certain unity. . . . it may be added that all natural precepts are united in one end; in one author or lawgiver, also; and in the one characteristic of avoiding evil because it is evil, and of prescribing good because it is right and necessary; so that these facts suffice to constitute a moral unity.

3. However, in order that the multitude of precepts may be reduced to some kind of order, they may be distinguished from one another under various heads. For example, they may be distinguished with reference to the persons for whom they are – objectively, so to speak – ordained. Thus, certain precepts relate to God; certain others to one's neighbour; and still others, to the individual himself. Or, the precepts in question may be distinguished according to the virtues [which they prescribe]. For some relate to justice; others to charity or natural love; and so on. Or, again, they may be distinguished according to their respective relations to the intellect. It is thus that natural precepts are classified by St. Thomas, Cajetan, and others, even as propositions necessarily true are classified by the philosophers. For certain of these precepts are manifest in and of themselves, and with respect to all men, as is the case with the most universal precepts. Others are manifest in and of themselves, and in an immediate sense, but not in so far as relates to our apprehension, although they may have this character in so far as relates to the wise. As examples of this group, we have certain precepts regarding individ-

ual virtues, and the Commandments of the Decalogue. However, there are still other precepts, which call for reflection [in order that they may be known], and this group, in turn, admits of gradations; for certain of these precepts are recognized easily, others with difficulty. The distinctions above set forth will be useful in examining the matter of ignorance in regard to natural law, a point which we shall presently discuss.

4. Lastly, St. Thomas,[13] followed by Cajetan and others, traces this variety in the natural precepts to the varied natural inclinations of mankind. For man is (as it were) an individual entity and as such has an inclination to preserve his own being, and to safeguard his own welfare; he is also a being corruptible – that is to say, mortal – and as such is inclined towards the preservation of the species, and towards the actions necessary to that end; and finally, he is a rational being and as such is inclined towards the preservation of the species, and towards the actions necessary to that end; and finally, he is a rational being and as such is suited for immortality, for spiritual perfection, and for communication with God and social intercourse with rational creatures. Hence, the natural law brings man to perfection, with regard to every one of his tendencies and, in this capacity, it contains various precepts – for example, precepts of temperance and of fortitude, relating to the first tendency mentioned above; those of chastity and prudence, relating to the third tendency. For all these propensities in man must be viewed as being in some way determined and elevated by a process of rational gradation. For, if these propensities are considered merely in their natural aspect, or as animal propensities, they must be bridled, that virtue may be attained and on the other hand, if the same propensities are considered with respect to their capacity for being regulated by right reason, then proper and suitable precepts apply to each of them.

5. In answer to the second question, the statement must be made that this natural law is a unified whole with respect to all men and in all places.

The rational basis of this position is that the law in question is (so to speak) a peculiar quality accompanying not the particular rational faculty of any given individual, but rather that characteristic nature which is the same in all men. Furthermore, synteresis[14] is one and the same in all men; and, absolutely speaking, the recognition of the truth of conclusions might be one and the same; therefore, the law of nature is also one and the same [in all men].

At this point, one encounters the objection that various nations have followed laws contrary to natural precepts; and that consequently, the natural law is not the same in all nations.

To this objection, following St. Thomas (*ibid.*), I shall reply briefly that the natural law in so far as relates to its substance is one and the same among all men, but that, in so far as concerns the knowledge of it, that law is not complete (so to speak) among all.

6. I shall expound this statement briefly. For, as I have previously remarked, the natural law may be considered in its first act, and as such, it may be regarded as the intellectual understanding itself; so that it is therefore evident that in this sense, the natural law is one and the same in all men.

Furthermore, it may be the same with respect to the second act, that is, in actual cognition and judgment, or again, in a proximate habit induced by such act; and in this sense, the natural law is in part [the same] in all who have the use of reason. For in so far, at least, as regards the primary and most universal principles – no one can be ignorant of this law, inasmuch as those principles are by the very terms defining them completely known and to such a degree in harmony with and (as it were) fitted to the natural bent of the reason and will, that it is not possible to evade them. . . . On the other hand, one may [less reprehensibly] be ignorant of particular precepts; and, assuming the existence of such ignorance, some nations may have introduced rules contrary to the natural law, although these rules were never regarded by them as natural, but were considered as positive human rules.

7. In this connexion, however, a question arises as to whether such ignorance of natural precepts can be invincible. . . . my opinion shall be briefly stated here, as follows: it is not possible that one should in any way be ignorant of the primary principles of the natural law, much less invincibly ignorant of them; one may, however, be ignorant of the particular precepts, whether of those which are self-evident, or of those which are deduced with great ease from the self-evident precepts.

Yet such ignorance cannot exist without guilt; not, at least, for any great length of time; for knowledge of these precepts may be acquired by very little diligence; and nature itself, and conscience, are so insistent in the case of the acts relating to those [precepts] as to permit no inculpable ignorance of them. . . . However, with respect to other precepts, which require greater reflection, invincible ignorance is possible, especially on the part of the multitude.

Chapter IX: Is the Natural Law Binding in Conscience?

1. Thus far, we have expounded the nature and causes, that is to say, the subject-matter, of the natural law. Next in order we must treat of the effects of that law, of which the chief, or very nearly the sole effect, is its binding force, for if the natural law does have other effects, they too may be reduced to this one. Its binding obligation then, and the mode in which it so binds, must be discussed.

2. In the first place, we must establish the fact that the natural law is binding in conscience.

This conclusion is unquestionably true, being a matter of faith, according to the theologians. It may be deduced, moreover, from the words of Paul (Rom. 2: [12]): "For whosoever have sinned without the law," – the written law, undoubtedly – "shall perish with the law"; that is [they shall perish] because they have violated the natural law. With regard to the latter, Paul adds [14–15]: "The Gentiles, who have not the law, do by nature those things that are of the law [. . .], their conscience bearing witness to them."

As for the reasons in favour of the above proposition, however, the first is that the natural law is the law of God, as has been shown. Secondly, this law is the proximate rule of moral goodness; and therefore, moral evil is wont to result from defiance of this law, so that sin is defined as an act contrary to God's law. . . .

3. As against this truthful assertion, however, it may in the first place be urged that the natural law is a dictate of natural reason; but natural reason knows nothing of eternal punishment; hence, this law cannot be binding under pain of eternal punishment; and consequently, it cannot bind under pain of mortal guilt. The truth of the latter consequent is evident, because that sin is mortal which leads to eternal punishment. And the truth of the former consequent is proved, since a law cannot be binding with the sanction of a punishment which it can neither indicate nor inflict.

For the present, we simply assert that, according to the faith, it cannot be denied that a transgression of the natural law suffices for the incurring of eternal punishment, even if the transgressor be ignorant of every supernatural law. For this fact is convincingly established by the testimony of Paul, and by the arguments already adduced. Neither is it to be controverted by the objection set forth above, for even though, in us, the natural law is reason itself, nevertheless in God, it is the Divine reason or will, and therefore it suffices that God Himself should know the penalty due to transgressors of that law. For in order that the subject and transgressor of the law may incur a given penalty, it is not necessary that he himself shall be aware of the penalty attaching to his transgression; on the contrary, it suffices if he commits an act that deserves such punishment.

Chapter XIV: Is Natural Law Subject to Human Power?

7. . . . among the precepts of natural law, there are certain precepts – dealing with pacts, agreements, obligations – which are introduced through the will of men: for example, the laws relating to the observance of vows and of human promises, whether these be made in simple form or confirmed by oath; and the same is true of other contracts, according to the particular characteristics of each; and true, also, of rights, natural and legal, arising therefrom.

There are other natural laws, however, which are directly binding, in their very subject-matter and independently of any prior consent by human will: for example, the positive precepts of religion in relation to God, of filial piety, of mercy, and of almsgiving to one's neighbour; and the negative precepts against killing, those against slander, and similar prohibitions. In both kinds of precepts there is involved the same necessity in so far as concerns the formal character of law, and consequently, there are the same uniformity and immutability; but with respect to the subject-matter, the second group of precepts possesses a greater degree of immutability, since they have not for their subject-matter (so to speak) human free will, which is exceedingly changeable and frequently requires correction and alteration.

Editor's Notes

1. Saint Thomas Aquinas, *Summa Theologiae,* Ia IIae 90.1; hereafter referred to simply as *ST.*
2. Suarez here follows Aristotle and Saint Thomas in distinguishing between justice in a broad sense, which is the whole of virtue insofar as virtue affects others besides the agent, and justice in a more specific sense, in which it is the virtue that renders to each his or her due. The latter is closer to the modern sense of the term.
3. *ST* IIa IIae 57.1.
4. That is, not part of the created being's nature but always accompanying it, as regularly as if it were part of that nature.
5. *ST* Ia IIae 91.3.
6. Although Suarez talks of a prince in this paragraph, his point is meant to apply to God's legislation as well.
7. Positive divine laws are laws God has given to particular communities, for example, to the Jews, whereas natural laws are laws God has laid down for all people.
8. Suarez is referring to Martin Luther, who, as indicated in the section "Luther and Calvin" in the Introduction, held that the moral commandments were laid down by God in order to show us both what we absolutely ought to do and what we cannot do, at least not by our own unaided efforts. In this way, "the Law is a schoolmaster unto Christ," showing us our desperate need for grace. Suarez followed Saint Thomas's theory of grace, touched on in the section "Saint Augustine and Saint Thomas" in the Introduction, which is very different.
9. *ST* Ia IIae 90.4.
10. *ST* Ia Iae 91.2.
11. The reference is the *Commentary* on Saint Thomas's *Summa* by Thomas de Vio, Cardinal Cajetan (1468–1534).
12. Aristotle uses the term to mean "ready wit" (*Rhetoric* 1389b11, *Nicomachean Ethics* 1108a24) – plainly not something that includes obligation. (I owe this information to Prof. Russell M. Dancy.)
13. *ST,* Ia IIae 94.2.
14. A technical term, discussed briefly in the section "Saint Augustine and Saint Thomas" in the Introduction to this volume, referring to the aspect of conscience in which it is a "repository of principles"; that is, it is in possession of general precepts for guiding and judging action. Its other main aspect is its ability to subsume particular cases under these principles.

Further Reading

The translation from which the selections in this volume were taken does not include the whole of *On Law and God the Lawgiver,* but it is the fullest source available in English for the study of Suarez's views on morality. Parts of some of his political and metaphysical works have been translated as well.

The neglect of Suarez by English-language scholars of natural law is reflected in the scarcity of works on him written in English. J. H. Fichter, *Man of Spain: Francisco Suarez* (New York: Macmillan, 1940), is a general study. There is a useful monograph by Reijo Wilenius, *The Social and Political Theory of Francisco Suarez,* in *Acta Philosophica Fennica,* vol. 15 (Helsinki: Philosophical Society of Finland, 1963), which contains a bibliography. Henrich Rommen examined Suarez in his *The Natural Law,* trans. Thomas R. Hanley (St. Louis: Herder, 1947). Suarez's political views are the focus of an excellent discussion in Quentin Skinner, *The Foundations of Modern Political Thought* (Cambridge, England: Cambridge University Press, 1978), vol. 2, chap. 5, which also looks at some of the other Thomists of the period. For further background, consult Bernice Hamilton, *Political Thought in Sixteenth Century Spain* (Oxford: Clarendon Press, 1963).

Hugo Grotius

Introduction

In 1788 Thomas Reid praised the "immortal Hugo Grotius" as the author of the first noteworthy attempt to systematize the commonsense morality of the human race with the aid of the civil law's technical apparatus. Eighty years earlier Jean Barbeyrac, who translated Grotius's main work into French, claimed that Grotius was the "first who broke the ice" in the modern history of the "science of morality." It was Grotius who left behind the sterile debates of the Aristotelian scholastics and opened the way for the modern development of moral philosophy, and it was Grotius's position, Barbeyrac added, and not that of the brilliant but dangerous Hobbes, that was continued by Pufendorf and Locke. Nineteenth- and twentieth-century surveys of the history of moral philosophy do not give Grotius so important a place, but if we wish to see the subject as it looked in early modern Europe, we cannot ignore him.

Hugo Grotius was born in the Netherlands in 1583. A brilliant and precocious scholar, he was part of a diplomatic mission to France when he was only fifteen. He practiced law, held several high public offices, and wrote Latin dramas as well as treatises on maritime law and a history of his country. Much against his will Grotius became involved in the fierce religious controversies then dividing the Protestants of Holland, which were connected with continuing struggles for political power. As a result he was sentenced in 1619 to life imprisonment. A daring escape engineered by his wife enabled him to flee to France, where he wrote his main work, *De jure belli ac pacis* (*On the Law of War and Peace*), first published in 1625. After serving as the Swedish ambassador to France and writing works on theology and other subjects, he died in 1645.

Grotius is often described as the first "modern" natural law thinker. The title is meant to distinguish him from the Thomistic thinkers who, like Suarez, continued to write and be read well into and beyond Grotius's lifetime. The reader will find several reasons for thinking of Grotius as an innovator, but what is usually taken to entitle Grotius to special recognition is the passage in §11 of the "Prolegomena" to *On the Law of War and Peace* in which he claimed that there would be binding laws of nature even if God did not exist. This statement is central to Grotius's aims of freeing natural law theory from religious controversy and of making the study of natural law a discipline that could be pursued without regard to sectarian religious differences. If Grotius had claimed only that there are goods and ills independent of the existence of God, his view would not have been particularly original. Such claims had been made in one form or another by various earlier thinkers. They were what Suarez had in mind when he asserted that goods and ills alone do not give rise to obligation and that a sanction imposed by a lawgiver must be added if there are to be obligations. Grotius's innovation was his assertion that there would be obligations, and not simply goods and ills, even if God did not exist.

Grotius did not offer any abstract proof that Suarez was mistaken on this point. What gave weight to his view was his use of it in developing an explicit statement of a body of law that was both acceptable to people of all religious confessions and capable of guiding the most important aspects of international relations, in peace as well as war. In order to do this Grotius set out the principles he thought were behind the institutions of private property, promise and contract, and marriage. His proposals on all these matters continued to influence actual legislation in Germany and elsewhere in Europe well into the eighteenth century.

To open the way for his system, Grotius found it necessary to assert that it is possible to have definite knowledge of laws that bind all people alike. This involved him in an attempt to confront the skepticism that had been expressed by writers such as Montaigne. In taking on this issue, Grotius ventured into matters that were not addressed by the traditional natural lawyers, who simply did not see skepticism as a problem. Theorists like Suarez took themselves to be expounding and improving the work of their authoritative sources – Aristotle, the church fathers, or Saint Thomas himself. Grotius cited many authorities, among them writers from classical antiquity, theologians, and scholastic natural lawyers, but his aim was not to explain or even to accommodate their views. It was simply to call them as witnesses to the fact that everyone – or at least the wisest men in the civilized nations – had always agreed on the basic principles of natural law. Grotius was contending that there was far less disagreement about the laws of nature than there was said to be by the skeptics of his time, who were, of course, his real targets, rather than the ancient skeptic, Carneades, whom he named.

Grotius also offered a theory about the sources of this agreement, a theory about our basic desires. We are self-interested, but we also are sociable. We look out for ourselves – a point Hobbes later stressed – but we enjoy one another's company for its own sake. Society therefore must be organized to take account of our ineradicable tendency to engage in controversies as well as our inherent sociability, and natural law shows us how to do it. Grotius's point seems to be that no one can deny these claims about human beings; so if it can be shown that these are the facts on which the laws of nature depend, the skeptic will be overcome. This is not an epistemological argument about the nature of knowledge, and even if it is effective, it does not establish certainty about anything but the foundations of morals.

If Grotius was breaking new ground in taking on skepticism, he was also innovating by introducing a new understanding of rights. He treated rights as attributes that each individual possesses independently of membership in any group or society and prior to being under any law. He also held that any or all of an individual's rights could be given away, a point he took to be shown by the possibility of agreeing to be a slave if one is given the choice of slavery or death when one is captured during wartime. In asserting that rights are qualities of individuals as such, Grotius was breaking with older views and initiating a way of understanding the sphere of control belonging to individuals that is still important. Against the skeptic it would seem less effective to claim that all humans possess rights than to hold that all are moved to some extent by self-interest. Yet both claims are important to Grotius's theory.

Because Grotius wrote as a lawyer rather than as a philosopher, the philosophically important parts of his text, after the "Prolegomena," are widely scattered. He opened with a bewildering array of definitions of law and of kinds of rights, none of which he put to immediate use. It was only later, when Grotius discussed more specific issues such as the origins of political power or of property, that he began to apply the notions. I have therefore included some of these specific discussions, although they bear more directly on political than on moral philosophy. The reader will see in some of these selections that while writing at length of rights and laws, Grotius also referred occasionally to love as an important part of our relations with one another. If he did not elaborate a complete theory of the relations between law and love, he did include enough about it to lead his successors to say more.

The following selections are taken from *On the Law of War and Peace,* trans. Francis W. Kelsey (Oxford: Oxford University Press, 1925).

On the Law of War and Peace

PROLEGOMENA

1. The Municipal law of Rome and of other states has been treated by many, who have undertaken to elucidate it by means of commentaries or to reduce it to a convenient digest. That body of law, however, which is concerned with the mutual relations among states or rulers of states, whether derived from nature, or established by divine ordinances, or having its origin in custom and tacit agreement, few have touched upon. Up to the present time no one has treated it in a comprehensive and systematic manner; yet the welfare of mankind demands that this task be accomplished.

5. Since our discussion concerning law will have been undertaken in vain if there is no law, in order to open the way for a favourable reception of our work and at the same time to fortify it against attacks, this very serious error must be briefly refuted. In order that we may not be obliged to deal with a crowd of opponents, let us assign to them a pleader. And whom should we choose in preference to Carneades?[1] For he had attained to so perfect a mastery of the peculiar tenet of his Academy that he was able to devote the power of his eloquence to the service of falsehood not less readily than to that of truth.

Carneades, then, having undertaken to hold a brief against justice, in particular against the phase of justice with which we are concerned, was able to muster no argument stronger than this, that for reasons of expediency, men imposed upon themselves laws, which vary according to customs, and among the same peoples often undergo changes as times change; moreover that there is no law of nature, because all creatures, men as well as animals, are impelled by nature towards ends advantageous to themselves; that, consequently, there is no justice, or, if such there be, it is supreme folly, since one does violence to his own interests if he consults the advantage of others.

6. What the philosopher here says . . . must not for one moment be admitted. Man is, to be sure, an animal, but an animal of a superior kind, much farther removed from all other animals than the different kinds of animals are

from one another; evidence on this point may be found in the many traits peculiar to the human species. But among the traits characteristic of man is an impelling desire for society, that is, for the social life – not of any and every sort, but peaceful, and organized according to the measure of his intelligence, with those who are of his own kind; this social trend the Stoics called "sociableness." Stated as a universal truth, therefore the assertion that every animal is impelled by nature to seek only its own good cannot be conceded.

7. Some of the other animals, in fact, do in a way restrain the appetency for that which is good for themselves alone, to the advantage, now of their offspring, now of other animals of the same species. This aspect of their behaviour has its origin, we believe, in some extrinsic intelligent principle, because with regard to other actions, which involve no more difficulty than those referred to, a like degree of intelligence is not manifest in them. The same thing must be said of children. In children, even before their training has begun, some disposition to do good to others appears . . . ; thus sympathy for others comes out spontaneously at that age. The mature man in fact has knowledge which prompts him to similar actions under similar conditions, together with an impelling desire for society, for the gratification of which he alone among animals possesses a special instrument, speech. He has also been endowed with the faculty of knowing and of acting in accordance with general principles. Whatever accords with that faculty is not common to all animals, but peculiar to the nature of man.

8. This maintenance of the social order, which we have roughly sketched, and which is consonant with human intelligence, is the source of law properly so called. To this sphere of law belong the abstaining from that which is another's, the restoration to another of anything of his which we may have, together with any gain which we may have received from it; the obligation to fulfil promises, the making good of a loss incurred through our fault, and the inflicting of penalties upon men according to their deserts.

9. From this signification of the word law there has flowed another and more extended meaning. Since over other animals man has the advantage of possessing not only a strong bent towards social life, of which we have spoken, but also a power of discrimination which enables him to decide what things are agreeable or harmful (as to both things present and things to come), and what can lead to either alternative: in such things it is meet for the nature of man, within the limitations of human intelligence, to follow the direction of a well-tempered judgement, being neither led astray by fear or the allurement of immediate pleasure, nor carried away by rash impulse. Whatever is clearly at variance with such judgement is understood to be contrary also to the law of nature, that is, to the nature of man.

10. To this exercise of judgement belongs moreover the rational allotment to each man, or to each social group, of those things which are properly theirs, in such a way as to give the preference now to him who is more wise over the less wise, now to a kinsman rather than to a stranger, now to a poor man rather than to a man of means, as the conduct of each or the nature of the thing suggests.

Long ago the view came to be held by many, that this discriminating allotment is a part of law, properly and strictly so called; nevertheless law, properly defined, has a far different nature, because its essence lies in leaving to another that which belongs to him or in fulfilling our obligations to him.

11. What we have been saying would have a degree of validity even if we should concede that which cannot be conceded without the utmost wickedness, that there is no God, or that the affairs of men are of no concern to Him.[2] The very opposite of this view has been implanted in us partly by reason, partly by unbroken tradition, and confirmed by many proofs as well as by miracles attested by all ages. Hence it follows that we must without exception render obedience to God as our Creator, to Whom we owe all that we are and have; especially since in manifold ways, He has shown Himself supremely good and supremely powerful, so that to those who obey Him He is able to give supremely great rewards, even rewards that are eternal, since He Himself is eternal. We ought, moreover, to believe that He was willed to give rewards, and all the more should we cherish such a belief if He has so promised in plain words; that He has done this, we Christians believe, convinced by the indubitable assurance of testimonies.

12. Herein, then, is another source of law besides the source in nature, that is, the free will of God, to which beyond all cavil our reason tells us we must render obedience. But the law of nature of which we have spoken, comprising alike that which relates to the social life of man and that which is so called in a larger sense, proceeding as it does from the essential traits implanted in man, can nevertheless rightly be attributed to God, because of His having willed that such traits exist in us.

13. There is an additional consideration in that, by means of the laws which He has given, God has made those fundamental traits more manifest, even to those who possess feebler reasoning powers; and He has forbidden us to yield to impulses drawing us in opposite directions – affecting now our own interest, now the interest of others – in an effort to control more effectively our more violent impulses and to restrain them within proper limits.

15. Again, since it is a rule of the law of nature to abide by pacts (for it was necessary that among men there be some method of obligating themselves one to another, and no other natural method can be imagined), out of this source the bodies of municipal law have arisen. For those who had associated themselves with some group, or had subjected themselves to a man or to men, had either expressly promised, or from the nature of the transaction must be understood impliedly to have promised, that they would conform to that which should have been determined, in the one case by the majority, in the other by those upon whom authority had been conferred.

16. What is said, therefore, in accordance with the view not only of Carneades but also of others, that

> Expediency is, as it were, the mother
> Of what is just and fair,[3]

is not true, if we wish to speak accurately. For the very nature of man, which even if we had no lack of anything would lead us into the mutual relations of society, is the mother of the law of nature. But the mother of municipal law is that obligation which arises from mutual consent; and since this obligation derives its force from the law of nature, nature may be considered, so to say, the great-grandmother of municipal law.

The law of nature nevertheless has the reinforcement of expediency; for the Author of nature willed that as individuals we should be weak, and should lack many things needed in order to live properly, to the end that we might be the more constrained to cultivate the social life. But expediency afforded an opportunity also for municipal law, since that kind of association of which we have spoken, and subjection to authority, have their roots in expediency. From this it follows that those who prescribe laws for others in so doing are accustomed to have, or ought to have, some advantage in view.

18. Wrongly, moreover, does Carneades ridicule justice as folly. For since, by his own admission, the national who in his own country obeys its laws is not foolish, even though, out of regard for that law, he may be obliged to forgo certain advantages for himself, so that nation is not foolish which does not press its own advantage to the point of disregarding the laws common to nations. The reason in either case is the same. For just as the national, who violates the law of his country in order to obtain an immediate advantage,* breaks down that by which the advantages of himself and his posterity are for all future time assured, so the state which transgresses the laws of nature and of nations cuts away also the bulwarks which safeguard its own future peace. Even if no advantage were to be contemplated from the keeping of the law, it would be a mark of wisdom, not of folly, to allow ourselves to be drawn towards that to which we feel that our nature leads.

19. Wherefore, in general, it is by no means true that

> You must confess that laws were framed
> From fear of the unjust,[4]

a thought which in Plato some one explains thus, that laws were invented from fear of receiving injury, and that men are constrained by a kind of force to cultivate justice. For that relates only to the institutions and laws which have been devised to facilitate the enforcement of right; as when many persons in themselves weak, in order that they might not be overwhelmed by the more powerful, leagued themselves together to establish tribunals and by combined force to maintain these, that as a united whole they might prevail against those with whom as individuals they could not cope.

And in this sense we may readily admit also the truth of the saying that right is that which is acceptable to the stronger; so that we may understand that law fails of its outward effect unless it has a sanction behind it. . . .

20. Nevertheless law, even though without a sanction, is not entirely void of

---

* . . . Marcus Aurelius . . . says: "What is advantageous to the swarm is advantageous to the bee."

effect. For justice brings peace of conscience, while injustice causes torments and anguish, such as Plato describes, in the breast of tyrants. Justice is approved, and injustice condemned, by the common agreement of good men. But, most important of all, in God injustice finds an enemy, justice a protector. He reserves His judgements for the life after this, yet in such a way that He often causes their effects to become manifest even in this life, as history teaches by numerous examples.

25. Least of all should that be admitted which some people imagine, that in war all laws are in abeyance. On the contrary war ought not to be undertaken except for the enforcement of rights; when once undertaken, it should be carried on only within the bounds of law and good faith. . . .

39. . . . . I have made it my concern to refer the proofs of things touching the law of nature to certain fundamental conceptions which are beyond question, so that no one can deny them without doing violence to himself. For the principles of that law, if only you pay strict heed to them, are in themselves manifest and clear, almost as evident as are those things which we perceive by the external senses; and the senses do not err if the organs of perception are properly formed and if the other conditions requisite to perception are present. . . .

40. In order to prove the existence of this law of nature, I have furthermore, availed myself of the testimony of philosophers, historians, poets, finally also of orators. Not that confidence is to be reposed in them without discrimination; for they were accustomed to serve the interests of their sect, their subject, or their cause. But when many at different times, and in different places, affirm the same thing as certain, that ought to be referred to a universal cause; and this cause, in the lines of inquiry which we are following, must be either a correct conclusion drawn from the principles of nature, or common consent. The former points to the law of nature; the latter, to the law of nations.

The distinction between these kinds of law is not to be drawn from the testimonies themselves (for writers everywhere confuse the terms law of nature and law of nations), but from the character of the matter. For whatever cannot be deduced from certain principles by a sure process of reasoning, and yet is clearly observed everywhere, must have its origin in the free will of man.

43. . . . . it seems to me that not without reason some of the Platonists and early Christians departed from the teachings of Aristotle in this, that he considered the very nature of virtue as a mean in passions and actions.[5] That principle, once adopted, led him to unite distinct virtues, as generosity and frugality, into one; to assign to truth extremes between which, on any fair premiss, there is no possible co-ordination, boastfulness, and dissimulation; and to apply the designation of vice to certain things which either do not exist, or are not in themselves vices, such as contempt for pleasure and for honours, and freedom from anger against men.

44. That this basic principle, when broadly stated, is unsound, becomes clear even from the case of justice. For, being unable to find in passions and acts resulting therefrom the too much and the too little opposed to that virtue,

Aristotle sought each extreme in the things themselves with which justice is concerned.[6] Now in the first place this is simply to leap from one class of things over into another class, a fault which he rightly censures in others; then, for a person to accept less than belongs to him may in fact under unusual conditions constitute a fault, in view of that which, according to the circumstances, he owes to himself and to those dependent on him; but in any case the act cannot be a variance with justice, the essence of which lies in abstaining from that which belongs to another.

By equally faulty reasoning Aristotle tries to make out that adultery committed in a burst of passion, or a murder due to anger, is not properly an injustice. Whereas nevertheless injustice has no other essential quality than the unlawful seizure of that which belongs to another; and it does not matter whether injustice arises from avarice, from lust, from anger, or from ill-advised compassion; or from an overmastering desire to achieve eminence, out of which instances of the gravest injustice constantly arise. For to disparage such incitements, with the sole purpose in view that human society may not receive injury, is in truth the concern of justice.

45. To return to the point whence I started, the truth is that some virtues do tend to keep passions under control; but that is not because such control is a proper and essential characteristic of every virtue. Rather it is because right reason, which virtue everywhere follows, in some things prescribes the pursuing of a middle course, in others stimulates to the utmost degree. We cannot, for example, worship God too much; for superstition errs not by worshipping God too much, but by worshipping in a perverse way. Neither can we too much seek after the blessings that shall abide for ever, nor fear too much the everlasting evils, nor have too great hatred for sin. . . .

48. I frequently appeal to the authority of the books which men inspired by God have either written or approved, nevertheless with a distinction between the Old Testament and the New. There are some who urge that the Old Testament sets forth the law of nature. Without doubt they are in error, for many of its rules come from the free will of God. And yet this is never in conflict with the true law of nature; and up to this point the Old Testament can be used as a source of the law of nature, provided we carefully distinguish between the law of God, which God sometimes executes through men, and the law of men in their relations with one another.

This error we have, so far as possible, avoided, and also another opposed to it, which supposes that after the coming of the New Testament the Old Testament in this respect was no longer of use. We believe the contrary, partly for the reasons which we have already given, partly because the character of the New Testament is such that in its teachings respecting the moral virtues it enjoins the same as the Old Testament or even enjoins greater precepts. In this way we see that the early Christian writers used the witnesses of the Old Testament. . . .

50. The New Testament I use in order to explain – and this cannot be learned from any other source – what is permissible to Christians. This,

however – contrary to the practice of most men – I have distinguished from the law of nature, considering it as certain that in that most holy law a greater degree of moral perfection is enjoined upon us than the law of nature, alone and by itself, would require. And nevertheless I have not omitted to note the things that are recommended to us rather than enjoined, that we may know that, while the turning aside from what has been enjoined is wrong and involves the risk of punishment, a striving for the highest excellence implies a noble purpose and will not fail of its reward. . . .

58. If any one thinks that I have had in view any controversies of our own times, either those that have arisen or those which can be foreseen as likely to arise, he will do me an injustice. With all truthfulness I aver that, just as mathematicians treat their figures as abstracted from bodies, so in treating law I have withdrawn my mind from every particular fact.

Book I

Chapter I: What Is War? What Is Law?

I. Scope of the treatise

Controversies among those who are not held together by a common bond of municipal law are related either to time of war or to times of peace. Such controversies may arise among those who have not yet united to form a nation, and those who belong to different nations, both private persons and kings; also those who have the same body of rights that kings have, whether members of a ruling aristocracy, or free peoples.

War, however, is undertaken in order to secure peace, and there is no controversy which may not give rise to war. In undertaking to treat the law of war, therefore, it will be in order to treat such controversies, of any and every kind, as are likely to arise. War itself will finally conduct us to peace as its ultimate goal.

III. Law is considered as a rule of action . . .

1. In giving to our treatise the title "The Law of War," we mean first of all, as already stated, to inquire whether any war can be just, and then, what is just in war. For law in our use of the term here means nothing else than what is just, and that, too, rather in a negative than in an affirmative sense, that being lawful which is not unjust.

Now that is unjust which is in conflict with the nature of society of beings endowed with reason. . . .

IV. A body of rights in respect to quality is divided into faculties and aptitudes

There is another meaning of law viewed as a body of rights, different from the one just defined but growing out of it, which has reference to the person.

In this sense a right becomes a moral quality of a person, making it possible to have or to do something lawfully.

Such a right attaches to a person, even if sometimes it may follow a thing, as in the case of servitudes over lands, which are called real rights, in contrast with other rights purely personal; not because such rights do not also attach to a person, but because they do not attach to any other person than the one who is entitled to a certain thing.

When the moral quality is perfect[7] we call it *facultas*, "faculty"; when it is not perfect, *aptitudo*, "aptitude." To the former, in the range of natural things, "act" corresponds; to the latter, "potency."

V. Faculties, or legal rights strictly so called, are divided into powers, property rights, and contractual rights

A legal right (*facultas*) is called by the jurists the right to one's own (*suum*); after this we shall call it a legal right properly or strictly so called.

Under it are included power, now over oneself, which is called freedom, now over other, as that of the father (*patria potestas*) and that of the master over slaves; ownership, either absolute, or less than absolute, as usufruct[8] and the right of pledge; and contractual rights, to which on the opposite side contractual obligations correspond.

VIII. On expletive justice and attributive justice . . .

1. Legal rights are the concern of expletive justice (*iustitia expletrix*), which is entitled to the name of justice properly or strictly so called. This is called "contractual" justice by Aristotle, with too narrow a use of the term; for though the possessor of something belonging to me may give it back to me, that does not result "from a contract," and nevertheless the act falls within the purview of this type of justice; and so the same philosopher has more aptly termed it "restorative" justice.

Aptitudes are the concern of attributive justice (*iustitia attributrix*). This Aristotle called "distributive" justice. It is associated with those virtues which have as their purpose to do good to others, as generosity, compassion, and foresight in matters of government. . . .

IX. Law is defined as a rule, and divided into the law of nature and volitional law

1. There is a third meaning of the word law, which has the same force as statute whenever this work is taken in the broadest sense as a rule of moral actions imposing obligation to what is right. We have need of an obligation; for counsels and instructions of every sort, which enjoin what is honourable indeed but do not impose an obligation, do not come under the term statute or law. Permission, again, is not, strictly speaking, an operation of law, but a negation of operation, except in so far as it obligates another not to put any hindrance in the way of him to whom permission is given. We said, moreover, "imposing obligation to what is right," not merely to what is lawful, because

law in our use of the term here stands related to the matter not only of justice, as we have set it forth, but also of other virtues. Nevertheless that which, in accordance with this law, is right, in a broader sense is called just.

2. The best division of law thus conceived is found in Aristotle, that is, into natural law and volitional law, to which he applies the term statutory, with a rather strict use of the word statute; sometimes he calls it established law. . . .

X. Definition of the law of nature, division, and distinction from things which are not properly so called

1. The law of nature is a dictate of right reason, which points out that an act, according as it is or is not in conformity with rational nature, has in it a quality of moral baseness or moral necessity; and that in consequence, such an act is either forbidden or enjoined by the author of nature, God.

2. The acts in regard to which such a dictate exists are, in themselves, either obligatory or not permissible, and so it is understood that necessarily they are enjoined or forbidden by God. In this characteristic the law of nature differs not only from human law, but also from volitional divine law; for volitional divine law does not enjoin or forbid those things which in themselves and by their own nature are obligatory or not permissible, but by forbidding things it makes them unlawful, and by commanding things it makes them obligatory.

3. For the understanding of the law of nature, again, we must note that certain things are said to be according to this law not in a proper sense but – as the Schoolmen love to say – by reduction, the law of nature not being in conflict with them; just as we said above that things are called just which are free from injustice. Sometimes, also, by misuse of the term, things which reason declares are honourable, or better than their opposites, are said to be according to the law of nature, although not obligatory.

4. It is necessary to understand, further, that the law of nature deals not only with things which are outside the domain of the human will, but with many things also which result from an act of the human will. Thus ownership, such as now obtains, was introduced by the will of man; but, once introduced, the law of nature points out that it is wrong for me, against your will, to take away that which is subject to your ownership. . . .

5. The law of nature, again, is unchangeable – even in the sense that it cannot be changed by God. Measureless as is the power of God, nevertheless it can be said that there are certain things over which that power does not extend; for things of which this is said are spoken only, having no sense corresponding with reality and being mutually contradictory. Just as even God, then, cannot cause that two times two should not make four, so he cannot cause that that which is intrinsically evil be not evil.

XI. That the instinct common to other animals, or that peculiar to man, does not constitute another kind of law

1. The distinction, which appears in the books of Roman law, between an unchangeable law common to animals and man, which the Roman legal writ-

ers[9] call the law of nature in a more restricted sense, and a law peculiar to man, which they frequently call the law of nations, is of hardly any value. For, strictly speaking, only a being that applies general principles is capable of law. . . .

XII. *In what way the existence of the law of nature is proved*

1. In two ways men are wont to prove that something is according to the law of nature, from that which is antecedent and from that which is consequent. Of the two lines of proof the former is more subtle, the latter more familiar.

Proof *a priori* consists in demonstrating the necessary agreement or disagreement of anything with a rational and social nature; proof *a posteriori,* in concluding, if not with absolute assurance, at least with every probability, that that is according to the law of nature which is believed to be such among all nations, or among all those that are more advanced in civilization. For an effect that is universal demands a universal cause; and the cause of such an opinion can hardly be anything else than the feeling which is called the common sense of mankind.

Chapter II: Whether It Is Ever Lawful to Wage War

I. *That war is not in conflict with the law of nature is proved by several considerations*

1. Having seen what the sources of law are, let us come to the first and most general question, which is this: whether any war is lawful, or whether it is ever permissible to wage war. This question, as also the others which will follow, must first be taken up from the point of view of the law of nature.

Marcus Tullius Cicero, both in the third book of his treatise *On Ends*[10] and in other places, following Stoic writings learnedly argues that there are certain first principles of nature – "first according to nature," as the Greeks phrased it – and certain other principles which are later manifest but which are to have the preference over those first principles. He calls first principles of nature those in accordance with which every animal from the moment of its birth has regard for itself and is impelled to preserve itself, to have zealous consideration for its own condition and for those things which tend to preserve it, and also shrinks from destruction and things which appear likely to cause destruction. Hence also it happens, he says, that there is no one who, if the choice were presented to him, would not prefer to have all the parts of his body in proper order and whole rather than dwarfed or deformed; and that it is one's first duty to keep oneself in the condition which nature gave to him, then to reject those things that are contrary thereto.

2. But after these things have received due consideration [Cicero continues], there follows a notion of the conformity of things with reason, which is superior to the body. Now this conformity, in which moral goodness becomes the paramount object, ought to be accounted of higher import than the

things to which alone instinct first directed itself, because the first principles of nature commend us to right reason, and right reason ought to be more dear to us than those things through whose instrumentality we have been brought to it.

Since this is true and without other demonstration would easily receive the assent of all who are endowed with sound judgement, it follows that in investigating the law of nature it is necessary first to see what is consistent with those fundamental principles of nature, and then to come to that which, though of later origin, is nevertheless more worthy – that which ought not only to be grasped, if it appear, but to be sought out by every effort. . . .

4. In the first principles of nature there is nothing which is opposed to war; rather, all points are in its favour. The end and aim of war being the preservation of life and limb, and the keeping or acquiring of things useful to life, war is in perfect accord with those first principles of nature. If in order to achieve these ends it is necessary to use force, no inconsistency with the first principles of nature is involved, since nature has given to each animal strength sufficient for self-defence and self-assistance.

5. Right reason, moreover, and the nature of society, which must be studied in the second place and are of even greater importance, do not prohibit all use of force, but only that use of force which is in conflict with society, that is which attempts to take away the rights of another. For society has in view this object, that through community of resource and effort each individual be safeguarded in the possession of what belongs to him.

6. It is not, then, contrary to the nature of society to look out for oneself and advance one's own interests, provided the rights of others are not infringed; and consequently the use of force which does not violate the rights of others is not unjust. . . .

VI. Preliminary considerations bearing upon the question whether war is in conflict with the law of the Gospel

9. The third argument[11] is wont to be taken from the passage which follows in *Matthew* [v. 43]: "Ye have heard that it was said, Thou shalt love thy neighbour and hate thine enemy; but I say unto you, love your enemies, bless them that curse you, pray for them that despitefully use you and persecute you." For there are men who think that with such love and well-doing towards enemies and them that despitefully use us, both capital punishment and wars are irreconcilable.

The argument, however, is easily refuted if we take into consideration the precise provision of the Hebraic law. It was enjoined upon the Jews to love their neighbour, that is a Jew; . . . But magistrates were none the less commanded to put to death murderers and others guilty of heinous crimes; the eleven tribes none the less attacked the tribe of Benjamin in a just war on account of a monstrous crime (*Judg.*, v. 21); none the less did David, who "fought the battles of the Lord," undertake to wrest from Ishbosheth by arms, and rightly, the kingdom which had been promised to him.

10. Let us concede, then, a broader signification of the word "neighbour," to include all men – for all men have now been received into a common dispensation, there are no peoples doomed by God to destruction – nevertheless that will be permitted with respect to all men which was then permitted with respect to the Israelites; they were bidden to love one another, just as now all men are. And if you wish to believe also that a greater degree of love is commanded in the law of the Gospel, let this too be granted, provided also the fact is recognized that love is not due to all in the same degree, but that a greater love is due to a father than to a stranger. In like manner also, in accordance with the law of a well-ordered love, the good of an innocent person should receive consideration before the good of one who is guilty, and the public good before that of the individual.

Now it is in the love of innocent men that both capital punishment and just wars have their origin. . . . The teachings of Christ in regard to loving and helping men ought, therefore, to be carried into effect unless a greater and more just love stand in the way.

Chapter III: On the Distinction Between Public and Private War

VII. What sovereignty is

1. That power is called sovereign whose actions are not subject to the legal control of another, so that they cannot be rendered void by the operation of another human will. When I say "of another," I exclude from consideration him who exercises the sovereign power, who has the right to change his determinations; I exclude also his successor, who enjoys the same right, and therefore has the same power, not a different power. Let us, then, see who is the subject of sovereignty.

The subject of a power is either common or special. Just as the body is a common, the eye a special subject of the power of sight, so the state, which we have defined above as a perfect[12] association, is the common subject of sovereignty. . . .

VIII. The opinion that sovereignty always resides in the people is rejected, and arguments are answered

1. At this point first of all the opinion of those must be rejected who hold that everywhere and without exception sovereignty resides in the people, so that it is permissible for the people to restrain and punish kings whenever they make a bad use of their power. How many evils this opinion has given rise to, and can even now give rise to if it sinks deep into men's minds, no wise person fails to see. We refute it by means of the following arguments.

To every man it is permitted to enslave himself to any one he pleases for private ownership, as is evident both from the Hebraic and from the Roman Law.[13] Why, then, would it not be permitted to a people having legal competence to submit itself to some one person, or to several persons, in such a way as plainly to transfer to him the legal right to govern, retaining no vestige of that right for itself? And you should not say that such a presumption is not admissible; for we are not trying to ascertain what the presumption should be in case of doubt, but what can legally be done.

It is idle, too, to bring up the inconveniences which result, or may result, from such a procedure; for no matter what form of government you may devise, you will never be free from difficulties and dangers. . . .

2. Just as, in fact, there are many ways of living, one being better than another, and out of so many ways of living each is free to select that which he prefers, so also a people can select the form of government which it wishes; and the extent of its legal right in the matter is not to be measured by the superior excellence of this or that form of government, in regard to which different men hold different views, but by its free choice.

3. In truth it is possible to find not a few causes which may impel a people wholly to renounce the right to govern itself and to vest this in another, as, for example, if a people threatened with destruction cannot induce anyone to defend it on any other condition; again, if a people pinched by want can in no other way obtain the supplies needed to sustain life. . . .

Chapter IV: War of Subjects Against Superiors

I. State of the question
2. The question to be considered here is simply this, whether it is permissible for either private or official persons to wage war against those under whose authority they are, whether this authority be sovereign or subordinate. . . .

3. Among all good men one principle at any rate is established beyond controversy, that if the authorities issue any order that is contrary to the law of nature or to the commandments of God, the order should not be carried out. For when the Apostles said that obedience should be rendered to God rather than men, they appealed to an infallible rule of action, which is written in the hearts of all men, and which you may find in Plato[14] expressed in about as many words. But if from any such cause, or under other conditions as a result of caprice on the part of him who holds the sovereign power, unjust treatment be inflicted on us, we ought to endure it rather than resist by force. . . .

VII. What view is to be taken in case of extreme and in other respects unavoidable necessity
1. More serious is the question whether the law of nonresistance should bind us in case of extreme and imminent peril. Even some laws of God, although stated in general terms, carry a tacit exception in case of extreme necessity. . . .

2. I do not deny that even according to human law certain acts of a moral nature can be ordered which expose one to a sure danger of death; an example is the order not to leave one's post. We are not, however, rashly to assume

that such was the purpose of him who laid down the law; and it is apparent that men would not have received so drastic a law applying to themselves and others except as constrained by extreme necessity. For laws are formulated by men and ought to be formulated with an appreciation of human frailty.

Now this law which we are discussing – the law of nonresistance – seems to draw its validity from the will of those who associate themselves together in the first place to form a civil society; from the same source, furthermore, derives the right which passes into the hands of those who govern. If these men could be asked whether they purposed to impose upon all persons the obligation to prefer death rather than under any circumstances to take up arms in order to ward off the violence of those having superior authority, I do not know whether they would answer in the affirmative, unless, perhaps, with this qualification, in case resistance could not be made without a very great disturbance in the state, and without the destruction of a great many innocent people. I do not doubt that to human law also there can be applied what love under such circumstances would commend. . . .

Book II

Chapter I: The Causes of War – First, Defence of Self and Property

I. What causes of war may be called justifiable

1. Let us proceed to the causes of war – I mean justifiable causes; for there are also other causes which influence men through regard for what is expedient and differ from those that influence men through regard for what is right. . . .

IX. Defence is sometimes not permissible against a person useful to the state because at variance with the law of love

1. On the other hand, it may happen that, since the life of the assailant is useful to many, he cannot be killed without wrong. And this is true, not only according to divine law, whether of the old or the new dispensation – this we treated above, when we showed that the person of a king is sacred – but also by the law of nature. For the law of nature, in so far as it has the force of a law, holds in view not only the dictates of expletive justice, as we have called it, but also actions exemplifying other virtues, such as self-mastery, bravery, and prudence, as under certain circumstances not merely honourable, but even obligatory. And to such actions we are constrained by regard for others.

Chapter II: Of Things Which Belong to Men in Common

I. The division of that which is our own

Next in order among the causes of war[15] is an injury actually received; and first, an injury to that which belongs to us. Some things belong to us by a right common to mankind, others by our individual right.

Let us begin with the right which is common to all men. This right holds good directly over a corporeal thing, or over certain actions. Corporeal things free from private ownership are either such as cannot become subject to private ownership, or such as can. In order to understand the distinction fully, it will be necessary to know the origin of proprietorship, which jurists call the right of ownership.

II. *The origin and development of the right of private ownership*

1. Soon after the creation of the world, and a second time after the Flood, God conferred upon the human race a general right over things of a lower nature.[16] "All things," as Justin says, "were the common and undivided possession of all men, as if all possessed a common inheritance."[17] In consequence, each man could at once take whatever he wished for his own needs, and could consume whatever was capable of being consumed. The enjoyment of this universal right then served the purpose of private ownership; for whatever each had thus taken for his own needs another could not take from him except by an unjust act. This can be understood from the comparison used by Cicero in his third book *On Ends*.[18] "Although the theatre is a public place, yet it is correct to say that the seat which a man has taken belongs to him."

This primitive state might have lasted if men had continued in great simplicity, or had lived on terms of mutual affection such as rarely appears. . . .

2. Men did not, however, continue to live this simple and innocent life, but turned their thoughts to various kinds of knowledge, the symbol for which was the tree of knowledge of good and evil, that is a knowledge of the things of which it is possible to make at times a good use, at times a bad use. . . .

The most ancient arts, agriculture and grazing, were pursued by the first brothers, not without some interchange of commodities. From the difference in pursuits arose rivalry, and even murder; and at length, since the good were corrupted by contact with the wicked, there came the kind of life ascribed to the giants, that is given over to violence, like the life of those whom the Greeks characterized as "men that cultivate justice with the fist." After the world had been cleansed by the Deluge, that brutish life was succeeded by a passion for pleasure, to which wine ministered; whence came also unlawful loves.

3. Harmony, however, was destroyed chiefly by a less ignoble vice, ambition, of which the symbol was the tower of Babel.

4. From these sources we learn what was the cause on account of which the primitive common ownership, first of movable objects, later also of immovable property, was abandoned. The reason was that men were not content to feed on the spontaneous products of the earth, to dwell in caves, to have the body either naked or clothed with the bark of trees or skins of wild animals, but chose a more refined mode of life; this gave rise to industry, which some applied to one thing, others to another.

Moreover, the gathering of the products of the soil into a common store was hindered first by the remoteness of the places to which men had made their

way, then by the lack of justice and kindness; in consequence of such a lack
the proper fairness in making division was not observed, either in respect to
labour or in the consumption of the fruits.

5. At the same time we learn how things became subject to private ownership. This happened not by a mere act of will, for one could not know what
things another wished to have, in order to abstain from them – and besides
several might desire the same thing – but rather by a kind of agreement,
either expressed, as by a division, or implied, as by occupation. In fact, as
soon as community ownership was abandoned, and as yet no division had
been made, it is to be supposed that all agreed, that whatever each one had
taken possession of should be his property. . . .

VI. *That in case of necessity men have the right to use things which have
    become the property of another, and whence this right comes*

1. Now let us see whether men in general possess any right over things
which have already become the property of another.

Some perchance may think it strange that this question should be raised,
since the right of private ownership seems completely to have absorbed the
right which had its origin in a state of community of property. Such, however,
is not the case. We must, in fact, consider what the intention was of those who
first introduced individual ownership; and we are forced to believe that it was
their intention to depart as little as possible from natural equity. For as in this
sense even written laws are to be interpreted, much more should such a point
of view prevail in the interpretation of usages which are not held to exact
statement by the limitations of a written form.

2. Hence it follows, first, that in direst need the primitive right of user
revives, as if community of ownership had remained, since in respect to all
human laws – the law of ownership included – supreme necessity seems to
have been excepted.

3. Hence it follows, again, that on a voyage, if provisions fail, whatever
each person has ought to be contributed to the common stock. Thus, again, if
fire has broken out, in order to protect a building belonging to me I can
destroy a building of my neighbour. I can, furthermore, cut the ropes or nets
in which my ship has been caught, if it cannot otherwise be freed. None of
these rules was introduced by the civil law, but they have all come into existence through interpretations of it.

4. Even among the theologians the principle has been accepted that, if a
man under stress of such necessity takes from the property of another what is
necessary to preserve his own life, he does not commit a theft.

The reason which lies back of this principle is not, as some allege, that the
owner of a thing is bound by the rule of love to give to him who lacks; it is,
rather, that all things seem to have been distributed to individual owners with
the benign reservation in favour of the primitive right. For if those who made
the original distribution had been asked what they thought about this matter
they would have given the same answer that we do. . . .

Chapter XII: On Contracts

VII. What acts are called contracts

Now all acts of benefits to others, except mere acts of kindness, are called contracts.

*VIII. That equality is required in contracts; and first, equality as regards
     preceding acts*

The law of nature enjoins that there be equality in contracts, and in such a way that the party who receives less acquires a right of action from the inequality.

IX. That equality is required in contracts as regards knowledge of the facts

1. To the preceding acts the consideration pertains that the person who is making a contract with any one ought to point out to him the faults of the thing concerned in the transaction which are known to himself. This is not only prevailingly established by the civil laws but is also consistent with the nature of the act. For between the contracting parties there is a closer union than ordinarily obtains in human society.

2. The same thing, however, should not be said in regard to circumstances which have no direct connexion with the thing contracted for; as if any one should know that many ships were in route bringing grain. The giving of such information is, in fact, a part of one's duty, and praiseworthy, so that often it cannot be omitted without violating the rule of love. Yet such omission is not unjust, that is, it is not inconsistent with the right of the one with whom the contract is made.[19]

X. That equality is required in contracts as regards freedom of choice

Not only in the knowledge of facts but also in the freedom of choice there ought to be a kind of equality between the contracting parties. Not indeed that any preceding fear, if justly inspired, ought to be removed, for that is outside of the contract; but that no fear should be unjustly inspired for the sake of making the contract, or, if such fear has been inspired, that it should be removed.

Chapter XX: On Punishments

*XLI. The law of nature must be distinguished from widely current national
     customs*

But at this point certain precautions need to be stated.

First, national customs are not to be taken for the law of nature, although they have been received on reasonable grounds among many peoples.

XLII. The law of nature must be distinguished also from the Divine law that is not voluntarily recognized by all

Second, we should not hastily class with the things forbidden by nature those with regard to which this point is not sufficiently clear, and which are rather prohibited by the law of the Divine Will. In this class we may perhaps place unions not classed as marriages and those which are called incestuous, as well as usury.

XLIII. In the law of nature we must distinguish between what is evident and what is not evident

1. Third, we should carefully distinguish between general principles, as, for example, that one must live honourably, that is according to reason, and certain principles akin to these, but so evident that they do not admit of doubt, as that one must not seize what belongs to another, and inferences; such inferences in some cases easily gain recognition, as that, for example, accepting marriage we cannot admit adultery, but in other cases are not so easily accepted, as the inference that vengeance which is satisfied with the pain of another is wicked. Here we have almost the same thing as in mathematics, where there are certain primary notions, or notions akin to those that are primary, certain proofs which are at once recognized and admitted, and certain others which are true indeed but not evident to all.

2. Therefore, just as in the case of municipal laws we excuse those who lack knowledge or understanding of the laws, so also with regard to the laws of nature it is right to pardon those who are hampered by weakness of their powers of reasoning or deficient education. For as ignorance of the law, if it is unavoidable, cancels the sin, so also, when it is combined with a certain degree of negligence, it lessens the offence.

Chapter XXIII: On Doubtful Causes of War

I. On the source of the causes of doubt in moral questions

What Aristotle wrote[20] is perfectly true, that certainty is not to be found in moral questions in the same degree as in mathematical science. This comes from the fact that mathematical science completely separates forms from substance, and that the forms themselves are generally such that between two of them there is no intermediate form, just as there is no mean between a straight and a curved line. In moral questions, on the contrary, even trifling circumstances alter the substance, and the forms, which are the subject of inquiry, are wont to have something intermediate, which is of such scope that it approaches now more closely to this, now to that extreme.

Thus it comes about that between what should be done and what it is wrong to do there is a mean, that which is permissible; and this is now closer to the former, now to the latter. Hence there often comes a moment of doubt, just as when day passes into night, or when cold water slowly becomes warm. This is what Aristotle means when he says: "Oftentimes it is hard to decide what choice one should make." . . .

II. *Nothing is to be done contrary to the dictates of one's mind, however erroneous they may be*

1. First of all we must hold to the principle that, even if something is in itself just, when it is done by one who, taking everything into consideration, considers it unjust, the act is vicious. This in fact is what the Apostle Paul meant by saying, "Whatsoever is not of faith, is sin,"[21] where "faith" signifies the judgement of the mind on the matter. For God has given the power of judgement as a guide for human actions, and if this is treated with contempt the mind becomes brutish.

2. Nevertheless, it often happens that the judgement presents no certainty, but is undecided. If this indecision cannot be dissipated by careful consideration, we must follow the precept of Cicero:[22] "That is a good rule which they lay down who bid you not to do a thing when you are in doubt whether it is right or wrong." . . .

This course, however, cannot be pursued where one really must do one of two things, and yet is in doubt whether either is right. In that case he will be allowed to choose that which appears to him to be less wrong. For always, when a choice cannot be avoided, the lesser evil assumes the aspect of the good. . . .

Chapter XXV: On the Causes of Undertaking War on Behalf of Others

III. *Whether an innocent subject may be surrendered to an enemy, in order that danger may be avoided*

1. Thus if one citizen, although innocent, is demanded by an enemy, to be made away with, there is no doubt that he may be abandoned to them if it appears that the state is by no means a match for the power of the enemy.

This view is opposed by Fernando Vazquez;[23] but, if you consider his purpose rather than his words, he seems to be making this point, that such a citizen is not to be hastily abandoned, where there is hope that he may be defended. For he also cites the story of the Italian infantry who deserted Pompey when his cause was not yet clearly desperate, but when they had been assured of their safety by Caesar. This conduct he deservedly censures.

2. Still the learned do discuss the question whether an innocent citizen may be delivered into the hands of the enemy, in order to prevent the ruin otherwise threatening the state; and the same question was debated long ago, as when Demosthenes brought forward the notable fable of the dogs, which the wolves demanded should be surrendered to them by the sheep for the sake of peace. That such a surrender may be made is denied not merely by Vazquez but also by Soto, whose opinion is attacked by Vazquez as bordering on

treachery. Nevertheless, Soto holds that such a citizen is bound to surrender himself to the enemy; but this also is denied by Vazquez, on the ground that the nature of political society, which each enters for his own advantage, does not require it.

3. But from this nothing more follows than that a citizen is not bound to surrender himself by law properly so called; it does not follow also that love permits him to do otherwise. For there are many duties which are not in the domain of justice properly speaking, but in that of affection, which are not only discharged amid praise (this Vazquez does not recognize) but cannot even be omitted without blame.

Such a duty seems quite clearly to be this, that a person should value the lives of a very large number of innocent persons above his own life.

Editor's Notes

1. Carneades (c. 213–128 B.C.E.), head of the Platonic Academy, who developed skeptical arguments against the Epicureans and the Stoics. None of his writings has survived intact. Cicero's *De republica* contains some discussion of his views, in Book III.vff. Cicero's own work survives only in fragmentary form and does not contain much that came directly from Carneades. More fragments of Carneades' work were quoted in a treatise, the *Divine Institutes*, by the third-century Christian apologist Lactantius. Grotius could have known of Carneades from both these sources.

   The accuracy of Grotius's presentation of Carneades does not matter much, because his real concern, as I have indicated, was with contemporary skepticism.
2. The Latin *etiamsi daremus*, translated as "even if we should concede," is often taken as a shorthand way to identify this important statement. Denial that God is concerned about humans, or that he exercises providential care over his creation, was interpreted by many writers during the seventeenth and eighteenth centuries as amounting to a denial that God exists.
3. Horace, *Satires*, I.iii.98.
4. Horace, *Satires*, I.iii.111.
5. Aristotle, *Nicomachean Ethics* II.6–II.9.
6. Aristotle treats justice in *Nicomachean Ethics*, V.
7. The Latin *perfectus* means "complete." A perfect right is a complete right, with all the attributes of a right, including enforceability at law. An imperfect right is less complete. Creditors have a perfect right to be paid what is owed them; beggars have an imperfect right to be given alms. Grotius said little about this distinction, which nonetheless came to be of considerable significance to later writers.
8. A Roman legal term, meaning the right to enjoy the use of something such as land and what comes from using it, when it is owned by someone else.
9. The early codifier of Roman law, Ulpian, is said to have written a passage found near the opening of Justinian's *Digest* and the *Institutes:* "Natural law is that which nature has taught all animals. For it is not peculiar to the human race but belongs to all animals. From this law comes the union of male and female, which we call marriage, and the begetting and education of children. For we see that all other animals are likewise governed by a knowledge of this law." Quoted in Barry Nicholas, *An Introduction to Roman Law* (Oxford: Oxford University Press, 1984), pp. 55–56.
10. Cicero, *De finibus*, III.v.17; vi.20.

11. This is the third argument against the permissibility of war that is drawn from the gospel.
12. "Perfect" again in the sense of "complete": a state can be self-sufficient in a way that any lesser human association like the family or a club cannot be.
13. Grotius was referring to Exod. 21:6 and to various provisions of the Roman law.
14. In the *Apology*.
15. The first cause of war is preventing injury.
16. Gen. 1:29, 30.
17. *Institutes* XLIII [i.3].
18. *De finibus* III.xx.67.
19. This is one of the places where Grotius expands on his distinction between perfect and imperfect rights and shows its use in making important distinctions for legal transactions.
20. *Nicomachean Ethics* I.3.
21. Rom. 14:23.
22. *De officiis* I.ix.30.
23. Vazquez and de Soto, referred to a few lines later, were Catholic theologians of the sixteenth century. The case seems to have been widely discussed.

Further Reading

Although the secondary literature on Grotius is large, there is little that is relevant to the bearing of his work on moral philosophy. Usually it is Grotius's legal and political doctrines that are discussed, and he is accordingly treated at greater or lesser length in all the standard histories of political thought.

For older Catholic views of Grotius, the reader should consult Heinrich A. Rommen, *The Natural Law,* trans. Thomas R. Hanley (St. Louis: Herder, 1946), and Anton-Hermann Chroust, "Hugo Grotius and the Scholastic Natural Law Tradition," *The New Scholasticism* 17(2)(1943). More recently, M. B. Crowe challenged Grotius's originality in asserting the validity of law even if God does not exist, in *The Changing Profile of Natural Law* (The Hague: Nijhoff, 1972).

Charles Edwards, *Hugo Grotius* (Chicago: Nelson-Hall, 1981), is a readable general study of Grotius's life and his work on natural and international law, although it is not always accurate on details. Knud Haakonssen, "Hugo Grotius and the History of Political Thought," *Political Theory* 13(2)(1985):239–65, is an excellent overview, helpful on some matters of philosophical importance. Richard Tuck, *Natural Rights Theories* (Cambridge, England: Cambridge University Press, 1979), is a pioneering study of the origins of modern ideas of natural rights; Chapter 3, on Grotius, is indispensable. Tuck has also written three articles bearing on Grotius: "Grotius, Carneades, and Hobbes," in *Grotiana*, n.s. 4 (1983):43–62; "The 'Modern' Theory of Natural Law," in Anthony Pagden, ed., *The Languages of Political Theory in Early Modern Europe* (Cambridge, England: Cambridge University Press, 1987); and "Optics and Sceptics: The Philosophical Foundations of Hobbes' Political Thought," in Edmund Leites, ed., *Conscience and Casuistry in Early Modern Europe* (Cambridge, England: Cambridge University Press, 1988).

Thomas Hobbes

Introduction

The moral philosophy of Thomas Hobbes has been more frequently discussed in the past half century than has that of any other seventeenth-century thinker. There have been a number of different interpretations of what he meant both in general and on specific issues. And many philosophers have tried to show that his basic theory can be understood in a way that shows him to have been essentially right. Indeed, Hobbes transcends his age as few moral and political thinkers ever have.

Hobbes was born in 1588 and died in 1679, a long life at any time and especially in the seventeenth century. He studied at Oxford for five years, becoming acquainted there with Aristotelian philosophy and with extreme Puritan opinions. His rejection of both of these colored much of his later thought. When he was twenty he became a tutor for the Cavendish family, with which he remained closely associated for the rest of his life. The connection enabled Hobbes to travel to the Continent and to meet many scientific and literary leaders of the period, including Bacon and Descartes. He spent much of his time giving himself a humanistic education – his first work was a translation of Thucydides into English – and he did not learn geometry until he was forty. Hobbes's fascination with the demonstrative powers of geometric proof lasted the rest of his life, and he was equally impressed by the physical laws that the new science was revealing to the world.

Hobbes lived in extremely turbulent times. Protracted religious, political, and military struggles for the control of England took place while he was at the height of his powers, and he viewed his philosophy as a doctrine – as indeed the only doctrine – that could bring peace and stability back into his world. In 1640 he completed *Elements of Law,* which contained a sketch of his views but which he did not publish until 1650. His moral and political theory first appeared in *De cive* in 1642, and the fullest account of it came out in 1651, in *Leviathan.*

Between 1640 and 1651 Hobbes lived in Paris; he returned thereafter to England, wrote new accounts of various parts of his system, engaged in sometimes-heated controversies over his views, and, toward the end of his life, translated Homer into English.

Hobbes had some followers, but for the most part those who read him hated and feared his views. He came to rival Niccolò Machiavelli in the popular mind as an exponent of dangerous and immoral doctrines. His critics took it as obvious that he was an atheist and that as a materialist he denied the existence of the soul. He was universally held to teach that all people are always self-interested in their voluntary actions. Because he did not believe that people have free will, he was thought to deny

111

that we could be held accountable for our actions. Hobbes was generally considered an Epicurean, a proponent of the doctrine that pleasure alone is the good for man – and only the coarser pleasures at that. He taught, it was believed, that there are no universal standards of morality and that because only what the sovereign requires is obligatory, morality varies from country to country. In political matters, Hobbes was assumed to have provided justification for tyrannical or despotical rule.

No doubt many of these doctrines are unappealing: the reader must decide whether or not Hobbes held them, or something close enough to them to warrant the condemnations to which he was subjected. Whether or not he did, it was because such views were attributed to him that he was the main object of criticism for generations of philosophers who succeeded him. Many of these criticisms were uninteresting, resting on gross misreadings of what Hobbes said or taking for granted much that he thought false or irrelevant. But the better critics – such as Hutcheson and Butler – were able not only to make telling objections to what they took him to expound but to do so in ways that advanced our philosophical understanding of human motivation and of morality. For the value of the opposition he generated as well as for the depth and originality of his own thought, Hobbes is an indispensable central figure in the history of ethics.

The following selections are from the English translation of *De cive* published in 1651 under the title *Philosophical Rudiments Concerning Government and Society*. It is possible that this translation was written by Hobbes himself, although the evidence is not conclusive. I have taken the text from the nineteenth-century edition by Sir William Molesworth, who modernized to some extent the spelling and punctuation.

Philosophical Rudiments Concerning Government and Society

The Epistle Dedicatory

. . . Now look, how many sorts of things there are, which properly fall within the cognizance of human reason; into so many branches does the tree of philosophy divide itself. And from the diversity of the matter about which they are conversant, there hath been given to those branches a diversity of names too. For treating of figures, it is called *geometry;* of motion, *physic;* of natural right, *morals;* put altogether, and they make up *philosophy.* Just as the British, the Atlantic, and the Indian seas, being diversely christened from the diversity of their shores, do notwithstanding all together make up *the ocean.* And truly the geometricians have very admirably performed their part. For whatsoever assistance doth accrue to the life of man, whether from the observation of the heavens or from the description of the earth, from the notation of times, or from the remotest experiments of navigation; finally, whatsoever things they are in which this present age doth differ from the rude simpleness of antiquity, we must acknowledge to be a debt which we owe merely to geometry. If the moral philosophers had as happily discharged their duty, I know not what could have been added by human industry to the completion of that happiness, which is consistent with human life. For were the nature of human actions as distinctly known as the nature of *quantity* in geometrical figures, the strength of *avarice* and *ambition,* which is sustained by the erroneous opinions of the vulgar as touching the nature of *right* and *wrong,* would presently faint and languish; and mankind should enjoy such an immortal peace, that unless it were for habitation, on supposition that the earth should grow too narrow for her inhabitants, there would hardly be left any pretence for war. But now on the contrary, that neither the sword nor the pen should be allowed any cessation; that the knowledge of the law of nature should lose its growth, not advancing a whit beyond its ancient stature; that there should still be such siding with the several factions of philosophers, that the very same action should be decried by some, and as much elevated by others; that the very same man should at several times embrace his several opinions, and esteem has own actions far otherwise in himself than he does in others: these, I say, are so many signs, so many manifest arguments, that what hath hitherto been written by moral philosophers, hath not made any progress in the knowledge of the truth; but yet hath took with the world, not so much by giving any light to the understanding as entertainment to the affections, whilst by the successful rhetorications of their speech they have confirmed them in their rashly received opinions.

. . . when I applied my thoughts to the investigation of natural justice, I was presently advertised from the very word *justice,* (which signifies a steady will of giving every one his *own*),[1] that my first enquiry was to be, from whence it proceeded that any man should call anything rather his *own,* than *another man's.* And when I found that this proceeded not from nature, but consent; (for what nature at first laid forth in common, men did afterwards distribute into several *impropriations*);[2] I was conducted from thence to another inquiry; namely, to what end and upon what impulsives, when all was equally every man's in common, men did rather think it fitting that every man should have his inclosure. And I found the reason was, that from a community of goods there must needs arise contention, whose enjoyment should be greatest. And from that contention all kind of calamities must unavoidably ensue, which by the instinct of nature every man is taught to shun. Having therefore thus arrived at two maxims of human nature; the one arising from the *concupiscible* part, which desires to appropriate to itself the use of those things in which all others have a joint interest; the other proceeding from the *rational,* which teaches every man to fly a contra-natural dissolution, as the greatest mischief that can arrive to nature: which principles being laid down, I seem from them to have demonstrated by a most evident connexion, in this little work of mine, first, the absolute necessity of leagues and contracts, and thence the rudiments both of moral and of civil prudence. That appendage which is added concerning the regiment of God,[3] hath been done with this intent; that the dictates of God Almighty in the law of nature, might not seem repugnant to the written law, revealed to us in his word. I have also been very wary in the whole tenour of my discourse, not to meddle with the civil laws of any particular nation whatsoever. . . .

The Preface to the Reader

. . . The benefit of it,[4] when rightly delivered, that is, when derived from true principles by evident connection, we shall then best discern, when we shall but

well have considered the mischiefs that have befallen mankind from its counterfeit and babbling form. For in matters wherein we speculate for the exercise of our wits, if any error escape us, it is without hurt; neither is there any
loss, but of time only. But in those things which every man ought to meditate
for the steerage of his life, it necessarily happens that not only from errors,
but even from ignorance itself, there arise offences, contentions, nay, even
slaughter itself. Look now, how great a prejudice these are; such and so great
is the benefit arising from this doctrine of morality truly declared. How many
kings, and those good men too, hath this one error, that a tyrant king might
lawfully be put to death, been the slaughter of! How many throats hath this
false position cut, that a prince for some causes may by some certain men be
deposed! And what bloodshed hath not this erroneous doctrine caused, that
kings are not superiors to, but administrators for the multitude! Lastly, how
many rebellions hath this opinion been the cause of, which teacheth that the
knowledge whether the commands of kings be just or unjust, belongs to
private men; and that before they yield obedience, they not only may, but
ought to dispute them! . . .

Since therefore such opinions are daily seen to arise, if any man now shall
dispel those clouds, and by most firm reasons demonstrate that there are no
authentical doctrines concerning right and wrong, good and evil, besides the
constituted laws in each realm and government; and that the question whether
any future action will prove just or unjust, good or ill, is to be demanded of
none but those to whom the supreme[5] hath committed the interpretation of
his laws: surely he will not only show us the highway to peace, but will also
teach us how to avoid the close, dark, and dangerous by-paths of faction and
sedition; than which I know not what can be thought more profitable.

Concerning my method, I thought it not sufficient to use a plain and evident
style in what I have to deliver, except I took my beginning from the very
matter of civil government, and thence proceeded to its generation and form,
and the first beginning of justice. For everything is best understood by its
constitutive causes. For as in a watch, or some such small engine, the matter,
figure, and motion of the wheels cannot well be known, except it be taken
insunder and viewed in parts; so to make a more curious search into the rights
of states and duties of subjects, it is necessary, I say, not to take them
insunder, but yet that they be so considered as if they were dissolved; that is,
that we rightly understand what the quality of human nature is, in what
matters it is, in what not, fit to make up a civil government, and how men
must be agreed amongst themselves that intend to grow up into a well-
grounded state. Having therefore followed this kind of method, in the first
place I set down for a principle, by experience known to all men and denied by
none, to wit, that the dispositions of men are naturally such, that except they
be restrained through fear of some coercive power, every man will distrust
and dread each other; and as by natural right he may, so by necessity he will
be forced to make use of the strength he hath, toward the preservation of
himself. . . .

Some object that this principle being admitted, it would needs follow, not only that all men were wicked, (which perhaps though it seem hard, yet we must yield to, since it is so clearly declared by holy writ), but also wicked by nature, which cannot be granted without impiety. But this, that men are evil by nature, follows not from this principle. For though the wicked were fewer than the righteous, yet because we cannot distinguish them, there is a necessity of suspecting, heeding, anticipating, subjugating, self-defending, ever incident to the most honest and fairest conditioned. Much less does it follow, that those who are wicked, are so by nature. For though from nature, that is, from their first birth, as they are merely sensible creatures, they have this disposition, that immediately as much as in them lies they desire and do whatsoever is best pleasing to them, and that either through fear they fly from, or through hardness repel those dangers which approach them; yet are they not for this reason to be accounted wicked. For the affections of the mind, which arise only from the lower parts of the soul, are not wicked themselves; but the actions thence proceeding may be so sometimes, as when they are either offensive or against duty. . . .

. . . The foundation therefore which I have laid, standing firm, I demonstrate, in the first place, that the state of men without civil society, which state we may properly call the state of nature, is nothing else but a mere war of all against all; and in that war all men have equal right unto all things. Next, that all men as soon as they arrive to understanding of this hateful condition, do desire, even nature itself compelling them, to be freed from this misery. But that this cannot be done, except by compact, they all quit that right they have to all things. Furthermore, I declare and confirm what the nature of compact is; how and by what means the right of one might be transferred unto another to make their compacts valid; also what rights, and to whom they must necessarily be granted, for the establishing of peace; I mean, what those dictates of reason are, which may properly be termed the laws of nature. And all these are contained in that part of this book which I entitle *Liberty*.

These grounds thus laid, I show further what civil government, and the supreme power in it, and the divers kinds of it are; by what means it becomes so; and what rights particular men, who intend to constitute the civil government, must so necessarily transfer from themselves on the supreme power, whether it be one man or an assembly of men, that, except they do so, it will evidently appear to be no civil government, but the rights which all men have to all things, that is, the rights of war will still remain. . . .

PHILOSOPHICAL ELEMENTS OF A TRUE CITIZEN

Liberty

Chapter I: Of the State of Men Without Civil Society
1. The Introduction. 2. That the beginning of civil society is from mutual fear. 3. That men by nature are all equal. 4. Whence the will of mischieving each other ariseth.

5. The discord arising from comparison of wits. 6. From the appetite many have to the same thing. 7. The definition of *right*. 8. A right to the end, gives a right to the means necessary to that end. 9. By the right of nature, every man is judge of the means which tend to his own preservation. 10. By nature all men have equal right to all things. 11. This right which all men have to all things, is unprofitable. 12. The state of men without civil society, is a mere state of war: the definitions of *peace* and *war*. 13. War is an adversary to man's preservation. 14. It is lawful for any man, by material right, to compel another whom he hath gotten in his power, to give caution of his future obedience. 15. Nature dictates the seeking after peace.

The faculties of human nature may be reduced unto four kinds; bodily strength, experience, reason, passion. Taking the beginning of this following doctrine from these, we will declare, in the first place, what manner of inclinations men who are endued with these faculties bear towards each other, and whether, and by what faculty they are born apt for society, and to preserve themselves against mutual violence; then proceeding, we will shew what advice was necessary to be taken for this business, and what are the conditions of society, or of human peace; that is to say, (changing the words only), what are the fundamental *laws of nature*.

2. The greatest part of those men who have written aught concerning commonwealths, either suppose, or require us or beg of us to believe, that man is a creature born fit* for society. The Greeks call him ζῷον πολιτικον;[6] and on this foundation they so build up the doctrine of civil society, as if for the preservation of peace, and the government of mankind, there were nothing else necessary than that men should agree to make certain covenants and conditions together, which themselves should then call laws. Which axiom, though received by most, is yet certainly false; and an error proceeding from our too slight contemplation of human nature. For they who shall more narrowly look into the causes for which men come together, and delight in each other's company, shall easily find that this happens not because naturally it

---

* *Born fit.*] Since we now see actually a constituted society among men, and none living out of it, since we discern all desirous of congress and mutual correspondence, it may seem a wonderful kind of stupidity, to lay in the very threshold of this doctrine such a stumbling block before the reader, as to deny *man to be born fit for society*. Therefore I must more plainly say, that it is true indeed, that to man by nature, or as man, that is, as soon as he is born, solitude is an enemy; for infants have need of others to help them to live, and those of riper years to help them to live well. Wherefore I deny not that men (even nature compelling) desire to come together. But civil societies are not mere meetings, but bonds, to the making whereof faith and compacts are necessary; the virtue whereof to children and fools, and the profit whereof to those who have not yet tasted the miseries which accompany its defects, is altogether unknown; whence it happens, that those, because they know not what society is, cannot enter into it; these, because ignorant of the benefit it brings, care not for it. Manifest therefore it is, that all men, because they are born in infancy, are born unapt for society. Many also, perhaps most men, either through defect of mind or want of education, remain unfit during the whole course of their lives; yet have they, infants as well as those of riper years, a human nature. Wherefore man is made fit for society not by nature, but by education. Furthermore, although man were born in such a condition as to desire it, it follows not, that he therefore were born fit to enter into it. For it is one thing to desire, another to be in capacity fit for what we desire; for even they, who through their pride, will not stoop to equal conditions, without which there can be no society, do yet desire it.

could happen no otherwise, but by accident. For if by nature one man should love another, that is, as man, there could no reason be returned why every man should not equally love every man, as being equally man; or why he should rather frequent those, whose society affords him honour or profit. We do not therefore by nature seek society for its own sake, but that we may receive some honour or profit from it; these we desire primarily, that secondarily.

The same is also collected by reason out of the definitions themselves of *will, good, honour, profitable*. For when we voluntarily contract society, in all manner of society we look after the object of the will, that is, that which every one of those who gather together, propounds to himself for good. Now whatsoever seems good, is pleasant, and relates either to the senses, or the mind. But all the mind's pleasure is either glory, (or to have a good opinion of one's self), or refers to glory in the end; the rest are sensual, or conducing to sensuality, which may be all comprehended under the word *conveniences*. All society therefore is either for gain, or for glory; that is, not so much for love of our fellows, as for the love of ourselves. But no society can be great or lasting, which begins from vain glory. Because that glory is like honour; if all men have it no man hath it, for they consist in comparison and precellence.[7] Neither doth the society of others advance any whit the cause of my glorying in myself; for every man must account himself, such as he can make himself without the help of others. But though the benefits of this life may be much furthered by mutual help; since yet those may be better attained to by dominion than by the society of others, I hope no body will doubt, but that men would much more greedily be carried by nature, if all fear were removed, to obtain dominion, than to gain society. We must therefore resolve, that the original of all great and lasting societies consisted not in the mutual good will men had towards each other, but in the mutual fear they had of each other.

3. The cause of mutual fear consists partly in the natural equality of men, partly in their mutual will of hurting: whence it comes to pass, that we can neither expect from others, nor promise to ourselves the least security. For if we look on men full-grown, and consider how brittle the frame of our human body is, which perishing, all its strength, vigour, and wisdom itself perisheth with it; and how easy a matter it is, even for the weakest man to kill the strongest: there is no reason why any man, trusting to his own strength, should conceive himself made by nature above others. They are equals, who can do equal things one against the other; but they who can do the greatest things, namely, kill, can do equal things. All men therefore among themselves are by nature equal; the inequality we now discern, hath its spring from the civil law.

4. All men in the state of nature have a desire and will to hurt, but not proceeding from the same cause, neither equally to be condemned. For one man, according to that natural equality which is among us, permits as much to others as he assumes to himself; which is an argument of a temperate man, and one that rightly values his power. Another, supposing himself above others, will have a license to do what he lists, and challenges respect and

honour, as due to him before others; which is an argument of a fiery spirit. This man's will to hurt ariseth from vain glory, and the false esteem he hath of his own strength; the other's from the necessity of defending himself, his liberty, and his goods, against this man's violence.

5. Furthermore, since the combat of wits is the fiercest, the greatest discords which are, must necessarily arise from this contention. For in this case it is not only odious to contend against, but also not to consent. For not to approve of what a man saith, is no less than tacitly to accuse him of an error in that thing which he speaketh: as in very many things to dissent, is as much as if you accounted him a fool whom you dissent from. Which may appear hence, that there are no wars so sharply waged as between sects of the same religion, and factions of the same commonweal, where the contestation is either concerning doctrines or politic prudence. And since all the pleasure and jollity of the mind consists in this, even to get some, with whom comparing, it may find somewhat wherein to triumph and vaunt itself; it is impossible but men must declare sometimes some mutual scorn and contempt, either by laughter, or by words, or by gesture, or some sign or other; than which there is no greater vexation of mind, and than from which there cannot possibly arise a greater desire to do hurt.

6. But the most frequent reason why men desire to hurt each other, ariseth hence, that many men at the same time have an appetite to the same thing; which yet very often they can neither enjoy in common, nor yet divide it; whence it follows that the strongest must have it, and who is strongest must be decided by the sword.

7. Among so many dangers therefore, as the natural lusts of men do daily threaten each other withal, to have a care of one's self is so far from being a matter scornfully to be looked upon, that one has neither the power nor wish to have done otherwise. For every man is desirous of what is good for him, and shuns what is evil, but chiefly the chiefest of natural evils, which is death; and this he doth by a certain impulsion of nature, no less than that whereby a stone moves downward. It is therefore neither absurd nor reprehensible, neither against the dictates of true reason, for a man to use all his endeavours to preserve and defend his body and the members thereof from death and sorrows. But that which is not contrary to right reason, that all men account to be done justly, and with right. Neither by the word *right* is anything else signified, than that liberty which every man hath to make use of his natural faculties according to right reason. Therefore the first foundation of natural right is this, that *every man as much as in him lies endeavour to protect his life and members*.

8. But because it is in vain for a man to have a right to the end, if the right to the necessary means be denied him, it follows, that since every man hath a right to preserve himself, he must also be allowed a right *to use all the means, and do all the actions, without which he cannot preserve himself*.

9. Now whether the means which he is about to use, and the action he is performing, be necessary to the preservation of his life and members or not,

he himself, by the right of nature, must be judge. For if it be contrary to right reason that I should judge of mine own peril, say, that another man is judge. Why now, because he judgeth of what concerns me, by the same reason, because we are equal by nature, will I judge also of things which do belong to him. Therefore it agrees with right reason, that is, it is the right of nature that I judge of his opinion, that is, whether it conduce to my preservation or not.

10. Nature hath given to *every one a right to all;* that is, it was lawful for every man, in the bare state of nature,† or before such time as men had engaged themselves by any covenants or bonds, to do what he would, and against whom he thought fit, and to possess, use, and enjoy all what he would, or could get. Now because whatsoever a man would, it therefore seems good to him because he wills it, and either it really doth, or at least seems to him to contribute towards his preservation, (but we have already allowed him to be judge, in the foregoing article, whether it doth or not, insomuch as we are to hold all for necessary whatsoever he shall esteem so), and by the 7th article it appears that by the right of nature those things may be done, and must be had, which necessarily conduce to the protection of life and members, it follows, that in the state of nature, to have all, and do all, is lawful for all. And this is that which is meant by that common saying, *nature hath given all to all.* From whence we understand likewise, that in the state of nature profit is the measure of right.

11. But it was the least benefit for men thus to have a common right to all things. For the effects of this right are the same, almost, as if there had been no right at all. For although any man might say of every thing, *this is mine,* yet could he not enjoy it, by reason of his neighbour, who having equal right and equal power, would pretend the same thing to be his.

12. If now to this natural proclivity of men, to hurt each other, which they derive from their passions, but chiefly from a vain esteem of themselves, you add, the right of all to all, wherewith one by right invades, the other by right resists, and whence arise perpetual jealousies and suspicions on all hands, and

---

† *In the bare state of nature.*] This is thus to be understood: what any man does in the bare state of nature, is injurious to no man; not that in such a state he cannot offend God, or break the laws of nature; for injustice against men presupposeth human laws, such as in the state of nature there are none. Now the truth of this proposition thus conceived, is sufficiently demonstrated to the mindful reader in the articles immediately foregoing; but because in certain cases the difficulty of the conclusion makes us forget the premises, I will contract this argument, and make it most evident to a single view. Every man hath right to protect himself, as appears by the seventh article. The same man therefore hath a right to use all the means which necessarily conduce to this end, by the eighth article. But those are the necessary means which he shall judge to be such, by the ninth article. He therefore hath a right to make use of, and to do all whatsoever he shall judge requisite for his preservation; wherefore by the judgment of him that doth it, the thing done is either right or wrong, and therefore right. True it is therefore in the bare state of nature, &c. But if any man pretend somewhat to tend necessarily to his preservation, which yet he himself doth not confidently believe so, he may offend against the laws of nature, as in the third chapter of this book is more at large declared. It hath been objected by some: if a son kill his father, doth he him no injury? I have answered, that a son cannot be understood to be at any time in the state of nature, as being under the power and command of them to whom he owes his protection as soon as ever he is born, namely, either his father's or his mother's, or him that nourished him; as is demonstrated in the ninth chapter.

how hard a thing it is to provide against an enemy invading us with an intention to oppress and ruin, though he come with a small number, and no great provision; it cannot be denied but that the natural state of men, before they entered into society, was a mere war, and that not simply, but a war of all men against all men. For what is WAR, but that same time in which the will of contesting by force is fully declared, either by words or deeds? The time remaining is termed PEACE.

13. But it is easily judged how disagreeable a thing to the preservation either of mankind, or of each single man, a perpetual war is. But it is perpetual in its own nature; because in regard of the equality of those that strive, it cannot be ended by victory. For in this state the conqueror is subject to so much danger, as it were to be accounted a miracle, if any, even the most strong, should close up his life with many years and old age. They of America are examples hereof, even in this present age: other nations have been in former ages; which now indeed are become civil and flourishing, but were then few, fierce, short-lived, poor, nasty, and deprived of all that pleasure and beauty of life, which peace and society are wont to bring with them. Whosoever therefore holds, that it had been best to have continued in that state in which all things were lawful for all men, he contradicts himself. For every man by natural necessity desires that which is good for him: nor is there any that esteems a war of all against all, which necessarily adheres to such a state, to be good for him. And so it happens, that through fear of each other we think it fit to rid ourselves of this condition, and to get some fellows; that if there needs must be war, it may not yet be against all men, nor without some helps.

14. Fellows are gotten either by constraint, or by consent; by constraint, when after fight the conqueror makes the conquered serve him, either through fear of death, or by laying fetters on him: by consent, when men enter into society to help each other, both parties consenting without any constraint. But the conqueror may by right compel the conquered, or the strongest the weaker, (as a man in health may one that is sick, or he that is of riper years a child), unless he will choose to die, to give caution of his future obedience. For since the right of protecting ourselves according to our own wills, proceeded from our danger, and our danger from our equality, it is more consonant to reason, and more certain for our conservation, using the present advantage to secure ourselves by taking caution, than when they shall be full grown and strong, and got out of our power, to endeavour to recover that power again by doubtful fight. And on the other side, nothing can be thought more absurd, than by discharging whom you already have weak in your power, to make him at once both an enemy and a strong one. From whence we may understand likewise as a corollary in the natural state of men, that *a sure and irresistible power confers the right of dominion and ruling over those who cannot resist;* insomuch, as the right of all things that can be done, adheres essentially and immediately unto this omnipotence hence arising.

15. Yet cannot men expect any lasting preservation, continuing thus in the state of nature, that is, of war, by reason of that equality of power, and other

human faculties they are endued withal. Wherefore to seek peace, where there is any hopes of obtaining it, and where there is none, to enquire out for auxiliaries of war, is the dictate of right reason, that is, the law of nature; as shall be showed in the next chapter.

Chapter II: Of the Law of Nature Concerning Contracts
1. That the law of nature is not an agreement of men, but the dictate of reason. 2. That the fundamental law of nature, is to seek peace, where it may be had, and where not, to defend ourselves. 3. That the first special law of nature, is not to retain our right to all things. 4. What it is to quit our right: what to transfer it. 5. That in the transferring of our right, the will of him that receives it is necessarily required. 6. No words but those of the present tense, transfer any right. 7. Words of the future, if there be some other tokens to signify the will, are valid in the translation of right. 8. In matters of free gift, our right passeth not from us through any words of the future. 9. The definition of contract and compact. 10. In compacts, our right passeth from us through words of the future. 11. Compacts of mutual faith, in the state of nature are of no effect and vain; but not so in civil government. 12. That no man can make compacts with beasts, nor yet with God without revelation. 13. Nor yet make a vow to God. 14. That compacts oblige not beyond our utmost endeavour. 15. By what means we are freed from our compacts. 16. That promises extorted through fear of death, in the state of nature are valid. 17. A later compact contradicting the former, is invalid. 18. A compact not to resist him that shall prejudice my body, is invalid. 19. A compact to accuse one's self, is invalid. 20. The definition of swearing. 21. That swearing is to be conceived in that form which he useth that takes the oath. 22. An oath superadds nothing to the obligation which is made by compact. 23. An oath ought not to be pressed, but where the breach of compacts may be kept private, or cannot be punished but from God himself.

1. All authors agree not concerning the definition of *the natural law,* who notwithstanding do very often make use of this term in their writings. The method therefore wherein we begin from definitions and exclusion of all equivocation, is only proper to them who leave no place for contrary disputes. For the rest, if any man say that somewhat is done against the law of nature, one proves it hence; because it was done against the general agreement of all the most wise and learned nations: but this declares not who shall be the judge of the wisdom and learning of all nations. Another hence, that it was done against the general consent of all mankind; which definition is by no means to be admitted. For then it were impossible for any but children and fools, to offend against such a law; for sure, under the notion of mankind, they comprehend all men actually endued with reason. These therefore either do nought against it, or if they do aught, it is without their own consent, and therefore ought to be excused. But to receive the laws of nature from the consents of them who oftener break than observe them, is in truth unreasonable. Besides, men condemn the same things in others, which they approve in themselves; on the other side, they publicly commend what they privately condemn; and they deliver their opinions more by hearsay, than any speculation of their own; and they accord more through hatred of some object, through fear, hope, love, or some other perturbation of mind, than true reason. And therefore it comes to pass, that whole bodies of people often do those things with

the greatest unanimity and earnestness, which those writers most willingly acknowledge to be against the law of nature. But since all do grant, that is done by *right,* which is not done against reason, we ought to judge those actions only *wrong,* which are repugnant to right reason, that is, which contradict some certain truth collected by right reasoning from true principles. But that which is done *wrong,* we say it is done against some law. Therefore *true reason* is a certain *law;* which, since it is no less a part of human nature, than any other faculty or affection of the mind, is also termed natural. Therefore the *law of nature,* that I may define it, is the dictate of right reason,‡ conversant about those things which are either to be done or omitted for the constant preservation of life and members, as much as in us lies.

2. But the first and fundamental law of nature is, *that peace is to be sought after, where it may be found; and where not, there to provide ourselves for helps of war.* For we showed in the last article of the foregoing chapter, that this precept is the dictate of right reason; but that the dictates of right reason are natural laws, that hath been newly proved above. But this is the first, because the rest are derived from this, and they direct the ways either to peace or self-defence.

3. But one of the natural laws derived from this fundamental one is this: *that the right of all men to all things ought not to be retained; but that some certain rights ought to be transferred or relinquished.* For if every one should retain his right to all things, it must necessarily follow, that some by right might invade, and others, by the same right, might defend themselves against them. For every man by natural necessity endeavours to defend his body, and the things which he judgeth necessary towards the protection of his body. Therefore war would follow. He therefore acts against the reason of peace, that is, against the law of nature, whosoever he be, that doth not part with his right to all things.

4. But he is said to part with his right, who either absolutely renounceth it, or conveys it to another. He absolutely renounceth it, who by some sufficient sign or meet tokens declares, that he is willing that it shall never be lawful for him to do that again, which before *by right* he might have done. But he conveys it to another, who by some sufficient sign or meet tokens declares to that other, that he is willing it should be unlawful for him to resist him, in going about to do somewhat in the performance whereof he might before *with*

---

‡ *Right reason.*] By right reason in the natural state of men, I understand not, as many do, an infallible faculty, but the act of reasoning, that is, the peculiar and true ratiocination of every man concerning those actions of his, which may either redound to the damage or benefit of his neighbours. I call it peculiar, because although in a civil government the reason of the supreme, that is, the civil law, is to be received by each single subject for the right; yet being without this civil government, in which state no man can know right reason from false, but by comparing it with his own, every man's own reason is to be accounted, not only the rule of his own actions, which are done at his own peril, but also for the measure of another man's reason, in such things as do concern him. I call it true, that is, concluding from true principles rightly framed, because that the whole breach of the laws of nature consists in the false reasoning, or rather folly of those men, who see not those duties they are necessarily to perform towards others in order to their own conservation. But the principles of right reasoning about such like duties, are those which are explained in the second, third, fourth, fifth, sixth, and seventh articles of the first chapter.

right have resisted him. But that the conveyance of right consists merely in not resisting, is understood by this, that before it was conveyed, he to whom he conveyed it, had even then also a right to all; whence he could not give any new right; but the resisting right he had before he gave it, by reason whereof the other could not freely enjoy his rights, is utterly abolished. Whosoever therefore acquires some right in the natural state of men, he only procures himself security and freedom from just molestation in the enjoyment of his primitive right. As for example, if any man shall sell or give away a farm, he utterly deprives himself only from all right to this farm; but he does not so others also.

5. But in the conveyance of right, the will is requisite not only of him that conveys, but of him also that accepts it. If either be wanting, the right remains. For if I would have given what was mine to one who refused to accept of it, I have not therefore either simply renounced my right, or conveyed it to any man. For the cause which moved me to part with it to this man, was in him only, not in others too.

6. But if there be no other token extant of our will either to quit or convey our right, but only words; those words must either relate to the present or time past; for if they be of the future only, they convey nothing. For example, he that speaks thus of the time to come, *I will give to-morrow,* declares openly that yet he hath not given it. So that all this day his right remains, and abides tomorrow too, unless in the interim he actually bestows it: for what is mine, remains mine till I have parted with it. But if I shall speak of the time present, suppose thus; *I do give or have given you this to be received to-morrow:* by these words is signified that I have already given it, and that his right to receive it to-morrow is conveyed to him by me to-day.

7. Nevertheless, although words alone are not sufficient tokens to declare the will; if yet to words relating to the future there shall some other signs be added, they may become as valid as if they had been spoken of the present. If therefore, as by reason of those other signs, it appear that he that speaks of the future, intends those words should be effectual toward the perfect transferring of his right, they ought to be valid. For the conveyance of right depends not on words, but, as hath been instanced in the fourth article, on the declaration of the will.

8. If any man convey some part of his right to another, and doth not this for some certain benefit received, or for some compact, a conveyance in this kind is called a gift or free donation. But in free donation, those words only oblige us, which signify the present or the time past; for if they respect the future, they oblige not as *words,* for the reason given in the foregoing article. It must needs therefore be, that the obligation arise from some other tokens of the will. But, because whatsoever is voluntarily done, is done for some good to him that wills it; there can no other token be assigned of the will to give it, except some benefit either already received, or to be acquired. But it is supposed that no such benefit is acquired, nor any compact in being; for if so, it would cease to be a free gift. It remains therefore, that a mutual good turn

without agreement be expected. But no sign can be given, that he, who used future words toward him who was in no sort engaged to return a benefit, should desire to have his words so understood as to oblige himself thereby. Nor is it suitable to reason, that those who are easily inclined to do well to others, should be obliged by every promise, testifying their present good affection. And for this cause, a promiser in this kind must be understood to have time to deliberate, and power to change that affection, as well as he to whom he made that promise, may alter his desert. But he that deliberates, is so far forth free, nor can be said to have already given. But if he promise often, and yet give seldom, he ought to be condemned of levity. . . .

9. But the act of two, or more, mutually conveying their rights, is called a *contract*. But in every contract, either both parties instantly perform what they contract for, insomuch as there is no trust had from either to other; or the one performs, the other is trusted; or neither perform. Where both parties perform presently, there the contract is ended as soon as it is performed. But where there is credit given, either to one or both, there the party trusted promiseth after-performance; and this kind of promise is called a *covenant*.

10. But the covenant made by the party trusted with him who hath already performed, although the promise be made by words pointing at the future, doth no less transfer the right of future time, than if it had been made by words signifying the present or time past. For the other's performance is a most manifest sign that he so understood the speech of him whom he trusted, as that he would certainly make performance also at the appointed time; and by this sign the party trusted knew himself to be thus understood; which because he hindered not, was an evident token of his will to perform. The promises therefore which are made for some benefit received, which are also covenants, are tokens of the will; that is, as in the foregoing section hath been declared, of the last act of deliberating, whereby the liberty of non-performance is abolished, and by consequence are obligatory. For where liberty ceaseth, there beginneth obligation.

11. But the covenants which are made in contract of mutual trust, neither party performing out of hand, if there arise§ a just suspicion in either of them, are in the state of nature invalid. For he that first performs, by reason of the wicked disposition of the greatest part of men studying their own advantage either by right or wrong, exposeth himself to the perverse will of him with whom he hath contracted. For it suits not with reason, that any man should perform first, if it be not likely that the other will make good his promise after; which, whether it be probable or not, he that doubts it must be judge of, as hath been showed in the foregoing chapter in the ninth article. Thus, I say, things stand in the state of nature. But in a civil state, when there is a power which can compel both parties, he that hath contracted to perform first, must

---

§ *Arise.*] For, except there appear some new cause of fear, either from somewhat done, or some other token of the will not to perform from the other part, it cannot be judged to be a just fear; for the cause which was not sufficient to keep him from making compact, must not suffice to authorize the breach of it, being made.

first perform; because, that since the other may be compelled, the cause which made him fear the other's non-performance, ceaseth.

12. But from this reason, that in all free gifts and compacts there is an acceptance of the conveyance of right required: it follows that no man can compact with him who doth not declare his acceptance. And therefore we cannot compact with beasts, neither can we give or take from them any manner of right, by reason of their want of speech and understanding. Neither can any man covenant with God, or be obliged to him by vow; except so far forth as it appears to him by Holy Scriptures, that he hath substituted certain men who have authority to accept of such-like vows and covenants, as being in God's stead.

13. Those therefore do vow in vain, who are in the state of nature, where they are not tied by any civil law, except, by most certain revelation, the will of God to accept their vow or pact, be made known to them. For if what they vow be contrary to the law of nature, they are not tied by their vow; for no man is tied to perform an unlawful act. But if what is vowed, be commanded by some law of nature, it is not their vow, but the law itself which ties them. But if he were free, before his vow, either to do it or not do it, his liberty remains; because that the openly declared will of the obliger is requisite to make an obligation by vow; which, in the case propounded, is supposed not to be. Now I call him the obliger, to whom any one is tied; and the obliged, him who is tied.

14. Covenants are made of such things only as fall under our deliberation. For it can be no covenant without the will of the contractor. But the will is the last act of him who deliberates;[8] wherefore they only concern things *possible* and *to come*. No man, therefore, by his compact obligeth himself to an impossibility. But yet, though we often covenant to do such things as then seemed possible when we promised them, which yet afterward appear to be impossible, are we not therefore freed from all obligation. The reason whereof is, that he who promiseth a future, in certainty receives a present benefit, on condition that he return another for it. For his will, who performs the present benefit, hath simply before it for its object a certain good, equally valuable with the thing promised; but the thing itself not simply, but with condition if it could be done. But if it should so happen, that even this should prove impossible, why then he must perform as much as he can. Covenants, therefore, oblige us not to perform just the thing itself covenanted for, but our utmost endeavour; for this only is, the things themselves are not in our power.

15. We are freed from covenents two ways, either by performing, or by being forgiven. By performing, for beyond that we obliged not ourselves. By being forgiven, because he whom we obliged ourselves to, by forgiving is conceived to return us that right which we passed over to him. For forgiving implies giving, that is, by the fourth article of this chapter, a conveyance of right to him to whom the gift is made.

16. It is a usual question, whether compacts extorted from us through fear, do oblige or not. For example, if, to redeem my life from the power of a

robber, I promise to pay him 100*l*. next day, and that I will do no act whereby to apprehend and bring him to justice: whether I am tied to keep promise or not. But though such a promise must sometimes be judged to be of no effect, yet it is not to be accounted so because it proceedeth from fear. For then it would follow, that those promises which reduced men to a civil life, and by which laws were made, might likewise be of none effect; (for it proceeds from fear of mutual slaughter, that one man submits himself to the dominion of another); and he should play the fool finely, who should trust his captive covenanting with the price of his redemption. It holds universally true, that promises do oblige, when there is some benefit received, and when the promise, and the thing promised, be lawful. But it is lawful, for the redemption of my life, both to promise and to give what I will of mine own to any man, even to a thief. We are obliged, therefore, by promises proceeding from fear, except the civil law forbid them; by virtue whereof, that which is promised becomes unlawful.

17. Whosoever shall contract with one to do or omit somewhat, and shall after covenant the contrary with another, he maketh not the former, but the latter contract unlawful. For he hath no longer right to do or to omit aught, who by former contracts hath conveyed it to another. Wherefore he can convey no right by latter contracts, and what is promised is promised without right. He is therefore tied only to his first contract, to break which is unlawful.

18. No man is obliged by any contracts whatsoever not to resist him who shall offer to kill, wound, or any other way hurt his body. For there is in every man a certain high degree of fear, through which he apprehends that evil which is done to him to be the greatest; and therefore by natural necessity he shuns it all he can, and it is supposed he can do no otherwise. When a man is arrived to this degree of fear, we cannot expect but he will provide for himself either by flight or fight. Since therefore no man is tied to impossibilities, they who are threatened either with death, (which is the greatest evil to nature), or wounds, or some other bodily hurts, and are not stout enough to bear them, are not obliged to endure them. Furthermore, he that is tied by contract is trusted; for faith only is the bond of contracts; but they who are brought to punishment, either capital or more gentle, are fettered or strongly guarded; which is a most certain sign that they seemed not sufficiently bound from nonresistance by their contracts. It is one thing, if I promise thus: if I do it not at the day appointed, kill me. Another thing, if thus: if I do it not, though you should offer to kill me, I will not resist. All men, if need be, contract the first way, and there is need sometimes. This second way, none; neither is it ever needful. For in the mere state of nature, if you have a mind to kill, that state itself affords you a right; insomuch as you need not first trust him, if for breach of trust you will afterwards kill him. But in a civil state, where the right of life and death and of all corporal punishment is with the supreme,[9] that same right of killing cannot be granted to any private person. Neither need the supreme himself contract with any man patiently to yield to his punishment; but only this, that no man offer to defend others from him. If in the state of

nature, as between two realms, there should a contract be made on condition of killing if it were not performed, we must presuppose another contract of not killing before the appointed day. Wherefore on that day, if there be no performance, the right of war returns, that is a hostile state, in which all things are lawful, and therefore resistance also. Lastly, by the contract of not resisting, we are obliged, of two evils to make choice of that which seems the greater. For certain death is a greater evil than fighting. But of two evils it is impossible not to choose the least. By such a compact, therefore, we should be tied to impossibilities; which is contrary to the very nature of compacts.

19. Likewise no man is tied by any compacts whatsoever to accuse himself, or any other, by whose damage he is like to procure himself a bitter life. Wherefore neither is a father obliged to bear witness against his son, nor a husband against his wife, nor a son against his father, nor any man against any one by whose means he hath his subsistence; for in vain is that testimony which is presumed to be corrupted from nature. But although no man be tied to accuse himself by any compact, yet in a public trial he may by torture be forced to make answer. But such answers are no testimony of the fact, but helps for the searching out of truth; so that whether the party tortured his answer be true or false, or whether he answer not at all, whatsoever he doth, he doth it by right.

Chapter III: Of the Other Laws of Nature

1. The second law of nature, is to perform contracts. 2. That trust is to be held with all men without exception. 3. What injury is. 4. Injury can be done to none but those with whom we contract. 5. The distinction of justice into that of men, and that of actions. 6. The distinction of commutative and distributive justice examined. 7. No injury can be done to him that is willing. 8. The third law of nature, concerning ingratitude. 9. The fourth law of nature, that every man render himself useful. 10. The fifth law, of mercy. 11. The sixth law, that punishments regard the future only. 12. The seventh law, against reproach. 13. The eighth law, against pride. 14. The ninth law, of humility. 15. The tenth, of equity, or against acceptance of persons. 16. The eleventh, of things to be had in common. 17. The twelfth, of things to be divided by lot. 18. The thirteenth, of birthright and first possession. 19. The fourteenth, of the safeguard of them who are mediators for peace. 20. The fifteenth, of constituting an umpire. 21. The sixteenth, that no man is judge in his own cause. 22. The seventeenth, that umpires must be without all hope of reward from those whose cause is to be judged. 23. The eighteenth, of witnesses. 24. The nineteenth, that there can no contract be made with the umpire. 25. The twentieth, against gluttony, and all such things as hinder the use of reason. 26. The rule by which we may presently know, whether what we are doing be against the law of nature or not. 27. The laws of nature oblige only in the court of conscience. 28. The laws of nature are sometimes broke by doing things agreeable to those laws. 29. The laws of nature are unchangeable. 30. Whosoever endeavours to fulfil the laws of nature, is a just man. 31. The natural and moral law are one. 32. How it comes to pass, that what hath been said of the laws of nature, is not the same with what philosophers have delivered concerning the virtues. 33. The law of nature is not properly a law, but as it is delivered in Holy Writ.

1. Another of the laws of nature is, to *perform contracts*, or *to keep trust*. For it hath been showed in the foregoing chapter, that the law of nature

commands every man, as a thing necessary, to obtain peace, to convey certain rights from each to other; and that this, as often as it shall happen to be done, is called a contract. But this is so far forth only conducible to peace, as we shall perform ourselves what we contract with others shall be done or omitted; and in vain would contacts be made, unless we stood to them. Because therefore to stand to our covenants, or to keep faith, is a thing necessary for the obtaining of peace; it will prove, by the second article of the second chapter, to be a precept of the natural law.

2. Neither is there in this matter any exception of the persons with whom we contract; as if they keep no faith with others, or hold that none ought to be kept, or are guilty of any other kind of vice. For he that contracts, in that he doth contract, denies that action to be in vain; and it is against reason for a knowing man to do a thing in vain: and if he think himself not bound to keep it, in thinking so he affirms the contract to be made in vain. He therefore who contracts with one with whom he thinks he is not bound to keep faith, he doth at once think a contract to be a thing done in vain, and not in vain; which is absurd. Either therefore we must hold trust with all men, or else not bargain with them; that is, either there must be a declared war, or a sure and faithful peace.

3. The breaking of a bargain, as also the taking back of a gift, (which ever consists in some action or omission), is called an injury. But that action or omission is called unjust; insomuch as an injury, and an unjust action or omission, signify the same thing, and both are the same with breach of contract and trust. And it seems the word *injury* came to be given to any action or omission, because they were *without right;* he that acted or omitted, having before conveyed his right to some other. And there is some likeness between that which in the common course of life we call *injury,* and that which in the Schools is usually called *absurd.* For even as he who by arguments is driven to deny the assertion which he first maintained, is said to be brought to an absurdity; in like manner, he who through weakness of mind does or omits that which before he had by contract promised not to do or omit, commits an injury, and falls into no less contradiction than he who in the Schools is reduced to an absurdity. For by contracting for some future action, he wills it done; by not doing it, he wills it not done: which is to will a thing done and not done at the same time, which is a contradiction. An injury therefore is a kind of absurdity in conversation, as an absurdity is a kind of injury in disputation.

4. From these grounds it follows, that an injury can be done to no man‖ but

‖ *Injury can be done to no man,* &c.] The word *injustice* relates to some law: *injury,* to some person, as well as some law. For what is unjust, is unjust to all; but there may an injury be done, and yet not against me, nor thee, but some other; and sometimes against no private person, but the magistrate only; sometimes also neither against the magistrate, nor any private man, but only against God. For through contract and conveyance of right, we say, that an injury is done against this or that man. Hence it is, which we see in all kind of government, that what private men contract between themselves by word or writing, is released again at the will of the obliger. But those mischiefs which are done against the laws of the land, as theft, homicide, and the like, are punished, not as he wills to whom the hurt is done, but according to the will of the magistrate; that is, the constituted laws.

him with whom we enter covenant, or to whom somewhat is made over by deed of gift, or to whom somewhat is promised by way of bargain. And therefore damaging and injuring are often disjoined. For if a master command his servant, who hath promised to obey him, to pay a sum of money, or carry some present to a third man; the servant, if he do it not, hath indeed damaged this third party, but he injured his master only. So also in a civil government, if any man offend another with whom he hath made no contract, he damages him to whom the evil is done; but he injures none but him to whom the power of government belongs. For if he who receives the hurt should expostulate the mischief, he that did it should answer thus: *what art thou to me; why should I rather do according to your than mine own will, since I do not hinder but you may do your own, and not my mind?* In which speech, where there hath no manner of pre-contract passed, I see not, I confess, what is reprehensible.

5. These words, *just* and *unjust*, as also *justice* and *injustice*, are equivocal; for they signify one thing when they are attributed to persons, another when to actions. When they are attributed to actions, *just* signifies as much as what is done with right, and *unjust*, as what is done with injury. He who hath done some just thing, is not therefore said to be a *just* person, but *guiltless;* and he that hath done some unjust thing, we do not therefore say he is an *unjust*, but *guilty* man. But when the words are applied to persons, *to be just* signifies as much as to be delighted in just dealing, to study how to do righteousness, or to endeavour in all things to do that which is just; and *to be unjust* is to neglect righteous dealing, or to think it is to be measured not according to my contract, but some present benefit. So as the justice or injustice of the mind, the intention, or the man, is one thing, that of an action or omission another; and innumerable actions of a just man may be unjust, and of an unjust man, just. But that man is to be accounted just, who doth just things because the law commands it, unjust things only by reason of his infirmity; and he is properly said to be unjust, who doth righteousness for fear of the punishment annexed unto the law, and unrighteousness by reason of the iniquity of his mind.

7. It is an old saying, *volenti non fit injuria,* the willing man receives no injury; yet the truth of it may be derived from our principles. For grant that a man be willing that that should be done which he conceives to be an injury to him; why then, that is done by his will, which by contract was not lawful to be done. But he being willing that should be done which was not lawful by contract, the contract itself (by the fifteenth article of the foregoing chapter) becomes void. The right therefore of doing it returns; therefore it is done by right; wherefore it is no injury.

8. The third precept of the natural law is, *that you suffer not him to be the worse for you, who, out of the confidence he had in you, first did you a good turn; or that you accept not a gift, but with a mind to endeavour that the giver shall have no just occasion to repent him of his gift.* For without this, he should act without reason, that would confer a benefit where he sees it would be lost; and by this means all beneficence and trust, together with all kind of benevolence, would be taken from among men, neither would there be aught of

mutual assistance among them, nor any commencement of gaining grace and favour; by reason whereof the state of war would necessarily remain, contrary to the fundamental law of nature. But because the breach of this law is not a breach of trust or contract, (for we suppose no contracts to have passed among them), therefore is it not usually termed an injury; but because good turns and thanks have a mutual eye to each other, it is called *ingratitude*.

9. The fourth precept of nature is, *that every man render himself useful unto others:* which that we may rightly understand, we must remember that there is in men a diversity of dispositions to enter into society, arising from the diversity of their affections, not unlike that which is found in stones, brought together in the building, by reason of the diversity of their matter and figure. For as a stone, which in regard of its sharp and angular form takes up more room from other stones than it fills up itself, neither because of the hardness of its matter can it well be pressed together, or easily cut, and would hinder the building from being fitly compacted, is cast away, as not fit for use: so a man, for the harshness of his disposition in retaining superfluities for himself, and detaining of necessaries from others, and being incorrigible by reason of the stubbornness of his affections, is commonly said to be useless and troublesome unto others. Now, because each one not by right only, but even by natural necessity, is supposed with all his main might to intend the procurement of those things which are necessary to his own preservation; if any man will contend on the other side for superfluities, by his default there will arise a war; because that on him alone there lay no necessity of contending; he therefore acts against the fundamental law of nature. Whence it follows, (which we were to show), that it is a precept of nature, that every man accommodate himself to others. But he who breaks this law may be called *useless* and troublesome. Yet Cicero opposeth *inhumanity* to this *usefulness*, as having regard to this very law.

10. The fifth precept of the law of nature is, *that we must forgive him who repents and asks pardon for what is past, having first taken caution for the time to come.* The pardon of what is past, or the remission of an offence, is nothing else but the granting of peace to him that asketh it, after he hath warred against us, and now is become penitent. But peace granted to him that repents not, that is, to him that retains a hostile mind, or that gives not caution for the future, that is, seeks not peace, but opportunity; is not properly peace, but fear, and therefore is not commanded by nature. Now to him that will not pardon the penitent and that gives future caution, peace itself it seems is not pleasing: which is contrary to the natural law.

11. The sixth precept of the natural law is, *that in revenge and punishments we must have our eye not at the evil past, but the future good:* that is, it is not lawful to inflict punishment for any other end, but that the offender may be corrected, or that others warned by his punishment may become better. But this is confirmed chiefly from hence, that each man is bound by the law of nature to forgive one another, provided he give caution for the future, as hath been showed in the foregoing article. Furthermore, because revenge, if the

time past be only considered, is nothing else but a certain triumph and glory of mind, which points at no end; for it contemplates only what is past, but the end is a thing to come; but that which is directed to no end, is vain: that revenge therefore which regards not the future, proceeds from vain glory, and is therefore without reason. But to hurt another without reason, introduces a war, and is contrary to the fundamental law of nature. It is therefore a precept of the law of nature, that in revenge we look not backwards, but forward. Now the breach of this law is commonly called *cruelty*.

12. But because all signs of hatred and contempt provoke most of all to brawling and fighting, insomuch as most men would rather lose their lives (that I say not, their peace) than suffer slander; it follows in the seventh place, that it is prescribed by the law of nature, that no man, either by deeds or words, countenance or laughter, *do declare himself to hate or scorn another.* The breach of which law is called *reproach*. But although nothing be more frequent than the scoffs and jeers of the powerful against the weak, and namely, of judges against guilty persons, which neither relate to the offence of the guilty, nor the duty of the judges; yet these kind of men do act against the law of nature, and are to be esteemed for contumelious.

13. The question whether of two men be the more worthy, belongs not to the natural, but civil state. For it hath been showed before (Chap. 1. Art. 3) that all men by nature are equal; and therefore the inequality which now is, suppose from riches, power, nobility of kindred, is come from the civil law. I know that Aristotle, in his first book of Politics, affirms as a foundation of the whole political science, that some men by nature are made worthy to command, others only to serve; as if lord and servant were distinguished not by consent of men, but by an aptness, that is, a certain kind of natural knowledge or ignorance. Which foundation is not only against reason, (as but now hath been showed), but also against experience. For neither almost is any man so dull of understanding as not to judge it better to be ruled by himself, than to yield himself to the government of another; neither if the wiser and stronger do contest, have these always or often the upper hand of those. Whether therefore men be equal by nature, the equality is to be acknowledged; or whether unequal, because they are like to contest for dominion, it is necessary for the obtaining of peace, *that they be esteemed as equal;* and therefore it is in the eighth place a precept of the law of nature, *that every man be accounted by nature equal to another;* the contrary to which law is *pride*.

26. Perhaps some man, who sees all these precepts of nature derived by a certain artifice from the single dictate of reason advising us to look to the preservation and safeguard of ourselves, will say that the deduction of these laws is so hard, that it is not to be expected they will be vulgarly known, and therefore neither will they prove obliging: for laws, if they be not known, oblige not, nay indeed, are not laws. To this I answer, it is true, that hope, fear, anger, ambition, covetousness, vain glory, and other perturbations of mind, do hinder a man, so as he cannot attain to the knowledge of these laws whilst those passions prevail in him: but there is no man who is not sometimes

in a quiet mind. At that time therefore there is nothing easier for him to know, though he be never so rude and unlearned, than this only rule, that when he doubts whether what he is now doing to another may be done by the law of nature or not, he conceive himself to be in that other's stead. Here instantly those perturbations which persuaded him to the fact, being now cast into the other scale, dissuade him as much. And this rule is not only easy, but is anciently celebrated in these words, *quod tibi fieri non vis, alteri ne feceris: do not that to others, you would not have done to yourself.*

27. But because most men, by reason of their perverse desire of present profit, are very unapt to observe these laws, although acknowledged by them; if perhaps some, more humble than the rest, should exercise that equity and usefulness which reason dictates, the others not practising the same, surely they would not follow reason in so doing: nor would they hereby procure themselves peace, but a more certain quick destruction, and the keepers of the law become a mere prey to the breakers of it. It is not therefore to be imagined, that by nature, that is, by reason, men are obliged to the exercise of all these laws# in that state of men wherein they are not practised by others. We are obliged yet, in the interim, to a readiness of mind to observe them, whensoever their observation shall seem to conduce to the end for which they were ordained. We must therefore conclude, that the law of nature doth always and everywhere oblige in the internal court, or that of conscience; but not always in the external court, but then only when it may be done with safety.

28. But the laws which oblige conscience, may be broken by an act not only contrary to them, but also agreeable with them; if so be that he who does it, be of another opinion. For though the act itself be answerable to the laws, yet his conscience is against them.

29. *The laws of nature are immutable and eternal:* what they forbid, can never be lawful; what they command, can never be unlawful. For *pride, ingratitude, breach of contracts* (or *injury*), *inhumanity, contumely,* will never be lawful, nor the contrary virtues to these ever unlawful, as we take them for dispositions of the mind, that is, as they are considered in the court of conscience, where only they oblige and are laws. Yet actions may be so diversified by circumstances and the civil law, that what is done with equity at one time, is guilty of iniquity at another; and what suits with reason at one time, is con-

---

The exercise of all these laws.] Nay, among these laws some things there are, the omission whereof, provided it be done for peace or self-preservation, seems rather to be the fulfilling, than breach of the natural law. For he that doth all things against those that do all things, and plunders plunderers, doth equity. But on the contrary, to do that which in peace is a handsome action, and becoming an honest man, is dejectedness and poorness of spirit, and a betraying of one's self, in the time of war. But there are certain natural laws, whose exercise ceaseth not even in the time of war itself. For I cannot understand what drunkenness or cruelty, that is, revenge which respects not the future good, can advance toward peace, or the preservation of any man. Briefly, in the state of nature, what is just and unjust, is not to be esteemed by the actions but by the counsel and conscience of the actor. That which is done out of necessity, out of endeavour for peace, for the preservation of ourselves, is done with right, otherwise every damage done to a man would be a breach of the natural law, and an injury against God.

trary to it another. Yet reason is still the same, and changeth not her end, which is peace and defence, nor the means to attain them, to wit, those virtues of the mind which we have declared above, and which cannot be abrogated by any custom or law whatsoever.

30. It is evident by what hath hitherto been said, how easily the laws of nature are to be observed, because they require the endeavour only, (but that must be true and constant); which whoso shall perform, we may rightly call him *just.* For he who tends to this with his whole might, namely, that his actions be squared according to the precepts of nature, he shows clearly that he hath a mind to fulfil all those laws; which is all we are obliged to by rational nature. Now he that hath done all he is obliged to, is a just man.

31. All writers do agree, that the natural law is the same with the moral. Let us see wherefore this is true. We must know, therefore, that good and evil are names given to things to signify the inclination or aversion of them, by whom they were given. But the inclinations of men are diverse, according to their diverse constitutions, customs, opinions; as we may see in those things we apprehend by sense, as by tasting, touching, smelling; but much more in those which pertain to the common actions of life, where what this man commends, that is to say, calls *good,* the other undervalues, as being evil. Nay, very often the same man at diverse times praises and dispraises the same thing. Whilst thus they do, necessary it is there should be discord and strife. They are, therefore, so long in the state of war, as by reason of the diversity of the present appetite, they mete good and evil by diverse measures. All men easily acknowledge this state, as long as they are in it, to be evil, and by conse-quence that peace is good. They therefore who could not agree concerning a present, do agree concerning a future good; which indeed is a work of reason; for things present are obvious to the sense, things to come to our reason only. Reason declaring peace to be good, it follows by the same reason, that all the necessary means to peace be good also; and therefore that modesty, equity, trust, humanity, mercy, (which we have demonstrated to be necessary to peace), are good manners or habits, that is, virtues. The law therefore, in the means to peace, commands also good manners, or the practice of virtue; and therefore it is called *moral.*

32. But because men cannot put off this same irrational appetite, whereby they greedily prefer the present good (to which, by strict consequence, many unforseen evils do adhere) before the future; it happens, that though all men do agree in the commendation of the foresaid virtues, yet they disagree still concerning their nature, to wit, in what each of them doth consist. For as oft as another's good action displeaseth any man, that action hath the name given of some neighbouring vice; likewise the bad actions which please them, are ever intituled to some virtue. Whence it comes to pass that the same action is praised by these, and called virtue, and dispraised by those, and termed vice. Neither is there as yet any remedy found by philosophers for this matter. For since they could not observe the goodness of actions to consist in this, that it was in order to peace, and the evil in this, that it related to discord, they built

a moral philosophy wholly estranged from the moral law, and unconstant to itself. For they would have the nature of virtues seated in a certain kind of mediocrity between two extremes, and the vices in the extremes themselves; which is apparently false. For *to dare* is commended, and, under the name of *fortitude* is taken for a virtue, although it be an extreme, if the cause be approved. Also the quantity of a thing given, whether it be great or little, or between both, makes not liberality, but the cause of giving it. Neither is it injustice, if I give any man more of what is mine own than I owe him. The laws of nature, therefore, are the sum of *moral* philosophy; whereof I have only delivered such precepts in this place, as appertain to the preservation of ourselves against those dangers which arise from discord. But there are other precepts of *rational* nature, from whence spring other virtues; for temperance, also, is a precept of reason, because intemperance tends to sickness and death. And so fortitude too, that is, that same faculty of resisting stoutly in present dangers, and which are more hardly declined than overcome; because it is a means tending to the preservation of him that resists.

33. But those which we call the laws of nature, (since they are nothing else but certain conclusions, understood by reason, of things to be done and omitted; but a law, to speak properly and accurately, is the speech of him who by right commands somewhat to others to be done or omitted), are not in propriety of speech laws, as they proceed from nature. Yet, as they are delivered by God in holy Scriptures, as we shall see in the chapter following, they are most properly called by the name of laws. For the sacred Scripture is the speech of God commanding over all things by greatest right.

Chapter IV: That the Law of Nature Is a Divine Law

1. The same law which is *natural* and *moral,* is also wont to be called *divine,* nor undeservedly; as well because reason, which is the law of nature, is given by God to every man for the rule of his actions; as because the precepts of living which are thence derived, are the same with those which have been delivered from the divine Majesty for the *laws* of his heavenly kingdom, by our Lord Jesus Christ, and his holy prophets and apostles. What therefore by reasoning we have understood above concerning the law of nature, we will endeavour to confirm the same in this chapter by holy writ.

Chapter V: Of the Causes and First Beginning of Civil Government

1. It is of itself manifest, that the actions of men proceed from the will, and the will from hope and fear, insomuch as when they shall see a greater good, or less evil, likely to happen to them by the breach, than observation of the laws, they will wittingly violate them. The hope therefore which each man hath of his security and self-preservation, consists in this, that by force or craft he may disappoint his neighbour, either openly, or by stratagem. Whence we may understand, that the natural laws, though well understood, do not instantly secure any man in their practice, and consequently, that as long as there is no caution had from the invasion of others, there remains to every

man that same primitive right of self-defence, by such means as either he can or will make use of, that is, a right to all things, or the right of war. And it is sufficient for the fulfilling of the natural law, that a man be prepared in mind to embrace peace when it may be had.

3. Since therefore the exercise of the natural law is necessary for the preservation of peace, and that for the exercise of the natural law security is no less necessary, it is worth the considering what that is which affords such a security. For this matter nothing else can be imagined, but that each man provide himself of such meet helps, as the invasion of one on the other may be rendered so dangerous, as either of them may think it better to refrain, than to meddle. But first, it is plain, that the consent of two or three cannot make good such a security; because that the addition but of one, or some few on the other side, is sufficient to make the victory undoubtedly sure, and heartens the enemy to attack us. It is therefore necessary, to the end the security sought for may be obtained, that the number of them who conspire in a mutual assistance be so great, that the accession of some few to the enemy's party may not prove to them a matter of moment sufficient to assure the victory.

4. Furthermore, how great soever the number of them is who meet on self-defence, if yet they agree not among themselves of some excellent means whereby to compass this, but every man after his own manner shall make use of his endeavours, nothing will be done. . . .

6. Since therefore the conspiring of many wills to the same end doth not suffice to preserve peace, and to make a lasting defence, it is requisite that, in those necessary matters which concern peace and self-defence, there be but one will of all men. But this cannot be done, unless every man will so subject his will to some other one, to wit, either man or council, that whatsoever his will is in those things which are necessary to the common peace, it be received for the wills of all men in general, and of every one in particular. Now the gathering together of many men who deliberate of what is to be done, or not to be done, for the common good of all men, is that which I call a council.

7. This submission of the wills of all those men to the will of one man, or one council, is then made, when each one of them obligeth himself by contract to every one of the rest, not to resist the will of that one man, or council, to which he hath submitted himself; that is, that he refuse him not the use of his wealth and strength against any others whatsoever (for he is supposed still to retain a right of defending himself against violence) and this is called union. But we understand that to be the will of the council, which is the will of the major part of those men of whom the council consists.

8. But though the will itself be not voluntary, but only the beginning of voluntary actions (for we will not to will, but to act) and therefore falls least of all under deliberation and compact; yet he who submits his will to the will of another, conveys to that other the right of his strength and faculties; insomuch as when the rest have done the same, he to whom they have submitted hath so much power, as by the terror of it he can conform the wills of particular men unto unity and concord.

9. Now union thus made is called a city, or civil society. . . .

Editor's Notes

1. The traditional definition, first given by the Roman jurist Ulpian in the second century C.E.
2. To impropriate is to take as one's own property.
3. God's general rule or regime.
4. "Civil science," that is, the true science of government.
5. God.
6. Political animal.
7. Superior excellence or precedence.
8. In *Leviathan*, chap. 6, Hobbes stated:

   "When in the mind of man, appetites, and aversions, hopes, and fears, concerning one and the same thing, arise alternately; and divers good and evil consequences of the doing, or omitting the thing propounded, come successively into our thoughts; so that sometimes we have an appetite to it; sometimes an aversion from it; sometimes hope to be able to do it; sometimes despair, or fear to attempt it; the whole sum of desires, aversions, hopes and fears continued till the thing be either done, or thought impossible, is that we call *deliberation*. . . .

   "In deliberation, the last appetite, or aversion, immediately adhering to the action, or to the omission thereof, is that we call the *will;* the act, not the faculty, of willing. And beasts that have deliberation, must necessarily also have will. . . ."
9. That is, the supreme civil power, the sovereign.

Further Reading

The only complete edition of Hobbes's works is that compiled by Sir William Molesworth, dated 1839–45, in which the English works take up eleven volumes and the Latin five. Howard Warrender edited both *De cive* and its English translation, *Philosophical Rudiments Concerning Government and Society* (Oxford: Clarendon Press, 1983), for the Clarendon Edition of Hobbes's works, but Warrender's death has halted that edition at least for the near future. The reader will find Warrender's "Introduction" to *De cive* most helpful.

The secondary literature on Hobbes is enormous and shows no signs of ceasing to grow. The best brief introduction is by Richard Tuck, *Hobbes* (Oxford: Oxford University Press, 1989), which includes a discussion of various interpretations of Hobbes. Both Richard Peters, *Hobbes* (London: Penguin, 1956), and J. W. N. Watkins, *Hobbes's System of Ideas* (London: Hutchinson University Library, 1965), give good general introductions to Hobbes's philosophy, including his views of meaning, method, and knowledge. In Keith Brown, ed., *Hobbes Studies* (Oxford: Blackwell Publisher, 1965), the reader will find a number of useful essays on different aspects of Hobbes's views and their historical setting. Another collection of valuable essays is by G. A. J. Rogers and Alan Ryan, *Perspectives on Thomas Hobbes* (New York: Oxford University Press, 1989).

There are several systematic studies, among which the most useful are David Gauthier, *The Logic of Leviathan* (Oxford: Clarendon Press, 1969); Jean Hampton, *Hobbes and the Social Contract Tradition* (Cambridge, England: Cambridge University Press, 1986); and Gregory S. Kavka, *Hobbesian Moral and Political Theory* (Princeton, N.J.: Princeton University Press, 1986). Each offers a systematic reconstruction of Hobbesian doctrine. Hampton has an extensive bibliography. Howard Warrender, *The*

Political Philosophy of Hobbes (Oxford: Clarendon Press, 1957), offers an acute but controversial reading of Hobbes's theory.

On the reception of Hobbes, see John Bowle, *Hobbes and His Critics* (London: Jonathan Cape, 1951); Samuel I. Mintz, *The Hunting of Leviathan* (Cambridge, England: Cambridge University Press, 1969); and Quentin Skinner, "Thomas Hobbes and His Disciples in France and England," *Comparative Studies in Society and History* 8 (1965): 153–67.

There are many editions of Hobbes's major work, *Leviathan:* the "Introduction" to the one by Michael Oakeshott (Oxford: Blackwell Publisher, n.d.), is particularly interesting.

Richard Cumberland

Introduction

Born in 1631 in London, Cumberland studied at Cambridge University and was elected a fellow of Magdalene College there in 1656. His career was in the Church of England, of which, after serving in several different parishes, he was made a bishop in 1691. He had been a loyal Protestant through the troubled years when Catholicism threatened England under James II. If the bishopric of Peterborough was a reward, it was one Cumberland had not sought, and he was diligent in carrying out the duties of his office. His only philosophical work was *De legibus naturae* (*Treatise of the Laws of Nature*), published in 1672 and translated into English twice during the eighteenth century and also into French, by Barbeyrac, the translator of Grotius and Pufendorf. Cumberland's other interest was history. He loved antiquarian research into Jewish history and wrote several volumes on various aspects of it, some published posthumously. He died in 1718.

The *Treatise of the Laws of Nature* is a rambling, badly organized work, in which Cumberland tried to replace Hobbes's views with an outlook that is at once philosophically defensible and substantively Christian. He spent many pages arguing against Hobbes – against his method, against his psychology, against the moral conclusions he drew, against his atheism, and against his politics. Cumberland tried to argue as rigorously as possible, drawing on science for assistance (there is a long section on human physiology, complete with a foldout diagram of the nerves in the backbone) but abstaining from the kind of humanistic citation of classical authors that Grotius used. Cumberland offered extensive mathematical formulations or analogies for some of his ideas. Though aware that he had anti-Hobbesian allies among the Cambridge philosophers, he refrained from joining with them in an appeal to a Platonic idea of the good, because he knew such an appeal would carry no weight against Hobbes. Yet although Cumberland tried to be scientific and up to date, there is no question that his message is that love is the fulfillment of the law (Rom. 13:10, cited on his title page). Love, for Cumberland, is benevolence, and benevolence, as he understood it, moves us to increase the happiness of all rational beings. In his work we can see natural law theory being moved decisively in one of the directions inherent in it, the utilitarian.

According to the utilitarian view, the basic principle of morality is that we are to bring about the greatest good we can, and other moral concepts are defined in terms of the good. All the natural lawyers, whether Thomistic or "modern," would have agreed that one function of the laws of nature is to direct us to attain something good. For Hobbes they show each individual the way to attain his or her own good, but for the other lawyers they direct our actions toward the common good as well as toward our own. For the natural lawyers, however, the laws of nature do more than teach us how to attain the good. They show us what God wills us to do, and they bind or obligate us as well. Furthermore, the concept of obligation is not defined simply in terms of the good. Now Cumberland did not deny that the law shows us God's will and also carries obligation with it, but he takes the fact that the laws direct us to the common good as their central feature and tries to show that the other functions of law derive solely from it. He moved natural law theory in the direction of utilitarianism because he believed that the single basic law of nature is that we are to increase the good of all rational beings and also because he wanted to explain how obligation is itself a function of that requirement.

Did Cumberland manage to achieve all his aims – to defeat Hobbes, to argue in scientific terms, and to preserve Christian teaching – in a consistent and coherent way? One problem he faced was that as a Christian he had to demonstrate that God matters for morality. God matters because the laws of nature are proper laws; proper laws require a sanction; and God is the source of the sanction. Cumberland was a moderate in the Church of England and rejected the extreme voluntarism of the Calvinists, as well as, of course, the variant of voluntarism in Hobbes. Hence he wanted to say that the good is not made by will but is eternal. We perceive it and are moved by it, and this, somehow, must explain how there is a law of nature.

Cumberland also rejected the idea of a wrathful deity moving us only by threats. He accordingly treated the sanctions of the laws of nature as coming from the way we naturally respond to the world. Just as we find that temperance benefits us personally, so we find that being benevolent is enjoyable and that being selfish is, in the long run, self-defeating. Sanctions become the pleasures and pains that naturally attend various courses of action, not rewards and punishments in addition to them. One then wants to ask why God is really needed. Admitting that God made the world with this helpful structure, what more is left for him to do? Cumberland came close to believing that the world can run on its own and that we, as part of it, can direct our own lives.

There are other ways in which Cumberland revealed this position. One of the points of Hobbes's doctrine that his critics disliked most was his denial that there is anything properly called free will. Actions can be free, Hobbes held, but not the will as such. We simply are part of the mechanism of nature, and natural forces are as effectively at work in determining the course of our desires and aversions as they are in the external world. Although Cumberland made an effort to distance himself from the egoism he found in Hobbes's psychology, he evaded the issue of free will, stating that he was not interested in metaphysical subtleties. He did not accept Hobbesian materialism, but he did not try to show that our mode of action differs in principle from the behavior of nonhuman beings. This comes out most strikingly in Cumberland's refusal to distinguish between stating the law of nature in terms of what does in fact occur and stating it in terms of what ought to occur. It is as if Cumberland were saying, I shall tackle Hobbes on his own terms, showing that as parts of nature we are moved to obtain not our own personal greatest good but the greatest good for all rational beings. The reader may wish to ask whether this is an adequate reply or simply a confusion.

The following selections are from Cumberland's *Treatise of the Laws of Nature*, translated by John Maxwell, London, 1727. I have used fewer capital letters and italics than the translator did and have simplified some of the punctuation.

A Treatise of the Laws of Nature

The Introduction

§I. It concerns us both, friendly reader, that you should be briefly acquainted with the design and method of this treatise; for thence you will immediately perceive what I have performed, or at least attempted; and what is further to be supplied from your own understanding of the writings of others. The laws of nature are the foundations of all moral and civil knowledge, as in the following work will at large appear. But these, as all other conclusions discoverable by the light of nature, may be deduced two ways: either from those manifest effects which flow from them or from the causes whence they themselves arise. I have endeavoured to discover them in this latter method, by arguing from the cause to the effect. To the former method of proving their obligation (by arguing from the effect to the cause) belongs what has been written by Hugo Grotius . . . the work of Hugo Grotius, which was the first of the kind, I think worthy both of the author and of immortality. . . .

§IV. Wherefore, that the conclusions of reason in moral matters might more evidently appear to be laws, laws of God, I have thought it proper to make a philosophical inquiry into their causes, as well internal as external, the nearer and the more remote; for by this method we shall at last arrive at their first author or efficient cause, from whose essential perfections and internal sanction of them by rewards and punishments . . . their authority arises. Most others have been satisfied with saying in general terms that these conclusions, or actions conformable to them, are taught by nature; but to me it seems necessary, especially at this time, to trace more distinctly after what manner the powers of things, as well without as within us, conspire to imprint these conclusions upon our minds and to give a sanction to them.

§V. The Platonists,[1] indeed, clear up this difficulty in an easier manner, by the supposition of innate ideas, as well of the laws of nature themselves as of those matters about which they are conversant; but, truly, I have not been so happy as to learn the laws of nature in so short a way. Nor seems it to me well advised to build the doctrine of natural religion and morality upon an hypothesis which has been rejected by the generality of philosophers, as well heathen as Christian, and can never be proved against the Epicureans,[2] with whom is our chief controversy. I was resolved, however, not to oppose this opinion, because it is my earnest desire that whatever looks with a friendly aspect upon piety and morality might have its due weight (and I look upon these Platonists to be favourers of their cause) and because it is not impossible that such ideas might be both born with us and afterwards impressed upon us from without.

§VI. Moreover, the same reasons which hindered us from supposing innate ideas of the laws of nature in our minds hinder us likewise from supposing without proof that these laws have existed from eternity in the divine mind.[3] I have therefore thought it necessary to remove the difficulty, and assert and prove the authority and eternal existence of these conclusions in the divine mind, in the following method; assuming those notices which we have from sense and daily experience, I demonstrate that the nature of things, which subsists and is continually governed by its first cause, does necessarily imprint on our minds some practical propositions (which must be always true, and cannot without a contradiction be supposed otherwise) concerning the study of promoting the joint felicity of all rationals: and that the terms of these propositions do immediately and directly signify that the first cause, in his original constitution of things, has annexed the greatest rewards and punishments to the observance and neglect of these truths. Whence it manifestly follows that they are laws, laws being nothing but practical propositions, with rewards and punishments annexed, promulged[4] by competent authority. Having hence shewn that the knowledge and practice of these laws is the natural perfection or most happy state of our rational nature, I infer that there must be in the first cause (from whom proceed both this our perfection, and that most wise disposition which we see, every day, of effects without us, for the common preservation and perfection of the whole system) a perfection correspondent but infinitely superior to this knowledge and practice of the laws of nature. For I look upon it as most evident that we must first know what justice is and from whence those laws are derived in the observance whereof it wholly consists, before we can distinctly know that justice is to be attributed to God, and that we ought to propose his justice as our example. For we come not at the knowledge of God by immediate intuition of his perfections, but from his effects first known by sense and experience; nor can we safely ascribe to him attributes which from other considerations we do not sufficiently comprehend.

§IX. Lastly, upon a diligent consideration of all those propositions which deserve to be ranked amongst the general laws of nature, I have observed they may be reduced to one universal one, from the just explication whereof all the particular laws may be both duly limited and illustrated. This general proposition may be thus expressed: "The endeavour, to the utmost of our power, of promoting the common good of the whole system of rational agents conduces, as far as in us lies, to the good of every part, in which our own happiness as that of a part is contained. But contrary actions produce contrary effects, and consequently our own misery, among that of others."

§XV. That the summary of all the precepts and sanctions of the law of nature is contained in our proposition and its corollary concerning the opposite behaviour, I thus briefly shew. The subject (to borrow a school-term) of the proposition is "an endeavour, according to our ability, to promote the common good of the whole system of rationals." This includes our love of God and of all mankind, who are the parts of this system. God, indeed, is the principal part; men, the subordinate: a benevolence toward both includes piety and humanity, that is, both tables of the law of nature.[5] The predicate of the proposition (to borrow another phrase from the schools) is "conducing to the good of every part, in which our own happiness, as of a part, is contained." In which, as all those good things we can procure to all are said to be the effect of this endeavour, so among the rest is not omitted that collection of good things whence our own happiness arises, which is the greatest reward of obedience; as misery arising from actions of a contrary kind is the greatest punishment of wickedness. But the natural connexion of the predicate with the subject is both the foundation of the truth of the proposition and the proof of the natural connexion between obedience and rewards, transgression and punishments.

Hence the reader will easily observe the true reason why this practical proposition, and all those which may be deduced from thence, oblige all rational beings who understand them; whilst other practical propositions (suppose geometrical ones) equally impressed by nature and consequently by God upon the mind of man do not oblige him to conform his practice to them; but may safely be neglected by most, to whom the practice of geometry is not necessary: which is wholly owing to the nature of the effects arising from the one and the other practice. The effects of the practice of geometry are such as most people may want[6] without prejudice. But the effects of a care of the common good do so nearly concern all, of whom we ourselves are a part, and upon whose pleasure the happiness of each individual does in some measure depend, that such care cannot be rejected without the hazard of losing that happiness or the hope thereof: and this God has manifested to us by the very nature of things, and thereby he has sufficiently promulged that he himself is the author of the connexion of rewards and punishments with our actions; whence this proposition and all others which flow from thence commence laws by his authority.

§XVI. From the very terms of our proposition, it is manifest that the adequate and immediate effect of that practice which this law establishes is that which is acceptable to God and beneficial to all men; which is the natural good of the whole system of rationals, even the greatest of all those good things which can be procured for them, as being greater than the like good of any part of the same system. Moreover, it sufficiently implies that the happiness of each individual (from the prospect of enjoying which, or being deprived of it, the whole sanction is taken) is derived from the best state of the whole system, as the nourishment of each member of an animal depends upon the nourishment of the whole mass of blood diffused through the whole.

Hence it is manifest, that this greatest effect (not any small portion thereof, the private happiness suppose, of any single person) is the principal end of the lawgiver and of everyone who truly obeys his will. It is likewise hence evident that those human actions which from their own natural force or efficacy are apt to promote the common good are called naturally good, and indeed better than those actions which are subservient to the private good of any individual, in proportion as the public good is greater than a private.

In like manner, such actions as take the shortest way to this effect as to their end, are naturally right, because of their natural resemblance to a right line, which is the shortest that can be drawn between any two given points. Nevertheless, the same actions, afterward, when they are compared with the law, whether natural or positive, which is the rule of morality, and they are found conformable to it, are called morally good, as also right, that is, agreeing with the rule; but the rule itself is called right, as pointing out the shortest way to the end.

§XVII. But because the connexion of rewards and punishments with such actions as promote the public good, or the contrary, is somewhat obscured by those evil things which happen to the good and those good things which happen to the evil, it seems necessary to our purpose more carefully to shew that (notwithstanding these) that connexion is sufficiently constant and manifest in human nature so that thence may with certainty be inferred the sanction of the law of nature, commanding these actions, and forbidding those.

§XVIII. The causes of human actions are the powers of the mind and body of man. Wherefore, because I have observed it to be manifest that happiness, or the highest reward, is necessarily connected with the most full and constant exercise of all our powers about the best and greatest objects and effects which are adequate and proportionable to them; I hence collect, that men endowed with these faculties are naturally bound, under the penalty of forfeiting their happiness, to employ or exercise them about the noblest objects in nature, viz. God, and man his image. Nor can it be long a question whether our faculties may be more properly employed in cultivating friendship or enmity with these, in engaging with them in a state of peace or war. For it is plain that there can be no neutral state, in which God and men shall be neither loved nor hated and irritated, or in which we shall act neither acceptably nor unacceptably to either, especially when we make use of things without us. For of necessity we must either take care not to deprive others of things necessary to their happiness, which without benevolence cannot be supposed; or we shall willingly take them away, which is a sure indication of a malicious mind. But if it be acknowledged that there is an evident necessity in order to happiness of cultivating friendship with God and man, the sanction of that most general law of nature, which alone we are here tracing, is of course granted. For that alone establishes both all natural religion and everything that is necessary to the happiness of mankind.

§XXIII. I have thus briefly laid down the method by which I have deduced the sanction of the laws of nature; in which I have considered the happiness which naturally flows from good actions as the reward annexed to them by the author of nature; and the loss thereof as a punishment not less naturally connected with evil actions. For whatever good or evil is the necessary consequence of human actions must necessarily be contained in such practical propositions as truly declare the consequences of those actions. And God himself is supposed to declare those practical propositions which are necessarily suggested to our minds by the nature, as well of our own actions, as of those of other rational beings, and which truly foretell what consequences will follow. But those advantages and disadvantages which God himself pronounces annexed to human actions, and by which we are admonished to pursue those and avoid these, are really and truly rewards and punishments.

§XXIV. Moreover, this method, by which I have reduced all the precepts of the law of nature to one, seems useful, because the proof of this one proposition is more easy and expeditious than that of those many which are usually proposed by philosophers; and the ease of the memory is better consulted, to which daily calling to mind a single sentence is not a burden; and (which is the greatest advantage of all) from the very nature of the common good, which in this proposition we are directed to promote, a certain rule or measure is afforded to the prudent man's judgment by the help whereof he may ascertain that just measure in his actions and affections in which virtue consists. This task Aristotle has assigned to the judgment of the prudent, in his definition of virtue, but has not pointed out the rule by which such judgment is to be formed. Our proposition shews that the rule is to be taken from the nature of the best and greatest end, respect being had to all the parts of the whole system of rationals, or of that society of which God is the head, the members, all God's subjects.

CHAPTER 1: OF THE NATURE OF THINGS

§IV. . . . although there are innumerable things which, in the knowledge of the universe, may be made use of for the matter of particular propositions which are to form our manners, I have nevertheless thought proper to select only a few, and those the most general, which might in some measure explain that general description of the laws of nature which I at first proposed, and are a little more manifestly contained in one proposition, the fountain of all nature's laws. Which general proposition is this, "the greatest benevolence of every rational agent towards all, forms the happiest state of every, and of all the benevolent, as far as is in their power, and is necessarily requisite to the happiest state which they can attain, and therefore the common good is the supreme law."

§XV. The things now proposed concerning human happiness appear so plain by common experience or obvious reasoning that I know nothing belonging to human nature more evident; and they have the same respect to the direction of our practice in morality which the postulates of geometricians have to the construction of problems; such are for plain problems that we can draw a right line from any one point to any other, or that we can describe a circle with any center and radius, and other more difficult ones, for the construction of solid and linear problems. In all these cases are supposed actions depending upon the free powers of men; yet geometry does not become uncertain by any disputes arising from the explanation of free will. The like may be said of arithmetical operations; for it is sufficient for the truth of these sciences that the connexion is inseparable between such acts (which it supposes may be done and which we find placed in our power when we go about the practice of geometry), and the effects desired. And either the pleasure arising from such contemplations or the manifold uses in life are sufficient to invite men to search after such effects. By a like reasoning, the truth of moral philosophy is founded in the necessary connexion between the

greatest happiness human powers can reach, and those acts of universal benevolence, or of love towards God and men, which is branched out into all the
moral virtues. But in the mean time these things are supposed as postulates:
that the greatest happiness they can attain is sought by men; and, that they
can exercise love not only towards themselves but also towards God and
[towards] men partaking of the same rational nature with themselves.

§XXII. Secondly. If men or other things do, or afford, any thing for the use
of men, such service or benefit is naturally and necessarily limited to certain
persons, times, and places. Therefore, if right reason enjoins that the use of
things or the services of men should be useful to all men, it necessarily enjoins
that for a certain time and place that use of things and of human services
should be limited to certain persons. The consequence is manifest because
that is right reason in commanding which commands that to be done which is
possible to be done according to the nature of things. The consequence tends
to prove that a division of things and of human services, at least for the time
they may be of use to others, is necessary for the advantage of all.

And certainly that necessary limitation of the use of one thing to one man
for the time it benefits any person is a natural division, that is, separation from
the use of any other person for the same time. It is manifest that I here call
those things one that are necessarily wholly employed in one use at one time.
For other things are likewise called one which at the same time may be of use
to many, as one island, one wood, etc. concerning whose division I have yet
affirmed nothing. From the above-mentioned natural division of things and its
necessity to the preservation of all, is derived that primitive right to things by
first occupancy (which is so frequently mentioned by philosophers and lawyers, and which they teach is to take place supposing all things common). For
right is the liberty of acting any thing granted by a law. But in that supposed
state there is no other law but the conclusions of right reason, concerning
actions necessary to the common good, promulgated by God. . . .

§XXIII. Nor, upon these suppositions, will there be any right to do anything
except what right reason declares to be necessary to the common good or at
least consistent with it; of which the first is therefore commanded by reason,
the last permitted. . . . This, however, I thought proper here carefully to
inculcate, that all right, even to the use of those things which are absolutely
necessary to every one's preservation (as it is distinguished from the mere
force of seizing those things, in which sense only its original is here inquired
into) is founded in the command, or at least in the permission, of the law of
nature, that is, of right reason pronouncing concerning those things which are
necessary to the common good according to the nature of things; and that
therefore it cannot be known that any one has a right to preserve himself,
unless it be known that this will contribute to the common good or that it is at
least consistent with it. But if this be the rise of our right to our own preservation, our powers will be hereby so limited that we may not invade the equal
rights of others, nor break forth into a war against all; that is, make an
attempt towards the destruction of all.

CHAPTER 2: OF HUMAN NATURE AND RIGHT REASON

§VII. I think it proper to observe here, by the way, that by the dictates of practical reason I understand propositions which point out either the end or the means thereto in every man's power. For all practice is resolved into these; and that practical reason is then called right when it determines truly, or as the thing is in itself, in propositions declaring what is every man's best and most necessary end and what are the most proper means of obtaining it; or (which comes to the same thing) which pronounces according to truth what effects of our own counsel and will will render our selves and others happy, and how we shall with the greatest certainty produce them; just as in geometry that speculative reason is right which affirms a quantity which is really in its own nature greater to be greater than another. And that practical proposition is right, which teaches that method of constructing problems which if we pursue, we shall really produce the effect proposed. Nor is an opinion or proposition of this kind truer when affirmed by a king than when by a subject. Since then all right reason is conformable to those things about which we have formed a judgment, since each thing is in its nature but one and uniform with it self; it follows that right reason in one [person] cannot dictate that which contradicts right reason concerning the same things in any other person.

From this principle follows that precept of universal use concerning the actions of all men, that human actions ought to be uniform and consistent with themselves, through the whole course of every man's life; . . .

It is included in the notion of a true proposition (a practical one, for instance) and is consequently a necessary perfection of a man forming a right judgment in that affair, that it should agree with other true propositions framed about a like subject, though that like case should happen at another time or belong to another man. And therefore, if any one judge that his act of taking to himself the necessaries of life not yet possessed by any other would promote the common happiness, it is necessary that the judgment that the like action of another in like circumstances would equally conduce to the same end, must be undoubtedly right. Whoever therefore judges truly, must judge the same things which he thinks truly are lawful to himself to be lawful to others in a like case. In the same manner, whatever assistance any man rightly and truly believes he may or ought to demand according to right reason, it is equitable and consequently a dictate of right reason that he should think that any other in like circumstances justly may or ought to demand the like help from him.

§XII. Shall I not reckon among the perfections of the human understanding that it can reflect upon itself? Consider its habits as dispositions arising from past actions? Judge which way the mind inclines? And direct itself to the pursuit of what seems fittest to be done? Our mind is conscious to itself of all its own actions, and both can and often does observe what counsels produced them; it naturally sits a judge upon its own actions, and thence procures to itself either tranquillity and joy, or anxiety and sorrow. In this power of the mind, and the actions thence arising consists the whole force of conscience, by which it proposes laws to itself, examines its past and regulates its future conduct. Nor appear any traces in other animals of so noble a faculty. Great are the powers of this principle, both to the formation and increase of virtue, to the erecting and preserving civil societies, both among those who are not subject to the same civil power, and among fellow-subjects. And, indeed, the principal design of this treatise is to shew how this power of our mind, either of itself, or excited by external objects, forms certain universal practical propositions which give us a more distinct idea of the utmost possible happiness of mankind and pronounce by what actions of ours, in all variety of circumstances, that happiness may most effectually be obtained. For these are the rules of action, these are the laws of nature.

CHAPTER 3: OF NATURAL GOOD

§I. Good is that which preserves or enlarges and perfects the faculties of any one thing or of several. For in these effects is discovered that particular agreement of one thing with another which is requisite to denominate anything good to the nature of this thing rather than of others.

In the definition of "good" I chose to avoid the word "agreement" because of its very uncertain signification. Nevertheless, those things whose actions or motions conduce to the preservation or increase of the powers of other things consistently with the nature of the individual may justly be said to agree with them. . . . So that is good to man which preserves or enlarges the powers of the mind and body, or of either, without prejudice to the other. . . .

Good of this kind, of which we form an idea without the consideration of any laws whatsoever, I call natural good. . . .

It is distinguished by its greater extensiveness from that good which is called "moral," which is ascribed only to such actions and habits of rational agents as are agreeable to laws, whether natural or civil, and is ultimately resolved into the natural common good, to the preservation and increase of which alone all the laws of nature and all just civil laws do direct use. . . .

§II. I own, therefore, that to be called "good" which agrees with another and consequently that the term is relative. But it is not always referred to the desire, nor always to that one person only who desires it. In these two points Hobbes[7] has often erred grossly (though he sometimes comes out with the truth, in contradiction to himself) and on these fundamental mistakes is supported most of what he has writ amiss concerning the right of war of all against all in a state of nature, and a right of exercising arbitrary power in a state of society. . . .

I . . . am of opinion that things are first judged to be good and that they are afterwards desired only so far as they seem good; that anything is therefore truly judged good because its effect or force truly helps nature; that a private good is that which profits one, public, which is of advantage to many; not because it is desired from opinion whether true or false or delights for this or that moment of time. . . . And it is the part of brutes only to measure the goodness of things or of actions by affection only, without the guidance of reason. . . .

§IV. There is another error of Hobbes concerning good, which is, that "the object of the" human "will is that, which every man thinks good for himself."* Which he thus expresses elsewhere, "every one is presumed to pursue his own good naturally; that which is just, for peace only, and by accident."† What is just, respects the good of others, which he does not think any man seeks unless from a fear of those evils which arise from a state of war. Of a piece with these passages are the places above quoted out of him; and numberless others, scattered through his writings, insinuate the same thing. Upon this is grounded that passage, "whatever is done voluntarily, is done for some good to him who wills it."‡ . . .

But if we examine what led him into an opinion so contrary to that of all philosophers, I can see nothing but that one hint which he affords, by the bye, in the same section, where he explains "nature" by "the affections planted in every animal, till by inconvenient consequences or by precepts it is effected, that the desire of things present is checked by the remembrance of things past."§ He judges of human nature and the adequate object of the will from those affections, which are previous to the use of reason, to experience, and to discipline, such as are found in children and madmen; see his Preface to his treatise *De cive*. But I, as well as all other philosophers that I know of, think that we are to take an estimate of the nature of man rather from reason (and that therefore the will may extend it self to those things which reason dictates to be agreeable to the nature of any person) since such irrational affections are to be looked on rather as perturbations of the mind and consequently as preternatural; which even Hobbes himself, since the publishing his book *De cive,* confesses in his treatise *De homine.*[8] Nor see I any thing to hinder but that what I judge agreeable to any nature I may desire should happen to it; nay, that I should endeavour, as far as in me lies, that it should be effected.

Nay, this may be demonstrated *a priori* to those who acknowledge the nature of the will to consist in the consent of the mind with the judgment of the understanding concerning things agreeing among themselves. For it is certain that the understanding is capable of judging what promotes the good of others as well as what promotes our own; nor is there any reason why we cannot will those same things which we have judged to be good. (Nay, it is hardly possible that we should not will those things which we have judged to be good.) But it is to be observed that, whatever a man can will, he can also resolve to effect the same as far as it is in his power. Good thus willed by us is said to be intended, and, by virtue of this intention, it assumes the complete

---

* Hobbes, *De cive,* I.2. (The passage in the English version is as follows: "For when we voluntarily contract society, in all manner of society we look after the object of the will, that is, that which every one of those who gather together propounds to himself for good.")
† Ibid., III.21.
‡ Ibid., II.8.
§ Ibid.

nature of an end: therefore the common good of the universe may be an end proposed by men.

Chapter 4: Of the Practical Dictates of Reason

§I. . . . A practical proposition is sometimes thus expressed: "This possible human action (universal benevolence, for instance) will chiefly, beyond any other action at the same time possible, conduce to my happiness and that of all others, either as an essential part thereof or as a cause which will, some time or other, effect a principal essential part thereof." It is sometimes expressed, in the form of a command: "Let that action, which is in thy power, and which will most effectually, of all those which thou can'st exert, promote the common good in the present circumstances, be exerted"; often also, in the form of a gerund: "such an action ought to be done." In my opinion, these several forms of speech relating to the law of nature mean the same thing, whether the understanding judges this best to be done, or commands it, or tells me, in the form of a gerund, that I am bound to do it. For the understanding (which in this affair is called conscience) sufficiently hints the natural obligation when it says, "this is best to be done, both for your self and others." For, in omitting what is declared best for me it is thence evident that I bring mischief (which may be called punishment) upon my self. If the dictate be considered under the form of a command, the same thing is inculcated by representing every man's own understanding as a magistrate deputed and authorized to make laws: Which, because it sounds somewhat metaphorically is therefore less philosophical. It is useful however, because the comparison has a very just foundation in nature. The form of a gerund teaches the same thing; but as an inferior judge or counsellor admonishing concerning a law already made and requiring a conformity of the future action therewith. The first manner is most becoming a philosopher, which, if we consider the form, appears a speculative proposition; if the force, a practical, as teaching the natural foundation of obligation. The second best becomes a sovereign prince; the third, a divine. But they may all be used promiscuously, provided we retain in mind the distinction, such as it is, between these forms. The nature of things represents to the mind what is best to be done. The mind, considering the government of things, does, from the idea of God, conclude, that he wills or commands them to be done and in his name imposes the command on itself, in the second form. In the third, it reflects upon the two former, and pronounces that an action agreeable to that command will be just; the contrary, unjust.

§IV. But before we consider these laws more particularly, it will be worth while to insist somewhat longer on treating of the nature of practical propositions, and first to shew their great affinity or agreement in meaning, whether they be absolute or conditional, with speculative propositions. Secondly, that in them all the effect is looked upon as the end; actions in our power, as the means.

In order to which we are first to observe that those are properly called practical propositions which declare the origin of an effect from human actions, which definition I think proper to illustrate by examples. Such is this in arithmetic, "the addition of numbers forms the sum," or "the subtraction of one number from another leaves their difference."

Yet farther: the science of morality and politics both can and ought to imitate the analytic art (in which I comprehend not only the extraction of roots, but also the whole doctrine of specious arithmetic or algebra) as the noblest pattern of science.

1. By delivering the rules of its practice and the whole substance of its art in a few universal theorems. Where I think proper to observe that its certainty is no more weakened or usefulness lessened because we cannot exactly determine what is fit to be done in our external actions with relation to a subject involved in a vast variety of circumstances, than the truth or usefulness of geometrical principles about measuring lines, surfaces, or solids is overthrown because neither our senses nor instruments will enable us to form without us a line exactly straight, or a surface perfectly plane or spherical or a body in all respects regular. It is sufficient that we approach so near to exactness that what we want of it is of no consequence in practice.

2. . . . . moral philosophy begins with contemplating an end very intricate, and means variously involved. For the end is a collection of all those good things within our power which are capable of adorning the kingdom of God, the whole system of intelligent agents, and its several parts. The means, by which this end is to be obtained, are all our possible free actions, about what object soever. And, from an equality supposed between these two ideas, as between the powers of the cause and their adequate effect are to be drawn all moral rules and all virtuous actions enjoined by them. It is evident that these things are equal because the end is the entire effect to be produced, and all our possible actions make up the entire efficient cause.

3. As algebra supposes the quantity unknown and yet sought after in some sort already known, by a certain anticipation of the mind, and expresses it by a proper character, and is thus enabled to exhibit its given relation to the known quantities, by means whereof itself at last becomes known: so ethics, also, forms some kind of idea of the end or effect proposed; by the help of those relations which it bears to our operations in some measure known (at least in general) it distinguishes it by the name of the chief good, or of happiness, from other objects, although it knows that it does not yet exist, and although it does not distinctly know what shall at last be the effect of our operations, and of the concurrence of things without us; whence it may justly be called unknown: but by the help of those actions and faculties to which it is related as the effect to its causes, and on which consequently it most certainly entirely depends, it at last gradually becomes known. Hither also is to be referred that, whereas the end proposed by every one is that entire and greatest good which he can procure to the universe and to himself in his station, it follows that the end is to be conceived as the greatest aggregate or

sum of good effects, most acceptable to God and men, which can be effected by the greatest industry of all our future actions. It often happens (and we ought to endeavour that it should happen as often as may be) that the good effects of our power increase in a geometrical progression (as in increase arising from interest upon interest, or in husbandry, or merchandizing, when every year the increase of the former is added to the main stock) whence arises a vast increase, both of public and private happiness beyond what can be distinctly foreseen.

Chapter 5: Of the Law of Nature, and Its Obligation

§I. Having prepared the way for all that is to follow, I shall begin this chapter with the definition of the law of nature. *The law of nature is a proposition proposed to the observation of, or impressed upon, the mind with sufficient clearness by the nature of things, from the will of the first cause which points out that possible action of a rational agent which will chiefly promote the common good and by which only the entire happiness of particular persons can be obtained.* The former part of this definition contains the precept, the latter, the sanction; and the mind receives the impression of both, from the nature of things.

§XXII. The second method[9] of knowing that God wills that actions conducing to the common good of rational agents should be performed by men or that he wills that such actions should be honoured with rewards, or the contrary restrained by punishments, is taken from the effects of this will, that is, from the rewards and punishments themselves, which, by means of the inward constitution of all men and of this whole system of the world, framed by the appointment of the divine will, are the natural and ordinary consequences of human actions; and do render men either miserable by evil or happy by good. For it is not to be doubted but that God, who has so established the natural order of all things that the consequences of human actions with respect to the actors themselves should be such; and who has caused that these ordinary consequences may be foreknown or expected with the highest probability by them, willed that before they prepared for action they should consider these things, and be determined by them, as by arguments contained in the sanction of the laws.

Such kind of effects are those internal pleasures of mind, which accompany every noble action intended for the publick good; and, on the contrary, those fears and anxieties of mind, which, like furies, pursue the wicked: and also those external rewards and punishments by which other rational agents, according to the dictates of right reason concerning the best end and means, preserve mankind from destruction and promote the common happiness.

I thought it proper to insist the longer upon this argument in this treatise, because I hoped my antagonists, who are so intent upon their own preservation, would the more willingly acknowledge its force; and because the nature of things seemed to propose many proofs of this matter, which required a very particular explication. I therefore resolve moral obligation (which is the immediate effect of nature's laws) into their first and principal cause which is the will and counsel of God promoting the common good; and therefore by rewards and punishments enacting into laws the practical propositions which tend thereto. Men's care of their own happiness, which causes them to consider and be moved by rewards and punishments, is no cause of obligation; that proceeds wholly from the law and the lawgiver. It is only a necessary disposition in the subject, without which the rewards and penalties of the law would be of no force to induce men to the performance of their duty. As contact is necessary in the communication of motion from body to body, though force impressed be the only cause of that motion.

It ought also in confirmation of this point to be considered that the obligation lies upon them too whose mind is so stupid that they wholly neglect the divine will and the sanction thereby annexed to the law. I must add that the care of preserving and perfecting ourselves, which is natural and inseparable from man, and that which is superinduced by right reason and which I acknowledge has some place among the motives to good actions, tho' not a cause of our obligation to them, are both wholly from God. From thence it follows, that the force of this care detracts nothing from his authority or honour, and that it ought to have its due influence.

§XXVII. Here, lest I should be thought to use words in a sense different from what is usual, I shall briefly shew that what I have said is implied in the received definition of obligation.

There is nothing which can superinduce a necessity of doing or forbearing any thing upon a human mind deliberating upon a thing future except thoughts or propositions promising good or evil to our selves or others, consequent upon what we are about to do. But because we are determined by some sort of natural necessity to pursue good foreseen, especially the greatest, and to avoid evils; hence those dictates of reason which discover to us that these things will follow from certain of our actions are said to lay upon us some kind of necessity of performing or omitting those actions, and to oblige us; because those advantages are necessarily connected with our happiness, which we naturally desire, and our actions are evidently necessary to the attainment of them.

I therefore think that moral obligation may be thus universally and properly defined: "Obligation is that act of a legislator by which he declares that actions conformable to his law are necessary to those for whom the law is made." An action is then understood to be necessary to a rational agent when it is certainly one of the causes necessarily required to that happiness which he naturally and consequently necessarily desires. Thus we are obliged to pursue the common good when the nature of things (especially of rational causes) exposed to our observation discovers to our minds that this action is a cause necessarily requisite to complete our happiness; which, therefore, naturally depends upon the pursuit of the common good of all rational agents; as the soundness of a member depends upon the soundness and life of the whole animated body. It amounts to the same thing when we say that the obligation is an act of the legislator or of the first cause, as if in this place we had called it an act of the law of nature. For the legislator obliges by the law sufficiently promulged, and he sufficiently promulges it when he discovers to our minds that the prosecution of the common good is the cause necessarily requisite to that happiness which every one necessarily desires.

Upon discovering this all men are obliged, whether it be of so great weight with them as perfectly to incline their minds to what it persuades, or whether what is alleged in favour of the contrary opinion weigh more. Those bodies which, through a fault in the balance, are raised by a smaller weight in the opposite scale are yet in themselves heavier or have a greater tendency towards the center of the earth.

It is to be observed that those arguments which prove our obligation in this case would certainly prevail, unless the ignorance, turbulent affections, or rashness of men, like the fault in the balance, opposed their efficacy; as discovering, beside rewards and punishments manifested or expressed, that others greater (if there be occasion) will be added at the pleasure of the supreme governour of the world.

. . . the entire happiness of every particular man naturally depends upon the benevolence of God and of other men; but neither can the benevolence of God towards any one be separated from his regard to his own honour; nor the favourable inclination of others towards us, be disjoined from their care of their own happiness. Nay, we must needs acknowledge this to be stronger in them than their affection towards us. Wherefore it is impossible that he who duly considers the nature of rational beings should desire that they should assist us, except their own preservation were at the same time taken care of; and, therefore he cannot propose to himself his own happiness separately from that of others as his adequate end.

Chapter 7: Of the Original of Dominion, and the Moral Virtues

§XII. . . . Moreover; these general laws of nature concerning the care of the publick good and the settling and preserving dominion require that both God and men take care, whenever they please to enact any positive law, to give sufficient evidence of their doing so; for such discovery is necessary to the promulgation thereof, without which no one can be obliged. Hence it is necessary that if God would command anything by a revelation, it must first appear plain that the command is perfectly consistent with his unchangeable laws known from nature. For it is certain, that the divine reason cannot contradict itself. And it is farther required that his will to enforce this new law be discovered to those for whom it is enacted by enabling his messengers to fortell future contingencies without mistake or deceit, or else to work true miracles. Hence also human legislators, when they enact laws, do in the first place declare that they tend to the publick good and therefore have the same view with the laws of nature; and then add some signs, or testimonies, to make it known that they have been actually promulged by their authority.

CHAPTER 8: OF THE MORAL VIRTUES IN PARTICULAR

§I. . . . First, then, we are to observe that as universal justice is a moral perfection to which we are therefore obliged because such a will, or inclination of mind, is commanded by the universal law of nature, enjoining the settling and preserving to every one his rights; so we ought to possess all particular virtues, or we are therefore obliged by them because they are commanded by some particular law of nature, which is contained in that universal one which I have mentioned. They are indeed, in their own nature good though there were no law, because they conduce to the good state of the universe. But moral obligation and the nature of a debt thence arising is unintelligible without a respect to a law, at least, of nature. Nay, farther: the very honour from which actions are distinguished by the title of (*honestas*) laudable practice, or are called honourable, seems wholly to come from this, that they are praised by the law of the supreme ruler, discovered by the light of nature, and honoured with the greatest rewards, among which is to be reckoned the concurring praise of good men. And justly they are called naturally lawful and honourable, because the law, which makes them such does not depend upon the pleasure of the civil power but arises necessarily, in the manner already explained, from the very nature of things, and is altogether unchangeable whilst nature remains unchanged.

§II. The special laws of the moral virtues may after this manner be deduced from the law of universal justice. There being a law given which fixes and preserves the rights of particular persons, for this end only, that the common good of all be promoted by every one, all will be laid under these two obligations, in order to that end: (1) To contribute to others such a share of those things which are committed to their trust as may not destroy that part which is necessary to themselves for the same end: (2) To reserve to themselves that use of what is their own as may be most advantageous to, or at least consistent with, the good of others.

§IV. Having explained the measure of that mediocrity[10] which is usually required in moral virtues, it is easy to describe them separately, because their essence consists in the inclination of the will to obey the laws deduced from the general law of justice.

Editor's Notes

1. Cumberland refers not to the followers of Plato in antiquity but to the group of his contemporaries at Cambridge, known as the Cambridge Platonists. This book includes selections from one of these Platonists, Ralph Cudworth. Cudworth's writings on moral philosophy, however, were not published until the eighteenth century. Cumberland would have known of the – rather vague and diffuse – Platonism of this group from the works of Benjamin Whichcote, Henry More, and

John Smith. There is a good selection from these writers in C. A. Patrides, ed., *The Cambridge Platonists* (Cambridge, England: Cambridge University Press, 1980).

2. Cumberland had in mind chiefly Hobbes.
3. Cumberland here is declaring his opposition to voluntarism.
4. Promulgated.
5. Cumberland is referring to the first and second tables or parts of the Decalogue, the first covering our duties to God and the second those to our neighbor. He followed Saint Thomas in treating these as parts of the law of nature.
6. To lack, to be without.
7. In *Leviathan,* I.6 Hobbes stated: "Whatsoever is the object of any man's appetite, that is it which he for his part calleth *good:* and the object of his hate and aversion, *evil.* . . . For these words of good, evil, . . . are ever used with relation to the person that useth them; there being nothing simply and absolutely so; nor any common rule of good and evil to be taken from the nature of the objects themselves. . . ."
8. Hobbes's *De cive* – from which excerpts were presented earlier – was published in Latin in 1642 and in English translation in 1651. His *De homine* appeared in 1658; the sections most pertinent to ethics are available in English in Bernard Gert, ed., *Man and Citizen* (New York: Peter Smith, 1972).
9. In V.xix Cumberland observed that the will of God can be known a priori by arguing from his known attributes or the causes of his willing as he does, or it can be known from the effects of his willing as he does. Cumberland preferred the latter kind of argument, which he is discussing here. The argument from God's attributes is, he believed, less effective against his opponents.
10. The reference is to the Aristotelian mean, the middle amount between too little and too much, which is the measure of virtue.

Further Reading

There is no modern edition of Cumberland, and little has been written about his philosophy. Ernest Albee, *A History of English Utilitarianism* (London: Allen & Unwin, 1901) devotes two chapters to him. Linda Kirk, *Richard Cumberland and Natural Law* (Cambridge, England: James Clark, 1987), sketches Cumberland's life and his involvement in the politics of his time and analyzes his particular theory of natural law. Murray Forsyth, "The Place of Richard Cumberland in the History of Natural Law Doctrine," *Journal of the History of Philosophy* 20 (1982), also is helpful.

Samuel Pufendorf

Introduction

Samuel Pufendorf, son of a Lutheran pastor, was born in 1632 in Saxony. After receiving a conventional education at Leipzig, he went to Jena for further work. There he studied mathematics and first read Grotius and Hobbes. In 1658, while serving as a tutor for a Swedish family during a war between Sweden and Denmark, he was arrested and imprisoned. In prison he wrote his first work, *Elementorum jurisprudentiae universalis* (*Elements of Universal Jurisprudence*), published in 1660. He returned to Germany to accept the first professorship in natural and international law at Heidelberg. Pufendorf's interest in contemporary affairs led him to publish in 1667 an analysis of the constitution of the Holy Roman Empire, which, he argued, was not helpfully explained by any known model. He then moved to a professorship in Sweden, where he wrote his great *De jure naturae et gentium* (*On the Law of Nature and of Nations*), which was published in 1672. In the next year he published a compact summary of this work, *De officio hominis et civis* (*On the Duty of Man and Citizen*).

These two works had an amazing reception. Despite its enormous length, the *Law of Nature* went through many Latin editions and was translated into every major European language, and the *Duty of Man*, in Latin or in modern languages, became the textbook with which students in much of Europe and in many of the American colonies studied natural law until well into the eighteenth century. No other modern natural law theorist had so wide and enduring a readership as did Pufendorf. In addition, several commentaries on his works were written to help students. And although orthodox Lutherans as well as lawyers and philosophers wrote frequent, sometimes vicious attacks on Pufendorf (to which he often replied), his portrayal of himself as the successor to the founder of modern natural law – the great and admittedly devout Grotius – was generally accepted.

Pufendorf spent much of his later life as court historian for the king of Sweden. He then accepted a similar post with the ruler of Prussia and died in 1688 as a result of a winter trip to Sweden to try to retrieve his manuscripts from his disgruntled former employer.

More systematic than Grotius and more inclined to spell out every detail of his view, Pufendorf produced as complete a "system" of natural law as Europe has ever seen. It has its philosophical underpinnings and a host of definitions of key terms; it relates these key terms to one another, and it then applies all this apparatus first to the construction of a fundamental law of nature, then to proximate implications of the fundamental law, and finally, in more detail, to every area of human activity but especially commercial relations, politics, and international affairs. Indeed, a contemporary reviewer said that *The Law of Nature* would be valuable to everyone: the merchant, the lawyer, and the businessman as well as the teacher.

Although Pufendorf quoted far less often than Grotius did from the authors of antiquity, he frequently discussed those of his contemporaries whom he thought important, signaling his agreement or disagreement with them and sometimes engaging in meticulous arguments over fine points. Hobbes, in particular, was vital to Pufendorf's thinking. He agreed with many of Hobbes's assumptions but tried to avoid being associated with not only Hobbes's atheism but also many of his moral and political conclusions. Cumberland's treatise on the law of nature was published in the same year as was Pufendorf's own large work, and Cumberland, a severe critic of Hobbes, is frequently cited favorably in Pufendorf's second edition. Pufendorf also discussed many other writers, most of them wholly ignored at present. He plainly relished such encounters, enjoying showing his readers that he was right on these important matters and rooting out the errors spread by wrongheaded thinkers.

I have begun the following selections with excerpts from Pufendorf's own summary of his doctrine, *The Duty of Man and Citizen*, to enable the reader to see the main outlines of Pufendorf's understanding of natural law. After stressing the independence of the study of natural law from the study of theology, Pufendorf showed how the laws of nature are tailored to the facts about the human constitution. Our self-interested nature combines with our weakness to make sociability – a disposition toward life in common – a primary need for all of us, and from the basic law of sociability all other laws are derived. Some of our duties arise from laws to which we are obligated by virtue of being human. Pufendorf began with negative duties, such as not harming others, but considered certain positive duties no less important. Thus we are to treat others as equals, and we are to be helpful, even generous, to one another. These basic duties do not, however, encompass as wide and detailed a field as do the derivative duties and rights arising from the various agreements we make with one another. Property rights belong here, as do contractual rights, including those of marriage, and political rights. Much of Pufendorf's work is concerned with derivative duties, but I have had to omit his treatment of them here.

The next selections come from *The Law of Nature and of Nations*, in which Pufendorf presented philosophical matters in more detail than he did in the student compendium. Particularly important instances can be found in the opening chapters of *The Law of Nature*, which develop a voluntaristic position, criticize Grotius for not holding such a view, and discuss the possibility of attaining certainty in moral matters. Pufendorf's account of free will and his elaborations on the difference between perfect and imperfect duties, as well as on the relation between duties and rights, should help the reader get a better grasp of his account of obligation and of the general structure of morality.

Natural law, Pufendorf believed, can be studied without appeal to revealed religion or theology, but he did not think religious truth irrelevant to the subject. Reasoning from our experience of the world leads us to understand that there is an all-powerful and benevolent creator who has definite plans for the way in which his creation is to operate. The purely physical things God has created carry out his will automatically, but the human part is under a special kind of direction, which Pufendorf explained in his discussion of moral entities. God imposes certain directives on us so that human life may have an order and a decorum lacking among animals and not be taken up entirely with the pursuit of goods that animals also pursue. God imposes obligations by legislating for us, and from his laws arise natural duties and rights. We can legislate as well and, by enacting laws, can create positions and titles that everyone should respect. Our legislation should be directed to benefit everyone, and God's certainly is so directed. But moral attributes are not the same as natural attributes, nor can they be explained in terms of them.

The voluntarism that Pufendorf articulated in his doctrine of moral entities has been variously interpreted. Some commentators have seen it as an indication of Pufendorf's belief that human culture has a unique status in the universe and therefore must be studied in a special way. They claim him as a forerunner of those who declare the methodological independence of the social sciences from the natural sciences. Others see the voluntarism as making Pufendorf the first to assert that there is no way of deriving conclusions about how people ought to act from premises concerning how in fact they do act. But however we read him on these points, his voluntarism is certainly a way of making clear that without God's will there would be no such thing as morality. Pufendorf thus distanced himself from Grotius, Hobbes, and Cumberland, who all offered theories that in one way or another imply that morality is independent of divine volition. Pufendorf was in some matters extremely audacious. For instance, he rejected without argument the age-old equation of "good" with "being" and offered a new account of what goodness is. Yet in making God indispensable to morality he was holding on to one of the oldest strands of Christian thought.

The following excerpts are modern translations: *The Duty of Man and Citizen,* trans. Frank Gardner Moore (Oxford: Oxford University Press, 1927), and *The Law of Nature and of Nations,* trans. C. H. Oldfather and W. A. Oldfather (Oxford: Oxford University Press, 1934). The reader may also wish to consult the eighteenth-century English translation of the latter work by Basil Kennet, which includes useful annotations by Jean Barbeyrac, who added them to his own French translation.

On the Duty of Man and Citizen

To the benevolent reader, greeting!

. . . it is manifest that from three founts, so to speak, men derive the knowledge of their duty and what in this life they must do, as being morally good, and what not to do, as being morally bad: namely the light of reason, the civil laws and the particular revelation of the divine authority. From the first flow the commonest duties of man, especially those which make him sociable with other men; from the second, the duties of man in so far as he lives subject to a particular and definite State; from the third, the duties of a man who is a Christian. From this three separate studies arise, the first of which is the natural law, common to all nations; the second, the civil law of the single individual States, into which the human race departed. The third is called moral theology in contradistinction to that part of theology which explains what is to be believed [that is, dogmatic theology].

Each of these studies uses a method of proving its dogmas corresponding to its principle. In the natural law it is asserted that something must be done because the same is gathered by right reason as necessary for sociability between men. The last analysis of the precepts of the civil law is that the lawgiver so established. The moral theologian acquiesces in that ultimate proposition, because God has so ordered in the Holy Scriptures. . . .

The first distinction therefore, whereby those studies are mutually separated, results from the different source from which each derives its dogmas, and upon this point we have just touched. Consequently, if there be some actions which we are bid by divine literature to perform or not to perform, yet whose necessity can not be grasped by reason left to itself, those actions fall outside the natural law and properly look toward moral theology. Moreover in theology law is considered proportionately as it has annexed a divine promise and a certain sort of pact between God and man. From this consideration the natural law abstracts, obviously since that which reason alone can not discover proceeds from the particular revelation of God.

Furthermore, that is by far the most important distinction whereby the end and aim of the natural law is included only in the circuit of this life, and therefore it moulds man accordingly as he ought to lead this life in society with others. But moral theology moulds a man into a Christian, who should not only have the purpose of passing honorably through this life, but who especially hopes for the fruit of piety after this life and who on this account has his πολίτευμα[1] in heaven, while here he lives merely as a wayfarer or sojourner. For although the mind of man not only with a glowing desire leans, as it were, towards immortality and vigorously shrinks from self-destruction, and hence among many of the Gentiles the persuasion has become inveterate that the soul remains after its separation from the body and that then it will go well with the good and ill with the bad; nevertheless a persuasion of this sort on such matters, in which the mind of man might plainly and firmly acquiesce, is drawn only from the word of God. Hence the decrees of the natural law are adapted only to the human forum,[2] which does not extend beyond this life, and they are wrongly applied in many places to the divine forum, which is the especial care of theology.

From this also it follows that, because the human forum is busied with only the external actions of man, while to those which lie concealed within the breast and produce no effect or sign outside it does not penetrate and consequently is not disturbed about them, the natural law likewise is concerned to a great extent with the directing of the external actions of man. But for moral theology it is not sufficient that the external customs of men have been made in some way or another in keeping with decorum; but it is concerned chiefly with this, that the mind and its internal movements be fashioned after the will of the deity; and it reprobates those very actions which extrinsically indeed appear to be proper, but nevertheless emanate from an impure mind. . . .

Book I

Chapter II: On the Norm of Human Action, or Law in General

1. Because human actions depend upon the will, but the wills of individuals are not always consistent, and those of different men generally tend toward different things, therefore, in order to establish order and seemliness among

the human race, it was necessary that some norm should come into being, to which actions might be conformed. For otherwise, if with such freedom of the will, and such diversity of inclinations and tastes, each should do whatever came into his head, without reference to a fixed norm, nothing but the greatest confusion could arise among men.

2. That norm is called law, that is, a decree by which a superior obliges a subject to conform his acts to his own prescription.

3. That this definition may be better understood, we must develop the meaning of obligation, whence it arises, who can undertake an obligation, and who impose it upon another. Obligation, then, is commonly defined as a legal bond, by which we are of necessity bound to perform something. That is, a kind of bridle is thereby put upon our freedom, so that, though in actual fact the will can have a different aim, still it finds itself imbued with an inward sentiment due to the obligation, with the result that, if the action performed is not in conformity with the prescribed norm, the will is forced to acknowledge that it has not done what is right. And so if any ill should befall a man on that account, he would judge that it befalls him not undeservedly; since by following the norm, as was proper, he might have avoided it.

4. For the fact that man is fitted to undertake an obligation there are two reasons: one, because he has a will which can turn in different directions, and so also conform to the rule: the other, since man is not free from the power of a superior. For where an agent's powers have been bound by nature to a uniform mode of action, there we look in vain for free action; and it is vain to prescribe a rule for a man who cannot understand it nor conform to the same. Again, assuming that a man does not recognize a superior, there is for that reason no one who can rightfully impose a necessity upon him. And if he be ever so strict in observing a certain method of action, and consistently abstain from certain acts, still he is understood to do this not from any obligation, but from his own good pleasure. It follows then that he is capable of an obligation who not only has a superior, but also can recognize a prescribed rule, and further has a will flexible in different directions, but conscious of the fact that, when the rule has been prescribed by a superior, it does wrong to depart from the same. Such is evidently the nature with which man is endowed.

5. Obligation is properly introduced into the mind of a man by a superior, that is, a person who has not only the power to bring some harm at once upon those who resist, but also just grounds for his claim that the freedom of our will should be limited at his discretion. For when these conditions are found in anyone, he has only to intimate his wish, and there must arise in men's minds a fear that is tempered with respect, the former in view of his power, the latter in consideration of the reasons, which, were there no fear, must still induce one to embrace his will. For whoever is unable to assign any other reason why he wishes to impose an obligation upon me against my will, except mere power, can indeed frighten me into thinking it better for a time to obey him, to avoid a greater evil; but, once that fear is removed, nothing further remains to prevent my acting according to my will rather than his. Conversely, if he has

indeed the reasons which make it my duty to obey him, but lacks the power of inflicting any harm upon me, I may with impunity neglect his commands, unless a more powerful person comes to assert the authority upon which I have trampled. Now the reasons why one may rightly demand that another obey him are: in case some conspicuous benefits have come to the latter from the former; or if it be proved that he wishes the other well, and is also better able than the man himself to provide for him, and at the same time actually claims control over the other; and finally if a man has willingly subjected himself to another and agreed to his control. . . .

16. With respect to its author, the law is divided into divine and human, the one enacted by God, the other by men. But if law be considered according as it has a necessary and universal adaptation to men or not, it is divided into the natural and the positive. The former is so adapted to the rational and social nature of man, that an honorable and peaceful society cannot exist for mankind without it. Consequently it can be investigated and learned as a whole, by the light of man's inborn reason and a consideration of human nature. The latter kind of justice by no means flows from the common condition of human nature, but proceeds from the decision of the lawgiver alone. And yet it ought not to lack its own reason, and the utility which it effects for certain men or a particular society. But while the divine law is now natural and now positive, human law is, in the strict sense, altogether positive.

Chapter III: On Natural Law

1. What is the character of the natural law, what its necessity, and of what precepts it consists in the present state of mankind, are most clearly seen, after one has thoroughly examined the nature and disposition of man. For, just as for an accurate knowledge of civil laws, it is very important to have a clear understanding of the condition of the state, and of the habits and interests of its citizens, so if we have examined the common disposition of men and their condition, it will be readily apparent upon what laws their welfare depends.

2. Now man shares with all the animals that have consciousness the fact that he holds nothing dearer than himself, and is eager in every way to preserve himself; that he strives to gain what seem to him good things, and to reject the evil. This feeling is regularly so strong that all the others give way to it. And one cannot but resent it, if any man make an attack upon one's life, so much so that, even after the threatened danger had been averted, hatred usually still remains, and a desire for vengeance.

3. But in one respect man seems to be in a worse state even than the brutes – that scarcely any other animal is attended from birth by such weakness. Hence it would be a miracle, if anyone reached mature years, if he have not the aid of other men, since, as it is, among all the helps which have been invented for human needs, careful training for a number of years is required, to enable a man to gain his food and clothing by his own efforts. Let us imagine a man brought to maturity without any care and training bestowed

upon him by others, having no knowledge except what sprang up of itself in his own mind, and in a desert, deprived of all help and society of other men. Certainly a more miserable animal it will be hard to find. Speechless and naked, he has nothing left him but to pluck herbs and roots, or gather wild fruits, to slake his thirst from spring or river, or the first marsh he encountered, to seek shelter in a cave from the violence of the weather, or to cover his body somehow with moss or grass, to pass his time most tediously in idleness, to shudder at any noise or the encounter with another creature, finally to perish by hunger or cold or some wild beast. On the other hand, whatever advantages now attend human life have flowed entirely from the mutual help of men. It follows that, after God, there is nothing in this world from which greater advantage can come to man than from man himself.

4. Yet this animal, though so useful to his kind, suffers from not a few faults, and is endowed with no less power to injure; which facts make contact with him rather uncertain, and call for great caution, that one may not receive evil from him instead of good. First of all, there is generally a greater tendency to injure found in man than in any of the brutes. For the brutes are usually excited by the desire for food and for love, both of which, however, they can themselves easily satisfy. But having stilled that craving, they are not readily roused to anger or to injure people, unless someone provokes them. But man is an animal at no time disinclined to lust, and by its goad he is excited much more frequently than would seem necessary for the conservation of the race. And his belly desires not merely to be satisfied, but also to be tickled, and often craves more than nature is able to digest. That the brutes should not need clothing nature has provided. But man delights to clothe himself, not for necessity only, but also for display. Many more passions and desires unknown to the brutes are found in man, as the desire to have superfluities, avarice, the love of glory and eminence, envy, emulation, and rivalry of wits. Witness the fact that most wars, in which men clash with men, are waged for reasons unknown to the brutes. And all these things can, and usually do, incite men to desire to injure one another. Then too there is in many a notable insolence and passion for insulting their fellows, at which the rest, modest though they be by nature, cannot fail to take offense, and gird themselves to resist, from the desire to maintain and defend themselves and their freedom. At times also men are driven to mutual injury by want, and the fact that their present resources are insufficient for their desires or their need.

5. Moreover men have in them great power for the infliction of mutual injuries. For though not formidable because of teeth or claws or horns, as are many of the brutes, still manual dexterity can prove a most effective means of injury; and shrewdness gives a man the opportunity to attack by cunning and in ambush, where the enemy cannot be reached by open force. Hence it is very easy for man to inflict upon man the worst of natural evils, namely death.

6. Finally, we must also consider in mankind such a remarkable variety of gifts as is not observed in single species of animals, which, in fact, generally have like inclinations, and are led by the same passion and desire. But among

men there are as many emotions as there are heads, and each has his own idea of the attractive. Nor are all stirred by a single and uniform desire, but by one that is manifold and variously intermixed. Even one and the same man often appears unlike himself, and if he has eagerly sought a thing at one time, at another he is very averse to it. And there is no less variety in the tastes and habits, the inclinations to exert mental powers – a variety which we see now in the almost countless modes of life. That men may not thus be brought into collision, there is need of careful regulation and control.

7. Thus then man is indeed an animal most bent upon self-preservation, helpless in himself, unable to save himself without the aid of his fellows, highly adapted to promote mutual interests; but on the other hand no less malicious, insolent, and easily provoked, also as able as he is prone to inflict injury upon another. Whence it follows that, in order to be safe, he must be sociable, that is, must be united with men like himself, and so conduct himself toward them that they may have no good cause to injure him, but rather may be ready to maintain and promote his interests.

8. The laws then of this sociability, or those which teach how a man should conduct himself, to become a good member of human society, are called natural laws.

9. So much settled, it is clear that the fundamental natural law is this: that every man must cherish and maintain sociability, so far as in him lies. From this it follows that, as he who wishes an end, wishes also the means, without which the end cannot be obtained, all things which necessarily and universally make for that sociability are understood to be ordained by natural law, and all that confuse or destroy it forbidden. The remaining precepts are mere corollaries, so to speak, under this general law, and the natural light given to mankind declares that they are evident.

10. Again, although those precepts have manifest utility, still, if they are to have the force of law, it is necessary to presuppose that God exists, and by His providence rules all things; also that He has enjoined upon the human race that they observe those dictates of the reason, as laws promulgated by Himself by means of our natural light. For otherwise they might, to be sure, be observed perhaps, in view of their utility, like the prescriptions of physicians for the regimen of health, but not as laws; since these of necessity presuppose a superior, and in fact one who has actually undertaken the direction of another.

11. But that God is the author of the natural law, is proved by the natural reason, if only we limit ourselves strictly to the present condition of humanity, disregarding the question whether his primitive condition was different from the present, or whence that change has come about.[3] The nature of man is so constituted that the race cannot be preserved without the social life, and man's mind is found to be capable of all the notions which serve that end. And it is in fact clear, not only that the human race owes its origin, as do the other creatures, to God, but also that, whatever be its present state, God includes the race in the government of His providence. It follows from these arguments

that God wills that man use for the conservation of his own nature those special powers which he knows are peculiarly his own, as compared with the brutes, and thus that man's life be distinguished from the lawless life of the brutes. And as this cannot be secured except by observing the natural law, we understand too that man has been obliged to God to keep the same, as a means not devised by will of man, and changeable at their discretion, but expressly ordained by God Himself, in order to insure this end. For whoever binds a man to an end, is considered to have bound him also to employ the means necessary to that end. And besides, we have evidence that the social life has been enjoined upon men by God's authority, in the fact that in no other creature do we find the religious sentiment or fear of the Deity – a feeling which seems inconceivable in a lawless animal. Hence in the minds of men not entirely corrupt a very delicate sense is born, which convinces them that by sin against the natural law they offend Him who holds sway over the minds of men, and is to be feared even when the fear of men does not impend.

12. The common saying that the law is known by nature, should not be understood, it seems, as though actual and distinct propositions concerning things to be done or to be avoided were inherent in men's minds at the hour of their birth. But it means in part that the law can be investigated by the light of reason, in part that at least the common and important provisions of the natural law are so plain and clear that they at once find assent, and grow up in our minds, so that they can never again be destroyed, no matter how the impious man, in order to still the twinges of conscience, may endeavor to blot out the consciousness of those precepts. For this reason in Scripture too the law is said to be "written in the hearts" of men.[4] Hence, since we are imbued from childhood with a consciousness of those maxims, in accordance with our social training, and cannot remember the time when we first imbibed them, we think of this knowledge exactly as if we had had it already at birth. Everyone has the same experience with his mother tongue.

13. Of the duties incumbent upon man in accordance with natural law the most convenient division seems to be according to the objects in regard to which they are to be practiced. From this standpoint they are classified under three main heads: the first of which instructs us how, according to the dictate of sound reason alone, a man should conduct himself toward God, the second, how toward himself, the third, how toward other men. Although those precepts of natural law which concern other men may be derived primarily and directly from sociability, which we have laid down as a foundation, indirectly also the duties of man to God as creator can be derived from the same, since the ultimate confirmation of duties toward other men comes from religion and fear of the Deity, so that man would not be sociable either, if not imbued with religion; and since reason alone cannot go further in religion than in so far as the latter subserves the promotion of peace and sociability in this life. For, in so far as religion promotes the salvation of souls, it proceeds from a special divine revelation. But duties of man to himself spring from religion and sociability conjointly. For the reason why he cannot determine

certain acts concerning himself in accordance with his own free will, is partly that he may be a fit worshiper of the Deity, and partly that he may be a good and useful member of human society.

Chapter VI: On Mutual Duties, and First, That of Not Injuring Others

1. Next come the duties which a man must practice toward other men. Some of them spring from the common obligation, by which the Creator willed that all men as such should be bound together. But some flow from a definite institution, introduced or received by men, or from a certain adventitious status of men. The first are to be practiced by every man toward every other; the second only toward certain persons, a certain condition or status being assumed. Hence one may call the former absolute duties, the latter conditional.

2. Among the absolute duties, i.e., of anybody to anybody, the first place belongs to this one: let no one injure another. For this is the broadest of all duties, embracing all men as such. It is also the easiest, as consisting in mere refraining from action, unless the passions that resist reason have somehow to be checked at times. Again, it is likewise the most necessary duty, because without it the social life could in no way exist. For with the man who confers no benefit upon me, who makes no interchange even of the common duties with me, I can still live at peace, provided he injure me in no way. In fact, from the vast majority of men we desire nothing more than that. Benefits are generally exchanged by the few. But with the man who injures me, I cannot by any means live peaceably. For nature has implanted in each man so sensitive a love of self and one's own possessions, that one cannot help repelling by every means the man who essays to injure them.

3. Moreover, this same duty is a bulwark not only to what a man has by nature itself, for instance, life, body, members, chastity, freedom, but also to all that has been acquired through some institution and convention of men. Hence by this precept it is forbidden to carry off, spoil, injure, or withdraw from our use, in whole or in part, anything that by any legitimate title is ours. Consequently the same duty is understood to interdict any crimes by which injury is inflicted upon others, as bloodshed, wounding, beating, robbery, theft, fraud, violence, directly or indirectly, mediately or immediately, and the like. . . .

Chapter VII: On Recognition of the Natural Equality of Men

1. Man is an animal not only most devoted to self-preservation, but one in which has been implanted a sensitive self-esteem. And if this be in any way slighted, he is in general no less perturbed, than if an injury has been inflicted upon his person or property. Even the word *man* is thought to contain a certain dignity, so that the last and most effective argument in repelling the insolent contempt of others is this: "I am certainly not a dog, but a man as well as you." Inasmuch then as human nature is the same for all alike, and no one

is perfectly willing or able to be associated with another, who does not esteem him as at least equally a man and a sharer in the common nature; therefore, among the mutual duties the second place is given to this: that each esteem and treat the other as naturally his equal, that is, as a man just as much as himself.

2. But this equality of men consists not only in the fact that adult men are about equal in strength, in so far as the weaker can inflict death upon the stronger by ambush, or with the help of dexterity, or an effective weapon; but also in this, that, although one has been fitted out by nature with various gifts of mind and body beyond the other, he must none the less practice the precepts of natural law toward other men, and himself expects the same treatment from others; and in the fact that no more freedom is given the man to injure others on that account. So, conversely too, niggardliness of nature or straitened circumstances do not of themselves condemn a man to a lot inferior to that of others as regards the enjoyment of the common right. But what one can demand or expect from another, that others too must demand of him, other things being equal. And it is eminently proper that one should himself practice the law which he has set up for others. For the obligation to cultivate the social life with others binds all men equally, and one is no more permitted than another to violate the natural laws in their dealings with each other. And yet popular arguments are not lacking to illustrate that equality; for example, that we all descend from the same stock, and are born, fed, and die in the same manner; and that God has given no man assurance of a stable and unshaken fortune. So also the injunctions of the Christian religion do not commend nobility, power, or wealth, as a means of gaining the favor of God, but sincere piety, which can be found in the humble, just as well as in the great.

3. Moreover, it follows from this equality that he who wishes to use the services of others for his own advantage, is bound in turn to spend himself, that their wants may be satisfied. For the man who demands that others serve him, but on the other hand desires to be always immune himself, is certainly considering others not equal to himself. Hence, as those who readily allow the same permission to all as to themselves, are the best adapted to society, so those are plainly unsociable who, thinking themselves superior to others, wish to have all things permitted to themselves alone, and arrogate honor to themselves above the rest, and the lion's share of the things common to all, to which they have no better right than the others. Accordingly this too is one of the common duties of the natural law: that no one, who has not acquired a peculiar right, arrogate more to himself than the rest have, but permit others to enjoy the same right as himself.

4. The same equality shows how a man should conduct himself, when he must assign their various rights to others, viz., that he must treat them as equals, and not indulge the one as against the other, except on the merits of the case. For if this is not done, the man not favored is affronted as well as injured, and the esteem Nature gave him is taken away. It follows then that a

common thing must be duly divided in equal portions among equals. When it does not admit of division, those who have an equal right ought to use it in common, and this as much as each shall please, if the amount permits. But if this is impracticable, they should then use the thing after a manner prescribed, and in proportion to the number of the users. For no other method of respecting equality can be devised. But if the thing can neither be divided nor held in common, let the enjoyment of it be alternate; or if this also fails, or no equivalent can be furnished the rest, the thing must be awarded to one by lot. For in cases of this kind no better remedy than the lot can be found, since this takes away the sense of a slight, and if it fails to favor a man, it does not detract from his esteem. . . .

Chapter VIII: On the Common Duties of Humanity

1. Among the duties of men in general to others in general, and those which are to be practiced for the sake of the common sociability, the third place is taken by this: that every man promote the advantage of another, so far as he conveniently can. For since Nature has established a kind of kinship among men, it would not be enough to have refrained from injuring or despising others; but we must also bestow such attentions upon others – or mutually exchange them – that thus mutual benevolence may be fostered among men. Now we benefit others either definitely or indefinitely, and that with a loss, or else without loss, to ourselves.

2. A man tends to promote the advantage of others indefinitely, if he thoroughly cultivates his own soul and body, so that useful actions may emanate from him to others; or if by ingenuity he finds the means of making human life better equipped. Hence it is against this duty that they are to be thought sinners, who learn no honorable art, pass their life in silence, and have a soul "only as so much salt, to keep the body from decay"[5] – "mere numbers," and "born to consume the fruits of earth."[6] Also those who, content with the riches left by their ancestors, think they may with impunity offer sacrifice to indolence, since the industry of others has already gained for them means to live upon. . . .

3. But to those who endeavor to be benefactors of the human race, the rest owe this in return, that they be not envious, throw no obstacle in the way of their noble efforts. Also that, if there be no other way of compensating them, they at least promote their fame and memory, this being the chief reward of labors.

4. But especially is it regarded as contemptible malignity and inhumanity, not to bestow willingly upon others those blessings which can be accorded without loss, trouble, or labor to ourselves. These are usually called mere favors, that is, benefiting the recipient, and not burdening the giver. Examples are: not to exclude from running water, to allow taking fire from our fire, to give honest advice to one in doubt, to point out the way kindly to him who has lost it. . . .

5. A higher form of humanity is bestowing freely upon another, and out of rare benevolence, something costing money or painful effort, designed to meet his needs, or win for him some signal advantage. These are called benefits *par excellence,* and they offer the best opportunity to gain praise, if only nobility of spirit and prudence duly control them. The dispensing of these and their proper limits are governed generally by the situation of the giver and that of the recipient. And here we must take special care that our generosity do not injure both those to whom we think we are doing a kind turn, and the others too; also that the generosity be not greater than our means; and again that we give to each in proportion to his worth, and above all to those who have deserved well; also in proportion to their need of our help, and with regard also to the different degrees of closeness in the relations of men. We must also consider what each needs most, and what he can accomplish or not, with or without us. The manner of giving too adds much to the acceptability of favors, if we give with cheerful face, readily, and with assurance of our good-will.

6. In return there must be gratitude in the mind of the recipient. Thus he shows that the gift was acceptable to him, and for that reason he favors the giver, and seeks an occasion to make an equal or larger return, in so far as he can. For it is not necessary to return precisely the amount of the gift; but often zeal and endeavor satisfy the obligation. However there must be no reasonable exception which we can take, as against the man who claims to have done us a favor. For example, I owe nothing to the man who has pulled me out of the water, if he first threw me in.

Chapter IX: On the Duties of Contracting Parties in General

1. From the absolute duties we pass to the conditional, by way of agreements as a transition; since all the duties not already enumerated seem to presuppose an express or tacit agreement. We have then to treat here of the nature of agreements, and what is to be observed by those who enter into them.

2. Now it is sufficiently clear that it was necessary for men to enter into agreements. For, although the duties of humanity are widely diffused throughout human life, it is still impossible to deduce from that one source all that men were entitled to receive to advantage from one another. For not all have such natural goodness, that they are willing, out of mere humanity, to do all the things by means of which they may benefit others, without an assured hope of receiving the like in return. Often, too, favors which can come to us from others, are of a sort to make us unable to demand without a blush that they be done for us for nothing. And frequently it is unbecoming to our station or person to owe such a favor to another. And in fact, as the other is unable to give much, so we are often unwilling to accept, unless he receives an equivalent from us. Finally, not uncommonly others are in the dark as to how

they may serve our interests. Therefore, in order that the mutual duties of men (the fruit, that is of sociability) may be discharged more frequently and according to certain rules, it was necessary for men to agree among themselves, as to the mutual performance of all that they could not certainly promise themselves from others, on the basis of the law of humanity alone. And indeed it was necessary to determine in advance, what one was bound to perform for another, and what the latter should in turn expect and exact as his right from the former. And this is done by promises and agreements.

3. In regard to these, the general duty which we owe under natural law is, that a man keep his plighted word, that is, fulfill his promises and agreements. For, but for this, we should lose the greatest part of the advantage which is apt to arise for the race from the interchange of services and property. And were there not the necessity of keeping promises, one could not build one's calculations firmly upon the support of others. And also from a breach of faith there are apt to arise entirely just causes for quarrels and war. For when I have performed something in accordance with an agreement, if the other defaults his promise, I have lost my property, or my services, for nothing. But if, on the other hand, I have not yet performed anything, it is still an annoyance to have my calculations and plans disturbed, since I could have made other provision for my affairs, if he had not presented himself. And it is a shame to be mocked because I believed the other a prudent and honest man.

4. We must observe also, that what we owe under the mere duty of humanity differs from what is owed by virtue of a compact or perfect promise especially in this respect, viz., the things of the former class are properly asked, and honorably performed; but when the other has failed of his own motion to perform, I can complain merely of his inhumanity, barbarity, or harshness; but I cannot compel him to perform, by my own force or that of my superior. This is my privilege, however, when he does not of himself perform what is due in acordance with a perfect promise or a compact. Hence we are said in the former case to have an imperfect right, in the latter, a perfect right, as also to be obligated imperfectly in the one case, and perfectly in the other.

8. Moreover, that promises and compacts may bind us to give or do something not formerly required of us, or to omit what we previously had a right to do, our voluntary consent is most essential. For, since the fulfillment of any promise and agreement is associated with some burden, there is no better reason to prevent our justly complaining about it, than the fact that we voluntarily consented to what it was evidently in our own power to avoid.

22. Such are the absolute duties of man, as also those which serve as a transition to the other kind. The rest presuppose either some human institution, based upon a universal convention, and introduced among men, or else some particular form of government. Of such institutions we observe in particular three: language, ownership and value, and human government. We must next explain each of these, together with the resulting duties.

The Law of Nature and of Nations

BOOK I

Chapter I: On the Origin and Variety of Moral Entities

1. The task of prime philosophy [metaphysics], if it was to fulfil the calling of its own very nature, was to give the most comprehensive definitions of things and to divide them appropriately into distinct classes, giving in addition the general nature and condition of every kind of thing. Now the classification of natural things seems to have been sufficiently treated by those who have so far undertaken the consideration of that science, but it is perfectly clear that they have not been as much concerned with moral entities as the dignity of these requires. Many, indeed, have not considered them at all; others have but lightly touched upon them, as if they were unimportant or figments of no moment. And yet their nature should by all means be known by man, to whom has been given the power to produce them, and whose life is deeply penetrated by their influence. This consideration impels us to give by way of preface, in so far as shall seem necessary for our undertaking, a discussion of this field of knowledge which has been neglected so far by most writers. . . .

2. According as all things which this universe embraces consist of their own principles, which the Great and Good Creator has apportioned and assigned to the constitution of their essence, so each several thing is observed to have its own properties, which arise from the disposition and aptitude of its substance, and to exert itself in distinct actions according to the measure of strength imparted it by the Creator. These properties we usually call natural, since by the term "nature" has generally been designated not merely the entire sum of created things, but also their modes and acts which follow from that innate strength which produces those infinite varieties of motion, whereby, as we observe, all things in this universe are stirred. Now those things which act with no perception at all, or with mere downright perception, or with perception but slightly aided by reflection, are led solely by the instinct of nature, and can in no way temper their actions by any measures that are taken of themselves. But to man there has been given, not merely beauty and adaptability of body, but also the distinctive light of intelligence, by the aid of which he can understand things more accurately, compare them with one another, judge the unknown by the known, and decide how things agree among themselves; so that, as it would seem, not only is he freed from the necessity of confining his actions to any one mode, but he can even exert, suspend, or moderate them. Furthermore, to the same being, man, there has been granted the power to invent or apply certain aids to each faculty, whereby it is signally assisted and directed in its functioning. It is the task of others to set forth all that in the way of concepts has been discovered to help save the intellect from being confused by the infinite variety of things. It is for us to observe, how, chiefly for the direction of the acts of the will, a specific kind of attribute has been given to

things and their natural motions, from which there has arisen a certain propriety in the actions of man, and that outstanding seemliness and order which adorn the life of men. Now these attributes are called Moral Entities, because by them the morals and actions of men are judged and tempered, so that they may attain a character and appearance different from the rude simplicity of dumb animals.

3. We seem able, accordingly, to define moral ideas most conveniently as certain modes [qualities], added to physical things or motions, by intelligent beings, primarily to direct and temper the freedom of the voluntary acts of man, and thereby to secure a certain orderliness and decorum in civilized life. We use the term *modes,* for the term entity seems more fittingly to be divisible into the two great subdivisions of substance and mode, than into those of substance and accident. Furthermore, as mode is distinguished from substance, so moral ideas clearly do not exist of themselves, but have their basis only in substances and in their motions, which they can affect only to a limited extent. Now some modes flow, as it were, from the very nature of the thing itself, while others are superadded by intelligent agency to physical things and modes. For whatever has been endowed with intellect is able, by means of reflection and a comparison of one thing with another, to form concepts, which are suitable to be the guides of a consistent faculty. Moral entities also are of the same kind. You may justly call the Great and Good God their maker, who surely did not will that men should spend their lives like beasts without civilization and moral law, but that their life and actions should be tempered by a fixed mode of conduct, which was impossible without moral entities. Nevertheless, the majority of them have been superadded later at the pleasure of men themselves, according as they felt that the introduction of them would help to develop the life of man and to reduce it to order. And so of these latter the purpose is clear: It is not the perfection of this world of nature, as is the case with physical entities, but it is the perfection in a distinctive way of the life of man, in so far as it was capable of a certain beauty of order above that in the life of beasts, as also the production of a pleasing harmony in a thing so changeable as the human mind.

4. Now as the original way of producing physical entities is creation, so the way in which moral entities are produced can scarcely be better expressed than by the word *imposition.* For they do not arise out of the intrinsic nature of the physical properties of things, but they are superadded, at the will of intelligent entities, to things already existent and physically complete, and to their natural effects, and, indeed, come into existence only by the determination of their authors. And these authors give them also certain effects, which they can also remove at their own pleasure without any accompanying change in the object to which they had been added. Hence the active force which lies in them does not consist in their ability directly to produce any physical motion or change in any thing, but only in this, that it is made clear to men along what line they should govern their liberty of action, and that in a special way men are made capable of receiving some good or evil and of directing

certain actions towards other persons with a particular effect. Also the efficacy of moral entities instituted by God flows from the fact, that, as man's
creator, He has the right to set certain limits to the liberty of will which He has
designed to vouchsafe man, and to turn that will, when reluctant, by the
threat of some evil to whatever course He wishes. Nay, even men themselves
have been able to give a force to their own inventions, by threatening some
evil that lay within their power, on him who refused to conform to their
dictates. . . .

12. Moral entities, regarded on the analogy of substances, are termed moral
persons. These are either individual men, or men united by a moral bond into
one system, considered together with their status, or the function which they
perform in common life. Now moral persons are either *simple* or *composite*.
Simple persons, on the basis of a difference in their status or functions, are
either public or private, as their function is directly for the use of a civil group,
or for the advantage of individuals as such. In the usage of Christian peoples
public persons are divided into *civil* and *ecclesiastical*. The former are either
principal, or *inferior.* Some among them rule a commonwealth with supreme
authority; some, by virtue of the power given them from the supreme authority, have charge of a certain part of the administration and are properly called
magistrates, or aid in the proper administration of the state by their counsels.
Inferior persons render a less important service to the state and to the magistrates as such. In war the superior and inferior officers correspond to the
magistrates, and are in command of the common soldiers, who, in this respect, may be considered public persons, because they are authorized, directly or indirectly, by the highest civil power, to bear arms in behalf of the
state. . . .

15. . . . the imposition which produces real moral persons is not at all a free
thing, but it should presuppose such qualities as are appropriate, so that some
real benefit may thereby accrue to mankind; and he who has no respect for
this consideration in constituting persons, should be regarded as insulting
mankind with his recklessness and folly. . . .

18. A conspicuous place among moral attributes is occupied by titles, which
are designations for the distinctions, made in the civil life of persons, upon the
basis of their esteem and status. They are in the main of two kinds. Some,
indeed, denote the degree of the esteem of individuals in civil life, or the
qualities peculiar to them, but they only connote and hint more or less clearly
at the status, according as such and such a title is ordinarily applied to few or
many statuses. Such are those honorary titles which are commonly appended
to the names of persons of distinction, as "most serene," "most eminent,"
"most illustrious," &c., the implications of which is greater or less according
to the force of the substantives to which they are attached. Other titles directly signify some status or some seat or peculiar place in a status, while they
indirectly connote a degree of the esteem which commonly attaches to that
status or position. Such are the names of moral persons, at least of those who
occupy any post of honour. . . .

19. Moral operative qualities are either *active* or *passive*. Of the former the most noble species are *power, right,* and *obligation. Power* is that by which a man is able to do something legally and with a moral effect. This effect is that an obligation is laid upon another to perform some task, or to admit as valid some of his actions, or not to hinder them, or that he shall be able to confer upon another a power of action or possession, which the latter did not formerly possess. For this quality is, indeed, to a very high degree diffusive, as it were, of itself. On the side of its efficacy, power is divided into *perfect* and *imperfect.*[7] The former is that which can be exercised by force against those who unlawfully endeavour to oppose it (force being chiefly exercised inside the boundaries of a state by an action at law; outside the boundaries, by war). In the case of the latter, if any one be prohibited unlawfully from its exercise, he is being treated inhumanely, indeed, and yet he has no right to defend it either by a legal action or by war, unless it so happen that necessity has supplied what it lacks in efficacy.[8]

On the side of its subject, power is divided into *personal* and *communicable*. The former is that which one cannot lawfully transmit to another. But in this there are several differences, for some powers are so intimately connected with a person that the acts belonging to them cannot rightly be exercised at all through the instrumentality of another. Such is the power of a husband over the body of his wife, the exercise of which by another no laws would admit. Such are also the powers the possession of which cannot be transferred by us to another, although the commission of the acts proper to them can be delegated to others; provided, however, that the acts derive all their authority from him to whom those powers inherently belong. Of this nature is the power of kings who have been constituted as such by the will of the people. For they cannot transfer to any one else the right to rule, and yet they can employ the services of ministers for the exercise of the acts that belong to such a right. Communicable power is such as can properly be transferred from one person to another, whether that be at his own pleasure, or by the authority or consent of a superior.

Finally, with regard to objects, most kinds of power can be classified into four groups. For powers concern either *persons* or *things*, and both these according as they are *one's own* or *another's*. Power over one's own person and actions is called liberty (although the ambiguities under which this word labours will have to be set forth elsewhere). Liberty is not to be understood as a principle distinct from him who enjoys it, or as a right of forcing oneself to an abhorrent task . . . but rather as a man's faculty to dispose of himself and his actions in accordance with his own desires; which faculty of itself involves a negation of any hindrance arising from a superior power. Power over one's own possessions is called *ownership*. Power over the persons of other men is properly *command;* power over another's possessions is *easement.*[9]

20. The word "right" (*ius*) is highly ambiguous. For in addition to the meanings where it is used for law, and for a body or system of homogeneous

laws, as well as for the decision rendered by a judge, it very frequently happens that it is taken as the moral quality by which we legally either command persons, or possess things, or by virtue of which something is owed us. This difference, however, seems to exist between the words power and right, namely, that the former tends more to introduce into things or persons the actual presence of the quality mentioned, and less expressly connotes the mode by which one has secured it. Right, however, directly and clearly indicates that a thing has been lawfully acquired and is lawfully now retained. Because, however, most kinds of power have a distinguishing name, which that quality, whereby something is understood to be owed us, lacks, it is convenient to designate this quality in a special way by the word "right," although we have not seen fit to avoid the other meanings of this word, because of customary usage.

Now we class right among active qualities, since by virtue of it something can be demanded of another. But it is also placed among *passive moral qualities,* since it enables a man lawfully to receive something. For passive qualities are those by which one can lawfully have, suffer, admit, or receive something. Of these there are three kinds: The first is that whereby we properly receive something, in such a way, however, that we have no power to demand it, nor is there any obligation on another to render it. Such is the ability to receive a gift that is purely gratuitous. And that such a quality is not an absolute fiction, may be ascertained from the consideration, that, for example, a judge may be forbidden to receive under any consideration a gift from parties to a suit. The second is that whereby we are capacitated to receive something from another, not in such a way that it can be extorted from him against his will, unless a chance necessity requires it, but only in so far as he is obliged by some moral virtue to give it. This is called by Grotius an "aptitude."[10] The third is that whereby we are able to force a man, even against his will, to the performance of something, and he himself is fully obligated to such performance by a specific law that prescribes a definite penalty. . . .

21. An obligation is that whereby one is required under moral necessity to do, or admit, or suffer something; its divisions will be treated more in detail below. There are also moral "sensible" qualities which are understood to affect the judgement of men in a particular manner, just as among physical qualities this term is used for those which affect the faculty of sensation; such are honour, disgrace, authority, dignity, fame, obscurity, and the like.

23. In conclusion, as moral entities owe their origin to imposition, so from this they obtain their stability, as well as their variations, and when it has ceased to operate, as it were, they simultaneously disappear, just as a shadow disappears the instant a light is extinguished. Moreover, those which are of divine imposition are removed again only at the divine pleasure. Those which have been established by the will of men are abolished again by the same, even though the physical substance of the persons or things remain unchanged. . . .

Chapter II: On the Certainty of the Moral Sciences

1. The majority of scholars have for long firmly held, that moral science lacks that certitude, which is so characteristic of other knowledge, and especially of mathematics, because it has no place for demonstrations, from which alone is derived knowledge that is pure and free from fear of error; and because what is known of it rests on probability alone. This feeling has worked an immense injury to sciences most noble and most necessary to the life of man. . . .

4. . . . Now that knowledge, which considers what is upright and what base in human actions, the principal portion of which we have undertaken to present, rests entirely upon grounds so secure, that from it can be deduced genuine demonstrations which are capable of producing a solid science. So certainly can its conclusions be derived from distinct principles, that no further ground is left for doubt.

5. Some there are who maintain that things moral are always uncertain and changing, and that no greater certitude can attach to any science than to the objects with which it deals. The reply is, that, although moral entities owe their origin to imposition, and for that reason are not in an absolute sense necessary, yet they have not arisen in such a loose and general manner, that scientific knowledge about them is on that account utterly uncertain. For the very condition of man demanded the institution of most of them, a condition assigned him by the most Good and Great Creator out of His goodness and wisdom; hence such entities can by no means be uncertain and weak. . . .

6. Now in order that this knowledge of natural law with which we are now concerned, and which includes all moral and civil knowledge that is genuine and solid, may meet the full requirements of a science, we feel that we need not declare, with certain writers,[11] that some things are noble or base of themselves without any imposition, and that these form the object of natural and perpetual law, while those, the good repute or baseness of which depends upon the will of a legislator, fall under the head of positive laws. For since good repute, or moral necessity, and turpitude, are affections of human actions arising from their conformity or non-conformity to some norm or law, and law is the bidding of a superior, it does not appear that good repute or turpitude can be conceived to exist before law, and without the imposition of a superior. . . .

And, indeed, they who set up an eternal rule for the morality of human actions, beyond the imposition of God, seem to me to do nothing other than to join to God some co-eternal extrinsic principle which He Himself had to follow in the assignment of forms of things [at the moment of creation]. All, furthermore, admit that God created all things, man included, of His free will; it must follow, then, that it lay within His own pleasure to assign whatever nature He wished to this creature whom He was about to create. How, then, can an action of man be accorded any quality, if it takes its rise from an extrinsic and absolute necessity, without the imposition and pleasure of God?

On this argument, in very truth, all the movements and actions of man, if every law both divine and human be removed, are indifferent; while some of them are termed naturally reputable or base, because the condition of nature, which the Creator freely bestowed upon man, most rigorously requires either their execution or avoidance; it does not follow, however, that any morality can exist of itself, without any law, in its own motion and the application of physical power. . . .

Here it should be carefully noted that this indifference of physical motion in the actions of men is maintained by us only in respect to morality. For otherwise actions prescribed by the law of nature have, through the determination of the first cause, the native power to produce an effect good and useful to mankind, while actions similarly forbidden produce a contrary effect. But this natural goodness and evil does by no means constitute an action in the field of morals. For there are many things which contribute to the happiness and convenience of man and yet are not morally good, since they are not voluntary actions, nor are they enjoined by any law; while many acts which tend to the welfare of man have the same natural effect among beasts, although among the latter they possess no moral quality. . . .

The reason why many men cannot understand such an indifference in actions, is because from childhood on we have been imbued with a hatred of such vices; and this hatred, impressed on a mind still simple, appears to have grown to have the strength of a moral judgment, the result being that few have thought of distinguishing between the material and the formal in such actions. Hence it is patent that Grotius, *On the Law of War and Peace,* Bk. I, chap. i, § 10, had not considered this matter thoroughly, when he refers the wickedness of some human actions to the class of things to which the power of God Himself does not extend, because they involve a contradiction. Twice two, indeed, can only be four, because twice two and four are one and the same thing, differing only in name and in the point of view. It is, however, a contradiction for something simultaneously to be and not to be the same thing. But surely such a contradiction does not appear in the case of actions which are opposed to natural law. For the same reason Grotius shortly thereafter undertakes to derive this wickedness from a comparison with *nature when following sound reason.* And yet in the words *sound reason,* as attributed to man, there is involved a reference to the law of society as given to man by the Creator. Again in § 12, he says that the absolute existence of any natural law is tested by its necessary agreement or non-agreement *with rational and social nature.* And yet man received this social nature not from any immutable necessity, but from the pleasure of God. Therefore, the morality of actions as well, whether they do or do not suit him as a social being, must be derived from the same source. And so morality is fittingly attributed to these actions, not of an absolute necessity, but of a hypothetical necessity, since such a position is posited for man as God freely assigned him above all other creatures. . . .

10. But, as a matter of fact, a certain latitude *is* found in moral quantities, and principally for that reason mathematical knowledge is generally held to surpass

moral in the delicacy of its processes. That is due to the different nature of physical and moral quantity. For physical quantities can be exactly compared with one another, and measured and divided into distinct parts, because they are in a material way objects of our senses. Hence one can determine accurately what relation or proportion they have to one another, especially since with numbers, which we use, all such relations are most exactly set forth. And besides, those quantities are a product of nature, and hence unmoved and eternal. But moral quantities arise from imposition, and the judgement of intelligent and free agents, whose judgement and pleasure is in no way subject to physical measurement; and so the quantity which they conceive and determine by their imposition, cannot be referred to a like measure, but retains the liberty and laxness of its origin. Neither did the end, for which moral quantities were introduced, require such a measure of exactness, and such straining after details, but it was enough for the purpose of man's life that persons, things, and actions be roughly rated and compared. . . .

Chapter IV: On the Will of Man as It Concurs in Moral Actions

1. Since the most wise Creator wished to make man an animal to be governed by laws, He implanted in his soul a will, as an internal director of his actions, so that after objects were proposed and understood, he might be able to move himself to them by an intrinsic principle apart from any physical necessity, and be able to choose what seemed to him the most fitting; as well as turn from those which did not seem agreeable to him. . . .

2. Freedom, men call a faculty of the will, whereby, given all things requisite for acting, it is able, from among many objects before it, to choose one, or some, and to reject the rest; or, if but one object be presented, it may admit or not admit it, do or not do it. Requisites for acting are sometimes summed up under the single word "occasion," from which requisites the final determination of the agent is considered to be a separate thing; and when determination is added to the other requisites, action at once follows. Now the requisites connected with liberty are distinguished from that aid to actions which is furnished by the man himself. But more particularly the faculty of choosing, from among many objects, one or several, is called liberty of specification or contrariety; the faculty which is concerned with the choice or rejection of but one object, is called liberty of contradiction or of exercise.

Now liberty is supposed to add to spontaneity, firstly, an indifference as to the exercise of its acts, so that the will is under no necessity to exert one of its acts, that is, to will or to refuse, but, touching a particular object before it (for in general it cannot help but turn to that which is good as such, or renounce evil as such), it may choose whatever action it please, although chance may incline it more to one than to another. Liberty also adds a free determination, so that the will by an internal impulse may choose here and now either of its acts, that is, to will or to refuse.

It should, however, be added, that, even though it may seem to a man that something should be desired or avoided, this is not dependent on the will but on the state of the object, according as it presents an appearance of good or evil; although that desire or aversion, which thus follows the appearance of the object, is not so strong but that there still remains to the will the liberty to shape itself to some outward action upon the object; especially since the appearance of an evil thing can seem desirable only so long as another evil is at its side. . . .

3. But the chief affection of the will, which seems to rise immediately from its very nature, is that it is not restrained intrinsically to a definite, fixed, and invariable mode of acting, which affection we shall denominate indifference, and that this intrinsic indifference cannot be entirely destroyed by an extraneous means. And this must be maintained all the more firmly because upon its removal the morality of human actions is at once entirely destroyed.

4. But some preliminary remarks should be made concerning the nature of good, so that the indifference of the will may be correctly apprehended. Now good is considered in an absolute way by some philosophers, so that every entity, actually existing, may be considered good; but we pay no attention to such a meaning, and consider a thing as good only in so far as it has a respect to others, and it is understood to be good for some person, or on his behalf. Taken in this sense the nature of good seems to consist in an aptitude whereby one thing is fitted to help, preserve, or complete another. And since this aptitude depends on the very nature of things, whether this nature be native or adapted by some contrivance, that good which we can call natural, is firm and uniform, and in no way dependent on the erroneous or changeable opinions of men. . . .

From what has been said it is clear that it belongs to the nature of the will always to seek what is inherently good, and to avoid what is inherently evil. For it implies a clear contradiction that you should not incline to what you see is agreeable to you, and should incline to what you feel is not agreeable. And so this general inclination of the will can admit no indifference, as though the will might seek good and evil by an appetite of simple approbation. But the will of individuals exerts the force of its indifference on particular good and evils, as men incline to different things at particular times. And this is so because scarcely any things good or evil appear to a man uncontaminated and distinct, but intermixed, evil with good and good with evil. . . .

Chapter VII: On the Qualities of Moral Actions

7. . . . It should be observed, in conclusion, that some things are due us by a perfect, others by an imperfect right. When what is due us on the former score is not voluntarily given, it is the right of those in enjoyment of natural liberty to resort to violence and war in forcing another to furnish it, or, if we live within the same state, an action against him at law is allowed; but what is due on the latter score cannot be claimed by war or extorted by a threat of the

law. Writers frequently designate a perfect right by the additional words, "his own," as they say, for example, a man demands this by *his own* [*suo*] *right*. But the reason why some things are due us perfectly and others imperfectly, is because among those who live in a state of mutual natural law there is a diversity in the rules of this law, some of which conduce to the mere existence of society, others to an improved existence. And since it is less necessary that the latter be observed towards another than the former, it is, therefore, reasonable that the former can be exacted more rigorously than the latter, for it is foolish to prescribe a medicine far more troublesome and dangerous than the disease. There is, furthermore, in the case of the former usually an agreement, but not in the latter, and so, since the latter are left to a man's sense of decency and conscience, it would be inconsistent to extort them from another by force, unless a grave necessity happens to arise. In civil states this distinction arises from their civil laws, which either allow or deny an action, although in most instances states have followed in the footsteps of natural law, except where their own reasons persuaded them to take another course.

8. When, therefore, actions or things are extended to another, which are due him only by an imperfect right, or when actions are performed for another which have no relation to business, it is usually said that universal justice is observed; as when one comes to the aid of a man with counsel, goods, or personal assistance, and performs a service of piety, respect, gratitude, kindness, or generosity, for those to whom he was obligated to perform the same. The only concern of this kind of justice is that one should furnish what is due another, without observing whether the service furnished is equal to, or less than, that which was the reason for the obligation. Thus an office of gratitude is fulfilled if as much is shown as one's faculties permit, although the kindness done may have far surpassed that measure. But when acts which concern business relations are performed for another, or acts by which something is transferred to another to which he had a perfect right, that is called particular justice.

Book III

Chapter IV: On Keeping Faith and on the Divisions of Obligations

6. We may well discuss the division of obligations into natural and civil, not so much on the ground that such a division explains the origin of obligations, as that it suggests the basis of their force in common life. And so a natural obligation is that which binds only by the force of natural law; a civil obligation that which is reinforced by civil laws and authority. The efficacy of each is considered, either in him in whom it resides as the subject of the obligation, or in the other person, who is its object. From the point of view of the subject, the efficacy of a natural obligation consists principally in the fact that it binds the conscience of a man, or that a man realizes, when he has not fulfilled it,

that he is disobeying the will of God, whose law all men recognize that they should obey, just as they are indebted to Him for their very existence. And although penal sanctions are not to be found so expressly defined in natural law, there is no reason to feel that it lacks every kind of sanction, and that the man who breaks its obligation should expect no greater punishment from the hands of its author than he who fulfils the same. Among other arguments for this fact are those bitings of conscience with which the wicked are seized, even when they have hope of deceiving men and escaping human punishment; and that such a fear springs from no higher principle, from no realization of the divine sovereignty, but can be traced to mere simplicity, habit, or the fear of human punishment, no pious man is convinced. . . .

. . . Nor can I believe that any man has ever found for himself in the impiety of atheism a final relief from such terrors, but that his fear of God has at times got the upper hand, and shaken his impious mind in the end with even greater tumults. . . .

Now although the binding of a man's conscience is the most characteristic feature of a natural obligation, the same efficacy is found as well in a civil obligation, provided the latter is concerned with an object not repugnant to the former. And so civil laws also, which are not repugnant to natural law, have an influence on the conscience. Furthermore, both obligations agree in this respect, that a man should do, of his own accord and by an intrinsic motive, the things which they demand of him. This forms the main difference between obligation and compulsion, since in the latter the mind is forced to something by mere external violence contrary to its intrinsic inclination, while whatever we do from an obligation is understood to come from an intrinsic impulse of the mind, and with the full approbation of its own judgment.

But when these obligations are viewed from the effect which they produce on the person who is owed something by reason of them, they have this feature in common, namely, that whatever is furnished as a debt on this account may be rightfully received and kept. But when a man neglects or refuses to meet an obligation, there arises a distinction, in the manner of requiring its fulfilment, between natural and civil obligations, according as one lives in natural liberty, or in a civil state.

Among those who live in natural liberty there obtains, from the precepts of natural law, an inequality of obligation. For such things as natural law commands one man to show another, before any agreement has passed between them, such as the duties of charity and humanity, can be required only by peaceful means, as by persuasion, admonition, request, or entreaty. But it will not be allowable to use force against a person who persists in his refusal, unless it happen that extreme necessity impels us. The reason for this seems to lie in the fact that, without such duties, the intercourse of men cannot be sufficiently peaceful, and so nature is understood to have put them to one side, as a means by which men may bind others to themselves by a special exhibition of good will; since things which may be extorted by force have no such power to win the hearts of others, as those which may be denied without fear. But if what is owed by an agreement is not forthcoming, force may be used to extort it. In the same way we may defend any of our possessions by force, when another man inflicts injury upon them.

Now civil obligations, or such as secure authority from civil law, open the way for action in a civil court. . . .

Chapter V: On the Nature of Promises and Pacts in General

3. . . . not every natural faculty to do something is properly a right, but only that which concerns some moral effect, in the case of those who have the same nature as I. Thus, as in the fables . . . the horse had a natural faculty to graze in the meadow, and so had the stag as well, yet neither of them had a right to this, because their respective faculties did not concern the other. In the same way, when a man takes inanimate objects or animals for his use, he exercises only a purely natural faculty, if it is considered simply with regard to the objects and animals which he uses, without respect to other men. But this faculty takes on the nature of a real right, at the moment when this moral effect is produced in the rest of mankind, that other men may not hinder him, or compete with him, against his will, in using such objects or animals. Of course it is absurd to try to designate as a right that faculty which all other men have an equal right to prevent one from exercising.

Now we admit that man has by nature a faculty to take for his use all inanimate objects and animals. But that faculty, thus exactly defined, cannot properly be called a right, both because such things are under no obligation to present themselves for man's use, and because, by virtue of the natural equality of all men, one man cannot rightfully exclude the rest from such things, unless their consent, expressed or presumed, has let him have them as his very own. Only when this has been done, can he say that he has a proper right to the thing. To state it more concisely: A right to all things, previous to every human deed, must be understood not exclusively, but only indefinitely, that is, not that one man may claim everything for himself to the exclusion of the rest of mankind, but that nature does not define what particular things belong to one man, and what to another, before they agree among themselves on their divison and allocation. And even less does the same equality of men allow one man to claim that he has by nature a right over every other man. Nay rather, no man would ever have a right to rule over another, had he not acquired it in some special way from the other's consent, or from some other antecedent act of his, as is shown at greater length in its proper place.

Editor's Notes

1. "Polity," that is, city or abiding home.
2. The human court of judgment. The term *inner forum* was often used to refer to the conscience.
3. In a work on natural law Pufendorf did not discuss human origins or touch on matters of original sin.

4. Rom. 2:14–15.
5. Cicero *De natura deorum* II.160, attributed to Chrysippus, who was speaking of the function of the pig's soul.
6. Horace, *Epistulae* 1.2.27.
7. That is, complete or incomplete.
8. In dire emergencies – cases of necessity – a sufferer may use force to obtain what is needed to sustain life, even though such force would not normally be legitimate. For example, a beggar may not ordinarily use force to get what he requests; but a starving man, to prevent his own death, may take food that is not his.
9. An easement now is a legal permission to use another's property, for example, to allow my porch to extend over to your plot of ground.
10. *Law of War and Peace,* I.I.iv.
11. As Pufendorf soon made clear, he had in mind at least Grotius.

Further Reading

In addition to the translations of Pufendorf's major works on natural law mentioned in the Introduction, another essay of his is available in English, in Michael Seidler, trans., *Samuel Pufendorf's "On the Natural State of Men"* (New York: Mellen Press, 1990); Seidler has provided a substantial and useful introduction. The only book on Pufendorf in English is by Leonard Krieger, *The Politics of Discretion: Pufendorf and the Acceptance of Natural Law* (Chicago: University of Chicago Press, 1965). For a brief study of the main points of Pufendorf's moral philosophy, see J. B. Schneewind, "Pufendorf's Place in the History of Ethics," *Synthese* 72 (1987):123–55, which contains references to some of the important literature on Pufendorf in German and in French. Richard Tuck discusses Pufendorf on several points in *Natural Rights Theories* (Cambridge, England: Cambridge University Press, 1979). The same author, in "The 'Modern' Theory of Natural Law," in Anthony Pagden, ed., *The Languages of Political Theory in Early Modern Europe* (Cambridge, England: Cambridge University Press, 1987), presents an important examination of the distinguishing features of Grotian and post-Grotian natural law. The Pagden volume also includes an essay by Istvan Hont, "The Language of Sociability and Commerce: Samuel Pufendorf and the Theoretical Foundations of the 'Four States Theory,' " which reviews Pufendorf's role in the rise of a developmental view of human history that is important to the economic work of Adam Smith. Michael Nutkiewicz, "Samuel Pufendorf: Obligation As the Basis of the State," *Journal of the History of Philosophy* 21 (1983):15–29, illuminates Pufendorf's ethics as well as his political thought.

John Locke

Introduction

Locke claimed that a deductive science of moral principles could be produced, although he himself never produced one. His epistemological and political views were so influential, however, that they gave considerable weight to the ideas about morality that Locke expressed in his various works. Those interested in the history of ethics should therefore have some acquaintance with Locke's views.

Locke was born in 1632 and educated at Oxford, where he taught for a period and then studied medicine, eventually obtaining a degree in 1674. In 1667 he took a post as physician to Lord Ashley (after 1672 the earl of Shaftesbury), whom he served in many capacities until the earl's death in 1683. Shaftesbury was a major figure in the party opposing absolutist monarchy and working to keep the throne in Protestant hands. Indeed, his intrigues led to his being tried for treason. Although he was acquitted, Shaftesbury fled England, and after the earl's death, Locke, thinking that he also was in some danger, left Oxford for Holland. He stayed there until 1689, returning when William and Mary – to whom he had been an adviser in Holland – came to the English throne.

When Locke was a student, philosophy at Oxford was still scholastic, and he was not interested in it. He studied Descartes only after he had finished his formal education. Then, during a stay in Paris Locke met a number of leading philosophical figures, among them Gassendi's disciple Bernier, who encouraged him in following an empiricist line of thought. During his exile in Holland, Locke worked on his *Essay Concerning Human Understanding*, which was published in 1690. The *Two Treatises on Civil Government*, though also dated 1690, had appeared shortly before the *Essay*. Locke's health was poor, and after his return to England he lived much of the time with friends in the country, although he also held a position in the new government. His *Reasonableness of Christianity* was published anonymously in 1695. In his later years Locke revised the *Essay*, engaged in controversy about it, and wrote on many other subjects. He died in 1704.

In the final chapter of the *Essay*, Locke divided the objects of understanding into three classes: the nature of things as they are in themselves, those things that man ought to do, and the ways by which he is to attain these two kinds of knowledge. The second kind of knowledge, Locke stated, is

the skill of right applying our own powers and actions for the attainment of things good and useful. The most considerable under this head is *Ethics*, which is the seeking out those rules and measures of human actions which lead to happiness, and the means to practice them.

The point of this sort of knowledge, Locke explained, is not "bare speculation"; rather, it is the improvement of practice.

Locke had a long-standing interest in morals and politics. When he was about thirty, he wrote two tracts on political affairs and a set of essays or disputations on the law of nature, and the discussions with friends that stimulated Locke to write the *Essay* probably initially concerned ethics. In the *Essay* itself Locke treated morality almost entirely as part of his general effort to work out accounts of how our ideas are derived from experience, of the way language is built on our experientially based ideas, and of the roles of reason and experience in combining these ideas into the different kinds of knowledge we possess. Thus he argued against innate moral ideas as part of his wider argument against innate ideas of any sort, and his account of moral relations was included as part of the discussion of relational ideas generally.

Some aspects of Locke's own position regarding morality emerge during these primarily epistemological discussions. He made apparent his hedonism: *good* and *evil* are defined in terms of pleasure and pain, and happiness is the presence of the one and the absence of the other. We all pursue happiness, although we do not always pursue what seems to us at the moment the greatest attainable good. We can place our happiness in different things, Locke believed, and so, even if I know that something would give me pleasure, I need not pursue it, because I need not think of that particular good or pleasure as contributing to my happiness. Locke stressed the variety of goods that people pursue and concluded, in a Hobbesian way, that

the philosophers of old did in vain inquire whether *summum bonum* [highest good] consisted in riches, or bodily delights, or virtue or contemplation; and they might have as reasonably disputed whether the best relish were to be found in apples, plums, or nuts. (*Essay,* II. xxi.55)

If moral principles are somehow meant to show us how to attain happiness, it will not be easy to figure out what those principles are.

Another feature of morality, in Locke's view, is that God is central to it. God has given us a law to live by, and he enforces it by means of sanctions. No law without a lawgiver, no lawgiver without the power to enforce. Here Locke distanced himself from Grotius and aligned himself with Pufendorf, whom he admired and whose books he recommended for the education of gentlemen. God is needed not only to lay down the law but also to instruct us in it, and not by roundabout means such as reason. Revelation was originally necessary because reason was too weak to inform us of what God requires of us – although Locke firmly believed that once the requirements were revealed, reason could show us that they were reasonable.

Locke did not publish his early writings on natural law, and he refused later requests to publish them, made by the few people who knew of them. They must be studied for a full understanding of Locke's views on morality, but because they did not become available until this century, the following selections are drawn from his published works. The first excerpts are from the *Essay Concerning Human Understanding* and the second from *The Reasonableness of Christianity*. The texts are from Locke's *Works,* 3rd ed., 3 vols. (London, 1727). I have modernized the spelling and some of the punctuation.

An Essay Concerning Human Understanding

Book I

Chapter III

1. If those speculative maxims whereof we discoursed in the foregoing chapter have not an actual universal assent from all mankind, as we there

proved, it is much more visible concerning practical principles, that they come short of an universal reception; and I think it will be hard to instance any one moral rule which can pretend to so general and ready an assent as "What is, is" or to be so manifest a truth as this, "that it is impossible for the same thing to be and not to be." Whereby it is evident that they are farther removed from a title to be innate; and the doubt of their being native impressions on the mind is stronger against these moral principles than the other. Not that it brings their truth at all in question. They are equally true, though not equally evident. Those speculative maxims carry their own evidence with them. But moral principles require reasoning and discourse, and some exercise of the mind, to discover the certainty of their truth. They lie not open as natural characters ingraven on the mind; which if any such were, they must needs be visible by themselves, and by their own light be certain and known to everybody. But this is no derogation to their truth and certainty . . . these moral rules are capable of demonstration: and therefore it is our own faults, if we come not to a certain knowledge of them. But the ignorance wherein many men are of them, and the slowness of assent wherewith others receive them, are manifest proofs that they are not innate. . . .

2. Whether there be any such moral principles wherein all men do agree, I appeal to any who have been but moderately conversant in the history of mankind and looked abroad beyond the smoke of their own chimneys. Where is that practical truth that is universally received without doubt or question, as it must be if innate? Justice, and keeping contracts, is that which most men seem to agree in. This is a principle which is thought to extend itself to the dens of thieves, and the confederacies of the greatest villains; and they who have gone farthest towards the putting off of humanity itself keep faith and rules of justice one with another. I grant that outlaws themselves do this one amongst another, but 'tis without receiving these as the innate laws of nature. They practise them as rules of convenience within their own communities. But it is impossible to conceive that he embraces justice as a practical principle who acts fairly with his fellow highwaymen, and at the same time plunders or kills the next honest man he meets with. Justice and truth are the common ties of society; and therefore even outlaws and robbers, who break with all the world besides, must keep faith and rules of equity amongst themselves, or else they cannot hold together. But will any one say that those that live by fraud and rapine have innate principles of truth and justice which they allow and assent to?

4. Another reason that makes me doubt of any innate practical principles is that I think *there cannot any one moral rule be proposed whereof a man may not justly demand a reason,* which would be perfectly ridiculous and absurd if they were innate, or so much as self-evident; which every innate principle must needs be, and not need any proof to ascertain its truth, nor want any reason to gain it approbation. He would be thought void of common sense who asked on the one side or on the other side went about to give a reason why it is impossible for the same thing to be and not to be. It carries its own light and evidence with it and needs no other proof. He that understands the terms assents to it for its own sake, or else nothing will ever be able to prevail

with him to do it. But should that most unshaken rule of morality and foundation of all social virtue, that one should do as he would be done unto, be proposed to one who never heard it before, but yet is of capacity to understand its meaning, might he not without any absurdity ask a reason why? And were not he that proposed it bound to make out the truth and reasonableness of it to him? Which plainly shews it not to be innate, for if it were, it could neither want nor receive any proof. . . .

6. Hence naturally flows the great variety of opinions concerning moral rules which are to be found amongst men, according to the different sorts of happiness they have a prospect of or propose to themselves; which could not be if practical principles were innate and imprinted in our minds immediately by the hand of God. I grant the existence of God is so many ways manifest, and the obedience we owe him so congruous to the light of reason, that a great part of mankind give testimony to the law of nature. But yet I think it must be allowed that several moral rules may receive from mankind a very general approbation, without either knowing or admitting the true ground of morality; which can only be the will and law of a God who sees men in the dark, has in his hand rewards and punishments, and power enough to call to account the proudest offender. . . .

Book II

Chapter XXI

31. To return then to the enquiry, what is it that determines the will in regard to our actions? And that upon second thoughts[1] I am apt to imagine is not, as is generally supposed, the greater good in view, but some (and for the most part the most pressing) uneasiness a man is at present under. This is that which successively determines the will and sets us upon those actions we perform. This uneasiness we may call, as it is, desire; which is an uneasiness of the mind for want of some absent good. . . .

35. It seems so established and settled a maxim by the general consent of all mankind that good, the greater good, determines the will, that I do not at all wonder that when I first published my thoughts on this subject I took it for granted; and I imagine that by a great many I shall be thought more excusable for having then done so, than that now I have ventured to recede from so received an opinion. But yet upon a stricter enquiry, I am forced to conclude that good, the greater good, though apprehended and acknowledged to be so, does not determine the will until our desire, raised proportionably to it, makes us uneasy in the want of it. Convince a man never so much that plenty has its advantages over poverty; make him see and own that the handsome conveniences of life are better than nasty penury: yet as long as he is content with the latter and finds no uneasiness in it, he moves not; his will never is determined to any action that shall bring him out of it. Let a man be never so well persuaded of the advantages of virtue, that it is as necessary to a man who has

any great aims in this world or hopes in the next as food to life: yet till he hungers and thirsts after righteousness, till he feels an uneasiness in the want of it, his will will not be determined to any action in pursuit of this confessed greater good; but any other uneasiness he feels in himself shall take place and carry his will to other actions. . . .

38. Were the will determined by the views of good, as it appears in contemplation greater or less to the understanding, which is the state of all absent good and that which in the received opinion the will is supposed to move to and to be moved by, I do not see how it could ever get loose from the infinite eternal joys of Heaven, once proposed and considered as possible. For all absent good, by which alone barely proposed and coming in view the will is thought to be determined and so to set us on action, being only possible, but not infallibly certain, 'tis unavoidable that the infinitely greater possible good should regularly and constantly determine the will in all the successive actions it directs; and then we should keep constantly and steadily in our course towards Heaven. . . .

This would be the state of the mind and regular tendency of the will in all its determinations, were it determined by that which is considered and in view the greater good; but that it is not so is visible in experience. . . .

41. If it be farther asked, what 'tis moves desire? I answer happiness and that alone. Happiness and misery are the names of two extremes, the utmost bounds whereof we know not; 'tis what eye hath not seen, ear hath not heard, nor hath it entered into the heart of man to conceive.[2] But of some degrees of both we have very lively impressions, made by several instances of delight and joy on the one side, and torment and sorrow on the other; which, for shortness sake, I shall comprehend under the names of pleasure and pain, there being pleasure and pain of the mind as well as the body. With him is fullness of joy, and pleasure for evermore.[3] Or to speak truly, they are all of the mind, though some have their rise in the mind from thought, others in the body from certain modifications of motion.

42. Happiness then in its full extent is the utmost pleasure we are capable of, and misery the utmost pain. And the lowest degree of what can be called happiness is so much ease from all pain, and so much present pleasure, as without which any one cannot be content. Now because pleasure and pain are produced in us by operation of certain objects, either on our minds or our bodies, and in different degrees, therefore what has an aptness to produce pleasure in us is that we call good, and what is apt to produce pain in us we call evil, for no other reason but for its aptness to produce pleasure and pain in us, wherein consists our happiness and misery. . . .

43. Though this be that which is called good and evil, and all good be the proper object of desire in general; yet all good, even seen and confessed to be so, does not necessarily move every particular man's desire, but only that part, or so much of it, as is considered and taken to make a necessary part of his happiness. All other good, however great in reality or appearance, excites not a man's desires, who looks not on it to make a part of that happiness

wherewith he, in his present thought, can satisfy himself. Happiness, under this view, every one constantly pursues and desires what makes any part of it. Other things acknowledged to be good he can look upon without desire, pass by, and be content without. . . .

44. This, I think, anyone may observe in himself and others, that the greater visible good does not always raise men's desires in proportion to the greatness it appears and is acknowledged to have, though every little trouble moves us and sets us on work to get rid of it. The reason whereof is evident from the nature of our happiness and misery itself. All present pain, whatever it be, makes a part of our present misery. But all absent good does not at any time make a necessary part of our present happiness, nor the absence of it make a part of our misery. If it did, we should be constantly and infinitely miserable, there being infinite degrees of happiness, which are not in our possession. All uneasiness therefore being removed, a moderate portion of good serves at present to content men. . . .

47. There being in us a great many uneasinesses always soliciting and ready to determine the will, it is natural, as I have said, that the greatest and most pressing should determine the will to the next action; and so it does for the most part, but not always. For the mind having in most cases, as is evident in experience, a power to suspend the execution and satisfaction of any of its desires, and so all one after another, is at liberty to consider the objects of them, examine them on all sides, and weigh them with others. In this lies the liberty man has; and from the not using of it right comes all that variety of mistakes, errors, and faults which we run into in the conduct of our lives and our endeavours after happiness; whilst we precipitate the determination of our wills and engage too soon before due examination. To prevent this we have a power to suspend the prosecution of this or that desire, as every one daily may experiment in himself. This seems to me the source of all liberty; in this seems to consist that which is (as I think improperly) called free will. For during this suspension of any desire, before the will be determined to action, and the action (which follows that determination) done, we have opportunity to examine, view, and judge of the good or evil of what we are going to do: and when upon due examination we have judged, we have done our duty, all that we can or ought to do in pursuit of our happiness; and 'tis not a fault but a perfection of our nature to desire, will, and act according to the last result of a fair examination.

48. This is so far from being a restraint or diminution of freedom that it is the very improvement and benefit of it; 'tis not an abridgement, 'tis the end and use of our liberty. And the farther we are removed from such a determination, the nearer we are to misery and slavery. . . .

52. This is the hinge on which turns the liberty of intellectual beings in their constant endeavours after and a steady prosecution of true felicity, that they can suspend this prosecution in particular cases till they have looked before them and informed themselves whether that particular thing which is then proposed or desired lie in the way to their main end and make a real part of

that which is their greatest good. For the inclination and tendency of their nature to happiness is an obligation and motive to them to take care not to mistake or miss it; and so necessarily puts them upon caution, deliberation and wariness in the direction of their particular actions, which are the means to obtain it. Whatever necessity determines to the pursuit of real bliss, the same necessity with the same force establishes suspense, deliberation and scrutiny of each successive desire, whether the satisfaction of it does not interfere with our true happiness and mislead us from it. This as seems to me is the great privilege of finite intellectual Beings; and I desire it may be well considered whether the great inlet and exercise of all the liberty men have, are capable of, or can be useful to them, and that whereon depends the turn of their actions, does not lie in this. . . .

54. From what has been said, it is easy to give an account, how it comes to pass that though all men desire happiness, yet their wills carry them so contrarily, and consequently some of them to what is evil. And to this I say that the various and contrary choices that men make in the world do not argue that they do not all pursue good; but that the same thing is not good to every man alike. This variety of pursuits shows that every one does not place his happiness in the same thing or choose the same way to it. Were all the concerns of man terminated in this life, why one followed study and knowledge and another hawking and hunting; why one chose luxury and debauchery, and another sobriety and riches, would not be, because every one of these did not aim at his own happiness; but because their happiness was placed in different things. And therefore 'twas a right answer of the physician to his patient, that had sore eyes: if you have more pleasure in the taste of wine than in the use of your sight, wine is good for you; but if the pleasure of seeing be greater to you than that of drinking, wine is naught.

Chapter XXVIII

4. Fourthly, there is another sort of relation, which is the conformity or disagreement men's voluntary actions have to a rule to which they are referred, and by which they are judged of: which I think may be called *moral relations,* as being that which denominates our moral actions, and deserves well to be examined, there being no part of knowledge wherein we should be more careful to get determined ideas and avoid, as much as may be, obscurity and confusion.

5. Good and evil, as hath been shown (bk. II, chap. XX, sec. 2, and chap. XXI, sec. 42) are nothing but pleasure or pain, or that which occasions or procures pleasure or pain to us. *Moral good* and *evil* then is only the conformity or disagreement of our voluntary actions to some law whereby good or evil is drawn on us from the will and power of the law-maker; which good and evil, pleasure or pain, attending our observance or breach of the law by the decree of the law-maker, is that we call reward and punishment.

6. Of these moral rules, or laws, to which men generally refer and by which

they judge of the rectitude or pravity[4] of their actions, there seem to me to be three sorts, with their three different enforcements, or rewards and punishments. For since it would be utterly in vain to suppose a rule set to the free actions of man without annexing to it some enforcement of good and evil to determine his will, we must, wherever we suppose a law, suppose also some reward or punishment annexed to that law. It would be in vain for one intelligent being to set a rule to the action of another if he had it not in his power to reward the compliance with, and punish deviation from his rule by some good and evil that is not the natural product and consequence of the action itself. For that being a natural convenience or inconvenience would operate of itself without a law. This, if I mistake not, is the true nature of all law properly so called.

7. The laws that men generally refer their actions to, to judge of their rectitude or obliquity, seem to me to be these three: (1) the *divine* law; (2) the *civil* law; (3) the law of *opinion* or *reputation,* if I may so call it. By the relation they bear to the first of these, men judge whether their actions are sins or duties; by the second, whether they be criminal or innocent; and by the third, whether they be virtues or vices.

8. First, the divine law, whereby I mean that law which God has set to the actions of men, whether promulgated to them by the light of nature or the voice of revelation. That God has given a rule whereby men should govern themselves, I think there is nobody so brutish as to deny. He has a right to do it; we are his creatures. He has goodness and wisdom to direct our actions to that which is best, and he has power to enforce it by rewards and punishments of infinite weight and duration, in another life, for nobody can take us out of his hands. This is the only true touchstone of moral rectitude; and by comparing them to this law it is, that men judge of the most considerable moral good or evil of their actions; that is, whether as duties or sins they are like to procure them happiness or misery from the hand of the ALMIGHTY.

9. Secondly, the civil law, the rule set by the commonwealth to the actions of those who belong to it, is another rule to which men refer their actions to judge whether they be criminal, or no. This law nobody overlooks, the rewards and punishments that enforce it being ready at hand and suitable to the power that makes it, which is the force of the commonwealth engaged to protect the lives, liberties and possessions of those who live according to its laws, and has power to take away life, liberty or goods from him who disobeys; which is the punishment of offences committed against this Law.

10. Thirdly, the law of opinion or reputation. Virtue and vice are names pretended and supposed everywhere to stand for actions in their own nature right and wrong. And as far as they really are so applied, they so far are coincident with the divine law above-mentioned. But yet, whatever is pretended, this is visible, that these names, virtue and vice, in the particular instances of their application, through the several nations and societies of men in the world, are constantly attributed only to such actions as in each country and society are in reputation or discredit. Nor is it to be thought strange that

men everywhere should give the name of virtue to those actions which amongst them are judged praiseworthy, and call that vice which they account blamable, since otherwise they would condemn themselves if they should think any thing right to which they allowed not commendation; anything wrong, which they let pass without blame. Thus the measure of what is everywhere called and esteemed virtue and vice is this approbation or dislike, praise or blame, which by a secret and tacit consent establishes itself in the several societies, tribes and clubs of men in the world, whereby several actions come to find credit or disgrace amongst them according to the judgment, maxims or fashions of that place. For though men, uniting into politic societies, have resigned up to the public the disposing of all their force so that they cannot employ it against any fellow-citizen any farther than the law of the country directs, yet they retain still the power of thinking well or ill, approving or disapproving of the actions of those whom they live amongst and converse with. And by this approbation and dislike they establish amongst themselves what they will call virtue and vice.

11. That this is the common measure of virtue and vice will appear to anyone who considers that though that passes for vice in one country which is counted a virtue or at least not vice in another, yet everywhere virtue and praise, vice and blame, go together. Virtue is everywhere that which is thought praiseworthy, and nothing else but that which has the allowance of public esteem is called virtue. . . .

12. If any one shall imagine that I have forgot my own notion of a law when I make the law whereby men judge of virtue and vice to be nothing else but the consent of private men, who have not authority enough to make a law, especially wanting that which is so necessary and essential to a law, a power to inforce it, I think I may say that he who imagines commendation and disgrace not to be strong motives on men to accommodate themselves to the opinions and rules of those with whom they converse seems little skilled in the nature or history of mankind; the greatest part whereof he shall find to govern themselves chiefly, if not solely, by this law of fashion; and, so they do that which keeps them in reputation with their company, little regard the laws of God or the magistrate. The penalties that attend the breach of God's laws, some, nay, perhaps most men seldom seriously reflect on. And amongst those that do many, whilst they break the law, entertain thoughts of future reconciliation and making their peace for such breaches. And as to the punishments due from the laws of the commonwealth, they frequently flatter themselves with the hopes of impunity. But no man escapes the punishment of their censure and dislike who offends against the fashion and opinion of the company he keeps, and would recommend himself to.

13. These three then: first, the law of God; secondly, the law of politic societies; thirdly, the law of fashion, or private censure, are those to which men variously compare their actions. And 'tis by their conformity to one of these laws that they take their measures when they would judge of their moral rectitude and denominate their actions good or bad.

14. Whether the rule to which, as to a touchstone, we bring our voluntary actions to examine them by and try their goodness, and accordingly to name them, which is, as it were, the mark of the value we set upon them, whether, I say, we take that rule from the fashion of the country or the will of a law-maker, the mind is easily able to observe the relation any action hath to it, and to judge whether the action agrees or disagrees with the Rule; and so hath a notion of moral goodness or evil which is either conformity or not conformity of any action to that rule, and therefore is often called moral rectitude. This rule being nothing but a collection of several simple ideas, the conformity thereto is but so ordering the action that the simple ideas belonging to it may correspond to those which the law requires. And thus we see how moral beings and notions are founded on and terminated in these simple ideas we have received from sensation or reflections. . . .

15. To conceive rightly of moral actions, we must take notice of them under this two-fold consideration. First, as they are in themselves each made up of such a collection of simple ideas. Thus "drunkenness" or "lying" signify such or such a collection of simple ideas which I call mixed modes.[5] And in this sense they are as much positive absolute ideas as the drinking of a horse or speaking of a parrot. Secondly, our actions are considered as good, bad, or indifferent; and in this respect they are relative, it being their conformity to or disagreement with some rule that makes them to be regular or irregular, good or bad. And so as far as they are compared with a rule and thereupon denomi-nated, they come under relation. Thus the challenging and fighting with a man, as it is a certain positive mode or particular sort of action, by particular ideas distinguished from all others, is called duelling; which, when considered in relation to the law of God, will deserve the name sin; to the law of fashion in some countries, valour and virtue; and to the municipal laws of some governments, a capital crime. In this case, when the positive mode has one name and another name as it stands in relation to the law, the distinction may as easily be observed as it is in substances, where one name, e.g. man, is used to signify the thing, another, e.g. father, to signify the relation.

BOOK IV

Chapter III

18. As to the third sort of our knowledge, viz. the agreement or disagree-ment of any of our ideas in any other relation, this, as it is the largest field of our knowledge, so it is hard to determine how far it may extend, because the advances that are made in this part of knowledge, depending on our sagacity in finding intermediate ideas that may shew the relations and habitudes of ideas whose co-existence is not considered, 'tis a hard matter to tell when we are at an end of such discoveries, and when reason has all the helps it is capable of for the finding of proofs or examining the agreement or disagree-ment of remote ideas. They that are ignorant of algebra cannot imagine the

wonders in this kind are to be done by it: and what farther improvements and helps advantageous to other parts of knowledge the sagacious mind of man may yet find out, 'tis not easy to determine. This at least I believe, that the ideas of quantity are not those alone that are capable of demonstration and knowledge; and that other and perhaps more useful parts of contemplation would afford us certainty, if vices, passions, and domineering interest did not oppose or menace such endeavours.

The idea of a supreme Being, infinite in power, goodness, and wisdom, whose workmanship we are and on whom we depend, and the idea of ourselves, as understanding, rational beings, being such as are clear in us, would, I suppose, if duly considered and pursued, afford such foundations of our duty and rules of action, as might place *morality amongst the sciences capable of demonstration;* wherein I doubt not but from self-evident propositions, by necessary consequences as incontestable as those in mathematics, the measures of right and wrong might be made out to any one that will apply himself with the same indifference and attention to the one as he does to the other of these sciences. The relation of other modes may certainly be perceived as well as those of number and extension. And I cannot see why they should not also be capable of demonstration, if due methods were thought on to examine or pursue their agreement or disagreement. "Where there is no property there is no injustice" is a proposition as certain as any demonstration in Euclid. For the idea of property being a right to any thing, and the idea to which the name "injustice" is given being the invasion or violation of that right, it is evident that these ideas being thus established and these names annexed to them, I can as certainly know this proposition to be true as that a triangle has three angles equal to two right ones. Again, "No government allows absolute liberty": the idea of government being the establishment of society upon certain rules or laws which require conformity to them, and the idea of absolute liberty being for any one to do whatever he pleases, I am as capable of being certain of the truth of this proposition as of any in mathematics.

19. That which in this respect has given the advantage to the ideas of quantity and made them thought more capable of certainty and demonstration, is,

First, that they can be set down and represented by sensible marks which have a greater and nearer correspondence with them than any words or sounds whatsoever. Diagrams drawn on paper are copies of the ideas in the mind, and not liable to the uncertainty that words carry in their signification. An angle, circle, or square, drawn in lines, lies open to the view and cannot be mistaken. It remains unchangeable and may at leisure be considered and examined, and the demonstration be revised, and all the parts of it may be gone over more than once without any danger of the least change in the ideas. This cannot be thus done in moral Ideas. We have no sensible marks that resemble them whereby we can set them down. We have nothing but words to express them by, which though when written they remain the same, yet the ideas they stand for may change in the same man, and 'tis very seldom that they are not different in different persons.

Secondly, another thing that makes the greater difficulty in ethics is that moral ideas are commonly more complex than those of the figures ordinarily considered in mathematics. From whence these two inconveniences follow. First, that their names are of more uncertain signification, the precise collection of simple ideas they stand for not being so easily agreed on, and so the sign that is used for them in communication always and in thinking often does not steadily carry with it the same idea. Upon which the same disorder, confusion, and error follows as would if a man going to demonstrate something of an heptagon should in the diagram he took to do it leave out one of the angles, or by oversight make the figure with one angle more than the name ordinarily imported, or he intended it should, when at first he thought of his demonstration. This often happens and is hardly avoidable in very complex moral ideas, where the same name being retained, one angle, i.e. one simple idea is left out or put in, in the complex one (still called by the same name) more at one time than another. Secondly, from the complexedness of these moral ideas there follows another inconvenience, viz. that the mind cannot easily retain those precise combinations so exactly and perfectly as is necessary in the examination of the habitudes and correspondencies, agreements or disagreements, of several of them one with another; especially where it is to be judged of by long deductions and the intervention of several other complex ideas to shew the agreement or disagreement of two remote ones.

20. One part of these disadvantages in moral ideas which has made them be thought not capable of demonstration may in a good measure be remedied by definitions, setting down that collection of simple ideas which every term shall stand for; and then using the terms steadily and constantly for that precise collection. And what methods algebra or something of that kind may hereafter suggest to remove the other difficulties is not easy to foretell. Confident I am that if men would in the same method and with the same indifferency search after moral as they do mathematical truths, they would find them to have a stronger connection one with another, and a more necessary consequence from our clear and distinct ideas, and to come nearer perfect demonstration, than is commonly imagined.

The Reasonableness of Christianity

It will possibly here be asked . . . What need was there of a Saviour? What advantage have we by Jesus Christ? . . .

2. Next to the knowledge of one God, maker of all things, a clear knowledge of their duty was wanting to mankind. . . . It should seem by the little that has hitherto been done in it that 'tis too hard a task for unassisted reason to establish morality in all its parts upon its true foundation, with a clear and convincing light. And 'tis at least a surer and shorter way to the apprehensions

of the vulgar and mass of mankind that one manifestly sent from God and coming with visible authority from him should as a king and law-maker tell them their duties, and require their obedience, than leave it to the long and sometimes intricate deductions of reason to be made out to them. Such trains of reasonings the greatest part of mankind have neither leisure to weigh nor, for want of education and use, skill to judge of. We see how unsuccessful in this the attempts of philosophers were before our Saviour's time. How short their several systems came of the perfection of a true and complete morality is very visible. And if, since that, the Christian philosophers have much out-done them, yet we may observe that the first knowledge of the truths they have added [is] owing to revelation, though as soon as they are heard and considered they are found to be agreeable to reason, and such as can by no means be contradicted. . . . 'tis plain in fact that human reason unassisted failed men in its great and proper business of morality. It never from unquestionable principles, by clear deductions, made out an entire body of the Law of Nature. And he that shall collect all the moral rules of the philosophers and compare them with those contained in the New Testament shall find them to come short of the morality delivered by our Saviour. . . .

Though yet if any one should think that out of the sayings of the wise heathens, before our Saviour's time, there might be a collection made of all those rules of morality which are to be found in the Christian religion, yet this would not at all hinder but that the world nevertheless stood as much in need of our Saviour and the morality delivered by him. Let it be granted (though not true) that all the moral precepts of the Gospel were known by somebody or other amongst mankind before. But where or how or of what use is not considered. Suppose they may be picked up here and there. . . . What will all this do to give the world a complete morality that may be to mankind the unquestionable rule of life and manners? . . . What would this amount to towards being a steady rule, a certain transcript of a law that we are under? . . . Was Zeno[6] a law-giver to mankind? If not, what he or any other philosopher delivered was but a saying of his. . . . 'Tis not enough that there were up and down scattered sayings of wise men, conformable to right reason. The law of nature is the law of convenience too, and 'tis no wonder that those men of parts, and studious of virtue . . . should by meditation light on the right, even from the observable convenience and beauty of it, without making out its obligation from the true principles of the law of nature and foundations of morality. . . . 'Tis not every writer of morals, or compiler of it from others, that can thereby be erected into a law-giver to mankind, and a dictator of rules which are therefore valid because they are to be found in his books. . . . He that anyone will pretend to set up in this kind, and have his rules pass for authentic directions, must show that either he builds his doctrine upon principles of reason, self-evident in themselves, or that he deduces all the parts of it from thence, by clear and evident demonstration, or must show his commission from heaven, that he comes with authority from God to deliver his will and commands to the world. In the former way nobody that I know before our Saviour's time ever did or went about to give us a morality. 'Tis true there is a law of nature; but who is there that ever did or undertook to give it us all entire, as a law, no more nor no less than what was contained in and had the obligation of law? Who ever made out all the parts of it, put them together, and showed the world their obligation? Where was there any such code that mankind might have recourse to as their unerring rule, before our Saviour's time? If there was not, 'tis plain there was need of one to give us such a morality. . . .

. . . A great many things which we have been bred up in the belief of from our cradles (and are notions grown familiar and as it were natural to us, under the Gospel) we take for unquestionable obvious truths, and easily demonstrable, without considering how long we might have been in doubt or ignorance of them had revelation been silent. And many are beholden to revelation who do not acknowledge it. 'Tis no diminishing to revelation that reason gives its suffrage too to the truths revelation has discovered. But 'tis our mistake to think that because reason confirms them to us, we had the first certain knowledge of them from thence, and in that clear evidence we now possess them. The contrary is manifest in the defective morality of the Gentiles before our Saviour's time; and the want of reformation in the principles and measures of it as well as practice. Philosophy seemed to have spent its strength and done its utmost; or if it should have gone further, as we see it did not, and from undeniable principles given us ethics in a science like mathematics, in every part demonstrable, this yet would not have been so effectual to man in this imperfect state, nor proper for the cure. The greatest part of mankind want leisure or capacity for demonstration, nor can carry a train of proofs, which in that way they must always depend upon for conviction, and cannot be required to assent to till they see the demonstration. Wherever they stick, the teachers are always put upon proof and must clear the doubt by a threat of coherent deductions from the first principle, how long or how intricate soever that be. And you may as soon hope to have all the day-laborers and tradesmen, the spinsters and dairy maids perfect mathematicians, as to have them perfect in ethics this way. Hearing plain commands is the sure and only course to bring them to obedience and practice. The greatest part cannot know and therefore they must believe. And I ask whether one coming from Heaven in the power of God, in full and clear evidence and demonstration of miracles, giving plain and direct rules of morality and obedience be not likelier to enlighten the bulk of mankind, and set them right in their duties, and bring them to do them, than by reasoning with them from general notions and principles of human reason? And were all the duties of human life clearly demonstrated, yet I conclude, when well considered, that method of teaching men their duties would be thought proper only for a few, who had much leisure, improved understandings, and were used to abstract reasonings. But the instruction of the people were best still to be left to the precepts and principles of the Gospel. . . .

4. Another great advantage received by our Saviour is the great encouragement he brought to a virtuous and pious life. . . . The portion of the righteous

has been in all ages taken notice of to be pretty scanty in this world. Virtue and prosperity do not often accompany one another, and therefore virtue seldom had many followers. . . . Mankind, who are and must be allowed to pursue their happiness, nay, cannot be hindered, could not but think themselves excused from a strict observation of rules which appeared so little to consist with their chief end, happiness, whilst they kept them from the enjoyments of this life; and they had little evidence and security of another. 'Tis true, they might have argued the other way and concluded that, because the good were most of them ill treated here, there was another place where they should meet with better usage; but 'tis plain they did not. Their thoughts of another life were at best obscure, and their expectations uncertain. . . . Before our Saviour's time the doctrine of a future state, though it were not wholly hid, yet it was not clearly known in the world. . . . How hath this one truth changed the nature of things in the world, and given advantage to piety over all that could tempt or deter men from it? The philosophers, indeed, showed the beauty of virtue; . . . but leaving her unendowed, very few were willing to espouse her. . . . But now there being put into the scales, on her side, an exceeding and immortal weight of glory, interest is come about to her, and virtue now is visible to most enriching purchase and by much the best bargain. . . . The view of heaven and hell will cast a slight upon the short pleasures and pains of the present state, and give attractions and encouragements to virtue which reason and interest and the care of our selves cannot but allow and prefer. Upon this foundation, and upon this only, morality stands firm and may defy all competition. This makes it more than a name, a substantial good, worth all our aims and endeavors; and thus the Gospel of Jesus Christ has delivered it to us.

Editor's Notes

1. Second thoughts, because Locke changed his mind on this matter after the first edition. In the first edition he said that "good . . . the greater good is that alone which determines the will" (II.29). In section 35 (immediately following), he rejected this view.
2. 1 Cor. 2:9.
3. Ps. 16:11.
4. That is, depravity.
5. Locke explained mixed modes in II.xxii. The mind actively assembles several of the ideas that it has passively received and considers them together as forming a single idea. It marks the unity of the collection by using a single word as its name. Locke offered "obligation," "sacrilege," "murder," and "parricide" as examples, but evaluative terms are not the only terms standing for mixed modes.
6. Zeno of Citium (c. 336–265 B.C.E.), the founder of Stoicism.

Further Reading

Locke's early writings on the law of nature and on politics are available in W. von Leyden, ed., *John Locke: Essays on the Law of Nature* (Oxford: Clarendon Press,

1954), and Philip Abrams, ed., *John Locke: Two Tracts on Government* (Cambridge, England: Cambridge University Press, 1967). The best edition of Locke's *Two Treatises of Government* is that by Peter Laslett (Cambridge, England: Cambridge University Press, 1988).

For an overview of Locke's philosophy, the reader may wish to consult Richard Aaron, *John Locke*, 3rd ed. (Oxford: Clarendon Press, 1971); D. J. O'Connor, *John Locke* (London: Penguin, 1952); R. S. Woolhouse, *Locke* (Minneapolis: University of Minnesota Press, 1983); or John W. Yolton, *Locke, an Introduction* (Oxford: Blackwell Publisher, 1985), which opens with discussion of Locke's moral views.

John Colman, *John Locke's Moral Philosophy* (Edinburgh: Edinburgh University Press, 1983) – the only book in English on the subject – is an excellent study with a good bibliography. For a discussion of Locke's religious views and their connection with his ethics, see W. M. Spellman, *John Locke and the Problem of Depravity* (Oxford: Clarendon Press, 1988).

John Dunn, *The Political Thought of John Locke* (Cambridge, England: Cambridge University Press, 1969), is an important study of the way Locke understood his own political thought. James Tully, *A Discourse on Property* (Cambridge, England: Cambridge University Press, 1980), though largely concerned with Locke's political views, sheds considerable light on his ethics.

Part II.
Intellect and Morality

Guillaume Du Vair

Introduction

Guillaume Du Vair was born into an old family in France in 1556. After receiving a good education, he toured Italy and later served for a time as a courtier. He then turned to reflecting on life and published in 1584 a book that combined Stoic and Christian themes, the *Sainte philosophie* (*Holy Philosophy*). Du Vair then began a more intensive study of Epictetus, whose *Encheiridion* or *Manual* he translated into French, and in 1585 he published his own rewriting of Epictetus, the short *Philosophie morale des Stoiques* (*The Moral Philosophy of the Stoics*). Thereafter he became active in politics, rising to high provincial office. In 1603 he was made a bishop, and in 1615 he was required to return to the service of the king. He died in 1621 while on a military campaign.

Of Du Vair's several writings, *The Moral Philosophy of the Stoics* was the most widely read. Its philosophy, as Du Vair himself pointed out, comes directly from Epictetus, with several passages, such as the advice about how to respond to the death of one's own child, being little more than paraphrases. In general, Du Vair recommended that we follow nature, live according to reason, concern ourselves only with what is within our power and remain unmoved by whatever we cannot control, recognize that reason is the highest part of the self, and see that the good is virtue. He was not interested in spelling out these teachings in detail, much less in proving them. Rather, his aim was to expound them briefly and attractively, providing thereby a manual that would be more accessible to his contemporaries than Epictetus's classic work was.

Only in one regard did Du Vair depart somewhat from his model – and then in a way that made Stoicism more acceptable to modern readers attracted to its austere teaching. Toward the end of his book, Du Vair managed to insert a distinctly Christian interpretation of the Stoic teachings. He urged the reader to practice Christian piety, thereby transforming Stoic aloofness from one's feelings into Christian acceptance of whatever God providentially sends, even though one cannot see the good that will come of it. The neo-Stoicism that was so influential in the seventeenth century thus was usually Christianized, to varying degrees.

Another effort to rewrite Stoicism for modern times was made by the Dutch scholar and political thinker Justus Lipsius, who in 1584 published *De constantia* (*On Constancy*), an exposition of the proper Stoic attitude toward political misfortune and personal hardship, which went through innumerable editions and was translated into several languages. The religious warfare of the period made it a time of great insecurity for everyone, not least for those serving their country as soldiers or in positions of command. A Christianized Stoicism, therefore, was a fit doctrine for both armies and those whose political fortunes might radically change overnight. Although Lipsius was a distinguished scholar who worked carefully on the ancient sources of our knowledge of Stoicism, his *On Constancy* was not meant to be an academic treatise. Like Du Vair's book, it paid no attention to the elaborate distinctions worked into the expositions of Stoicism preserved in Cicero. Both authors were writing for an unscholarly audience that needed a doctrine to live by, and the popularity of both of their works showed that they were meeting this need.

As Du Vair made clear at the beginning of his book, the Stoic believes that knowledge of the good is sufficient to achieve the good life. If we see clearly what is good, we will infallibly pursue it, because will follows the guidance of intellect. It is only when we "do not know wherein consisteth our good" that we "shoot wide from our general mark and intention." Du Vair did not argue for the trustworthiness of intellect as Descartes later did, but Descartes, like the rationalists who succeeded him, held the view that we need only know the constitution of things in the fullest sense to be moved to act for the good, an aspect of Stoicism that lived on well into the eighteenth century.

The following selections are from the English translation of Du Vair by Thomas James, published in 1598 and reprinted with an introduction and notes by Rudolf Kirk (New Brunswick, N.J.: Rutgers University Press, 1951). I have modernized the spelling and punctuation somewhat but have left James's English otherwise intact.

The Moral Philosophy of the Stoics

There is nothing in the world which tendeth not to one end or other: yea, even things insensible do advance themselves (as it seemeth) and make themselves fit for that use unto which they do properly belong: and being applied thereunto do shew forth a kind of joy, and seem to have a feeling of the perfection and happiness of their estates. Things that have action in them move of themselves in such sort as we see; all creatures in general, and every one severally in his kind, with great vehemence and contention, followeth and pursueth after that for which they are born and bred, and do most certainly rejoice and exult in the fruition of that which they seek, when they have found it out.

What then ought man to do, whom nature, besides this inclination and motion which dead things do partake with him, hath endowed with sense, and over and besides sense, which is common to him and other creatures, hath given the benefit of discourse and reason, to be able to discern and choose the best things of all things which present themselves unto his consideration, and that which is most fit and proper to his use? May we not safely conclude that man also has his end, as well as all other creatures; which is set before him as the furthermost mark and butt, whereto all his actions should be directed: and since the happiness of all things is their perfection, and their perfection the fruition of their end, shall not the happiness and felicity of man consist in the full obtaining and attaining unto that which is proposed unto him, and whereunto all his actions are to be referred?

Now the end of man and of all his thoughts and meditations is good. And truly, there is not one among many, so diverse in nature and condition of life, which desireth not that which is good, and escheweth not that which is evil: and being demanded wherefore he does this or that, answereth not, but that he doth it or thinks that he doth it for his good and welfare. And albeit in our actions a man may find a great many more bad than good; yet the general intention whereby we are directed and guided is to come unto that which is good.

But as it fareth many times with him which aims at a mark, if his sight be hindered, either by some disease of the eye or fault in the air, or if he take one thing for another, although he desire to hit the mark, so that he covet nothing more, yet it is impossible but he should be wide from it: so likewise we, because we do not know wherein consisteth our good, but oftentimes take that which is about it, for it, do therefore in our particular actions take our aim amiss, and shoot wide from our general mark and intention.

Good, in good truth, is not so placed that all the world may see and perceive it; nature has sowed and scattered here beneath amongst us certain weak and feeble sparklings of that heat, which notwithstanding[1] being rightly applied unto our minds, are able to kindle a pure light in them, and cause us to see good as it is and not as it seems. So then, we must seek it, and we shall find it; and having found it, we must acknowledge it; acknowledging it, we cannot choose but love it; and loving it, we shall fasten all our desires thereunto, and enjoy it with great happiness. For even as truth presenting itself unto our understanding is there entertained with great joy and contentedness: even so good offering itself unto our will, is received by her with great pleasure, as being her natural object.

And therefore I think that if a man would properly define good, he must affirm it to be nothing else but the essence and usage of a thing according unto his nature.[2] For this same nature is so prudent and provident a mistress that she always disposeth all things unto their greatest good, and therefore hath given them a first motion unto that which is good, and unto that end which they should seek and search after: in such sort, that he that will follow after it cannot choose but compass and obtain it.

Now by the rules of nature, man should be so composed and fashioned that that which is most excellent in him should bear rule and command, and that reason should use all that which is presented unto her as best beseemeth her, and shall most serve for her purpose. Well then, the good and happiness of man consists in the right use of reason, and what is that but virtue, which is nothing else but a constant disposition of will to follow that which is honest and convenient.[3] There is no man, as I suppose, but will avow this to be good: but yet for all that there will be a great many found out which will affirm that herein only consisteth not man's good and happiness, but that he must have a sound and well disposed body, and a hundred more commodities, without the which it is not possible for man's life to be, much less to be happy and fortunate.

But if our position which we have set down unto you at the first be true (as true it is), that the end of every thing is his good, and his good is his end, and that these two are so reciprocable and convertible the one with the other, that the one cannot be without the other, then may we not justly say that health, or riches, are man's good, seeing that they are not his end which he regardeth. For he cannot possess or use them but to some other end. And so too, that the greatest part of his time, while he enjoys them, he cannot joy in them, but is with them unfortunate and unhappy: unless peradventure some man will say that they are happy which make their riches and health serve them (as they do full many in the world) to nourish their vices, and cherish them up in their wicked passions and affections.

But happily will some man say, they do serve as means and instruments disposed unto the attainment of this good, without which it is not possible that a man should get it, and therefore by a necessary consequent they are to be accounted necessary to the obtaining thereof, and therefore good. Truly it is a harsh and improper kind of speech to call that good which serves to the procurement and obtaining of that which is good; or that which is the subject and matter of good. For virtue, which we have proved before to be the true good, is of such a nature that she can make her benefit indifferently of things contrary in nature; she profits and helps her self as well by poverty as by riches, by sickness as by health. For we do as much commend him that can patiently endure his poverty, and constantly bear his griefs of disease, as we do him that liberally bestoweth his goods, and being in health, honestly laboureth in his vocation. So that if you will needs call riches good, because they serve to the obtaining and getting of virtue, why may you not as well call poverty by the same name, seeing that it serves to the self same use, and that more profitable also? Now to call things so contrary and repugnant as riches and poverty are by the same name hath not so much as any show or appearance of any truth. Wherefore, let all these things remain indifferent, as being made good or evil by the mind of man which knoweth how to use them rightly, which if he want, yet will he not want the means of attaining unto his end, which is to be fashioned and framed rightly according unto reason, and to make use and benefit of all things which shall happen whatsoever, and consequently to purchase his chief good and felicity.

If we will truly know wherein consisteth this good, let us consider within ourselves what that is which seeks it: for it must needs be the good of that part. Nothing seeks after that [good] which is another's, unless it be coupled and joined with his own. Now then there is no doubt but that the beginning and first motion of all our actions cometh from the understanding and will, and therefore the good which we seek after must needs be the perfection, rest and contentment of the same. But if we place riches and health in this account, and esteem them for things good, and by a consequent repute all things contrary unto them evil; what do we else but testify unto all men that there is no true felicity in this world, and that our minds are here held in perpetual torment? For a man must needs have death and grief continually before his eyes, both which are esteemed evils, and whereof one is oftentimes present with him, the other never ceaseth to threaten and menace him. If then they be things evil, the fear of them is just, and if he be always in fear, how can he be at any time happy? Let us therefore confess that either man hath no good ordained and prepared for him in this world which he may compass and attain unto, or else acknowledge that his good doth wholly and entirely consist in virtue. For it must needs be that the end of every thing should be proportionable unto the strength and nature of the thing itself: for otherwise, if the end were impossible to be achieved, instead of being man's good it would turn to be man's further torment. And so he should nothing but labour and travail in vain, as the daughters of Danaus[4] are said to do in hell, striving to fill certain bottomless vessels with water, which can hold no water at all.

Again, if there be no science nor art in the world, which hath not one end or other which they may come unto by keeping certain precepts and rules, shall we think that nature, the mother of Arts and Sciences, hath proposed unto man (which is her chief work) an end which it is impossible for him to come unto because it is out of his power? Will (as we say) is that which seeketh after our good: now a ruled and well governed will never coveteth (as indeed it ought not to do) but that which she may, and which it is in her power to procure. She busieth not herself about having of that which it is not in her power to have when she will; as health, riches, and honours. For if our good did consist and depend of them, we should not need to employ reason or will to the procurement of them, but we might as well compass them by prayers and wishes: for it is a thing which is subject unto a thousand casualties, which cannot be prevented or foreseen, as not being in our hands to dispose of them as we list, but subject unto the rule of Fortune, their good Lady and mistress. What show or probability of reason is there I pray you in this, that Nature should so create man, the perfection of all other creatures, that his good, which is his perfection, should depend not only upon other matters, but upon so many things that a man hath not hope to have them all favourable unto him; but that he should here beneath with Tantalus[5] lie miserably thirsting and crying after water.

Nay doubtless Nature doth offer you so much to the getting of this good as a mind well disposed and fit to use anything which shall be laid before it, and to pass over those things which do far pass his reach and capacity. Will you then rather choose to run unto Fortune, and wait at her deceitful hands for that good which you may give unto yourself if you will? For this is a divine and inviolable law, which hath been made since the beginning of the world, that if we will have any good, we must purchase and get it our selves, by our own labour and industry. For nature hath provided a rich storehouse of all good things, and inclosed it in our minds: let us then but stretch forth the hands of our will, and we shall take as much as we will. For if the will of man be well guided and ordered, it will turn all things to her good, as Midas turned all things that he touched into gold. There is no accident so grievous, which can befall a man either in body or riches, whence a man may not reap some rest and comfort of mind: so that if we can here rest content our selves, we have already found out our end. For though we should remit so much of the severity of this sect,[6] as to confess that the body or goods, which are but instruments of man's life, were a part of man's substance and might by their qualities alter the quality of the soul; yet may we not avouch this for good, that loss either in goods or body is unable to hinder the felicity and happiness of man, if his mind enjoy quiet rest and content.

In things which are compounded of many parts, the most noble part giveth both name and laws unto the rest, and they take their denomination from her: what doubt then can there be, but that man should be wholly happy, if his mind enjoyeth his happiness. And so we say that a Commonwealth is happy after a great victory, although there be many citizens lost, because the happiness thereof is measured by the person of the Prince, or else of the state, to the good and service of whom all the rest must be obedient. Hence is it that particular men do even glory in their wounds, do even brag and boast of them, if they have received them in the defence of either Prince or country. Shall we then assign unto the body any other motion or desire than that by which it referreth all things that come unto him, unto the joy and happiness of the mind? Shall we, I say, be so foolish as to link and knit the soul so fast unto the body that the good thereof should remain as a slave within his members, and so far forth depend on them that accordingly as the body should be well or ill disposed, the mind should be altered, and accounted either happy or unhappy? Truly, if so be that nature would have had man's happiness and perfection to have depended on his body, or consisted in his goods, she would have given unto all men like bodies and like measure and quantity of goods: for so she should not have been partial, but equal unto all, and so have passed from the general unto every particular of that kind. But on the contrary side, she having made all men of very diverse natures and conditions, both in respect of their bodies as also in regard of their goods, hath notwithstanding granted unto all men like power and ability of well using their bodies or riches of what sort soever they be, in such sort that the action of the mind may be as honourable and glorious in one sort as in another: yea, the excellency thereof doth appear and shine forth more gloriously and merit more praise then, when being destitute of means and instruments he cometh of himself unto his wished end. For so in my opinion we are to judge him to be the skilfuller pilot in a ship, which can in a great tempest, amidst the raging floods, guide an old sea-beaten ship full of holes, whose sails are rent and ropes broken, than he which can tell how to govern a new ship well rigged and furnished with all necessaries, having wind at will and seas favourable. Therefore we will here conclude this point thus: seeing that the happiness of man doth lie in procuring of his good, and that his good is to live according unto nature; and to live according unto nature, is not to be troubled with any passions or perturbations of the mind, but so to behave himself, happen what happen may, as that he do not exceed patience, or pass the bounds of reason; that if we will be truly happy, we must purge our minds of all manner of passions, and learn how to be affected in mind towards all things which shall happen.

Now there is nothing which can so soon set us in this way and learn us how to obtain the right course of ordering our affections, minds and wills according unto reason, as Wisdom, which is (in my simple opinion) both the beginning and end of all virtues. For causing us to have an exact and true knowledge of the condition and quality of things which come into our considerations and views, she teacheth and telleth us what is according unto nature, and what not, and likewise what is to be desired and followed, or shunned and avoided. She removes all false opinions out of our heads which trouble our brains, makes our affections kind and natural, and finally upon her wait all other virtues, as being their mother, nurse, and keeper. O how happy would man's life be, if it were always led and guided by her direction? But alas, as this virtue is most fair and excellent, so she is most rare and hard to be found: For she is so hidden in the bottom of our minds, as the veins of gold lie secret in the bowels of the earth, and are found but in few places. . . . we must go to school to Philosophy to know the right use of wisdom. And if we will hearken unto her, she will tell us, that wisdom hath two properties and uses, the one to prick us forward to that which is good, the other to pull us back from following that which is evil. Now because when we come unto Philosophy, we do not bring with us a mind pure and neat, but already distempered, evilly disposed, and possessed with filthy humours, and such as are incident unto the common sort of people; because, I say, we come unto her as unto a skilfull leech[7] or cunning physician: therefore if we will be cured, we must do as surgeons do which have to do with sores and wounds, who before they apply any medicine or salve to cure them do first draw out all the bad humours and dead flesh: and so must we also in like manner begin first of all to purge our minds of all such passions as do arise in them, and with the smoke of them darken and obscure the eye of reason: for otherwise precepts of manners and wholesome instructions would profit our souls as little as plenty of meat doth a corrupted body, which the more you feed the more you offend.

Now to know what these passions are, you must understand that we do term them a violent or vehement motion of the soul in the sensitive part, which is caused in the following or eschewing of that which seemeth to be either good or evil. For albeit there be but one soul in every one of us, which is the cause of life, and fountain of all our actions, and is all in all, and all in every part: yet there be many faculties in the soul, which it is strange to see how diverse, yea how contrary they be many times one towards another, according unto the diversity of instruments and vessels where it is kept, and variety of objects which are offered unto her. In one place she causeth vegetation,[8] in another motion, in another sense, in another desire or appetite, in another imagination, in another remembrance, in another reason and discourse: even as the Sun, which though he be all in his own essence, yet dividing and parting his beams in diverse places, he bringeth heat to one place, and light to another, softeneth wax and hardens clay, scattereth the clouds, and drieth up standing pools and lakes. And when the parts where the soul lieth inclosed do retain and use her but in a proportion of their capacities, and as far forth as it is necessary for their convenient use, then she bringeth forth gentle, sweet, and orderly effects: but contrariwise, if her parts do take more heat and motion then is requisite and convenient, you shall have clean contrary operations, and such as will prove very hurtful and prejudicial unto the soul. . . . Now it hath pleased nature to grant unto sense this power and strength which cometh from the soul, to apply itself unto things and extract their forms,[9] and afterwards either to choose or refuse them, as they shall best please or displease him, and agree or disagree with his nature. And this is done for two reasons: one because they should be instead of sentinels unto the body still watching and warding for his good: the other, which is a principal cause indeed, because they should be messengers and vant-couriers[10] from the sovereign and chiefest part of the soul, and also serve for ministers and instruments of bettering our discourse and reason. But as she hath allotted them this power and authority: so she doth most straitly will and command them to content themselves with their office, which is to call to mind things past, and thereupon to advise themselves what is best to be done: not presuming or daring to disquiet the higher and stronger faculties, or breed any further uproar or confusion. For so it falleth out many times in an army, that the watch, because they know not the purpose of the General whose direction they should follow, may be deceived and take the enemy coming unto them disguised for friends, and their friends which come in good will to succour and relieve them for enemies: and even so the senses, because they cannot throughly conceive and comprehend things appertaining unto reason, as being above their reach, are beguiled with show and appearance of things, and do oft time judge that for a friend unto us, which is our greatest adversary. And so while they presently rush forward without staying, or looking for any commandment from reason, they provoke and stir up that part of the soul where concupiscence and anger doth lodge, whereby springeth such a tumult and hurly burly in the mind, that reason during this fury cannot be heard, nor understanding obeyed, no more then laws or Magistrates are regarded in a state rent and torn with evil dissention. But in this trouble, the passions which do wax most mutinous and troublesome unto the quiet rest of the spirit, do first arise in the appetible or concupiscible part, that is to say, in that place where the soul doth exercise this faculty of desiring or rejecting things presented unto her, as being things proper or contrary unto her welfare and preservation. So then, their first moving and springing is upon a show and appearance or imagination of some good or evil. Now if it be of some present good which she doth already begin to possess, we call this motion by the name of pleasure: but if it be of some good to come, which is as yet far estranged from us, we call it desire: if it be of a present evil, the inconvenience and grief whereof we do already feel, being moved and incensed against another, we call it hatred or horror: and being moved within our selves, discontentedness, which if it happen upon occasion of anything which concerns us, we call it sorrow: if by reason of another man's evil, pity: if by occasion of an apparent good where we pretend a part, jealousy: if otherwise, envy. Again, to fall back unto the second part of our second general division: if it be of some after ensuing evil, it is rightly termed by the name of fear.

See here the first band of these seditious passions, which so much trouble the quiet rest of our soul, which are accompanied with most dangerous effects, and yet nothing like so dangerous as are those which follow after. For why? These first motions being bred and formed in that part, by means of the object which presents itself, do pass forth incontinently unto the irascible part of the mind, that is to say, to the place where the soul seeks all means possible of obtaining or avoiding that which seemeth unto her good or evil. And then, forthwith as a wheel which is already moved being to receive a fresh motion is carried about with greater swiftness: so the mind being moved with the first apprehension, having a second strength added unto the former, is whirled about with greater violence than before, and stirs up more strong and untameable passions, because they are doubled and coupled with the former, and so being joined together do stay and strengthen one another with mutual help and consent. For the first passions, which are formed from some imagined or seeming good, considering with themselves of the means how to obtain and acquire it, do stir up in us either hope or despair: but those affections which are made of the object of some seeming evil, do bring forth fear and anger: which four passions are wonderfully strong and violent, and do wholly overturn the frame of reason which they find already tottering.

Here behold and mark the four winds (as I verily suppose) from whence spring the cruel tempests of our souls. Their den from whence they come, is nothing else (as hath been already showed you) but a false imagination which we have that those things which are presented unto us are either good or evil. For by this means attributing that quality unto them, which indeed is not in them, we fly or follow after them with vehemence: and this is the very original and spring of these passions. Well then to stop this den, assure the rest of our souls, and provide that they be not otherwise moved then it is meet for them to be, let us call to mind that which was proved unto us in the very beginning and entrance into this discourse. To wit, that the good of a man, and the perfection of his nature, consisteth in the disposing and fashioning of his will to the right use of things according unto reason: and contrariwise, that his evil cometh from a disordered or unskilful using, or rather abusing of them. For by the first he shall reap much profit, receive much content and quietness, and chance what chance, nay he may set up his rest, and remain as stable and immoveable as a rock in the midst of the sea: by the second, every small thing that chanceth will trouble him and turn to his great grief and disadvantage. Now this disposition of our will lieth wholly in our power, and consequently our good and evil. Wherefore, if at any time there be presented unto us any object, to the end that we may not be troubled at all as with some good or evil which doth follow us, let us consider whether the thing which happeneth be in our power or no. If it be in our power well and good, it may be good or ill unto us. And yet in this case too, we must not be too passionately affected in any sort: for if we can but moderate and guide our wills aright, we shall make it good, and so continue it still. If it be out of our power, then it is neither good nor evil, and consequently we ought not to seek or provide it.

Now the things which are in our power are these; to approve, undertake, desire, and eschew a matter, and in a word, all our actions. For our will hath authority and power to rule and govern them according unto reason, till they come unto the place from whence our good and happiness must come. As, for example's sake, she is able to dispose our opinion, so that it yield not consent but to that which it is meet it should, and which shall be examined either by sense or reason, that she shall cleave fast unto things which are evidently true of themselves, and keep her self in suspense in things doubtful, and utterly reject things which are of themselves plainly untrue and false. Besides, she can so rule our desire, that it shall follow after nothing but that which is agreeable with nature, and eschew the contrary. The things which are out of our power are these; our riches, reputation, and briefly, that which doth no way depend of our wills: and here, if anything do happen, we may not say that it is contrary to our natures: because it happeneth either by the universal and continual order of things, and ordinary continuance of causes, and therefore should not seem strange unto us: or else cometh to pass by some particular providence so ordering it, and then we must know that nature hath made us subject thereunto. Furthermore, she hath given us a power and ability in the soul of well using and applying ourselves to all that which shall happen unto us from without; which showeth that she hath not made us fit and proper to one thing, but to every thing which shall come unto us whatsoever: in such sort that we may not desire or fly any such external thing which is not in our power, as well for that is a very foolish and vain affection to will that which it is not in our power to have, as also because that howsoever it happen, it may prove good unto us, and be the subject of many worthy and laudable actions. Now then if we can so command ourselves and our minds as not to desire or fly anything which is out of our powers, but with a sober and moderate affection receive and entertain it when it cometh, we shall be altogether exempted from all troubles and perturbations of the mind, we shall be free and happy, and never frustrated of our expectations, or hindered in our affairs and enterprises: we shall not need to hate any man, to complain of any man, to fear any man, or to be angry with any man: for no man shall be able to do us harm. On the other side, if we desire and labour to avoid that which is out of our powers, we shall oftentimes fall from our hopes and wished ends, and miss of our purposes, and light upon that which we so much abhor, we shall trouble ourselves, vex and torment ourselves, and all to no purpose or end in the world. . . .

Therefore when anything doth use to trouble us, let us consider two things: the one, the nature of that which hath chanced unto us: the other, the nature of that which is in us: and then let us learn to use everything according unto his nature, and so we shall be sure never to receive any loathing or discontentment at all. For discontent being a disease of the soul is contrary unto nature, and therefore we may not suffer it to take deep root within us. Now there is nothing that causeth more offence or discontentment than the newness or strangeness of a thing when it happeneth. And this appeareth most evidently in that the things which displease us most are made pleasant and sweet by custom and continuance. The galley slaves when they go to sea weep at first shipping, but after three or four months they sing as merrily as birds. So that you see custom is all: for they which have not been accustomed to the sea are afraid and look pale when they see them weigh anchors and launch forth into the sea, though it be in a calm: where contrarily the old and tried mariners laugh and are merry in a tempest. And look what good custom bringeth unto the common sort of people, the same meditation bringeth unto a Philosopher: for by often thinking and meditation upon things, he maketh them seem most familiar and ordinary unto him. Let us therefore exactly consider and ruminate with ourselves the nature of each thing that may molest and trouble us, and let us cast beforehand the worst that may happen; as sickness, poverty, banishment and injuries, and let us sift them narrowly to find out the nature of them, or else that which is most contrary unto their natures. It so falleth out that some of us are diseased in body: well, it is not we that are offended but our bodies; for the offence being taken, many times hindereth the excellency and perfection of the thing: whereas otherwise the disease may happen to be a great deal fitter subject and occasion to exercise our patience with praise and commendation than health: now where there is most occasion of praise, is there least good to be gotten?

As much as the mind is more to be accounted of than the body, so much the goods of the mind are more to be valued and esteemed of then the goods of the body. If then the body be the instrument of the mind, who will be so foolish as to complain, when he seeth the instrument applied unto that use for which it is ordained? A man's body is sick and diseased: no great marvel, for seeing it is a compound thing, therefore it is subject unto alteration. Yea sir, it is true, as you say: but yet for all that the grief of the disease is felt so violently that it makes us cry out in spite of our teeth. I grant indeed that it is felt, I must needs confess that, but it is felt only in body, and it makes us cry too and if we will be so foolish. Grief is not intolerable but unto them which think that it is so: for there be which can endure and suffer it when it is at the sharpest. Posidonius the philosopher[11] discoursing at large of certain matters in the presence of Pompey,[12] was sorely troubled with the gout, and when the disease pained him most, he said no more but this: Sir grief, you have attempted your worst against me, what remedy but patience: you think to make me curse and speak ill of you: no, no, far be it from me that ever I should say that you are evil: and so he went forward with his discourse, and made as if he had never felt it. Now I pray tell me and if you can, what new remedies had this Philosopher found out against this grief? What plasters and ointments had he stored up against the gout? Truly these two, the knowledge of things, and courage of mind. For he was thoroughly resolved, that the body was made to serve the soul, and that if so be the soul should be grieved for that which happened unto the body, that then it must of force be subject to the body. Now if it ought not to be troubled for that which happeneth unto the body, how much less ought she be grieved for the loss of goods? For the loss of a man's goods doth not touch a man so near as the want of his health. Indeed both of them are things merely without us, yet of the two the body is nearer unto us than goods. . . .

Do you know how to suffer loss of things so that it shall not trouble you? It is quickly learned, there is no more in it but this, not to accustom your self to love anything otherwise then it is, or better than it deserveth. If a man have an earthen vessel, let him love it as a vessel of earth, which may be broken, and so if it chance to be broken, the matter will never trouble him much. Let us pass from smaller things to greater things, from vile and baser things to things of greater value and more account, and let us do the like. If we love our children, let us love them as men, that is to say, as men subject unto infinite casualties of death, and then afterwards when they happen to die their deaths will be neither strange nor grievous unto us.

Indeed it is an imagination and opinion that vexeth and tormenteth us more then the things themselves, which is formed of those words which a man useth when he is surprised with such accidents: for we call one thing by the name of another, and imagine it to be like unto that other, and the image and idea thereof remaineth so in our minds. And therefore let us mollify and sweeten our words as well as we can: for if one of our children chance to die, say not I have lost one of my children: but this, I have restored one of my children to God, of whom I borrowed them. And likewise if we lose any other of our goods, let us use the like words. If a naughty fellow take away our goods from us, and it grieves us at the very heart, say no more but this: Was it not meet that God should have that again which he had lent me for a time? For the rest, remember your own opinion of the like mishaps when they did happen unto others, and consider with your self how then you were not much moved, but rather how you did blame them, and neglect their frivolous and vain complaints. Suppose that the judgement which you give of them is a prejudice against yourself which cannot be avoided. For our judgements in another man's behalf are always more just and favourable than in a man's own cause. If a servant of your neighbour's chance to break a glass, you say, there is no great harm done, it was but a glass broken. If his son die, you say, he was of estate mortal, not born to live ever: and I pray why can you not say as much when your own son dieth, without crying out, tormenting your self, or accusing God and men for the loss of that which is so ordinary? . . .

O that we could be once fully persuaded in this point not to fear death, good God how happy should we then be? For in this one thing more than in any other, opinion taketh occasion to band herself against reason, that so she might terrify us by wearing the ugly vizar of death. And albeit there be but one death in all the world, yet she painteth him forth unto us after an infinite kind of fashions. Believe me there is nothing in death which is to be feared: But here is the mischief, she sendeth forth certain fearful and cowardly spies abroad, to spy what is done, which report not the truth what they have seen, but what they have heard men say, and which they themselves fear is likely for to happen. Indeed we trust too much unto the sayings of the vulgar sort of people, which are most inconsiderate, affirming it to be a great evil, and yield no credit unto Philosophy, which teacheth us that it is the haven of man's life. If Socrates be to be believed, death is not to be feared. If Cato[13] have any credit with us, he will persuade us to run and meet her coming unto us. . . .

Let us therefore accustom ourselves to forgive all the whole world. Let not the greatness or grievousness of the injury withhold us from pardoning them: but on the contrary side let us think that the greater the injury is the better it deserveth to be pardoned, and that the more just our revenge is, the more our gentleness is to be praised. But especially such as are seated by fortune in the highest degree of honour, should take heed to their motions that they be remiss and temperate: for as their actions are of greater importance, so their faults are harder to be cured. The heaven itself presenteth them daily with an example and doctrine of avoiding all manner of haste and precipitation, in shewing them that Saturn the very highest of all the planets is most remiss and slowest in his course. And astronomers say that Jupiter alone by himself is able to shoot forth profitable and pleasing lightnings and good auguries; but when there is a question or sending forth hurtful and revenging storms and lightnings, then he cannot do this of his own authority, but is to crave the counsel and assistance of twelve other gods. And is it not a very strange case, that he that is the greatest of all the gods, that can do good unto all the whole world, is not able to hurt one person, but after a solemn counsel and delibera-tion? So that Jupiter himself, though that he be very wise, yet is he afraid lest he should overshoot himself in a matter of revenge, and therefore thinketh he had need of good counsel to advise him. Wherefore if at any time we happen to have feeling of this passion within us, let us repair unto our friends, and ripen our cholers with their pleasant discourses. For take the best man that is in the world when he is moved, and you shall see whether he be able to do anything as he ought to do. For reason being hindered with passions, stands a man in as much stead as wings do birds when they are caught with lime-twigs fast by the feet. And this is the reason why we should study to lift up our hearts from the earth, and place them in a quiet and peaceable estate, if we desire to make our souls capable of all good and virtuous actions. We must never leave til we have brought our minds to be of such a disposition, as the highest region of the air is, which is never darkened with clouds, nor shaken with thunderbolts, but enjoyeth a continual fairness: for so the mind should never be darkened with sorrow, nor moved with choler. And if once a man could bring his mind unto this pass, he should very easily rule his other actions, and bring them unto their wished end: for then doubtless he would follow nature hard by the heels, tread altogether in her steps, and join himself by a pleasant and temperate affection unto those other parts of the world, of which man is the knot, the marriage knot which linketh heavenly and earthly things together.

The effects of this soft and temperate affection which man beareth towards other things of the world, are called duties,[14] as if they did shew us our duties[15] and behaviours towards other things. Therefore if we would learn to rule and moderate this duty, and to be informed in the right use thereof, we cannot have a better mistress then Nature to teach and inform us. For she hath established an order and disposition in everything, by virtue whereof she committeth things one under another, and yet chaineth them altogether with the links of mutual respect which they owe one to another, which she hath engraven in the forehead of each thing, as Princes stamp their images in their coin, to show that they are good and lawful money. Let us therefore in every thing consider the order and course of nature, and we shall straightways know the value of it, whether it be current or no, and how much will be given for it. Good being the object of man's will, where perfect and true good is to be found, there our will ought to be moved.

This being granted, it must needs follow that the strongest and chiefest affection of man ought to be accounted that which joineth us together with the author and fountain of all good, to wit, godliness: for by it a man is reunited and substantially engrafted in his first cause, as being the root which keepeth him (as long as he abideth and dwelleth in it) in his full perfection: but contrarily, being separated from it withereth and drieth away incontinently. Now the principal effect of piety is to teach us how to know God: For the honour and respect which we bear unto anything proceedeth from the true knowledge of it. Therefore first of all we must believe that there is a God: secondly, that he hath created the world by his mighty power, bounty and wisdom, and by them governeth it: then, that his providence watcheth over all things, yea the smallest things in the world. Again, that whatsoever he sendeth unto us is for our good and that our evil cometh not but from our selves. For if we esteem those chances evil which God sendeth unto us, we shall oftentimes take occasion to blaspheme him; because that naturally we honour them which seek our good, and hate them which procure us any evil. And therefore we must resolve with our selves to be obedient unto him, and take in good part whatsoever cometh from his hands. And seeing that his knowledge is most perfect, his power thrice infinite, and his will most loving and charitable: what resteth then, but that we should conclude that God sendeth nothing unto us, but tendeth to our great good? and albeit we for our parts cannot conceive the good which we ought to receive of that which he sendeth us; yet nevertheless we hope all is for the best: supposing, that as the physician doth oftentimes many things for the safety of the body, which may seem at the beginning to hurt it: so God in the guiding of our lives doth save us by means which may seem grievous and hurtful.

The physician diverse times pricketh the eye to recover a man's sight: and oftentime God almighty useth to prick and wound our hearts with sharp afflictions to restore our minds unto their brightness. Under the seal of this assurance we ought to commit and submit ourselves unto him, confessing that we come into the world not to command, but to obey, finding laws already made which we ought to follow. . . .

Editor's Notes

1. That is, even though the sparklings are weak and feeble.
2. More accurately, "to be and to act according to nature" – the fundamental Stoic principle.
3. *Convenable,* that is, suitable.
4. In Greek mythology, Danaus ordered his fifty daughters to slay the husbands to whom he had been forced to give them. All but one obeyed him, and for punishment they were condemned to try to fill with water a jar with holes in the bottom.
5. Tantalus, a Greek mythological figure, was punished by the gods by being left beside a pool that receded whenever he tried to drink from it.
6. That is, of the Stoics.
7. One who lets blood.
8. That is, simple bodily growth.
9. Du Vair assumed that sense perception is explained by saying that perceptible forms enter the senses, thereby conveying information about the things whose forms they are.
10. Advance runners.
11. Lived around 135–151 B.C.E., head of the Stoic school in Rhodes.
12. Roman general, 106–48 B.C.E.
13. Roman soldier and official, 234–149 B.C.E., taken as a model of the Stoic sage.
14. Du Vair used the term *offices.*
15. Here Du Vair used *le devoir.*

Further Reading

Aside from Rudolf Kirk's helpful introduction to his edition of *The Moral Philosophie of the Stoicks,* there is not much to recommend to the reader anxious to know more about Du Vair. He is discussed in some histories of French literature but is lucky to get even a mention in historics of philosophy.

Hiram Haydn, *The Counter-Renaissance* (New York: Harcourt Brace & World, 1950), talks about neo-Stoicism in various passages and often mentions Du Vair. The reader wishing to know more about neo-Stoicism will also want to consult Rudolf Kirk's edition of Justus Lipsius, *Two Bookes of Constancie* (New Brunswick, N.J.: Rutgers University Press, 1939). Lipsius is also the focus of an important study of the political significance of neo-Stoicism in early modern Europe by Gerhard Oestreich, *Neostoicism and the Early Modern State* (Cambridge, England: Cambridge University Press, 1982).

René Descartes

Introduction

Descartes was born in 1596. He attended the Jesuit school at La Fleche from 1606 to 1614 and then obtained a law degree at Poitiers. While spending some time learning military skills and traveling, Descartes began to work on mathematics and physics, and on the night of November 10, 1619, he had three dreams that he took as indications that he should devote his life to developing some of the new ideas about science that he had been considering. During the next few years Descartes traveled and spent time in Paris, in contact with many of the leading scientists and other thinkers of the time.

In 1628 Descartes moved to Holland, where he lived for most of the rest of his life. He was upset enough by the condemnation of Galileo in 1633 to drop his plan for publishing a scientific treatise he had written. It thus was not until 1637 that he published his first book, *Discourse on Method,* which was accompanied by three scientific essays illustrating how successfully the method he advocated could be used. In 1641 he published his *Meditations on First Philosophy,* which also contained six sets of objections to Descartes's views, by some philosophers and theologians to whom the *Meditations* had been sent in manuscript, and his own replies. A systematic exposition of his views, the *Principles of Philosophy* appeared in 1644. In 1649 Descartes went to Sweden at the invitation of Queen Christina, with whom he had corresponded and who wanted him to teach her philosophy. Shortly after he arrived he published his psychology, the *Passions of the Soul.* Then, during the winter, he caught pneumonia, from which he died in 1650.

Descartes's views were extremely controversial, and his efforts to placate the established educational and religious powers did not succeed. In 1663 his works were put on the Roman Catholic index of prohibited books; but whatever the orthodox thought of him, his philosophy captured educated Europe. Descartes offered a comprehensive alternative to the then-dominant Aristotelian understanding of the world. Moreover, he submitted examples to show in detail how his program worked. As he was a master of the new science (including its mathematics, to which he made major contributions), he could integrate what we now distinguish as his specifically philosophical theory with the work of Galileo, Harvey, and other discoverers of the time, to produce a synthesis more convincing than anything hitherto available. It was not until Isaac Newton produced an alternative that the hold of Cartesian physics was broken.

The Cartesian system had some omissions. Most notably, perhaps, Descartes did not develop the hints he dropped here and there about morality. Why not? In a letter dated November 20, 1647, to Chanut, the French ambassador to Sweden, Descartes stated:

It is true that I am accustomed to refuse to write down my thoughts concerning morality, and that for two reasons: first, that there is no subject from which malicious people can more easily draw pretexts for slandering one; second, that I believe it is proper only for sovereigns, or for those who are authorized by them, to busy themselves with regulating the morals [*les moeurs*] of others.

In Part Six of the *Discourse* Descartes again noted the role of authority in establishing morality: "As regards conduct," he observed,

everyone is so full of his own wisdom that we might find as many reformers as heads if permission to institute change in these matters were granted to anyone other than those whom God has set up as sovereigns over his people or those on whom he has bestowed sufficient grace and zeal to be prophets.

Descartes here seems to be thinking of morality as centering on laws that must come either from God through his prophets or from secular authority, thus leaving no room for private reflection on it. In other places Descartes made quite different suggestions. Morality, he wrote, is part of the tree of knowledge. Along with medicine and mechanics, it is one of the fruit-bearing twigs that grow on a trunk firmly rooted in the first principles of metaphysical truth, which Descartes had established. These principles give rise to or warrant our knowledge of the physical world, and in due time they will enable us to explain both human psychology and the mechanisms of the human body. If this much of the tree is independent of religious or political authority, why should not moral knowledge be so as well?

It all depends on what moral knowledge is. When Descartes reached that issue, he did not tell us that we must know the rules or laws that we are commanded to obey. Instead, he discussed the sovereign good. Does wisdom constitute the supreme good, and is it composed of the knowledge of physics and the other sciences? At one point Descartes suggested that this was so, but at his most explicit, in his letters, he took a different approach. He mentioned contentment, happiness, and the satisfaction of desire, which come, he asserted, from attaining the perfections of body and soul. Reason can tell us what the perfections are, and we can then pursue what will bring us the greatest perfection, and with it the greatest pleasure – at least if we control the passions that make us distort the values of things.

Descartes did not explain what he meant by the perfections of body and soul. Not, surely, what the Aristotelians meant: he rejected the natural teleology on which their notions of perfection rested. But he offered no alternative account, nor did he tell his correspondents how his emphasis on personal virtue as being what makes its possessor happy fits in with the morality that God or the sovereign imposes on us. He thus left a problem for later philosophers who wanted to understand – more fully than Descartes cared to – the place of morality in the new world picture he had done so much to create.

Descartes left another problem as well, or rather he gave an old problem new life. In letters and in published work he let it be known, without going into much detail, that he accepted a voluntarist view of the principles that underlie knowledge and morality. They are as they are, he confirmed, because God willed them to be so, and he could have willed them to be otherwise. This reversion to voluntarism (see the section "Luther and Calvin" in the Introduction to this anthology) caused his contemporaries – as it causes his present commentators – no end of headache. For recent commentators, the problem is one of interpreting Descartes on the status of logic and mathematics. For his contemporaries, it raised serious issues about religion and morality. Many Catholics regarded voluntarism as a specifically Protestant view, and to thinkers of both confessions

Hobbesianism was its ultimate implication. But Descartes himself did not discuss the bearing of his voluntarist view on his moral outlook.

On Cartesian principles a provable morality and a science of medicine can someday be obtained. Descartes allowed that he could not produce either of them. In his *Discourse,* however, he told us what code he proposed to live by until the true morality is proved. In other places as well, particularly in *The Passions of the Soul,* we can catch glimpses of Descartes's own moral outlook, which is often described as Stoic or neo-Stoic. Change oneself rather than the world; control one's passions by means of virtue; do not be upset by what is beyond one's control – all this, indeed, sounds rather Stoic. But other passages sound less so. For instance, as Descartes pointed out in Part Six of the *Discourse,* through his philosophy we can attain sufficient knowledge of the physical world to make ourselves "lords and masters of nature." We shall be able to invent innumerable devices to make life more convenient and enjoyable, and when medicine is perfected we shall be able to use it even to improve the condition of our minds, as bodily health greatly affects the mind. These are hardly Stoic sentiments, and passages in his letters defending the enjoyment of life also sound somewhat less than Stoic. The reader will need, therefore, to consider whether Descartes was simply wavering at these points or whether a deeper outlook unified all his attitudes.

The following selections are from three sources. The first is from the *Discourse on Method,* in John Cottingham, Robert Stoothof, and Dugald Murdoch, trans., *The Philosophical Writings of Descartes,* vol. 1 (Cambridge, England: Cambridge University Press, 1985). The third is from the "Replies" to the Sixth Set of Objections, in the second volume of the same translation. Both are reprinted by permission of the Cambridge University Press. The second set of excerpts is from Anthony Kenny, trans., *Descartes: Philosophical Letters* (Oxford: Clarendon Press, 1970), reprinted by permission of Anthony Kenny.

Discourse on Method

Part Three

Now, before starting to rebuild your house, it is not enough simply to pull it down, to make provision for materials and architects (or else train yourself in architecture), and to have carefully drawn up the plans; you must also provide yourself with some other place where you can live comfortably while building is in progress. Likewise, lest I should remain indecisive in my actions while reason obliged me to be so in my judgements, and in order to live as happily as I could during this time, I formed for myself a provisional moral code consisting of just three or four maxims, which I should like to tell you about.

The first was to obey the laws and customs of my country, holding constantly to the religion in which by God's grace I had been instructed from my childhood, and governing myself in all other matters according to the most moderate and least extreme opinions – the opinions commonly accepted in practice by the most sensible of those with whom I should have to live. For I had begun at this time to count my own opinions as worthless, because I wished to submit them all to examination, and so I was sure I could do no better than follow those of the most sensible men. And although there may be men as sensible among the Persians or Chinese as among ourselves, I thought it would be most useful for me to be guided by those with whom I should have to live. I thought too that in order to discover what opinions they really held I had to attend to what they did rather than what they said. For with our declining standards of behaviour, few people are willing to say everything that they believe; and besides, many people do not know what they believe, since believing something and knowing that one believes it are different acts of thinking, and the one often occurs without the other. Where many opinions were equally well accepted, I chose only the most moderate, both because these are always the easiest to act upon and probably the best (excess being usually bad), and also so that if I made a mistake, I should depart less from the right path than I would if I chose one extreme when I ought to have pursued the other. In particular, I counted as excessive all promises by which we give up some of our freedom. It was not that I disapproved of laws which remedy the inconstancy of weak minds by allowing us to make vows or contracts that oblige perseverance in some worthy project (or even, for the security of commerce, in some indifferent one). But I saw nothing in the world which remained always in the same state, and for my part I was determined to make my judgements more and more perfect, rather than worse. For these reasons I thought I would be sinning against good sense if I were to take my previous approval of something as obliging me to regard it as good later on, when it had perhaps ceased to be good or I no longer regarded it as such.

My second maxim was to be as firm and decisive in my actions as I could, and to follow even the most doubtful opinions, once I had adopted them, with no less constancy than if they had been quite certain. In this respect I would be imitating a traveller who, upon finding himself lost in a forest, should not wander about turning this way and that, and still less stay in one place, but should keep walking as straight as he can in one direction, never changing it for slight reasons even if mere chance made him choose it in the first place; for in this way, even if he does not go exactly where he wishes, he will at least end up in a place where he is likely to be better off than in the middle of a forest. Similarly, since in everyday life we must often act without delay, it is a most certain truth that when it is not in our power to discern the truest opinions, we must follow the most probable. Even when no opinions appear more probable than any others, we must still adopt some; and having done so we must then regard them not as doubtful, from a practical point of view, but as most true and certain, on the grounds that the reason which made us adopt them is itself true and certain. By following this maxim I could free myself from all the regrets and remorse which usually trouble the consciences of those weak and faltering spirits who allow themselves to set out on some supposedly good course of action which later, in their inconstancy, they judge to be bad.

My third maxim was to try always to master myself rather than fortune, and change my desires rather than the order of the world. In general I would become accustomed to believing that nothing lies entirely within our power except our thoughts, so that after doing our best in dealing with matters external to us, whatever we fail to achieve is absolutely impossible so far as we are concerned. This alone, I thought, would be sufficient to prevent me from desiring in future something I could not get, and so to make me content. For our will naturally tends to desire only what our intellect represents to it as somehow possible; and so it is certain that if we consider all external goods as equally beyond our power, we shall not regret the absence of goods which seem to be our birthright when we are deprived of them through no fault of our own, any more than we regret not possessing the kingdom of China or of Mexico. Making a virtue of necessity, as they say, we shall not desire to be healthy when ill or free when imprisoned, any more than we now desire to have bodies of a material as indestructible as diamond or wings to fly like the birds. But I admit that it takes long practice and repeated meditation to become accustomed to seeing everything in this light. In this, I believe, lay the secret of those philosophers who in earlier times were able to escape from the dominion of fortune and, despite suffering and poverty, rival their gods in happiness. Through constant reflection upon the limits prescribed for them by nature, they became perfectly convinced that nothing was in their power but their thoughts, and this alone was sufficient to prevent them from being attracted to other things. Their mastery over their thoughts was so absolute that they had reason to count themselves richer, more powerful, freer and happier than other men who, because they lack this philosophy, never achieve such mastery over all their desires, however favoured by nature and fortune they may be.[1]

Finally, to conclude this moral code, I decided to review the various occupations which men have in this life, in order to try to choose the best. Without wishing to say anything about the occupations of others, I thought I could do no better than to continue with the very one I was engaged in, and devote my whole life to cultivating my reason and advancing as far as I could in the knowledge of the truth, following the method I had prescribed for myself. Since beginning to use this method I had felt such extreme contentment that I did not think one could enjoy any sweeter or purer one in this life. Every day I discovered by its means truths which, it seemed to me, were quite important and were generally unknown by other men; and the satisfaction they gave me so filled my mind that nothing else mattered to me. Besides, the sole basis of the foregoing three maxims was the plan I had to continue my self-instruction. For since God has given each of us a light to distinguish truth from falsehood, I should not have thought myself obliged to rest content with the opinions of others for a single moment if I had not intended in due course to examine them using my own judgement; and I could not have avoided having scruples about following these opinions, if I had not hoped to lose no opportunity to discover better ones, in case there were any. Lastly, I could not have limited my desires, or been happy, had I not been following a path by which I thought I was sure to acquire all the knowledge of which I was capable, and in this way all the true goods within my reach. For since our will tends to pursue or avoid only what our intellect represents as good or bad, we need only to judge well in order to act well, and to judge as well as we can in order to do our best – that is to say, in order to acquire all the virtues and in general all the other goods we can acquire. And when we are certain of this, we cannot fail to be happy.

Once I had established these maxims and set them on one side together with the truths of faith, which have always been foremost among my beliefs, I judged that I could freely undertake to rid myself of all the rest of my opinions.[2] . . .

Principles of Philosophy

PREFACE TO THE FRENCH EDITION

Author's Letter to the Translator of the Book Which May Here Serve as a Preface

First of all, I would have wished to explain what philosophy is, beginning with the most commonplace points. For example, the word "philosophy" means the study of wisdom, and by "wisdom" is meant not only prudence in our everyday affairs but also a perfect knowledge of all things that mankind is capable of knowing, both for the conduct of life and for the preservation of health and the discovery of all manner of skills. In order for this kind of knowledge to be perfect it must be deduced from first causes; thus, in order to set about acquiring it – and it is this activity to which the term "to philosophize" strictly refers – we must start with the search for first causes or principles. These principles must satisfy two conditions. First, they must be so clear and so evident that the human mind cannot doubt their truth when it attentively concentrates on them; and, secondly, the knowledge of other things must depend on them, in the sense that the principles must be capable of being known without knowledge of these other matters, but not *vice versa*. Next, in deducing from these principles the knowledge of things which depend on them, we must try to ensure that everything in the entire chain of deductions which we draw is very manifest. In truth it is only God who is perfectly wise, that is to say, who possesses complete knowledge of the truth of all things; but men can be said to possess more or less wisdom depending on how much knowledge they possess of the most important truths. I think that everything I have just said would be accepted by all people of learning.

Next, I would have looked at the benefits of this philosophy and shown that it encompasses everything which the human mind is capable of knowing. Thus we should consider that it is this philosophy alone which distinguishes us from the most savage and barbarous peoples, and that a nation's civilization and refinement depends on the superiority of the philosophy which is practised there. Hence the greatest good that a state can enjoy is to possess true philosophers. As for the individual, it is not only beneficial to live with those who apply themselves to this study; it is incomparably better to undertake it oneself. For by the same token it is undoubtedly much better to use one's own eyes to get about, and also to enjoy the beauty of colours and light, than to close one's eyes and be led around by someone else. Yet even the latter is much better than keeping one's eyes closed and having no guide but oneself. Living without philosophizing is exactly like having one's eyes closed without ever trying to open them; and the pleasure of seeing everything which our sight reveals is in no way comparable to the satisfaction accorded by knowledge of the things which philosophy enables us to discover. Lastly, the study of philosophy is more necessary for the regulation of our morals and our conduct in this life than is the use of our eyes to guide our steps. The brute beasts, who have only their bodies to preserve, are continually occupied in looking for food to nourish them; but human beings, whose most important part is the mind, should devote their main efforts to the search for wisdom, which is the true food of the mind. And I am sure that there are many people who would not fail to make the search if they had some hope of success and knew how much they were capable of. No soul, however base, is so strongly attached to the objects of the senses that it does not sometimes turn aside and desire some other, greater good, even though it may often not know what this good consists in. Those who are most favoured by fortune and possess health, honour and riches in abundance are no more exempt from this desire than anyone else. On the contrary, I am convinced that it is just such people who long most ardently for another good – a higher good than all those that they already possess. Now this supreme good, considered by natural reason without the light of faith, is nothing other than the knowledge of the truth through its first causes, that is to say wisdom, of which philosophy is the study. Since all these points are absolutely true, they would easily carry conviction if they were properly argued.

What prevents these points being accepted is the widespread experience that those who profess to be philosophers are often less wise and less reasonable than those who have never applied themselves to philosophy. And so at this point I would have explained briefly what all the knowledge which we now possess consists in and the levels of wisdom that have so far been attained. The first level contains only notions which are so clear in themselves that they can be acquired without meditation. The second comprises everything we are acquainted with through sensory experience. The third comprises what we learn by conversing with other people. And one may add a fourth category, namely what is learned by reading books – not all books, but those which have been written by people who are capable of instructing as well; for in such cases we hold a kind of conversation with the authors. I think that all the wisdom which is generally possessed is acquired in these four ways. I am not including divine revelation in the list, because it does not lead us on by degrees but raises us at a stroke to infallible faith. Now in all ages there have been great men who have tried to find a fifth way of reaching wisdom – a way which is incomparably more elevated and more sure than the other four. This consists in the search for the first causes and the true principles which enable us to deduce the reasons for everything we are capable of knowing; and it is above all those who have laboured to this end who have been called philosophers. I am not sure, however, that there has been anyone up till now who has succeeded in this project. . . .

After fully explaining these matters, I would have wanted next to put down the reasons which serve to prove that the true principles, enabling one to reach the highest degree of wisdom which constitutes the supreme good of human life, are the principles which I have set down in this book. Just two reasons are enough to prove the point: the first is that the principles are very clear, and the second is that they enable all other things to be deduced from them. These are the only two conditions that such principles must meet. Now I can easily prove that the principles are very clear. This is shown by the way in which I discovered them, namely by rejecting everything in which I could discover the least occasion for doubt; for it is certain that principles which it was impossible to reject in this way, when one attentively considered them, are the clearest and most evident that the human mind can know. Thus I considered that someone who wishes to doubt everything cannot, for all that, doubt that he exists while he is doubting; and that what reasons in this way, being unable to doubt itself while doubting everything else, is not what we call our body but what we call our soul or our thought. Accordingly I took the being or existence of this thought as my first principle, and from it I deduced very clearly the following principles. There is a God who is the author of everything there is in the world; further, since he is the source of all truth, he certainly did not create in us an understanding of the kind which would be capable of making a mistake in its judgements concerning the things of which it possesses a very clear and very distinct perception. These are all the principles that I make use of with regard to immaterial or metaphysical things, and from them I deduce very clearly the principles of corporeal or physical things, namely that there are bodies which are extended in length, breadth and depth, and which have various shapes and move in various ways. Here, in total, are all the principles which I use to deduce the truth of other things. The other reason which proves the clarity of these principles is that they have been known for all time and indeed accepted as true and indubitable by everyone, with the sole exception of the existence of God, which some people have called into doubt because they have attributed too much to sensory perceptions, and God cannot be seen or touched. Yet although all the truths which I include among my principles have been known for all time by everyone, there has, so far as I know, been no one up till now who has recognized them as the principles of philosophy, that is to say, as the principles which enable us to deduce the knowledge of all the other things to be found in the world. This is why it remains for me here to prove that they do indeed qualify as principles of this sort; and I think that the best way of doing this is to get people to see by experience that this is so, that is to say, to invite my readers to read this book. Admittedly, I have not dealt with all things, for this would be impossible. But I think I have explained all the things I have had occasion to deal with in such a way that those who read the book attentively will be convinced that in order to arrive at the highest knowledge of which the human mind is capable there is no need to look for any principles other than those I have provided. . . .

Following on from this, in order to get people to see the purpose I had in publishing my work, I would wish to explain here the order which I think we should follow when we aim to instruct ourselves. First of all, a man who still possesses only the ordinary and imperfect knowledge that can be acquired in the four ways explained above should try before anything else to devise for himself a code of morals which is sufficient to regulate the actions of his life. For this is something which permits no delay, since we should endeavour above all else to live well. After that, he should study logic. I do not mean the logic of the Schools, for this is strictly speaking nothing but a dialectic which teaches ways of expounding to others what one already knows or even of holding forth without judgement about things one does not know. Such logic corrupts good sense rather than increasing it. I mean instead the kind of logic which teaches us to direct our reason with a view to discovering the truths of which we are ignorant. Since this depends to a great extent on practice, it is good for the student to work for a long time at practising the rules on very easy and simple questions like those of mathematics. Then, when he has acquired some skill in finding the truth on these questions, he should begin to tackle true philosophy in earnest. The first part of philosophy is metaphysics, which contains the principles of knowledge, including the explanation of the principal attributes of God, the non-material nature of our souls and all the clear and distinct notions which are in us. The second part is physics, where, after discovering the true principles of material things, we examine the general composition of the entire universe and then, in particular, the nature of this earth and all the bodies which are most commonly found upon it, such as air, water, fire, magnetic ore and other minerals. Next we need to examine individually the nature of plants, of animals and, above all, of man, so that we may be capable later on of discovering the other sciences which are beneficial to man. Thus the whole of philosophy is like a tree. The roots are metaphysics, the trunk is physics, and the branches emerging from the trunk are all the other sciences, which may be reduced to three principal ones, namely medicine, mechanics and morals. By "morals" I understand the highest and most perfect moral system, which presupposes a complete knowledge of the other sciences and is the ultimate level of wisdom.

Now just as it is not the roots or the trunk of a tree from which one gathers the fruit, but only the ends of the branches, so the principal benefit of philosophy depends on those parts of it which can only be learnt last of all. I am ignorant of almost all of these. . . .

Correspondence with Princess Elizabeth and Queen Christina

DESCARTES TO ELIZABETH, 4 AUGUST 1645[3]

Madame,

When I chose Seneca's *de vita beata*[4] to suggest to your Highness as an agreeable topic of discussion, I took account only of the reputation of the author and the importance of his topic, without thinking of his manner of treating it. I have since given some thought to this and find it not sufficiently accurate to deserve to be followed. To assist your Highness to make a judgement on the topic, I will try to explain how I think the topic should have been treated by such a philosopher, unenlightened by faith, with only natural reason to guide him.

At the beginning he says very well that all men want to live happily (*vivere beate*), but not all see clearly what makes a life happy. But first we must know what *vivere beate* means; I would translate it into French *vivre heureusement,* if there were not a difference between *heur*[5] and *beatitude*. The former depends only on outward things: a man is thought more fortunate (*heureux*) than wise if some good happens to him without his own effort; but happiness (*beatitude*) consists, it seems to me, in a perfect contentment of mind and inner satisfaction, which is not commonly possessed by those who are most favoured by fortune, and which is acquired by the wise without fortune's favour. So *vivere beate,* to live happily, is to have a perfectly content and satisfied mind.

Next we must consider what makes a life happy, i.e. what are the things which can give us this supreme contentment. Such things, I observe, can be divided into two classes: those which depend on us, like virtue and wisdom, and those which do not, like honours, riches, and health. For it is certain that a man of good birth who is not ill, and who lacks nothing can enjoy a more perfect contentment than another who is poor, unhealthy and deformed provided that the two are equally wise and virtuous. None the less a small vessel may be just as full as a large one, although it contains less liquid; and similarly if we regard each man's contentment as the full satisfaction of all his reasonable desires, I do not doubt that the poorest man, least blest by nature and fortune, can be entirely content and satisfied just as much as every one else, although he does not enjoy as many good things. It is only this sort of contentment which is here in question; to seek the other sort would be a waste of time, since it is not in our own power.

It seems to me that every man can make himself content without any external assistance, provided that he respects three conditions, which are related to the three rules of morality which I put in the *Discourse on Method.*[6]

The first is always to employ his mind as well as he can to discover what he should or should not do in all the circumstances of life.

The second is to have a firm and constant resolution to carry out whatever reason recommends without being diverted by passion or appetite. Virtue, I believe, consists precisely in firmness in this resolution; though I do not know that anyone has ever so described it. Instead, they have divided it into different species to which they have given various names, because of the various objects to which it applies.

The third is to bear in mind that while one thus guides oneself, as far as one can, by reason, all the good things which one does not possess are all equally outside one's power. In this way one will accustom oneself not to desire them. Nothing can impede our contentment except desire, regret, and repentance; but if we always do what reason tells us, even if events show us afterwards that we were mistaken, we will never have any grounds for repentance, because it was not our own fault. We do not desire to have more arms or more tongues than we have, and yet we do desire to have more health or more riches. The reason is simply that we imagine that the latter, unlike the former, can be acquired by our exertions, or are due to our nature. We can rid ourselves of that opinion by bearing in mind that since we have always followed the advice of our reason, we have left undone nothing that was in our power; and that sickness and misfortune are no less natural to man than prosperity and health.

Of course not every kind of desire is incompatible with happiness: only those which are accompanied with impatience and sadness. It is also not necessary that our reason should be free from error; it is sufficient if our conscience testifies that we have never lacked resolution and virtue to carry out whatever we judge the best course. So virtue by itself is sufficient to make us happy in this life. But virtue unenlightened by intellect can be false: that is to say, the will and resolution to do well can carry us to evil courses, if we think them good; and in such a case the contentment which virtue brings is not solid. Moreover, such virtue is commonly set in opposition to pleasure, appetite and passion, and is accordingly very difficult to practise. The right use of reason on the other hand, by giving a true knowledge of good, prevents virtue from being false; by accommodating it to licit pleasures makes it easy to practise; and by making us realize the condition of our nature sets bounds to our desires. So we must conclude that the greatest felicity of man depends on the right use of reason; and consequently the study which leads to its acquisition is the most useful occupation one can take up. Certainly it is the most agreeable and delightful.

After this, it seems to me, Seneca should have taught us all the principal truths whose knowledge is necessary to facilitate the practice of virtue and to regulate our desires and passions, and thus to enjoy natural happiness. That would have made his book the finest and most useful that a pagan philosopher could have written. . . .

Descartes to Elizabeth, 1 September 1645

Madame,

When last I wrote I was uncertain whether your Highness was at the Hague or at Rhenen, so I addressed my letter via Leyden; and the one you condescended to write me was only delivered to me after the departure of the messenger who had brought it to Alkmaar. So I have been unable to tell you earlier how proud I am that my judgement of the book you read is no different from yours, and that my manner of reasoning seems natural to you. I am sure that if you had had as much leisure as I have had to think about these topics, I could not write anything which you would not have observed better than I;

but because your Highness' age, birth, and business have not permitted this, perhaps what I write can save you time.

Even my faults will give you opportunities for observing the truth. For instance, I spoke of a happiness which depends entirely on our free will, which all men can acquire without assistance from without. You observe very truly that there are diseases which take away the power of reasoning and with it the power of enjoying the satisfaction proper to a rational mind. This shows me that what I said about all men without exception applies only to those who have the free use of their reason, and in addition know the way to reach such happiness. For everybody wants to make himself happy; but most people do not know how to, and often a bodily indisposition prevents their will from being free. This happens too when we are asleep; because nobody, however philosophical, can prevent himself having bad dreams when his temperament so disposes him. However, experience shows that if one has often had a certain thought while one's mind was at liberty, it returns again however indisposed one's body may be. Thus I can boast that my own dreams never portray anything distressing, and there is no doubt that it is a great advantage to have long accustomed oneself to drive away sad thoughts. But we cannot altogether answer for ourselves except when we are in our own power. It is better to lose one's life than to lose the use of reason, because even without the teachings of faith, natural philosophy by itself makes us hope that our soul will be in a happier state after death than now; and makes us fear nothing more than being attached to a body which altogether takes away its liberty.

There are other indispositions which do no harm to one's reason but which merely alter the humours, and make a man unusually inclined to sadness, or anger, or some other passion. These certainly cause distress, but they can be overcome; and the harder they are to conquer, the more satisfaction the soul can take in doing so. The same is true of all exterior handicaps, such as the splendour of high birth, the flatteries of courts, the adversities of fortune, and also great prosperity, which commonly does more than misfortune to hamper the would-be philosopher. When everything goes according to our wishes we forget to think of ourselves; when fortune changes we are the more surprised the more we trusted it. Altogether, we can say, nothing can completely take away our power of making ourselves happy provided that it does not trouble our reason. It is not always the things which seem the most distressing which do the most harm.

But in order to discover what contribution each thing can make to our contentment, we must consider what are its possible causes. This information is also most valuable in making it easy to practise virtue; because all actions of our soul that acquire us some perfection are virtuous, and all our contentment consists in our interior awareness of possessing some perfection. Thus whenever we practise any virtue – that is to say, do what reason tells us we should do – we automatically receive satisfaction and pleasure from so doing. But pleasures are of two kinds: those that belong to the mind by itself, and those that belong to the whole human being, that is to say to the mind as joined to the body. These last present themselves in a confused manner to the imagination and often appear much greater than they are, especially before we possess them; and this is the source of all the evils and all the errors of life. For according to the rule of reason, each pleasure should be measured by the size of the perfection which produces it; it is thus that we measure those whose causes are clearly known to us. But often passion makes us believe certain things to be much better and more desirable than they are; then, when we have taken much trouble to acquire them, and in the process lost the chance of possessing other more genuine goods, possession of them brings home to us their defects; and thence arises dissatisfaction, regret, and remorse. And so the true function of reason is to examine the just value of all the goods whose acquisition seems to depend in some way on our conduct, so that we always devote our efforts to obtaining those which are in truth the most desirable. If, in such cases, fortune opposes our plans and makes them fail, we shall at least have the satisfaction that our loss was not our fault; and despite our failure we shall enjoy all the natural happiness whose acquisition was really within our power.

Anger, for instance, can sometimes excite in us such violent desires for vengeance that it makes us imagine more pleasure in chastising our enemy than in preserving our honour or our life, and makes us risk both imprudently in the attempt. Whereas, if reason examines what is the good or perfection on which the pleasure derived from vengeance is based, it will find – unless the vengeance serves to prevent future offences – that there is nothing except our imagination that we have some superiority and advantage over the person on whom we are taking vengeance. And this is often only a vain imagination, which is worthless in comparison with honour or life, or even the satisfaction to be had from seeing one's own mastery of one's anger when one abstains from revenge.

The same is true of the other passions. They all represent the goods to which they tend with greater splendour than they deserve, and before we experience pleasures they make them seem greater than experience shows them to be. This is why pleasure is commonly dispraised, because the word is used to mean only the pleasures which frequently deceive us by their appearance, and make us neglect other much solider pleasures, such as the pleasures of the mind commonly are, which are not so impressive in anticipation. I say "commonly" because not all pleasures of the mind are praiseworthy: they can be founded on some false opinion. An instance is the pleasure we take in slander, which is based only on the belief that the worse others are esteemed, the better esteemed we shall be ourselves. Also, they can deceive us by their appearance, when some strong passion accompanies them, as can be seen in the pleasure arising from ambition.

But the main difference between the pleasures of the body and those of the mind is the following. The body is subject to perpetual change, and indeed its preservation and well-being depend on change; so the pleasures proper to it last a very short time, since they arise from the acquisition of something useful to the body at the moment of reception, and cease as soon as it stops being useful. The pleasures of the soul, on the other hand, can be as immortal as the soul itself, provided they are so solidly founded that neither the knowledge of truth nor any false persuasion can destroy them.

The true function of reason, then, in the conduct of life is to examine and consider without passion the value of all perfections of body and soul that can be acquired by our conduct, so that since we are commonly obliged to deprive ourselves of some goods in order to acquire others, we shall always choose the better. Because the pleasures of the body are minor, it can be said in general that it is possible to make oneself happy without them. However, I do not think that they should be altogether despised, nor even that one should free oneself altogether from passion. It is enough to subject one's passions to reason; and once they are thus tamed they are sometimes useful precisely to the degree that they tend to excess. I will never have a more excessive passion than that which impels me to the respect and veneration which I owe you and makes me, etc.

DESCARTES TO ELIZABETH, 15 SEPTEMBER 1645

Madame,

Your Highness has so accurately observed all the reasons which prevented Seneca from expounding clearly his opinion on the supreme good, and you have read his book so carefully, that I would fear to be tedious if I continued examining his chapters one by one. Moreover, I do not want to put off replying to your question how to fortify one's understanding so as to discern what is the best in all the actions of life. And so, without following Seneca any further, I will try simply to explain my own opinion on the topic.

In order to be always disposed to judge well only two things seem to me necessary. One is the knowledge of truth, the other is practice in remembering and assenting to this knowledge whenever the occasion demands. But because nobody except God knows everything perfectly, we have to content ourselves with knowing the truths most useful to us.

The first and chief of these is that there is a God on whom all things depend, whose perfections are infinite, whose power is immense, and whose decrees are infallible. This teaches us to accept calmly all the things which happen to us as expressly sent by God. Moreover, since the true object of love is perfection, when we lift up our minds to consider Him as He is, we find ourselves naturally so inclined to love Him, that we even rejoice in our afflictions at the thought that they are an expression of His will.

The second thing we must know is the nature of our soul. We must know that it is a substance independent of, and nobler than, the body, and that it is capable of enjoying many satisfactions not to be found in this life. This prevents us from fearing death, and so detaches our affections from the things of this world that we scorn whatever is in the power of fortune.

Here it is important to judge worthily of the works of God and to have a vast idea of the extent of the universe, such as I tried to convey in the third book of my *Principles*.[7] For if we imagine that beyond the heavens there is nothing but imaginary spaces, and that all the heavens are made only for the service of the earth, and the earth only for man, we will be inclined to think that this earth is our principal abode and this life our best. Instead of discovering the perfections that are truly within us, we will attribute to other creatures imperfections which they do not have, so as to raise ourselves above them. We will be so absurdly presumptuous as to wish to belong to God's council and assist Him in the government of the world; and this will bring us a mass of vain anxiety and distress.

After acknowledging the goodness of God, the immortality of our souls, and the immensity of the universe, there is yet another truth that is, in my opinion, most useful to know. That is, that though each of us is a person distinct from others, whose interests are accordingly in some way different from those of the rest of the world, we must still think that none of us could subsist alone and each one of us is really one of the many parts of the universe, and more particularly a part of the earth, the State, the society, and the family to which we belong by our domicile, our oath of allegiance, and our birth. And the interests of the whole, of which each of us is a part, must always be preferred to those of our individual personality – with measure, of course, and discretion, because it would be wrong to expose ourselves to a great evil to produce only a slight benefit to our kinsfolk or our country. (Indeed if a man were worth more, by himself, than all his fellow citizens he would have no reason to destroy himself to save his city.) But if a man saw everything in relation to himself, he would not hesitate to injure others greatly when he thought he could draw some slight advantage; and he would have no true friendship, no fidelity, no virtue at all. On the other hand, if a man considers himself a part of the community he delights in doing good to everyone, and does not hesitate even to risk his life in the service of others, when the occasion demands. If he could, he would even be willing to lose his soul to save others. So that this consideration is the source and origin of all the most heroic actions done by men. A man seems to me more pitiful than admirable if he risks death from vanity, in the hope of praise, or through stupidity, because he does not apprehend the danger. But when a man risks death because he believes it to be his duty, or when he suffers some other evil to bring good to others, then he acts in virtue of the consideration that he owes more to the community of which he is a part than to himself as an individual, though this thought may be only confusedly in his mind without his reflecting upon it. Once a man knows and loves God as he should he has a natural impulse to think in this way; because, abandoning himself altogether to God's will, he strips himself of his own interests, and has no other passion than to do what he thinks pleasing to Him. Thus he acquires a mental satisfaction and contentment incomparably more valuable than all the passing joys which depend upon the senses.

In addition to these truths which concern all our actions in general, others must be known which concern more particularly each individual action. The chief of these, in my view, are those I mentioned in my last letter: namely, that all our passions represent to us the goods to whose pursuit they impel us as being much greater than they really are; and that the pleasures of the body are never as lasting as those of the soul, nor as great in possession as they appear in anticipation. We must pay great attention to this, so that when we feel ourselves moved by some passion we should suspend our judgement until it is calmed, and not let ourselves easily be deceived by the false appearance of the goods of this world.

I have only this to add, that one must also examine minutely all the customs of one's place of abode to see how far they should be followed. Though we cannot have certain proofs of everything, still we must take sides, and in matters of custom embrace the opinions that seem the most probable, so that we may never be irresolute when we need to act. For nothing causes regret and remorse except irresolution.

I said above that besides the knowledge of truth, practice also is required if one is to be always disposed to judge well. We cannot continually pay attention to the same thing; and so however clear and evident the reasons may have been that persuaded us of some truth in the past, we can later be turned away from believing it by some false appearances unless we have so imprinted it on our mind by long and frequent meditation that it has become a settled disposition with us. In this sense the scholastics are right when they say that virtues are *habitus;* because our failings are rarely due to the lack of theoretical knowledge of what one should do, but to lack of knowledge in practice, that is for lack of a firm habit of belief. And since in examining these truths I am also increasing in myself the corresponding habit, I am particularly obliged to your Highness for allowing me to correspond with her about them. There is no activity in which I think my leisure better spent than one in which I can prove that I am, etc.

DESCARTES TO CHRISTINE OF SWEDEN, 20 NOVEMBER 1647[8]

Madame,

I learn from M. Chanut[9] that it pleases your Majesty that I should have the honour to expound to you my view of the supreme good understood in the sense of the ancient philosophers. I count this command such a great favour that my desire to obey it turns away all other thoughts; so without making excuses for my insufficiency I will put in a few words all that I have been able to discover on the topic.

The goodness of each thing can be considered in itself without reference to anything else, and in this sense it is evident that God is the supreme good, since He is incomparably more perfect than any creature. But goodness can also be considered in relation to ourselves, and in this sense I do not see anything which we can esteem good unless it somehow belongs to us and makes us more perfect. Thus, the ancient philosophers, unenlightened by the light of faith and knowing nothing about supernatural beatitude, considered only the goods we can possess in this life; and what they were trying to discover was which of these is the supreme, that is, the chief and greatest good.

In trying to decide this, my first observation is that we should not consider as good, in relation to ourselves, anything which we do not possess and is not in our power to acquire. Once this is agreed, it seems to me that the supreme good of all men together is the total or aggregate of all the goods, of soul, of body and of fortune, which can belong to any human being; but that the supreme good of each individual is quite a different thing, and consists only in a firm will to do well and the contentment which this produces. My reason for this is that I can discover no other good which seems so great or so entirely within each man's power. For the goods of the body and of fortune do not depend absolutely upon us; and those of the soul can be all reduced to two heads, the one being to know, and the other to will, what is good. But knowledge is often beyond our powers, and so there remains only our will of which we can dispose outright. I do not see that it is possible to dispose it better than by a regular and constant resolution to carry out to the letter whatever one judges best, and to employ all the powers of one's mind in informing this judgement. This by itself constitutes all the virtues; this alone really deserves praise and glory; this alone, finally, produces the greatest and most solid contentment of life. So I conclude that it is this which constitutes the supreme good.

In this way I think I can reconcile the most opposed and famous opinions of the ancient philosophers, that of Zeno[10] who thought virtue or honour the supreme good, and that of Epicurus,[11] who thought the supreme good was contentment, to which he gave the name of pleasure. All vices arise only from the uncertainty and weakness consequent on ignorance – and virtue consists only in the resolution and vigour with which a man is inclined to do the things which he thinks good – this vigour, of course, must not stem from stubbornness, but from the consciousness of having examined the matter as well as one morally can. What a man does after such examination may be bad, but none the less he can be sure of having done his duty; whereas, if he does a virtuous action thinking he is doing wrong, or takes no trouble to find out whether he is doing right or wrong, he is not acting like a virtuous man. As for honour and praise, these are often awarded to the other goods of fortune; but because I am sure that your Majesty values virtue more than her crown, I shall not hesitate to express my opinion that nothing except virtue really deserves praise. All other goods deserve only to be esteemed and not to be honoured or praised, except in so far as they are supposed to have been acquired or obtained from God by the good use of free will. For honour and praise is a kind of reward, and only what depends on the will provides grounds for reward or punishment.

I still have to show that the good use of free will is what produces the greatest and most solid happiness in life. This does not seem difficult if we consider carefully what constitutes pleasure, or delight, and in general all the happinesses we can have. I observe first that all of them are entirely within the soul, though many of them depend on the body; just as it is the soul that sees, though through the medium of the eyes. Next I observe that there is nothing that can content the soul except its belief that it possesses some good, and that often this belief is only a very confused representation in the soul. Moreover, the soul's union with the body causes it commonly to represent certain goods to itself as being incomparably greater than they are; but if it knew distinctly their just value, its contentment would always be in proportion to the greatness of the good from which it proceeded. I observe also that the greatness of a good, in relation to us, should not be measured only by the value of the thing which constitutes it but principally also by the manner in which it is related to us. Now free will is in itself the noblest thing we can have because it makes us in a certain manner equal to God and exempts us from being his subjects; and so its rightful use is the greatest of all the goods we possess, and further there is nothing that is more our own or that matters more to us. From all this it follows that nothing but free will can produce our greatest contentments. Thus we see that the repose of mind and interior satisfaction felt by those who know they never fail to do their best is a pleasure incomparably sweeter, more lasting and more solid than all those which come from elsewhere.

I omit here many other things, because when I call to mind how much business is involved in ruling a great Kingdom, and how much of it your Majesty attends to in person, I do not dare to ask for longer audience. But I am sending to M. Chanut some papers in which I have expressed my sentiments on the matter at greater length.[12] If it pleases your Majesty to look at them, he will oblige me by presenting them to her, and show that I am etc.

Replies to Objections

SIXTH SET OF REPLIES

6. As for the freedom of the will, the way in which it exists in God is quite different from the way in which it exists in us. It is self-contradictory to suppose that the will of God was not indifferent from eternity with respect to everything which has happened or will ever happen; for it is impossible to imagine that anything is thought of in the divine intellect as good or true, or worthy of belief or action or omission, prior to the decision of the divine will to make it so. I am not speaking here of temporal priority: I mean that there is not even any priority of order, or nature, or of "rationally determined reason" as they call it, such that God's idea of the good impelled him to choose one thing rather than another. For example, God did not will the creation of the world in time because he saw that it would be better this way than if he had created it from eternity; nor did he will that the three angles of a triangle

should be equal to two right angles because he recognized that it could not be otherwise, and so on. On the contrary, it is because he willed to create the world in time that it is better this way than if he had created it from eternity; and it is because he willed that the three angles of a triangle should necessarily equal two right angles that this is true and cannot be otherwise; and so on in other cases. There is no problem in the fact that the merit of the saints may be said to be the cause of their obtaining eternal life; for it is not the cause of this reward in the sense that it determines God to will anything, but is merely the cause of an effect of which God willed from eternity that it should be the cause. Thus the supreme indifference to be found in God is the supreme indication of his omnipotence. But as for man, since he finds that the nature of all goodness and truth is already determined by God, and his will cannot tend towards anything else, it is evident that he will embrace what is good and true all the more willingly, and hence more freely, in proportion as he sees it more clearly. He is never indifferent except when he does not know which of the two alternatives is the better or truer, or at least when he does not see this clearly enough to rule out any possibility of doubt. Hence the indifference which belongs to human freedom is very different from that which belongs to divine freedom.

8. If anyone attends to the immeasurable greatness of God he will find it manifestly clear that there can be nothing whatsoever which does not depend on him. This applies not just to everything that subsists, but to all order, every law, and every reason for anything's being true or good. If this were not so, then, as noted a little earlier, God would not have been completely indifferent with respect to the creation of what he did in fact create. If some reason for something's being good had existed prior to his preordination, this would have determined God to prefer those things which it was best to do. But on the contrary, just because he resolved to prefer those things which are now to be done, for this very reason, in the words of Genesis, "they are very good"; in other words, the reason for their goodness depends on the fact that he exercised his will to make them so. There is no need to ask what category of causality is applicable to the dependence of this goodness upon God, or to the dependence on him of other truths, both mathematical and metaphysical. For since the various kinds of cause were enumerated by thinkers who did not, perhaps, attend to this type of causality, it is hardly surprising that they gave no name to it. But in fact they did give it a name, for it can be called efficient causality, in the sense that a king may be called the efficient cause of a law, although the law itself is not a thing which has physical existence, but is merely what they call a "moral entity." Again, there is no need to ask how God could have brought it about from eternity that it was not true that twice four make eight, and so on; for I admit this is unintelligible to us. Yet on the other hand I do understand, quite correctly, that there cannot be any class of entity that does not depend on God; I also understand that it would have been easy for God to ordain certain things such that we men cannot understand the possibility of their being otherwise than they are. And therefore it would be

irrational for us to doubt what we do understand correctly just because there is something which we do not understand and which, so far as we can see, there is no reason why we should understand. Hence we should not suppose that eternal truths "depend on the human intellect or on other existing things"; they depend on God alone, who, as the supreme legislator, has ordained them from eternity.

Editor's Notes

1. This is a portrait of the Stoic wise man.
2. Descartes gives, in the fourth section of the *Discourse*, a brief account of how he rid himself of all his opinions; the main account is in the first of the *Meditations on First Philosophy*.
3. Princess Elizabeth (1618–88) was one of thirteen children of King Frederick V of Bohemia and Elizabeth Stuart of England. She lived in exile, devoting herself to intellectual endeavors.
4. Seneca's essay "On the Happy Life," written in the latter half of the first century C.E., is a short treatment, Stoic in tone, of what constitutes the happy life and how to attain it. According to Seneca, the happy life is one in harmony with nature, and it can be obtained by studying philosophy. See Seneca, *Moral Essays* II, trans. John Basore (Cambridge, Mass.: Harvard University Press, 1932), for the text and a translation.
5. The French *heur* means "chance" or "luck."
6. Given in the previous selection.
7. Part III of the *Principles of Philosophy* gives a scientific account of the visible universe, including the stars, the solar system, and the principles of their movements.
8. Queen Christine (or Christina) of Sweden (1626–89), daughter of Gustavus Adolphus, reigned from 1632 until her abdication in 1654.
9. Chanut was the French ambassador at the Swedish court.
10. Zeno of Citium, fl. c. 300 B.C.E., was the founder of Stoicism.
11. The founder of Epicureanism, lived from 341 to 270 B.C.E.
12. Copies of his letters to Elizabeth.

Further Reading

The best translation of Descartes's works is that by John Cottingham, Robert Stoothof, and Dugald Murdoch, *The Philosophical Writings of Descartes*, 2 vols. (Cambridge, England: Cambridge University Press, 1985). John J. Blom, in *Descartes: His Moral Philosophy and Psychology* (New York: New York University Press, 1978), translated more of the letters pertinent to ethics than did Anthony Kenny in the volume from which the present excerpts from the correspondence were taken.

Several good general studies of Descartes's philosophy are available. Among them are Tom Sorrell, *Descartes* (New York: Oxford University Press, 1987), which is very brief; Margaret Wilson, *Descartes* (London: Routledge & Kegan Paul, 1978); Anthony Kenny, *Descartes* (New York: Random House, 1968); Jonathan Rée, *Descartes* (London: Lane, 1974); and E. M. Curley, *Descartes Against the Skeptics* (Cambridge, Mass.: Harvard University Press, 1978). These, however, do not discuss Descartes's ethics.

A. Boyce Gibson, *The Philosophy of Descartes* (London: Methuen, 1932), chap. 10,

"Free Will and the Moral Life," is helpful regarding Descartes and ethics. The great French scholar Martial Gueroult discussed Descartes's moral philosophy in chapters 19 and 20 of his *Descartes' Philosophy Interpreted According to the Order of Reasons,* trans. Roger Ariew, 2 vols. (Minneapolis: University of Minnesota Press, 1984). See also Robert Cumming, "Descartes' Provisional Morality," *Review of Metaphysics* 9 (1955): 208–35.

Benedict de Spinoza

Introduction

Spinoza was born in Amsterdam in 1632, a descendant of Portuguese Jews who had fled persecution. ("Benedict" was the conventional Latin equivalent of his given name, Baruch.) Spinoza received a traditional Hebrew education and learned several modern languages. As he grew up, he found it more and more difficult to reconcile the Bible with the new sciences. His skepticism increased, and as he would not keep it to himself, he was excommunicated and thus cut off from the Jewish community. Determined to be independent, he learned the highly skilled craft of grinding lenses for the optical instruments that scientists needed, and he maintained himself by this work. Spinoza lived in Amsterdam until 1660 and then moved to a quiet village close to Leyden, where he wrote his first book, the *Short Treatise on the Improvement of the Understanding*, which was not published until more than a century later. He also wrote an exposition of Descartes's philosophy, presenting it in geometrical order, and began work on what eventually became his masterpiece, the *Ethics*. Spinoza's account of Descartes was published in 1663 under his name, with a preface explaining that he did not accept all of Descartes's views.

Spinoza let some of his own views be known in correspondence with friends and with scientists with whom he worked, and gradually he acquired a wide reputation as an important philosopher. Leibniz corresponded with him and even came to the Netherlands to talk with him. When Spinoza was asked to become the professor of philosophy at Heidelberg, he refused in order to maintain his independence. Although he lived quietly, he was concerned enough about Dutch political affairs to have tried once or twice to become active in them. Spinoza's political interests and protracted investigation of the Bible as a book written by human beings and calling for purely rational study culminated in an important work on politics and biblical interpretation, the *Tractatus theologico-politicus (Treatise on Religion and Politics)*, published anonymously in 1670.

When Spinoza died in 1677 of lung disease, probably aggravated by the constant inhalation of glass particles while grinding lenses, he left behind an unfinished treatise on politics, as well as his *Ethics*. His works were published posthumously and were generally ignored. Spinoza had the reputation of being an atheist, and insofar as the *Ethics* was read, it was initially dismissed as an irreligious tract. Not until the latter part of the eighteenth century was more careful and more favorable attention paid to his work.

Everyone agrees that the theory Spinoza presented in the *Ethics* is difficult. Part of the difficulty comes from the geometrical form into which he cast his thought, and part of it from having to grasp the whole system in order to understand its parts. The interconnection of parts within his theory corresponds to his belief that none of the things we usually assume to be individual entities can be understood by itself. For Spinoza each such thing is a part or aspect of the one substance that exists, and each expresses that substance's being in a special way. We can understand things only by seeing how they are connected to the one substance, which may be called indifferently God or Nature, and we can understand Spinoza's thought only when we grasp the connections of all its parts through the idea of God or Nature.

Like Hobbes and unlike Descartes, Spinoza tried to show that human life is completely contained within the natural order. "Most of those who have written about the Affects, and men's way of living," he stated at the beginning of Part III of the *Ethics,* "seem to treat, not of natural things, which follow the common laws of nature, but of things which are outside nature. Indeed they seem to conceive man in nature as a dominion within a dominion." Spinoza's system, by contrast, shows us a wholly deterministic nature, which includes thoughts and desires no less than the motions of bodies. Like Descartes, we may think we are free to control our feelings and our actions, Spinoza pointed out, but this is because we are aware only of our present ideas and emotions and not of their causes. But if we had adequate knowledge of the world, we would see that everything has to be as it is.

The implications of this thesis for the moral life are considerable. As the reader will see, Spinoza believed that a drastic revision of our understanding of the whole moral vocabulary was needed. When speaking of what one ought to do, or of what would be better than the way things now are, we seem to suppose that things might be other than they are. If we were completely informed about the world, would we not think such talk mistaken? There is a sense in which Spinoza thinks we would. But for us, who have far less than adequate knowledge of the world, such language does have uses. Spinoza's political and ethical writings explain what these uses are. They also go well beyond that topic to provide substantive views on how to live. In his political works Spinoza argued in favor of a limited democracy, extending, as far as possible, freedom and toleration of diversity of opinion. Parts IV and V of the *Ethics* offer a deeply felt and moving portrait of the wise or virtuous man, which we can use as a model in our own search for the good.

The usefulness of the model is based on a fundamental point about human psychology. In Proposition 6 (P6) or Part III of the *Ethics* Spinoza stated that "each thing, as far as it can by its own power, strives to persevere in its being." The *conatus*, or striving to persevere, is displayed at one level in the adhesion of a stone's parts to one another, and at another level in human efforts to satisfy desires. Spinoza used his proposition to imply that each of us always seeks to advance his or her own interests. But we, unlike stones, can modify the direction of our striving. Hence reason is not, as it was for Hobbes, only a tool by which we can find out how to get what we want; it also can change our aims. We need not be narrowly selfish, as Hobbesian men in a state of nature seem to be. The transformation is effected by knowledge – but knowledge of what?

The knowledge that a wise man possesses is not specifically moral knowledge, for according to Spinoza, there is really no such thing. God does not command, and there are no eternal and immutable laws of morality, only the laws that determine how everything in the universe actually and necessarily behaves. Neither is the good something built into the nature of things, waiting there for us to discover and pursue it. The good, to both Spinoza and Hobbes, is always relative to our conative response to things. What virtuous agents know, then, is the necessary connections of all things. The more clearly and distinctly they know the metaphysical and physical workings of the universe, the freer and more blessed they will be. Because Spinoza thought that skepticism was a mistake, he was sure that this kind of knowledge was available in principle. But he would have admitted – or, rather, insisted – that most people would never acquire it.

The excerpts in the first section are from *A Treatise on Religion and Politics*, in Benedict de Spinoza, *The Political Works*, ed. and trans. A. G. Wernham (Oxford: Oxford University Press, 1958), reprinted by permission of Oxford University Press. Those in the second section are from the *Ethics*, in Edwin Curley, ed. and trans., *The Collected Works of Spinoza*, vol. 1 (Princeton, N.J.: Princeton University Press, 1985). Copyright © 1985 by Princeton University Press and reprinted by permission of Princeton University Press.

In structuring the *Ethics*, Spinoza used the format of the Euclidean geometry of his day. Each of its "parts" is, therefore, divided into numbered "propositions," with accompanying "demonstrations," and these are sometimes accompanied by "corollaries" (further propositions following from or easily shown in conjunction with a main proposition) and by "scholia" (explanatory notes appended to propositions). In the translation used here, these labels are abbreviated as "P" (Proposition), "Dem" (Demonstration), "Cor" (Corollary), and "Schol" (Scholium). In the references, the part from which a proposition comes is indicated by a roman numeral before the letter "P." The general direction of Spinoza's thought can often be gathered from the propositions, corollaries, and scholia without working through the demonstrations, some of which I have accordingly omitted.

A Treatise on Religion and Politics

Chapter IV: Of the Divine Law

The word "law" in the widest sense means a rule in accordance with which all individual things, or all things of the same species, or some of them, act in one and the same fixed and determinate way; and this either by natural necessity or by the will of men. A law based on natural necessity is one which follows necessarily from the actual nature or definition of the thing in question; while a law based on the will of men – more properly called an ordinance – is one which men prescribe for themselves and others in order to live in greater security and comfort, or for some other purpose. E.g. that any body impinging on a smaller body loses as much of its own motion as it imparts to the other is a law which is common to all bodies and depends on natural necessity. Similarly, that on thinking of one thing a man immediately thinks of something else like it, or associated with it in his previous experience, is a law which follows necessarily from human nature. But that men should surrender, or be forced to surrender, the right which they hold from nature, and should bind themselves to follow a definite rule of life, depends on human volition. . . .

But the application of the word "law" to natural things seems to be metaphorical, and the ordinary meaning of law is simply a command which men can either obey or disobey, since it confines human power within definite bounds which are narrower than its natural limits, and requires nothing that is beyond man's strength. This makes it advisable, I think, to restrict the word to its second meaning, and to define law as a rule of life which man prescribes to himself or to others for some object. Yet the real object of law is seldom obvious to more than a few; most men are practically incapable of seeing it, and do anything but live by reason's guidance. Thus in order to bind all men equally legislators have wisely introduced another motive for obedience – very different from the one which follows necessarily from the nature of law – by holding out the sort of reward for active support, and the sort of penalty for transgression, that appeals most strongly to the hopes and fears of the masses; and in this way they have tried to keep them on the tightest possible rein. In consequence, law is apt to be regarded as a rule of life prescribed for men by the command of others; accordingly, those who obey law are said to live under law, and are thought to be slaves. Now it is true that he who gives every man his own because he fears the gallows acts by the command of another and under compulsion of evil, so that he cannot be called just; still, he who gives every man his own because he knows the real reason and necessity for law acts with constancy of purpose and of his own volition, not another's, and hence is rightly called just. . . . Law, then, is simply a rule of living which men prescribe to themselves or to others for some object; and since this is so, it seems necessary to divide it into two categories, human and divine. By human law I mean a rule of living which serves no other purpose than to preserve life and the state; while by divine law I mean one whose sole object is the supreme good, i.e. true knowledge and love of God. I call the latter divine because of the nature of the supreme good, which I shall now explain as briefly and as clearly as possible.

Since the better part of us is our understanding, it follows that, if we really wish to seek our own good, our primary aim must be to make our understanding as perfect as possible; for it is in its perfection that our supreme good must lie. Now since all our knowledge, and the certainty which really removes all doubt, depends wholly on our knowledge of God – not only because nothing can either be or be conceived without God, but also because complete scepticism is possible as long as we have no clear and distinct idea of God – our supreme good and perfection is wholly dependent on our knowledge of God and the consequences of that knowledge. Again, since nothing can either be or be conceived without God it necessarily follows that everything in nature involves and expresses the concept of God in proportion to its essence and perfection; so that the more we learn of things in nature, the greater and more perfect is the knowledge of God we acquire: or (since to understand an effect through its cause is simply to understand a particular property of the cause) the more we learn of things in nature the more perfect becomes our knowledge of God's essence, which is the cause of all things. Hence all our knowledge, i.e. our supreme good, not only depends upon, but wholly consists in our knowledge of God. This also follows from the fact that a man is more perfect as the main object of his love is more perfect, and vice versa; so that the man whose main love and chief delight is the intellectual knowledge of the most perfect being, God, is necessarily most perfect, and shares most fully in supreme blessedness. Our highest good and blessedness, then, is summed up in this – knowledge and love of God. Accordingly, the means required by this object of all human actions, i.e. by God himself in so far as we have the idea of him in our minds, can be called the commands of God, since they are, so to speak, prescribed to us by God himself in so far as he exists in our minds; and so the rule of living which has this object in view is well named the divine law. What these means are, what rule of living this object requires, and how the principles of the best state, and the best way of living among men, are derived from it, are questions for a comprehensive treatise on ethics. Here I shall confine myself to discussing the divine law in general terms.

Since love of God is the supreme happiness and blessedness of man, and the highest object and aim of all human actions, the only man who fulfils the divine law is he who seeks to love God, not from fear of punishment, or through love for other things like pleasure, fame, and so forth, but simply because he knows God, or knows that knowledge and love of God is the supreme good. Hence the sum of the divine law, and its fundamental precept, is to love God as the supreme good; that is – to repeat what I have said already – not from fear of any punishment or penalty, or through love of anything else which we desire to enjoy. For what the idea of God teaches us is that God is our supreme good, i.e. that knowledge and love of God is the ultimate object to which all our actions should be directed. The sensual man cannot understand this, and to him it seems empty talk, because he has too slight a knowledge of God, and also because in the supreme good, which consists entirely in contemplation and purity of spirit, he has found nothing to fondle or eat, nothing, in short, to appeal to the carnal nature which is his chief source of pleasure. But those who know that they have no possessions more precious than understanding and soundness of mind will doubtless regard these blessings as pretty substantial. I have thus explained the main content of the divine law, and shown which laws are human; they are all that have a different aim. . . . If we now consider the nature of natural divine law in the sense just explained, we shall see:

I. That it is universal, i.e. common to all men; for I have deduced it from human nature in general.

II. That it requires no belief in historical narratives[1] of any kind; for since reflection on human nature is all that is needed to understand it, this law can certainly be conceived in Adam as easily as in any other man, in a solitary as easily as in a social being. In any case, belief in historical narratives, however well-grounded, cannot give us knowledge of God, and hence cannot give us love for him either. For love of God arises from knowledge of him, and knowledge of him must be derived from common notions which are self-validating and self-evident; hence it is quite untrue that belief in historical narratives is a necessary condition of our attaining our supreme good. Nevertheless, although belief in historical narratives cannot give us knowledge and love of God, I do not deny that a perusal of them gives very useful guidance for living in society; for the more we have observed, and the better we know, men's characters and dispositions – which are best discovered from their actions – the more we shall be able to live discreetly among them, and to make reasonable allowances for their nature in the conduct of our lives.

III. We see that this natural divine law does not require ceremonies, i.e. actions which are indifferent in themselves and are called good only by convention, or symbolize some good necessary for salvation, or, if you like, have a justification which is beyond human understanding. For the light of nature requires nothing that is beyond its own compass, but only what it can clearly show us to be good, i.e. a means to our blessedness. Actions whose only claim to goodness is the fact that they are prescribed by convention, or that they symbolize some good, can do nothing to perfect our understanding, but are simply empty forms, and no part of conduct which is the product or fruit of understanding and sound sense. But there is no need to show this more fully here.

IV. Finally, we see that the supreme reward of the divine law is the law itself, i.e. to know God and love him in true freedom with a pure and constant mind; while its penalty is lack of these blessings and slavery to the flesh, or a troubled and inconstant mind.

Having noted these points we must now inquire:

I. Whether the light of nature allows us to conceive God as a legislator or king who lays down laws for men.

II. What Holy Writ teaches regarding the light of nature and this natural law. . . .

The answer we must give to the first is easily deduced from the nature of God's will, which is distinguished from his understanding only from the viewpoint of our reason; that is to say, God's will and God's understanding are in themselves really one and the same, and the distinction between them has no basis but our different ways of conceiving God's understanding. For example, when we confine our attention to the fact that the nature of a triangle is eternally contained in the divine nature as an eternal truth, we say that God has an idea of the triangle, or understands the nature of the triangle. But when we afterwards consider that it is only through the necessity of the divine nature that the triangle's nature is thus contained in it, and not through the necessity of the essence and nature of the triangle, indeed, that the necessity of the essence and properties of the triangle, again in so far as they are conceived as eternal truths, depends wholly on the necessity of the divine nature and understanding, and not on the nature of the triangle; then what we called God's understanding we now call God's will or decree. Hence we make one and the same assertion about God in saying that he has eternally decreed and willed the three angles of the triangle to be equal to two right angles, and in saying that he has understood this to be so. It follows that God's affirmations and negations always involve eternal necessity or truth. Thus if God, for example, had told Adam that he willed him not to eat of the tree of the knowledge of good and evil, it would have involved a contradiction for Adam to be able to eat of that tree, and so it would have been impossible that Adam should eat of it; for that divine decree would necessarily have involved eternal necessity and truth. But since Scripture nevertheless relates that Adam did eat of the tree in spite of what God had told him, we must hold that God only revealed to Adam the evil which would befall him if he ate of it, and did not reveal the necessity with which that evil would follow. In consequence, Adam did not regard the revelation as an eternal and necessary truth, but as a law, i.e. as an ordinance involving rewards and penalties which do not follow necessarily from the nature of the action performed, but are wholly dependent on the whim and absolute authority of some king. Hence that revelation was a law, and God a legislator or king, only in Adam's eyes, and only because of his lack of knowledge did he conceive them in this way. Similarly, the Decalogue was a law only in the eyes of the Jews; and this for the same reason, lack of knowledge. For since they did not apprehend God's existence as an eternal truth, they had to regard what was revealed to them in the Decalogue, i.e. that God exists and that God alone must be worshipped, as a law: whereas if God had spoken to them directly, without using any physical means, they would have understood this revelation as an eternal truth, and not as a law. What I have just said about the Israelites and Adam applies with equal force to all the prophets who wrote laws in God's name; none of them understood God's decrees adequately, as eternal truths. It applies even to Moses himself. For through revelation, or the fundamental laws revealed to him, Moses merely saw how the people of Israel could be united in a particular strip of territory, could form an independent community, i.e. establish a state, and could be compelled to obedience; he did not see or have revealed to him that the means prescribed were the best, and that the general obedience of the people in such a strip of territory would necessarily lead to the end they sought. He thus conceived all his discoveries, not as eternal truths, but as precepts and ordinances, and commanded them as God's laws; accordingly, he imagined God as a ruler, a legislator, a king, as merciful, just, and so on; although all such characteristics belong to human nature only, and must be eliminated completely from our conception of the divine nature. . . . I conclude then that the stupidity of the masses, and their failure to think, is the only reason why God is described as a legislator or king, and called just, merciful, and so on; that in fact God acts and directs everything by the necessity of his own nature and perfection alone; and, finally, that his decrees and volitions are eternal truths, and always involve necessity. This was the first point which I proposed to explain and prove.

Let us therefore pass to the second question, and run through the pages of Holy Writ to see what it teaches about the light of nature and this divine law. The first thing we find is the story of the first man, which tells how God commanded Adam not to eat the fruit of the tree of the knowledge of good and evil. This seems to mean that God told Adam to do and pursue good as good, and not as the opposite of evil, i.e. to pursue good from love of good, and not from fear of evil. For, as I have already shown, he who does good from true knowledge and love of good acts with freedom and constancy of purpose; while he who does good from fear of evil acts under compulsion of evil, like a slave, and lives under the control of another. Thus this single command laid by God upon Adam comprehends the whole of the natural divine law, and is in complete agreement with the dictate of the light of nature. . . .

CHAPTER XVI: THE BASIS OF THE STATE; THE RIGHT OF THE INDIVIDUAL, BOTH NATURAL AND CIVIL; AND THE RIGHT OF THE SOVEREIGN

. . . we must discuss the basis of the state; and we must begin with the natural right of the individual, paying no attention for the present to either state or religion.

By the right and law of nature I simply mean the rules of each individual thing's nature, the rules whereby we conceive it as naturally determined to exist and act in a definite way. Fish, for example, are determined by nature to swim, and the large to eat the smaller; so fish occupy the water, and the large eat the smaller, with perfect natural right. For there is no doubt that nature in the absolute sense has a perfect right to do everything in its power, i.e. that the right of nature extends as far as its power; the power of nature being nothing but the power of God, who has a perfect right to do everything. But the universal power of nature as a whole is simply the power of all individual things combined; hence each individual thing has a perfect right to do everything it can, in other words, its right extends to the limit of its power. And since the supreme law of nature is that everything does its utmost to preserve its own condition, and this without regard to anything but itself, everything has a perfect right to do this, i.e. (as I said) to exist and act as nature has determined it to do. Nor do I recognize any difference in this respect between men and other individual things in nature, or between men endowed with reason and others to whom true reason is unknown, or between the foolish, the mad, and the sane: for whatever anything does by the laws of its nature it does with perfect right, simply because it acts as it has been determined by nature to act, and can do nothing else. Hence as long as men are regarded as living under the sway of nature alone, he who is still blind to reason, or has still to acquire a virtuous disposition, lives wholly by the laws of appetite with as perfect a right as he who guides his life by the laws of reason. In other words, just as an enlightened man has a perfect right to do everything which reason dictates, or to live by the laws of reason, so too an unenlightened and weak-minded man has a perfect right to do everything that appetite suggests, or to live by the laws of appetite. . . .

Thus man's natural right is not determined by sound reason, but by his desire and his power. For men are not all determined by nature to act in accordance with the rules and laws of reason; on the contrary, all men are born in complete ignorance, and, even although they are well brought up, much of their life must pass before they can discover the true way of living and acquire a virtuous disposition. Yet meanwhile they have to live and preserve themselves as best they can; that is, by the prompting of appetite alone, since nature has given them nothing else, and has denied them the effective power to live by sound reason. Hence they are no more bound to live by the laws of a sound understanding than a cat is bound to live by the laws of a lion's nature. Anything, then, that an individual who is considered as subject only to nature judges to be useful to himself – either through the guidance of sound reason or through the impetus of passion – he has a perfect natural right to desire and indeed to appropriate by any means in his power – by force, fraud, entreaty, or however he finds it easiest; and hence a perfect natural right to regard as an enemy anyone who wishes to prevent him from satisfying his desire.

It follows that the right and law of nature, under which all are born and for the most part live, forbids nothing save what nobody desires and nobody can do: it forbids neither strife, nor hatred, nor anger, nor deceit; in short, it is opposed to nothing that appetite can suggest. Nor is this surprising; for nature is not bounded by the laws of human reason, which aim only at men's true interest and preservation, but by other laws of infinite scope governing the eternal order of the whole of nature, in which man is a tiny part: and it is by the necessity of this order alone that all individual things are determined to exist and act in a definite way. Hence if anything in nature seems to us ridiculous, absurd, or bad, this is because we know things only in part, being almost entirely ignorant of how they are linked together in the universal system of nature; and because we wish everything to be directed in conformity with our own reason. Yet what reason declares to be bad is not bad in relation to the order and laws of nature as a whole, but only in relation to the laws of our nature in particular.

Still, nobody can doubt that it is much more advantageous for men to live by the laws and sure dictates of our reason, which, as I said, aim at nothing but the true interest of men. Moreover everyone desires to enjoy the maximum safety and security (which is impossible as long as each may do anything he pleases, and reason is allowed no more influence than hatred and anger); for everyone lives a life of anxiety when surrounded by hostility, hatred, anger, and treachery, and so does his utmost to escape such things. If we also reflect . . . that without mutual help men live in utter wretchedness, and are inevitably debarred from the cultivation of reason, we shall see very clearly that to live safely and well men had necessarily to join together. They therefore arranged that the right to do everything which each had by nature should be held collectively, and should be determined no longer by the force and appetite of each but by the power and will of all together. But they would not have succeeded in this had they been willing to follow nothing but the prompting of appetite (for by the laws of appetite individuals are drawn in different ways); so each must have firmly resolved and contracted to direct everything by the dictate of reason alone (which no one dares to oppose openly lest he appear to lack understanding), to bridle his appetite when it suggested anything harmful to another, to do to nobody what he would not wish done to himself, and, finally, to defend his neighbour's right as if it were his own.

But we must now inquire how this contract must be made if it is to be permanently binding: for it is a universal law of human nature that no one forgoes anything he thinks good save from hope of a greater good or fear of a greater loss, or tolerates any evil save to avoid a greater, or from hope of a greater good. In other words, of two goods everyone will choose the one which he thinks the greater, and of two evils the one which he thinks the lesser. I say expressly "which he (the chooser) thinks the greater or lesser"; not that his judgement is necessarily correct. Now this law is graven so deeply upon human nature that it must be set among the eternal truths which everyone must know. . . .

Ethics

FOURTH PART OF THE ETHICS: ON HUMAN BONDAGE, OR THE POWERS OF THE AFFECTS

Preface

Man's lack of power to moderate and restrain the affects[2] I call Bondage. For the man who is subject to affects is under the control, not of himself, but of fortune, in whose power he so greatly is that often, though he sees the better for himself, he is still forced to follow the worse.[3] In this Part, I have undertaken to demonstrate the cause of this, and what there is of good and evil in the affects. But before I begin, I choose to say a few words first on perfection and imperfection, good and evil.

If someone has decided to make something, and has finished it, then he will call his thing perfect[4] – and so will anyone who rightly knows, or thinks he knows, the mind and purpose of the Author of the work. For example, if someone sees a work (which I suppose to be not yet completed), and knows that the purpose of the Author of that work is to build a house, he will say that it is imperfect. On the other hand, he will call it perfect as soon as he sees that the work has been carried through to the end which its Author has decided to give it. But if someone sees a work whose like he has never seen, and does not know the mind of its maker, he will, of course, not be able to know whether that work is perfect or imperfect. And this seems to have been the first meaning of these words.

But after men began to form universal ideas, and devise models of houses, buildings, towers, etc., and to prefer some models of things to others, it came about that each one called perfect what he saw agreed with the universal idea he had formed of this kind of thing, and imperfect, what he saw agreed less with the model he had conceived, even though its maker thought he had entirely finished it.

Nor does there seem to be any other reason why men also commonly call perfect or imperfect natural things, which have not been made by human hand. For they are accustomed to form universal ideas of natural things as much as they do of artificial ones. They regard these universal ideas as models of things, and believe that nature (which they think does nothing except for the sake of some end) looks to them, and sets them before itself as models. So when they see something happen in nature which does not agree with the model they have conceived of this kind of thing, they believe that Nature itself has failed or sinned, and left the thing imperfect.

We see, therefore, that men are accustomed to call natural things perfect or imperfect more from prejudice than from true knowledge of those things. For we have shown in the Appendix of Part I, that Nature does nothing on account of an end. That eternal and infinite being we call God, *or* Nature, acts from the same necessity from which he exists. For we have shown (IP16) that the necessity of nature from which he acts is the same as that from which he exists. The reason, therefore, *or* cause, why God, *or* Nature, acts, and the reason why he exists, are one and the same. As he exists for the sake of no end, he also acts for the sake of no end. Rather, as he has no principle or end of existing, so he also has none of acting. What is called a final cause is nothing but a human appetite insofar as it is considered as a principle, *or* primary cause, of some thing.

For example, when we say that habitation was the final cause of this or that house, surely we understand nothing but that a man, because he imagined the conveniences of domestic life, had an appetite to build a house. So habitation, insofar as it is considered as a final cause, is nothing more than this singular appetite. It is really an efficient cause, which is considered as a first cause, because men are commonly ignorant of the causes of their appetites. For as I have often said before, they are conscious of their actions and appetites, but not aware of the causes by which they are determined to want something.

As for what they commonly say – that Nature sometimes fails or sins, and produces imperfect things – I number this among the fictions I treated in the Appendix of Part I.

Perfection and imperfection, therefore, are only modes of thinking, i.e., notions we are accustomed to feign because we compare individuals of the same species or genus to one another. This is why I said above (IID6) that by reality and perfection I understand the same thing. For we are accustomed to refer all individuals in Nature to one genus, which is called the most general, i.e., to the notion of being, which pertains absolutely to all individuals in Nature. So insofar as we refer all individuals in Nature to this genus, compare them to one another, and find that some have more being, *or* reality, than others, we say that some are more perfect than others. And insofar as we attribute something to them that involves negation, like a limit, an end, lack of power, etc., we call them imperfect, because they do not affect our Mind as much as those we call perfect, and not because something is lacking in them which is theirs, or because Nature has sinned. For nothing belongs to the nature of anything except what follows from the necessity of the nature of the efficient cause. And whatever follows from the necessity of the nature of the efficient cause happens necessarily.

As far as good and evil are concerned, they also indicate nothing positive in things, considered in themselves, nor are they anything other than modes of thinking, *or* notions we form because we compare things to one another. For one and the same thing can, at the same time, be good, and bad, and also indifferent. For example, Music is good for one who is Melancholy, bad for one who is mourning, and neither good nor bad to one who is deaf.

But though this is so, still we must retain these words. For because we desire to form an idea of man, as a model of human nature which we may look to, it will be useful to us to retain these same words with the meaning I have indicated. In what follows, therefore, I shall understand by good what we know certainly is a means by which we may approach nearer and nearer to the model of human nature that we set before ourselves. By evil, what we certainly know prevents us from becoming like that model. Next, we shall say that men are more perfect or imperfect, insofar as they approach more or less near to this model. . . .

P36: *The greatest good of those who seek virtue is common to all, and can be enjoyed by all equally.* . . .

Schol.: But suppose someone should ask: what if the greatest good of those who seek virtue were not common to all? Would it not follow from that, as above (see P34), that men who live according to the guidance of reason, i.e. (by P35), men, insofar as they agree in nature, would be contrary to one another?

To this the answer is that it is not by accident that man's greatest good is common to all; rather, it arises from the very nature of reason, because it is deduced from the very essence of man, insofar as [that essence] is defined by reason, and because man could neither be nor be conceived if he did not have the power to enjoy this greatest good. For it pertains to the essence of the human Mind (by IIP47) to have an adequate knowledge of God's eternal and infinite essence.

P37: *The good which everyone who seeks virtue wants for himself, he also desires for other men; and this Desire is greater as his knowledge of God is greater.* . . .

Schol. 1: He who strives, only because of an affect, that others should love what he loves, and live according to his temperament, acts only from impulse and is hateful – especially to those to whom other things are pleasing, and who also, therefore, strive eagerly, from the same impulse, to have other men live according to their own temperament. And since the greatest good men seek from an affect is often such that only one can possess it fully, those who love are not of one mind in their love – while they rejoice to sing the praises of the thing they love, they fear to be believed. But he who strives from reason to guide others acts not by impulse, but kindly, generously, and with the greatest steadfastness of mind.

Again, whatever we desire and do of which we are the cause insofar as we have the idea of God, *or* insofar as we know God, I relate to Religion. The Desire to do good generated in us by our living according to the guidance of reason, I call Morality. The Desire by which a man who lives according to the guidance of reason is bound to join others to himself in friendship, I call Being Honorable,[5] and I call that honorable which men who live according to the guidance of reason praise; on the other hand, what is contrary to the formation of friendship, I call dishonorable. . . .

P50: *Pity, in a man who lives according to the guidance of reason, is evil of itself, and useless:*

Cor.: From this it follows that man who lives according to the dictate of reason, strives, as far as he can, not to be touched by pity.

Schol.: He who rightly knows that all things follow from the necessity of the divine nature, and happen according to the eternal laws and rules of nature, will surely find nothing worthy of Hate, Mockery or Disdain, nor anyone whom he will pity. Instead he will strive, as far as human virtue allows, to act well, as they say, and rejoice.

To this we may add that he who is easily touched by the affect of Pity, and moved by another's suffering or tears, often does something he later repents – both because, from an affect, we do nothing which we certainly know to be good, and because we are easily deceived by false tears.

Here I am speaking expressly of a man who lives according to the guidance of reason. For one who is moved to aid others neither by reason nor by pity is rightly called inhuman. For (by IIIP27) he seems to be unlike a man.

P53: *Humility is not a virtue, or does not arise from reason.*

P54: *Repentance is not a virtue, or does not arise from reason; instead, he who repents what he has done is twice wretched, or lacking in power.*

Schol.: Because men rarely live from the dictate of reason, these two affects, Humility and Repentance, and in addition, Hope and Fear, bring more advantage than disadvantage. So since men must sin, they ought rather to sin in that direction. If weak-minded men were all equally proud, ashamed of nothing, and afraid of nothing, how could they be united or restrained by any bonds?

The mob is terrifying, if unafraid. So it is no wonder that the Prophets, who considered the common advantage, not that of the few, commended Humility, Repentance, and Reverence so greatly. Really, those who are subject to these affects can be guided far more easily than others, so that in the end they may live from the guidance of reason, i.e., may be free and enjoy the life of the blessed.

P64: *Knowledge of evil is an inadequate knowledge.*

Cor.: From this it follows that if the human Mind had only adequate ideas, it would form no notion of evil.

P66: *From the guidance of reason we want a greater future good in preference to a lesser present one, and a lesser present evil in preference to a greater future one.*

Schol.: If these things are compared with those we have shown in this Part up to P18, concerning the powers of the affects, we shall easily see what the difference is between a man who is led only by an affect, *or* by opinion, and one who is led by reason. For the former, whether he will or no, does those things he is most ignorant of, whereas the latter complies with no one's wishes but his own, and does only those things he knows to be the most important in life, and therefore desires very greatly. Hence, I call the former a slave, but the latter, a free man.

I wish now to note a few more things concerning the free man's temperament and manner of living.

P67: *A free man thinks of nothing less than of death, and his wisdom is a meditation on life, not on death.*

Dem.: A free man, i.e., one who lives according to the dictate of reason alone, is not led by Fear (by P63), but desires the good directly (by P63C), i.e. (by P24), acts, lives, and preserves his being from the foundation of seeking his own advantage. And so he thinks of nothing less than of death. Instead his wisdom is a meditation on life, q.e.d.

P68: *If men were born free, they would form no concept of good and evil so long as they remained free.*

Dem.: I call him free who is led by reason alone. Therefore, he who is born free, and remains free, has only adequate ideas, and so has no concept of evil (by P64C). And since good and evil are correlates, he also has no concept of good, q.e.d.

P72: *A free man always acts honestly, not deceptively.*

Dem.: If a free man, insofar as he is free, did anything by deception, he would do it from the dictate of reason (for so far only do we call him free). And so it would be a virtue to act deceptively (by P24), and hence (by the same Prop.), everyone would be better advised to act deceptively to preserve his being. I.e. (as is known through itself), men would be better advised to agree only in words, and be contrary to one another in fact. But this is absurd (by P31C). Therefore, a free man etc., q.e.d.

Schol.: Suppose someone now asks: what if a man could save himself from the present danger of death by treachery? Would not the principle of preserving his own being recommend, without qualification, that he be treacherous?

The reply to this is the same. If reason should recommend that, it would recommend it to all men. And so reason would recommend, without qualification, that men make agreements, join forces, and have common rights only by deception – i.e., that really they have no common rights. This is absurd.

P73: *A man who is guided by reason is more free in a state, where he lives according to a common decision, than in solitude, where he obeys only himself.*

Dem.: A man who is guided by reason is not led to obey by Fear (by P63), but insofar as he strives to preserve his being from the dictate of reason, i.e. (by P66S), insofar as he strives to live freely, desires to maintain the principle of common life and common advantage (by P37). Consequently (as we have shown in P37S2), he desires to live according to the common decision of the state. Therefore, a man who is guided by reason desires, in order to live more freely, to keep the common laws of the state, q.e.d.

Schol.: These and similar things which we have shown concerning the true freedom of man are related to Strength of Character,[6] i.e. (by IIIP59S), to Tenacity[7] and Nobility.[8] I do not consider it worthwhile to demonstrate separately here all the properties of Strength of Character, much less that a man strong in character hates no one, is angry with no one, envies no one, is indignant with no one, scorns no one, and is not at all proud. For these and all things which relate to true life and Religion are easily proven from P37 and P46, viz. that Hate is to be conquered by returning Love, and that everyone who is led by reason desires for others also the good he wants for himself.

To this we may add what we have noted in P50S and in other places: a man strong in character considers this most of all, that all things follow from the necessity of the divine nature, and hence, that whatever he thinks is troublesome and evil, and moreover, whatever seems immoral, dreadful, unjust, and dishonorable, arises from the fact that he conceives the things themselves in a way that is disordered, mutilated, and confused. For this reason, he strives most of all to conceive things as they are in themselves, and to remove the obstacles to true knowledge, like Hate, Anger, Envy, Mockery, Pride, and the rest of the things we have noted in the preceding pages.

And so, as we have said [II/47/21], he strives, as far as he can, to act well and rejoice. In the following Part I shall demonstrate how far human virtue can go in the attainment of these things, and what it is capable of.

Fifth Part of the Ethics: On the Power of the Intellect, or on Human Freedom

Preface

I pass, finally, to the remaining Part of the Ethics, which concerns the means, or way, leading to Freedom. Here, then, I shall treat of the power of reason, showing what it can do against the affects, and what Freedom of Mind, or blessedness, is. From this we shall see how much more the wise man can do than the ignorant. . . .

P6: *Insofar as the Mind understands all things as necessary, it has a greater power over the affects, or is less acted on by them.*

Dem.: The Mind understands all things to be necessary (by IP29), and to be determined by an infinite connection of causes to exist and produce effects (by IP28). And so (by P5) to that extent [the mind] brings it about that it is less acted on by the affects springing from these things, and (by IIIP48) is less affected toward them, q.e.d.

Schol.: The more this knowledge that things are necessary is concerned with singular things, which we imagine more distinctly and vividly, the greater is this power of the Mind over the affects, as experience itself also testifies. For we see that Sadness over some good which has perished is lessened as soon as the man who has lost it realizes that this good could not, in any way, have been kept. Similarly, we see that no one pities infants because of their inability to speak, to walk, or to reason, or because they live so many years, as it were, unconscious of themselves. But if most people were born grown up, and only one or two were born infants, then everyone would pity the infants, because they would regard infancy itself, not as a natural and necessary thing, but as a vice of nature, *or* a sin. We could point out many other things along this line.

P20: *This love toward God cannot be tainted by an affect of Envy or Jealousy . . .*

Schol.: . . . the power of the Mind over the affects consists:

I. In the knowledge itself of the affects (see P4S);

II. In the fact that it separates the affects from the thought of an external cause, which we imagine confusedly (see P2 and P4S);

III. In the time by which the affections related to things we understand surpass those related to things we conceive confusedly, *or* in a mutilated way (see P7);

IV. In the multiplicity of causes by which affections related to common properties or to God are encouraged (see P9 and P11);

V. Finally, in the order by which the Mind can order its affects and connect them to one another (see P10, and in addition, P12, P13, and P14).

But to understand better this power of the Mind over the affects, the most important thing to note is that we call affects great when we compare the affect of one man with that of another, and see that the same affect troubles one more than the other, or when we compare the affects of one and the same man with each other, and find that he is affected, *or* moved, more by one affect than by another. For (by IVP5) the force of each affect is defined by the power of the external cause compared with our own. But the power of the Mind is defined by knowledge alone, whereas lack of power, *or* passion, is judged solely by the privation of knowledge, i.e., by that through which ideas are called inadequate.

From this it follows that that Mind is most acted on, of which inadequate ideas constitute the greatest part, so that it is distinguished more by what it undergoes than by what it does. On the other hand, that Mind acts most, of which adequate ideas constitute the greatest part, so that though it may have as many inadequate ideas as the other, it is still distinguished more by those which are attributed to human virtue than by those which betray man's lack of power.

Next, it should be noted that sickness of the mind and misfortunes take their origin especially from too much Love toward a thing which is liable to many variations and which we can never fully possess. For no one is disturbed or anxious concerning anything unless he loves it, nor do wrongs, suspicions, and enmities arise except from Love for a thing which no one can really fully possess.

From what we have said, we easily conceive what clear and distinct knowledge – and especially that third kind of knowledge (see IIP47S), whose foundation is the knowledge of God itself – can accomplish against the affects. Insofar as the affects are passions, if clear and distinct knowledge does not absolutely remove them (see P3 and P4S), at least it brings it about that they constitute the smallest part of the Mind (see P14). And then it begets a Love toward a thing immutable and eternal (see P15), which we really fully possess (see IIP45), and which therefore cannot be tainted by any of the vices which are in ordinary Love, but can always be greater and greater (by P15), and occupy the greatest part of the Mind (by P16), and affect it extensively. . . .

P41: *Even if we did not know that our Mind is eternal, we would still regard as of the first importance Morality, Religion, and absolutely all the things we have shown (in Part IV) to be related to Tenacity and Nobility.*

Dem.: The first and only foundation of virtue, *or* of the method of living rightly (by IVP22C and P24) is the seeking of our own advantage. But to determine what reason prescribes as useful, we took no account of the eternity of the Mind, which we only came to know in the Fifth Part. Therefore, though we did not know then that the Mind is eternal, we still regarded as of the first importance the things we showed to be related to Tenacity and Nobility. And so, even if we also did not know this now, we would still regard as of the first importance the same rules of reason, q.e.d.

Schol.: The usual conviction of the multitude seems to be different. For most people apparently believe that they are free to the extent that they are permitted to yield to their lust, and that they give up their right to the extent that they are bound to live according to the rule of the divine law. Morality, then, and Religion, and absolutely everything related to Strength of Character, they believe to be burdens, which they hope to put down after death, when they also hope to receive a reward for their bondage, that is, for their Morality and Religion. They are induced to live according to the rule of the divine law (as far as their weakness and lack of character allows) not only by this hope, but also, and especially, by the fear that they may be punished horribly after death. If men did not have this Hope and Fear, but believed instead that minds die with the body, and that the wretched, exhausted with the burden of Morality, cannot look foward to a life to come, they would return to their natural disposition, and would prefer to govern all their actions according to lust, and to obey fortune rather than themselves.

These opinions seem no less absurd to me than if someone, because he does not believe he can nourish his body with good food to eternity, should prefer to fill himself with poisons and other deadly things, or because he sees that the Mind is not eternal, *or* immortal, should prefer to be mindless, and to live without reason. These [common beliefs] are so absurd they are hardly worth mentioning.

P42: *Blessedness is not the reward of virtue, but virtue itself; nor do we enjoy it because we restrain our lusts; on the contrary, because we enjoy it, we are able to restrain them.*

Dem.: Blessedness consists in Love of God (by P36 and P36S), a Love which arises from the third kind of knowledge (by P32C). So this Love (by IIIP59 and P3) must be related to the Mind insofar as it acts. Therefore (by IVD8), it is virtue itself. This was the first point.

Next, the more the Mind enjoys this divine Love, *or* blessedness, the more it understands (by P32), i.e. (by P3C), the greater the power it has over the affects, and (by P38) the less it is acted on by evil affects. So because the Mind enjoys this divine Love *or* blessedness, it has the power of restraining lusts. And because human power to restrain the affects consists only in the intellect, no one enjoys blessedness because he has restrained the affects. Instead, the power to restrain lusts arises from blessedness itself, q.e.d.

Schol.: With this I have finished all the things I wished to show concerning the Mind's power over the affects and its Freedom. From what has been shown, it is clear how much the Wise man is capable of, and how much more powerful he is than one who is ignorant and is driven only by lust. For not only is the ignorant man troubled in many ways by external causes, and unable ever to possess true peace of mind, but he also lives as if he knew neither himself, nor God, nor things; and as soon as he ceases to be acted on, he ceases to be. On the other hand, the wise man, insofar as he is considered as such, is hardly troubled in spirit, but being, by a certain eternal necessity, conscious of himself, and of God, and of things, he never ceases to be, but always possesses true peace of mind.

If the way I have shown to lead to these things now seems very hard, still, it can be found. And of course, what is found so rarely must be hard. For if salvation were at hand, and could be found without great effort, how could nearly everyone neglect it? But all things excellent are as difficult as they are rare.

Editor's Notes

1. Spinoza is referring to biblical narratives.
2. "Affect" is a somewhat technical term, translating the Latin *affectus*. It refers to emotions, feelings, desires, and other mental states leading us to act, but because

for Spinoza the mental and the physical were always strictly correlated, the affects are bodily conditions as well.

3. Spinoza was echoing an often-quoted passage from Ovid's *Metamorphoses* VII.20–21: Medea is torn between reason, telling her to obey her father, and passion, urging her to yield to her desire for her beloved:

> One way desire, another reason calls;
> The better course I see and do approve –
> The worse I follow . . . (Melville translation)

4. Spinoza was relying on the Latin sense of *perfectus*, which means "completed or fully made."

5. This translates the Latin *honestas*.

6. This translates the Latin *fortitudo*.

7. This translates the Latin *animositas*, which another translator rendered as "strength of mind."

8. This translates the Latin *generositas*.

Further Reading

Stuart Hampshire, *Spinoza* (London: Penguin, 1951) provides a good general introduction to Spinoza's thought, as does Henry E. Allison, *Benedict de Spinoza* (New Haven, Conn.: Yale University Press, 1986). Edwin Curley, *Behind the Geometrical Method* (Princeton, N.J.: Princeton University Press, 1988), is an excellent brief treatment of the main themes in the *Ethics*. Alan Donagan, *Spinoza* (Chicago: University of Chicago Press, 1989), is a comprehensive study. For analytical commentary, see Jonathan Bennett, *A Study of Spinoza's Ethics* (Indianapolis: Hackett, 1984); and R. J. Delahunty, *Spinoza* (London: Routledge & Kegan Paul, 1985). Stuart Hampshire's *Two Theories of Morality* (Oxford: Oxford University Press, 1977), reprinted in Hampshire's *Morality and Conflict* (Cambridge, Mass.: Harvard University Press, 1983), is an insightful comparison of Aristotle's and Spinoza's moral outlooks. Hampshire's views are discussed in Bennett, *A Study*, pp. 347–55. David Bidney, *The Psychology and Ethics of Spinoza*, 2nd ed. (New Haven, Conn.: Yale University Press, 1940), is one of the few books concentrating on Spinoza's moral psychology and morality. Eugene Freeman and Maurice Mandelbaum, *Spinoza, Essays in Interpretation* (LaSalle, Ill.: Open Court, 1975), contains a number of essays concerning Spinoza's moral philosophy, as well as an extensive bibliography.

Nicholas Malebranche

Introduction

Born in Paris in 1638 into a prosperous and well-connected family, Malebranche studied theology at the Sorbonne and entered the religious order of the Oratory in 1660. It was a reading of Descartes's treatise *On Man* in 1664 that awoke his philosophical interests. His first, and in many ways his most important, book, *De la recherche de la vérité* (*The Search for Truth*), published in two volumes in 1674 and 1675, showed the intermingling of religious concern with philosophical argument that was characteristic of all of Malebranche's thought. In later books he presented arguments for the truth of Christianity, discussed the relations between nature and grace, and explained his theory in graceful dialogues. The *Traité de morale* (*Treatise of Morality*) was published in 1684.

Malebranche lived during a period of stormy religious controversy and spent much time replying to his critics and criticizing others in turn. Leibniz, his slightly younger contemporary, and Antoine Arnauld, the logician and controversialist of the Port Royal Jansenists, were among his antagonists. Eventually the religious authorities decided that Malebranche's views were dangerous, and two of his works – the *Search for Truth* and the *Treatise on Nature and Grace* – were put on the index of books forbidden by the Catholic church. Malebranche was widely read in his lifetime, and his major works were translated into English. Admired by Berkeley and Hume, he exercised a not inconsiderable influence on British thought. He died in 1715.

Malebranche held two remarkable basic views. The first concerned perception. Starting from the accepted theory of his time, that we do not perceive external objects directly but only through the mediation of something in our minds, Malebranche argued to the conclusion that what we perceive directly is always ideas in the mind of God. We perceive these ideas sometimes clearly and distinctly but more often confusedly, and in the latter case they come to us as sensations or feelings. Malebranche did not deny the existence of physical objects but simply insisted that all our knowledge of them is mediated through our awareness of ideas of them in the divine mind.

Malebranche's second unusual view concerned causation. He denied that either physical objects or our own thoughts have the power to influence or act on one another. There certainly are regular sequences of events, and we can learn what these are by observation. But we cannot form any clear idea of what it would be for one body or one thought to have sufficient power or force to alter another. No matter how much we learn about any single entity, we can never infer what changes it will bring about in any other entity. Hence there cannot be what our idea of cause supposes there is – a necessary connection between one entity and another.

The only conceivable causal power capable of affecting anything is God, and so we must believe that all the actions of things – and the continuity of things – depend on God as their cause. Physical objects and souls or minds have no more power to sustain themselves over time than they have to affect other things. Thus, instead of speaking of one event's causing another, Malebranche believed that we should say that one event is the occasion for God to produce another. Malebranche's view of causation is therefore called *occasionalism*.

According to Malebranche, then, philosophy proves that it is in God that we live and move and have our being. This rational support may be a boon to religion, but it is clear that Malebranche's view raises serious problems for the understanding of Christianity. Is God, who alone can cause anything to happen, then responsible for all the evil in the world? Malebranche believed that we have a power of free choice and can make choices that God does not make for us. But if my mind cannot cause my body to move and God causes it to move on the occasion of my choosing (say) to shoot someone, will it not really be God who pulls the trigger? Malebranche wrestled with this problem, as well as with the problem of explaining how, in his view, God's ordinary actions could differ from his special action of bestowing grace on us. Is not every happening in the universe as miraculous and specially caused by God as is the gift of grace to an individual?

Much of the reply rests on Malebranche's thesis that God acts by means of general laws and does not make exceptions. (Miracles pose another problem for Malebranche.) Natural evil, such as the ravaging of a forest by a flood, is due to the complex interactions of particular things working under general laws. Humans too must cope with the generality of God's laws. God will not stop a roof tile from falling toward you, but you will not be disobeying him if you step out of its way, because we are meant to use our power of free choice in directing our lives (admittedly with God making our bodies move). Likewise, for the evil we occasion through our choices, we, and not God, are responsible.

Malebranche's resolution of the problem of evil is very much in the spirit of Saint Augustine, and much of Malebranche's ethic is also Augustinian. (See the section "Saint Augustine and Saint Thomas" in the Introduction to this anthology.) Like Augustine, Malebranche made central to morality his ideas of right love and wrong love. And like him also, he made the rightness or wrongness of a love depend on its relation to its object. The different things in the world possess different degrees of perfection. We can see what these are when we perceive the ideas of things in the mind of God. When our love of the more perfect is greater than our love of the less perfect, we love with a right love. And a habitual right love – a habitual love of the order of things according to their perfections – is what constitutes virtue.

Malebranche thought that humans were always tempted to pursue their own good rather than to follow the immutable order of perfection. There is a good that is proper to us, and we would realize – if only we could see the order of perfection clearly and distinctly – that our own good is best attained by developing the habit of conforming to that order. This sounds like one more reiteration of the old assertion that virtue is the best means to happiness, and in a way it is. But what is interesting about Malebranche's way of developing the idea is that the order of perfection is conceptually quite distinct from the good proper to a finite being. Malebranche did not, as many other writers did, conceptually tie virtue to what brings good to the agent. Rather, he defined virtue in terms of conformity to order. The knowledge we need if we are to be virtuous is not knowledge of a deeper truth than we usually have about how to attain

our own good. We can nonetheless be moved by a love of order as such, and in being
so moved we are not motivated by a desire for our own good, not even our own long-
range good.

Prudence and morality were thus distinguished more sharply by Malebranche than
by his predecessors, and there are other ways in which Malebranche made morality a
special realm of knowledge. The knowledge we need in order to be virtuous is not
knowledge of God's commands, not even of those he imposes on everyone alike, as it
is for the natural lawyers. It is not scientific or metaphysical knowledge of the interconnection of everything in nature, as it is for Spinoza. Instead, it is knowledge of a
unique kind of relationship, and it is practical knowledge, knowledge essentially tied to
the guidance of action. Moral philosophy for the first time had a subject matter of its
own, capable of rational study.

The following readings are from the *Treatise of Morality,* translated by James Ship-
ton, London, 1699. I have modernized the spelling and punctuation and silently corrected the translation itself at a few points.

Treatise of Morality

Part I

Chapter I

I. The reason of man is the word or the wisdom of God himself; for every
creature is a particular being, but the reason of a man is universal.

II. If my own particular mind were my reason and my light, my mind would
also be the reason for all intelligent beings; for I am certain that my reason
enlightens all intelligent beings. No one can feel my pain but myself, but
everyone may see the truth which I contemplate; so that the pain which I feel
is a modification of my own proper substance, but truth is a possession common to all spiritual beings.

III. Thus by the means of reason I have or may have some society with God
and all other intelligent beings, because they all possess a good or a law in
common with me, to wit, reason.

IV. This spiritual society consists in a participation of the same intellectual
substance of the word, from which all spiritual beings may receive their nourishment. In contemplating this divine substance I am able to see some part of
what God thinks; for God sees all truths, and there are some which I can see. I
can also discover something of the will of God, for God wills nothing but
according to a certain order, and this order is not altogether unknown to me.
It is certain that God loves things according as they are worthy of love; and I
can discover that there are some things more perfect, more valuable, and
consequently more worthy of love than others.

V. It is true, indeed, that I cannot by contemplating the word or consulting
reason be assured whether God doth actually produce anything out of his own
being or no. For none of the creatures proceed naturally from the word, nor is
the world a necessary emanation of the deity. God is fully sufficient for

himself, and the idea of a being infinitely perfect can be conceived to subsist alone.[1] The creatures then suppose in God free and arbitrary decrees which give them their being.[2] So that the word as such not containing in it the existence of the creatures, we cannot by the contemplation of it be assured of the action of God; but supposing that God doth act, I am able to know something of the manner in which he acts, and may be certain that he doth not act in such and such a manner; for that which regulates his manner of acting, the law which he inviolably observes, is the word, the eternal wisdom, the universal reason which makes me rational and which I can in part contemplate according to my own desires.

VI. If we suppose man to be a rational creature, we cannot certainly deny him the knowledge of something that God thinks and of the manner in which he acts. For by contemplating the intelligible substance of the word, which alone makes me and all other intelligent beings rational, I can clearly discover the relations or proportions of greatness that are between the intellectual ideas comprehended in it; and these relations are the same eternal truths which God himself sees. For God sees as well as I that twice two is four and that triangles which have the same base and are between the same parallels are equal. I can also discover, at least confusedly, the relations of perfection, which are the immutable order which God consults when he acts and which ought also to regulate the esteem and love of all intelligent beings.[3]

VII. From hence it is evident that there are such things as true and false, just and unjust, and that too in respect of all intelligent beings; that whatsoever is true in respect of man is true also in respect of angels and of God himself; that what is injustice or disorder with relation to man is so also with relation to God. For all spiritual beings contemplating the same intellectual substance necessarily discover in it the same relations of greatness or the same speculative truths. They discover also the same practical truths, the same laws, and the same order when they see the relations of perfection that are between those intellectual beings comprehended in the substance of the word, which alone is the immediate object of all our knowledge.

VIII. I say, when they *see* these relations of perfection or greatness, and not when they *judge of* them; for only truth or the real relations of things are visible, and we ought to judge of nothing but what we see. When we judge before we see or of more things than we see, we are deceived in our judgment, or at least we judge ill, though we may happen by chance not to be deceived. For when we judge of things by chance, as well as when we judge by passion or interest, we judge ill. This is judging by our selves and not by reason, or according to the laws of universal reason; that reason, I say, which alone is superior to spirits and hath a right to judge of those judgments which are pronounced by them.

IX. The mind of man being finite cannot see all the relations that the objects of its knowledge bear to one another. So it may be deceived when it judges of relations which it does not see. But if it judged of nothing but just what it saw, which without doubt it may do, certainly though it be a finite spirit, though it be ignorant and in its own nature subject to error, it would never be deceived; for then the judgments framed by it would proceed not so much from itself as from the universal reason pronouncing the same judgments in it.

XIII. . . . that a beast is more valuable than a stone and less valuable than a man, is true, because a beast bears a greater proportion or relation of perfection to a stone than a stone doth to a beast; and a beast has less proportion of perfection compared to a man than a man hath compared to a beast. And he that sees these relations sees such truths as ought to regulate his esteem and consequently that sort of love which is determined by esteem. But he that esteems his horse more than his coachman or thinks a stone is in itself more valuable than a fly or than the very least of organized bodies doth not see that which perhaps he thinks he doth. It is not universal reason but his own particular reason that makes him judge after that manner. It is not the love of order but self-love [*l'amour-propre*] which inclines him to love as he doth. That which he thinks he sees is neither visible nor intelligible; 'tis a false and imaginary relation; and he that governs his esteem or love by this or the like relation must necessarily fall into error and irregularity.

XIV. Since truth and order are relations of greatness and perfection, real immutable and necessary relations, relations comprehended in the substance of the divine word, he that sees these relations sees that which God sees. He that regulates his love according to these relations observes a law which God invincibly loves. So that there is a perfect conformity of mind and will between God and him. In a word, seeing he knows that which God knows and loves that which God loves, he is like God as far as he is capable of being so. So likewise since God invincibly loves himself, he cannot but esteem and love his own image. And as he loves things in proportion to their being amiable, he cannot but prefer it before all those beings which either by their nature or corruption are far from resembling him.

XV. Man is a free agent, and I suppose him to have all necessary assistances. In respect of truth, he is capable of searching after it notwithstanding the difficulty he finds in meditation; and in respect of order, he is able to follow it in spite of all the efforts of concupiscence. He can sacrifice his ease to truth and his pleasures to order. On the other side he can prefer his actual and present happiness before his duties, and fall into error and disorder. In a word, he can be deserving or not. Now God is just; he loves his creatures as they are loveable or as they resemble him. His will therefore is that every good action should be rewarded and every evil one punished; that he who hath made a good use of his liberty, and by that means hath rendered himself in part perfect and like God, should be in part happy as he is, and, on the contrary, etc.

XVII. He therefore that labors for his perfection and endeavors to make himself like God labors for his happiness and advancement. If he doth that which in some sort depends upon himself, that is to say, if he deserves well by making himself perfect, God will do that which in no sort depends upon him, in making him happy. . . . He that incessantly consults his reason and loves order, having a share in the perfection of God shall have also a share in his happiness, glory, and greatness.

XIX. This then is the first and greatest duty, that for which God hath created us, the love of which is the mother of all virtue, the universal, the fundamental virtue, the virtue which makes us just and which will one day make us happy. We are rational creatures; our virtue and perfection is to love reason or rather to love order. For the knowledge of speculative truths, or relations of greatness, doth not regulate our duties. It is principally the knowledge and love of the relations of perfection, or practical truths, wherein consist our perfection. Let us apply ourselves then to know, to love and follow order. . . .

XX. The obedience which we pay to order and submission to the law of God is virtue in all senses. Submission to the divine decrees or to the power of God is rather necessity than virtue. . . .

XXI. If all the motions of bodies were caused by particular acts of the will of God, it would be a sin to avoid the ruins of a falling house by flight, for we cannot without injustice refuse to render back to God that life which he hath given us when he requires it again. At this rate it would be an affront to the wisdom of God to alter the course of rivers and to turn them to places that want water; we should follow the order of nature and be quiet. But since God acts in consequence of certain general laws, we correct his work without injuring his wisdom. We resist his action without opposing his will, because he doth not will positively and directly every thing that he doth. For example, he doth not directly will unjust actions, though he alone gives motion to those that commit them. And though it be only he who sends rain, yet every man hath a liberty to shelter himself when it rains. For God doth not send rain but by a necessary consequence of general laws, laws which he hath established not that such or such a man should be wet through but for greater ends. . . .

Chapter II

I. The love of order is not only the chief of all moral virtues but the only virtue. It is the mother virtue, the fundamental, universal virtue, the virtue which alone makes the habits or dispositions of the mind virtuous. He that bestows his goods on the poor out of vanity or natural compassion is not liberal,[4] because it is not reason that guides him, nor order that governs him, it is nothing but pride or mechanism. . . . The same may be said of all the other virtues. If the love of order be not the foundation of them, they are false and vain and altogether unbecoming a reasonable nature which bears the image of God himself and hath a communication with him. They derive their original from the body only . . . whatever the rebellious imagination may think, it is not mean and servile to submit to the law of God himself. Nothing is more just than to be conformable to order. Nothing is more brave and generous than to follow the party of reason with an unshaken constancy and inviolable fidelity, not only when one may follow it with honor, but then more especially when the circumstances of times and places are such that one cannot do it without the greatest shame and disgrace. For he that passes for a fool in following reason loves reason more than himself, but he that follows order only when it shines and sparkles in the eyes of the world seeks only glory; and though he may be very glorious in the eyes of men, he is an abomination in the sight of God.

II. I know not whether I may be mistaken or no, but I believe there are abundance of people that do not rightly know what true virtue is, and even those that have writ of morality do not always speak very clearly and exactly of it. It is certain that all those great names which they give to virtues and vices produce rather confused sensations in the mind than clear ideas. But because the sensations affect the soul, and abstracted ideas, though clear in themselves, do not diffuse their light but in attentive minds, men most commonly rest satisfied with these words which please the senses but leave the mind in the dark. . . .

IV. One of the greatest defects observable in the moral writings of some philosophers is that they confound duties with virtues, or that they give the name of virtues to simple duties, so that though properly there be but one virtue, to wit the love of order, they make an infinite number of them. This is it which causes such confusion and so perplexes that science, that it is very hard to understand thoroughly what a man must do to be perfectly good and virtuous.

VII. It is certain that universal reason is always the same. Order is immutable, and yet morality changes according to places and times. It is a virtue among the Germans to drink hard, and a man can have no conversation with them if he be not drunk. It is not reason but wine that unites their societies. . . . Duelling was for a long time a lawful action amongst the French, and as if reason was not worthy to determine their differences, they decided them by force. . . .

VIII. . . . From whence can this diversity proceed, if the reason of man be always the same? From hence, no doubt, that they leave off consulting reason and suffer themselves to be guided by imagination, its enemy. Instead of observing the immutable order as their inviolable and natural law, they frame to themselves ideas of virtue conformable at least in some things to their own inclinations. . . .

X. I must confess that the immutable order is not easy to be found. It dwells within us, but we are always roving abroad. Our senses unite our soul to all the parts of the body, our imagination and passions extend it to all the objects which surround us and often carry it into a world that hath no more reality than imaginary spaces. This is undeniably so. But then we should endeavor to silence our sense, imagination and passions, and not fancy that we can be reasonable without consulting reason. . . .

XII. I grant then that those who have not light enough to guide themselves may attain to virtue as well as those who retire into themselves to consult reason and contemplate the beauty of order, because the grace of sense or prevenient delectation[5] may supply the want of light and keep them firm and steadfast in their duty. But that which I maintain is, first, that supposing all other things equal, he that enters farthest into himself and harkens to the truth within him in the greatest silence of his sense, imagination and passions is the most solidly virtuous. Secondly, that such a love of order as hath for its foundation more of reason than of faith, that is, more of light than of pleasure, is more solid, meritorious and valuable than another love which I suppose equal. For indeed the true good, the good of the soul, should be loved by reason and not by the instinct of pleasure. But the condition to which sin hath reduced us makes the grace of delight necessary to counterpoise the continual endeavors of our concupiscence. Lastly I assert that if a man should never, I say, never retire into himself, his imaginary faith would be wholly useless to him. For the word became sensible only to render truth intelligible. Reason was made incarnate for no other end but to guide men to reason by their senses; and he that should do and suffer all that Jesus Christ did and suffered would be neither reasonable nor a Christian if he did it not in the spirit of Christ, the spirit of order and reason. . . .

Chapter III

I. Though I have not expressed the principal or mother virtue by the authentic name of charity, I would not have anyone imagine that I pretend to deliver to men any other virtue than that which Christ himself hath established in these words: "All the law and the prophets depend on these two commandments: thou shalt love the Lord thy God with all thy heart and with all thy strength, and thy neighbor as thyself." . . .

II. These words are clear, but it is chiefly to those who are inwardly taught by the unction of the spirit. For as to others, they are more obscure than is commonly imagined. To "love" is an equivocal term. It signifies two things among many others: first, to unite ourselves by the will to any object as to our good or the cause of our happiness; and secondly to wish well to anyone. We may love God in the first sense and our neighbor in the second. But it would be impiety or at least stupidity to love God in the latter sense, and a kind of idolatry to love our neighbor in the former.

IV. . . . Our Saviour tells us in the parable of the Samaritan that all mankind is our neighbor. . . . Certainly there are none but those that love the true and real good who fulfil this commandment in loving their neighbor as themselves. For a father who loves his son with great tenderness and carefully procures for him all sensible good things, what love soever he may have for him, is very far from loving him as God commands us to love our neighbor.

VI. I think then I may say that justifying charity, or that virtue which renders the possessors of it truly just and virtuous, is properly a ruling love of the immutable order. But that I may clear those obscurities which ordinarily attend abstract ideas, I must explain these terms a little more at large.

VII. I have already said that the immutable order consists in nothing else but in those proportions or relations of perfection which are between the intellectual ideas comprehended in the substance of the eternal word. Now we ought to esteem and love nothing but perfection. And therefore our esteem and love should be conformable to order. I mean there should be the same proportion between two degrees of love as there is between the perfection or reality or the objects which cause them. For if there be not, they are not conformable to order. From hence it is evident that charity or the love of God is a consequence of the love of order, and that we ought to esteem and love God not only more, but infinitely more, than all other things. For there can be no finite relation between infinite and finite.

VIII. There are two principal kinds of love, a love of benevolence and a love which may be called love of union. A sensual man loves the object of his passion with a love of union, because he looks upon that object as the cause of his happiness, and therefore he desires to be united to it that it may act upon him and make him happy. He is carried towards it as well by the motion of his heart or by his affections as by the motion of his body. The love which we bear to persons of worth and merit is a love of benevolence. For we love them even when they are not in a condition to do us any good. We love them because they have more perfection and virtue than other men. So that the power to do us good, or that kind of perfection which relates to our happiness, in one word, goodness, excites in us a love of union, and all other perfections a love of benevolence. Now God only is good. He alone hath the power of acting on us.[6] He does not really communicate that perfection to his creatures, but only makes them occasional causes for the producing of some effects. For real and true power is incommunicable. Therefore all our love of union ought to tend toward God.

IX. We may, for instance, bring our body to the fire, because fire is the occasional cause of heat, which is necessary for it. But we cannot love it with a love of union without offending against order, because fire is so far from having any power over that part of us which is capable of loving that it hath no power at all. The same may be said of all other creatures, even angels and demons. . . . When I speak of loving, I mean also fearing and hating . . . the soul should remain unmoved in their presence. . . .

X. But the case is not the same with the love of benevolence as with the love of union. God is infinitely more amiable with this sort of love than all his creatures together. But as he hath really communicated to them some perfection, as they are capable of happiness, they really deserve our love and esteem. Order itself requires that we should esteem and love them according to the measure of perfection which they enjoy, or rather according to that which we know to be in them. For to esteem and love them exactly in proportion to their being amiable is utterly impossible, because many times their perfections are unknown to us, and we can never know exactly the proportions that are between perfections; for we cannot express them either by numbers or by incommensurable lines. Nevertheless faith takes away a great many difficulties in this matter. For since a finite being, by the relation it hath to infinity, acquires an infinite value, it is evident that we ought to love those creatures which have or may have a great relation to God infinitely more than those which do not bear his image. . . .

XII. Self-love, the irreconcilable enemy of virtue, or a ruling love of the immutable order, may agree with the love of union which is referred to and honors a power capable of acting on us. For it is sufficient for that purpose that this self-love be enlightened. Man invincibly desires to be happy, and he sees clearly that God alone is able to make him so. This being supposed and all the rest excluded, of which I do not speak, it is evident that he may desire to be united to God. For to take away everything that may be equivocal, I do not speak of a man who knows that God rewards only merit and who finds none in himself; but I speak of one who considers only the power and goodness of God, or one to whom the testimony of his conscience and his faith give a free access, as I may so say, to draw near to God and join himself with him.

XIII. But the case is different with the love of esteem or benevolence which a man ought to bear to himself. Self-love makes it always irregular. Order requires that the reward should be proportionable to the merit and the happiness to the perfection of the soul, which it hath gained by a good use of its liberty. But self-love can endure no bounds to its happiness and glory. Though it be never so much enlightened, yet if it be not just it must of necessity be contrary to order; and it cannot be just without diminishing or destroying itself. Nevertheless, when self-love is both enlightened and just, whether it be destroyed by, or confounded with, the love of order, a man hath then the greatest perfection that he is capable of. For certainly he that always places himself in the rank that belongs to him, who desires to be happy no farther than he deserves to be so and seeks his happiness in the justice which he expects from the righteous judge, who lives by faith and rests contented, steadfast and patient in the hope of foretaste of the true good; he, I say, is really a good man, though the love he bears to himself, reformed indeed and corrected by grace, be the natural foundation of his love of order above all things.

XVI. . . . to obtain the possession of virtue, it is not sufficient that we love order with a natural love but we must also love it with a free, enlightened and reasonable love. It is not sufficient to love it when it agrees with our self-love. We must sacrifice everything to it, our actual happiness and if it should require it of us our very being. . . .

Chapter IV

I. That I may give a clear explication of the means of acquiring or preserving the ruling love of the immutable order, I shall lay down two fundamental truths belonging to the first part of this treatise. First, that virtues are generally acquired and fortified by acts. Secondly, that when we act we do not always produce the acts of the ruling virtue. What I say of virtue must be also understood of all habits good or bad, and even of the passions which are natural to us.

XVI. All then that we have to do to acquire and preserve the ruling love of immutable order . . . consists in searching diligently what are the things that excite this love and make it produce its proper acts, and what those are that can stop the actual motion of self-love. Now I know but two principles which determine the natural motion of the will and stir up the habits, to wit, light and sense. Without one of these principles no habit is formed naturally, and those which are formed remain unactive. If anyone will take the pains to consult what he finds within himself, he will easily be satisfied that the will never actually loves any good except the light discovers it or pleasure renders it present to the soul. And if we consult reason we shall be convinced that it must be so, for otherwise the author of nature would imprint useless motions on the will.

XVII. There is nothing then but light and pleasure which can produce any motion in the soul. Light discovers to it the good which it loves by an irresistible impression, and pleasure assures it that the good is actually present. For the soul is never more fully convinced of its good than when it makes itself actually touched with the pleasure which makes it happy. Let us therefore enquire into the means by which we may cause the light to diffuse itself in our minds, and make our hearts be touched with such sensations as are suitable to our design, which is to produce in us the acts of the love of order, or to hinder us from forming those of self-love. For it is evident that all the precepts of morality absolutely depend on these means.

Chapter V

XII. The only rule which I would have carefully observed is to meditate only on clear ideas and undeniable experiences. To meditate on confused sensations and doubtful experiences is lost labor. This is to contemplate nothing but chimeras and to follow error. The immutable and necessary order, the divine law, is also our law. This ought to be the principal subject of our meditations. Now there is nothing more abstracted and less subject to sense than this order. I grant that we may also be guided by order made sensible and visible by the actions and precepts of Jesus Christ. Yet that is because that sensible order raises the mind to the knowledge of the intellectual order, for the word made flesh is our model only to conform us to reason, the indispensable model of all intelligent beings. . . .

XV. By clear ideas, which I make the principal object of those who would know and love order, I mean not only those between which the mind can discover the precise and exact relations such as are all those which are the object of mathematical knowledge and may be expressed by numbers or represented by lines. But I understand in general by clear ideas all such as produce any light in the mind of those who contemplate them, and from which one may draw certain consequences. So that I reckon among clear ideas not only simple ideas but also those truths which contain the relations that are between ideas. I comprehend also in this number common notions and principles of morality and in a word all clear truths which are evident either of themselves, or by demonstration, or by an infallible authority, though to speak more nicely these last are rather certain than clear and evident.

XVI. By undeniable experiences I mean chiefly those matters of fact which faith informs us of and those of which we are convinced by the inward sense we have of what passes within ourselves. . . .

XIX. The knowledge of order, which is our indispensable law, is compounded of both these, clear ideas and inward sensations. Every man knows that it is better to be good, than rich, a prince, or a conqueror; but every man doth not see it by a clear idea. Children and ignorant people know well enough when they do ill; but 'tis because the secret check of reason reproves them for it, and not always because the light discovers it to them. For order considered speculatively and precisely, only as it contains the relations of perfection, enlightens the mind without moving it; if it be taken only for the law of God, the law of all spiritual beings, and considered only so far as it hath the force of a law (for God loves order himself and irresistibly wills that we should love it or that we should love everything in proportion to its being amiable); order, I say, as it is the natural and necessary principle and rule of all the motions of the soul touches, penetrates and convinces the mind without enlightening it. So that we may discover order by a clear idea, but we know it also by a sensation. For since God loves order and continually imprints on us a love and motion like his own, we must necessarily be informed by the sure and compendious way of sensations when we follow or forsake the immutable order.

XX. But we must observe that this way of discovering order by sensation or instinct is often rendered uncertain by sin, which hath introduced concupiscence, because the secret influences of the passions are of the same nature with that inward sensation. For when we act contrary to opinion and custom we often feel such inward checks as very much resemble those of reason and order. Before sin entered the world, the sense of inward reproof was a sign that could not be mistaken . . . but since that time the secret inspirations of our passions are not subject to our wills, so that they are easily confounded with the inspirations of inward truth when the mind is not enlightened. Hence it is that there are so many people who seriously and in good earnest maintain abominable errors. A false idea of religion and morality which agrees with their interests and passions appears truth itself to them. . . .

XXI. There is nothing then more certain and secure than light. We cannot fix our attention too long on clear ideas, and though we may suffer ourselves to be animated by the inward sense yet we must never be guided by it. We must contemplate order in itself and permit this sensation only to keep up our attention by the motion which it excites in us. Otherwise our meditations will never be rewarded with a clear prospect of truth. . . .

Chapter VI

I. We cannot discover truth without the labor of attention, because this labor alone is rewarded with light. Before a man can support and continue the labor of attention, he must have attained some strength of mind. . . .to keep [a man] from falling into error it is not sufficient to have a strong mind to endure labor, but he must also have another virtue which I cannot better express than by the equivocal name of *liberty of mind,* by which a man withholds his assent until he be irresistibly forced to give it.

II. When we examine any very compounded question and our mind finds itself surrounded on all sides with very great difficulties, reason permits us to give over our labor, but it indispensably requires us to suspend our assent and to judge of nothing when nothing is evident. To make use of our liberty as much as we can is an essential and indispensable precept both of logic and of morality. For we ought never to believe till evidence obliges us to it; we ought never to love that which we may without remorse hinder ourselves from loving. . . .

IV. . . . he that loves nothing but what he evidently knows to be the true good, nothing but what he cannot help loving, is not irregular in his love. He loves nothing but God, for there is nothing else which we cannot without remorse hinder ourselves from loving. There is nothing but God which we clearly and evidently know to be really good. . . .

V. Strength and liberty of mind then are two virtues which we may call general or to use the common term cardinal virtues. For since we ought never to love anything nor do any action without good consideration, we must make use of the strength and liberty of our mind every moment. . . .

XV. That we may clearly comprehend the necessity of endeavoring to gain some liberty of mind, or some facility of suspending the assent of the will, we must know that when two or more goods are actually present to the mind and the mind determines its choice in relation to them, it never fails to choose that which at that instant appears to be the best, supposing equality in everything else. For the soul being capable of loving only by the natural tendency which it hath toward good must of necessity love that which hath the greatest conformity with what it loves irresistibly.

XVI. But we must observe that the soul may still suspend its assent and not determine itself finally, even when it doth determine itself . . . we may withhold our assent till evidence obliges us to yield it. Now we can never evidently see that false goods are true ones because we can never evidently see that which is not. So that though we cannot hinder ourselves from determining in favor of the most apparent goods, yet by suspending our assent we may love none but those that are most solid. . . . There is nothing then more necessary than the liberty of the mind to make us love none but the true good, live according to order, inviolably obey reason, and procure us true and solid virtue. . . .

Chapter VII

I. The facility of rendering the mind attentive and of withholding its assent till evidence obliges it are habits necessary for such as would be substantially virtuous. But solid virtue, virtue every way complete, doth not consist only in those two noble and extraordinary dispositions of the mind. There is required besides an exact obedience to the law of God, general nicety in all our duties, a firm and governing disposition of regulating all the motions of our hearts by the known order, in a word the love of order. . . .

II. But how must we gain this fixed and ruling disposition of governing all the motions of our heart and all the actions of our lives by the known order? . . . Habits are formed by acts. We must therefore frequently make firm and constant resolutions of obeying order and sacrificing everything to it. For by often repeating these actual resolutions and pursuing them at least in part, we may by degrees form some kind of habitual disposition. This is easy enough to be conceived, but it is by no means easy to be practiced. For which way can we frame this heroic resolution of sacrificing even our predominant passion to the divine law? Certainly it is not possible to be done without grace. . . . the desire of happiness is invincible and irresistible. And therefore without a firm faith and the hope of enjoying a happiness more solid than that which we part with, self-love, though never so much enlightened, cannot beget in us a bare resolution of sacrificing our predominant passion. This is without dispute.

III. Now . . . this faith and hope are the gifts of God. . . .

Chapter VIII

II. But when our faith is not lively nor our hope strong enough to make us resolve to sacrifice a passion which hath got such a dominion over our heart that it corrupts our mind every moment and draws it to its party, the only thing we ought to do, and perhaps the only thing we can do in this case, is to seek for that in the fear of Hell and the just indignation of an avenging God which we cannot find in the hope of an eternal happiness. . . .

XIV. I know very well that many people condemn the fear of hell as a motive of self-love. Notwithstanding I have made use of it as being the most lively and the most common motive to excite us to do those things which may contribute to our justification. . . . to desire to be happy or to desire not to be miserable is the same thing. . . . The fear of pain and the desire of pleasure are both of them but motions of self-love. Now self-love in itself is not evil. God continually produces it in us. He irresistibly inclines us to good and by the same motion irresistibly diverts us from evil. We cannot hinder ourselves from desiring to be happy and consequently from desiring not to be miserable. So then the fear of Hell and the hope of Heaven are two motives equally good: only that of fear hath this advantage over the other, that it is more lively, strong and efficacious, because generally, supposing all other things equal, we fear pain more than we desire pleasure. . . . besides it hath this advantage, that it is proper to awaken the most drowsy and stupid; and for this reason it is that the Scripture and the Fathers make use of this motive*

---

* By motive I understand that which excites in the soul an actual motion of that kind of love which I called before the love of union.

upon all occasions. For after all, it is not properly the motive which regulates the heart but the love of order. Every motive is grounded on self-love. . . .

XV. . . . There is a difference between the motives and the end. We are excited by the motives to act for the end. It is the greatest crime imaginable to place our end in ourselves. We should do everything for God. All our actions should be referred to him from whom alone we have the power to do them. Otherwise we violate order, we offend God and are guilty of injustice. This is undeniable. But we should seek for the motives which may make us love order in that invincible love which God hath given us for happiness. For since God is just, we cannot be happy if we are not subservient to order. It matters not whether those motives be of fear or of hope, if they do but animate and support us. . . .

PART II

Chapter I

II. So then, though it be sufficient to make us just and acceptable to God that the love of order be our predominant habit, yet if we would be perfect and complete, we must be able to govern this love by an exact knowledge of our duties. Nay, I would say that he who neglects or slights this knowledge, what zeal soever he may find within himself for order, his heart is by no means rightly disposed. . . .

III. Indeed those whose mind is so weak and their passions so strong that they are not capable of giving counsel to themselves, or rather of taking counsel of him who enlightens all men, are excusable before God if they sincerely desire and follow the advice of such as they believe to be the best and wisest of men. . . .

V. But since it is impossible for a man that is not versed in the science of morality to discover the order of his duties in sudden and unexpected occasions, though he have never so great strength and liberty of mind, it is necessary for him to provide against those occasions which leave him no time for examination, and by a prudent foresight to inform himself of his duties in general, or of some certain and undeniable principles to govern his actions by in particular cases. This study of a man's duties ought without doubt to be preferred before all others. Its end and reward is eternity. . . .

Chapter IV

VII. Now that the natural love which God continually imprints on us may still continue love and not be turned into hatred, that the love of happiness may make us happy, that it may carry us toward good and unite us to him . . . our love must always be conformable to or resembling the divine love. We must love perfection as well as happiness. We must remain united to the wisdom of God as well as to his power. For God when he created man gave him . . . as it were two sorts of love, one of happiness and the other of perfection. By the love of happiness he united him to his power, which alone can make him happy; and by the love of perfection he united him to his wisdom, by which alone as his inviolable law he ought to be governed. . . .

VIII. For we must observe that in the condition we are now in, our happiness and our perfection often clash, and we cannot avoid engaging on one side or the other. . . . when we sacrifice our happiness to our perfection, or our pleasure to the love of order, we merit, for then we obey the divine law, though we suffer by it, and thereby we give honor to the wisdom of God. . . . God is certainly just and faithful. He will give us all the happiness we deserve; our patience shall not be fruitless. . . .

Chapter VI

I. Having explained in general the duties which we owe to God, we must now examine those which we owe to other men. . . .

II. We are capable of forming two sorts of society with other men: a society for some years, and an eternal society; a society of commerce and a society of religion. . . .

III. The great, or indeed the only, design of God is the holy city, the heavenly Jerusalem, where truth and justice inhabit. All other societies shall perish. . . .

V. So when our savior bids us love one another, we must not imagine that he absolutely commands us any other thing than to procure one another the true and spiritual goods. . . . We must assist our neighbor and preserve his life as we are obliged to preserve our own, but we must prefer the salvation of our neighbor before his and our own life.

VII. . . . we may and ought to love [our neighbor] with a love of benevolence. We must love him in that sense of the word which signifies to desire his happiness and perfection, and . . . use all our endeavors to procure him solid virtue that he may merit the true goods which are the reward of it.

X. There is this difference between the duties which religion obliges us to pay to God and those which society requires us to pay to men: that the principal duties of religion are inward and spiritual, because God searches the hearts and absolutely speaking hath no need of his creatures; whereas the duties of society are almost all external. . . .

XI. Therefore to expect from other men inward and spiritual duties which are due to God alone . . . is a diabolical pride. . . . If they faithfully perform what we desire of them, what can we complain of?

Chapter VII

I. The three general heads to which all the particular duties that we owe to other men may be reduced are . . . simple esteem, which ought to be proportioned to the excellence or perfection of every being; respect, or a relative submission of the mind proportionable to the subordinate power of intelligent occasional causes;[7] and the love of benevolence. . . .

II. Simple esteem is a duty which we owe to all mankind. Contempt is an injury, and the greatest of injuries. There is nothing contemptible but nothing, for every real being deserves esteem. And as man is the noblest of creatures, it is a false judgment and an irregular motion to despise any man, let him be what he will. . . .

VII. As to our enemies and persecutors, it is certain that esteem is a duty more general than benevolence. There are some goods which we are not bound to wish our enemies. . . . But the persecution of our enemies ought not of itself to diminish the esteem that is due to them. . . .

Chapter XIV

I. The duties which we owe to ourselves as well as those which we owe to our neighbors may be reduced to this general head, of laboring for our happiness and perfection: our perfection, which consists chiefly in a perfect conformity of our will with the immutable order; and our happiness, which consists wholly in the enjoyment of pleasure. . . .

II. The perfection of the mind consists chiefly in the conformity of the will to order. For he that loves order above all things hath virtue. He that obeys order in all things fulfils his duty. And he that sacrifices his present pleasure to order, that suffers pain and despises himself out of respect to the divine law, merits a solid happiness, the genuine and suitable reward of a tried and approved virtue. That almighty and all-righteous law shall judge his cause and shall reward him to all eternity.

III. To seek after happiness is not virtue but necessity. For virtue is free and voluntary but the desire of happiness is not in our own choice. Self-love, properly speaking, is not a quality which may be increased or diminished. We cannot cease to love ourselves, though we may cease to love ourselves amiss. We cannot stop the motion of self-love, but we may regulate it according to the divine law. We may by the motion of self-love enlightened, supported by faith and hope, and governed by charity, we may, I say, sacrifice present for future pleasures and make ourselves miserable for a time to escape the eternal vengeance of the righteous judge. For grace doth not destroy nature. The motion which God continually imprints on us toward good in general never stops. The wicked and the righteous equally desire to be happy. They equally tend toward the source of their felicity. Only the righteous doth not suffer himself to be deceived and corrupted by pleasing appearances. The foretaste of the true good supports him in his course. But the sinner, being blinded by his passions, forgets God, his rewards and punishments, and employs all the motion which God gives him for the true good in the pursuit of phantoms and illusions.

IV. Self-love therefore or the desire of being happy is neither virtue nor vice. But it is the natural motive to virtue and in wicked men becomes the motive to vice. God alone is our end; he alone is our good; reason alone is our law; and self-love . . . is the motive which should make us love God, unite ourselves to him, and submit to his law. For we are not our own good nor our own law. . . .

V. Our self-love then is the motive which being assisted by grace unites us to God as our good or the cause of our happiness, and subjects us to reason as our law or the model of our perfection. But we must not make the motive our End or our law. We must truly and sincerely love order and unite ourselves to God by reason. . . .

Editor's Notes

1. And consequently, following the Cartesian principle that what can be conceived can be, such a being can exist all alone, without creating other beings.
2. Particular beings must be created by God's volition, but not the eternal order itself or the essences of things, which determine their degrees of perfection. Malebranche was opposed to Descartes's voluntarism. See the tenth "Clarification" of the *Search for Truth*.
3. For Malebranche, relations of greatness hold between ideas of the same nature, as between a fathom and a foot, whereas relations of perfection hold between ideas of different natures, as between body and spirit or mind.
4. "Liberal" in the sense of displaying the virtue of liberality or generosity.
5. Malebranche was arguing here that unenlightened religious faith may do something to lead men to virtue because it may facilitate the acquisition of a grace that comes before merit, a prevenient grace, and this may show itself by one's taking pleasure in virtue. But, as he continued, virtue arising from the love of clearly seen order is firmer and much better.
6. This is the core of Malebranche's occasionalism, here turned to show that we ought to love God above all else.
7. Malebranche considered all human actions (like every other motion) as only occasional causes, that is, as not having any real power to do anything. Only God has such power. Within this metaphysical framework, Malebranche was telling us we must respect what are commonly thought to be earthly superior powers.

Further Reading

Volume 11 of André Robinet, ed., *Oeuvres complètes de Malebranche* (Paris: Vrin, 1966), is a modern edition of the *Traité de morale*.

Malebranche's major philosophical work, *De la recherche de la vérité*, was translated into English by Thomas M. Lennon and Paul Olscamp as *The Search After Truth* (Columbus: Ohio State University Press, 1980). Another of his works available in English, *Dialogues on Metaphysics*, trans. M. Ginsberg (London: Allen & Unwin, 1923), is a good introduction to Malebranche's epistemological and metaphysical views.

Although Malebranche has been much studied by the French, there is little about him in English, no recent general review of his philosophy, and only one book on his ethics: Craig Walton, *De la Recherche du Bien, A Study of Malebranche's Science of Ethics* (The Hague: Nijhoff, 1972). Michael E. Hobart, *Science and Religion in the Thought of Nicholas Malebranche* (Chapel Hill: University of North Carolina Press, 1982), does not discuss the ethics. Patrick Riley discusses the political bearing of

Malebranche's metaphysical, religious, and moral views – particularly the thesis that God always acts by general laws – in *The General Will Before Rousseau* (Princeton, N.J.: Princeton University Press, 1986). For the political context of Malebranche's work, see Nannerl O. Keohane, *Philosophy and the State in France* (Princeton, N.J.: Princeton University Press, 1980), pp. 308–10. Ira O. Wade, *Intellectual Origins of the French Enlightenment* (Princeton, N.J.: Princeton University Press, 1971), esp. pp. 418–36, explains Malebranche's importance to later French thought.

Charles McCracken, *Malebranche and British Philosophy* (Oxford: Clarendon Press, 1983), is a good study of the influence of Malebranche's views on British thought.

Ralph Cudworth

Introduction

Cudworth was born in 1617 and died in 1688, thus living through the troubled years of rebellion and restoration in England. It was a time during which the Puritans' Calvinist views attained and then lost dominance. Conflicting philosophies and theologies moved rapidly from the bookshelf to the battlefield, and ecclesiastical and academic positions were given and taken away on doctrinal grounds; never before had public life been so divided by ideology. The concurrent growth of scientific knowledge was proving as unsettling to some thinkers as was Hobbes's powerful secular vision of morals and politics.

Cudworth attended Emmanuel College, Cambridge, and was elected a fellow in 1639. While a student, he came under the influence of Benjamin Whichcote, a leading figure among the opponents of strongly Calvinistic versions of Christianity. Cudworth was sympathetic enough to the Puritans, however, to be appointed by them to the mastership of Clare College and to serve on committees for the Parliament they controlled. Nonetheless, in the sermon he gave at the invitation of Parliament in 1647, Cudworth spoke as a follower of Whichcote's. He argued eloquently against making matters of doctrine and ritual central to the Christian life, defended the independence of standards of good and evil from God's will, and stressed the importance of a moral life that all people could lead regardless of their differences regarding religious doctrines.

After a few years away from Cambridge, Cudworth returned in 1654 as master of Christ's College. He wrote a great deal but hesitated to publish anything. In 1678, however, his massive treatise *The True Intellectual System of the Universe* was issued, but it was not until 1731 that his *Treatise Concerning Eternal and Immutable Morality* appeared, and his incomplete *Treatise of Freewill* was not published until 1838. Cudworth's influence, however, may have been greater than this publication record suggests, as his manuscripts were available to a few people before their publication, and his daughter, Damaris Lady Masham, who was a close friend of John Locke's, did much to disseminate her father's thought. Cudworth's substantial extant manuscripts are now being studied by scholars, but until more work is done on them, our knowledge of his views will remain incomplete.

Cudworth served as professor of Hebrew at Cambridge and was a man of enormous erudition. His *True Intellectual System* is so crammed with learning and quotations that it was long considered valuable mainly for the historical lessons offered. Yet Cudworth was an acute philosopher, with a far greater ability to work out a systematic view than that of any of the other Cambridge thinkers with whom he was allied. Centered at Emmanuel College and known as the Cambridge Platonists, this group was united by a

275

desire to present Christianity as teaching that morality matters more than dogma does and that morality is chiefly a matter of love, of showing to one another God's love to us. The Platonists were strongly opposed to Puritan interpretations of their religion, and they welcomed the advances of the new science, seeing in them nothing to threaten the core of faith. For they held that religion is wholly reasonable and that reason cannot conflict with itself.

"In the use of reason and the exercise of virtue, we enjoy God," stated Benjamin Whichcote, summing up two key points of the Platonists' view. And in one of his most famous aphorisms, he observed, "There are but two things in religion: morals and institutions. Morals may be known by the reason of the thing; morals are owned [i.e., accepted] as soon as spoken, and they are nineteen parts in twenty of all religion." Against the voluntarism of the Puritans – and with the belief that Hobbes was also a voluntarist – Whichcote remarked, "The moral part of religion never alters. Moral laws are laws of themselves, without sanction by will; and the necessity of them arises from the things themselves." He approached this also from another angle: "The spirit of God in us is a living law, informing the soul; not constrained by a law without, that enlivens not; but we act in the power of an inward principle of life, which enables, inclines, facilitates, determines." We can be moved by this law within us, Whichcote believed with his colleagues, because we are free. The Platonists thus opposed the predestinarianism of the Puritans and the determinism of Hobbes. They were equally opposed to materialistic doctrines, as these cut at the root of their belief that it is in our communion with God, through reason, that we acquire the living knowledge of morality that is indispensable to salvation.

Some of the Platonists, like Henry More, wrote philosophical treatises; others, like Whichcote and John Smith, confined themselves to sermons and tracts. Even More found it difficult to write a convincing philosophical articulation and defense of the Platonists' position. If anyone provided a philosophy for the Platonists, it was Cudworth.

Cudworth's *True Intellectual System* is an attempt to refute determinism. It begins by attacking atheism, which Cudworth assumed was implied by materialism. Hence he attacked Hobbes's materialism and also the more complex materialism attributing to matter its own kind of soul – an ancient doctrine that, Cudworth thought, was being revived by Spinoza. Cudworth tried to replace these views with a dualism of active and passive entities, of which the active ones are like the human mind, although there are other kinds of active entities as well. The view that the human mind is active is central to Cudworth's ethics, but unfortunately in the published work the details are not spelled out. In the treatise on morality, however, Cudworth argued on epistemological grounds that the mind cannot only be a passive recipient of sensations; it must also contribute substantially from its own resources in order for us to have the knowledge we have. This holds for both scientific and moral knowledge. The mind brings to the world its innate understanding of God's mind, of which we can have a rational, if only a partial, grasp. This knowledge is gathered from outside the self and is also involved in its central identity. Hence it can provide us with reason to act as it directs: external inducements, punishments and rewards, are unnecessary.

Cudworth's opposition to voluntarism is evident throughout the *Treatise Concerning Eternal and Immutable Morality*. He meant to oppose both the voluntarist view of the ultimate unintelligibility of God's direction of our lives and the model of morality as laws backed by sanctions. In the published work Cudworth offered little or nothing of an alternative vision of morality. But it would be consonant with the general views of the Platonists to assume that, for him, morality was an expression of proper love and that immorality was excessive self-love. What is perhaps less evident in the *Treatise* is Cudworth's insistence that although morality requires no punishment-wielding legislator, God is nonetheless indispensable to the moral life. In knowing what morality requires, we are knowing God's mind, without which we would be able to know only our own, separate minds. Because we would then have no common moral knowledge, it is plain that the human community is held together through God. Cudworth's *Treatise* is essentially a work of moral epistemology. It shows us the subject emerging as part of an overall defense of a Christian view.

The following selections are from *A Treatise Concerning Eternal and Immutable Morality,* London, 1731. I have modernized some of the spelling, capitalization, italics, and punctuation.

A Treatise Concerning Eternal and Immutable Morality

Book I

Chapter I

1. As the vulgar generally look no higher for the original of moral good and evil, just and unjust, than the codes and pandects, the tables and laws of their country and religion; so there have not wanted pretended philosophers in all ages who have asserted nothing to be good and evil, just and unjust, naturally and immutably; but that all these things were positive, arbitrary and factitious only. . . .

Of this sort is that late writer of ethics and politics[1] who asserts "that there are no authentic doctrines concerning just and unjust, good and evil, except the laws which are established in every city; and that it concerns none to inquire whether an action shall be reputed just or unjust, good or evil, except such only whom the community have appointed to be the interpreters of their laws."

And again, "even a Christian government hath power to determine what is righteous, and what is the transgression of it."

And he gives us the same over again in English: "In the state of nature nothing can be unjust; the notions of right and wrong, justice and injustice have there no place; where there is no common power, there is no law; where no law, no transgression. No law can be unjust." Nay, temperance is no more naturally according to this civil (or rather uncivil) philosopher, than justice. "Sensuality in that sense in which it is condemned, hath no place till there be laws."

5. But whatsoever was the true meaning of these philosophers, that affirm justice and injustice to be only by law and not by nature (of which I shall discourse afterwards,) certain it is that divers modern theologers do not only seriously but zealously contend in like manner that there is nothing absolutely, intrinsically and naturally good and evil, just and unjust antecedently to any positive command or prohibition of God; but that the arbitrary will and

pleasure of God (that is, an omnipotent being devoid of all essential and natural justice), by its commands and prohibitions, is the first and only rule and measure thereof. Whence it follows unavoidably that nothing can be imagined so grossly wicked or so foully unjust or dishonest but if it were supposed to be commanded by this omnipotent deity, must needs upon that hypothesis forthwith become holy, just and righteous. For though the ancient fathers of the Christian church were very abhorrent from this doctrine (as shall be shewed hereafter) yet it crept up afterward in the scholastic age, Ockham[2] being among the first that maintained that there is no act evil but as it is prohibited by God, and which cannot be made good if it be commanded by God. And so on the other hand as to good. . . .

But this doctrine hath been since chiefly promoted and advanced by such as think nothing so essential to the deity as uncontrollable power and arbitrary will, and therefore that God could not be God if there should be anything evil in its own nature which he could not do; and who impute such dark counsels and dismal actions unto God, as cannot be justified otherwise than by saying that whatsoever God can be supposed to do or will, will be for that reason good or just, because he wills it.

Now the necessary and unavoidable consequences of this opinion are such as these, that to love God is by nature an indifferent thing, and is morally good only because it is commanded by God; that to prohibit the love of God, or command the hatred of God, is not inconsistent with the nature of God, but only with his free will;[3] that it is not inconsistent with the natural equity of God to command blasphemy, perjury, lying, etc. That God may command what is contrary, as to all the precepts of the decalogue, so especially to the first, second, third; that holiness is not a conformity with the nature of God; that God may oblige man to what is impossible;[4] that God hath no natural inclination to the good of the creatures; that God can justly doom an innocent creature to eternal torment.[5] All which propositions with others of like kind are word for word asserted by some late authors. . . . And yet [none of these writers] are to be thought any more blame-worthy herein, than many others that holding the same premises have either dissembled or disowned those conclusions which unavoidably follow therefrom, but rather to be commended for their openness, simplicity and ingenuity,[6] in representing their opinion nakedly to the world, such as indeed it is, without any veil or mask.

Wherefore since there are so many, both philosophers and theologers, that seemingly and verbally acknowledge such things as moral good and evil, just and unjust, that contend notwithstanding that these are not by nature but institution,[7] and that there is nothing naturally or immutably just or unjust, I shall from hence fetch the rise of this ethical discourse or inquiry concerning things good and evil, just and unjust, laudable and shameful (for so I find these words frequently used as synonymous in Plato and other ancient authors) demonstrating in the first place that if there be anything at all good or evil, just or unjust, there must of necessity be something naturally and immutable good and just. And from thence I shall proceed afterward to shew what this natural, immutable, and eternal justice is, with the branches and species of it.

Chapter II

1. Wherefore in the first place, it is a thing which we shall very easily demonstrate that moral good and evil, just and unjust, honest and dishonest (if they be not mere names without any signification, or names for nothing else, but willed and commanded, but have a reality in respect of the persons obliged to do and avoid them) cannot possibly be arbitrary things, made by will without nature; because it is universally true that things are what they are, not by will but by nature. As for example, things are white by whiteness, and black by blackness, triangular by triangularity, and round by rotundity, like by likeness, and equal by equality, that is, by such certain natures of their own. Neither can omnipotence itself (to speak with reverence) by mere will make a thing white or black without whiteness or blackness; that is, without such certain natures, whether we consider them as qualities in the objects without us according to the peripatetical philosophy, or as certain dispositions of parts in respect of magnitude, figure, site and motion, which beget those sensations or phantasms of white and black in us.[8] Or, for instance in geometrical figures, omnipotence itself cannot by mere will make a body triangular, without having the nature and properties of a triangle in it; that is, without having three angles equal to two right ones, nor circular without the nature of a circle; that is, without having a circumference equidistant everywhere from the center or middle point. Or lastly, to instance in things relative only; omnipotent will cannot make things like or equal one to another, without the natures of likeness and equality. The reason whereof is plain, because all these things imply a manifest contradiction; that things should be what they are not. And this is truth fundamentally necessary to all knowledge, that contradictories cannot be true: For otherwise, nothing would be certainly true or false. Now things may as well be made white or black by mere will, without whiteness or blackness, equal and unequal, without equality and inequality, as morally good and evil, just and unjust, honest and dishonest, *debita* and *illicita*,[9] by mere will, without any nature of goodness, justice, honesty. For though the will of God be the supreme efficient cause of all things and can produce into being or existence or reduce into nothing what it pleaseth, yet it is not the formal cause of anything besides itself, as the schoolmen have determined in these words, that God himself cannot supply the place of a formal cause.[10] And therefore it cannot supply the formal cause or nature of justice or injustice, honestly or dishonestly. Now all that we have hitherto said amounts to no more than this, that it is impossible anything should be by will only, that is, without a nature or entity, or that the nature and essence of any thing should be arbitrary.

2. And since a thing cannot be made anything by mere will without a being or nature, everything must be necessarily and immutably determined by its

own nature, and the nature of things be that which it is, and nothing else. For though the will and power of God have an absolute, infinite and unlimited command upon the existences of all created things to make them to be, or not to be at pleasure; yet when things exist, they are what they are, this or that, absolutely or relatively, not by will or arbitrary command, but by the necessity of their own nature. . . .

3. Now the necessary consequence of that which we have hitherto said is this, that it is so far from being true that all moral good and evil, just and unjust are mere arbitrary and factitious things that are created wholly by will, that (if we would speak properly) we must needs say that nothing is morally good or evil, just or unjust by mere will without nature, because everything is what it is by nature, and not by will. For though it will be objected here that when God or civil powers command a thing to be done that was not before obligatory or unlawful, the thing willed or commanded doth forthwith become obligatory; that which ought to be done by creatures and subjects respectively; in which the nature of moral good or evil is commonly conceived to consist. And therefore if all good and evil, just and unjust be not the creatures of mere will (as many assert) yet at least positive things must needs owe all their morality, their good and evil to mere will without nature. Yet notwithstanding, if we well consider it we shall find that even in positive commands themselves, mere will doth not make the thing commanded just or obligatory, or beget and create any obligation to obedience; but that it is natural justice or equity, which gives to one the right or authority of commanding, and begets in another duty and obligation to obedience. Therefore it is observable that laws and commands do not run thus, to will that this or that thing shall become just or unjust, obligatory or unlawful; or that men shall be obliged or bound to obey; but only to require that something be done or not done, or otherwise to menace punishment to the transgressors thereof. For it was never heard of that any one founded all his authority of commanding others and others' obligation or duty to obey his commands in a law of his own making, that men should be required, obliged, or bound to obey him. Wherefore since the thing willed in all laws is not that men should be bound or obliged to obey, this thing cannot be the product of the mere will of the commander, but it must proceed from something else; namely, the right or authority of the commander, which is founded in natural justice and equity, and an antecedent obligation to obedience in the subjects; which things are not made by laws but presupposed before all laws to make them valid. And if it should be imagined that anyone should make a positive law to require that others should be obliged or bound to obey him, everyone would think such a law ridiculous and absurd; for if they were obliged before, then this law would be in vain, and to no purpose; and if they were not before obliged, then they could not be obliged by any positive law, because they were not previously bound to obey such a person's commands. So that obligation to obey all positive laws is older than all laws, and previous or antecedent to them. Neither is it a thing that is arbitrarily made by will or can be the object of command, but that which either is or is

not by nature. And if this were not morally good and just in its own nature before any positive command of God, that God should be obeyed by his creatures, the bare will of God himself could not beget an obligation upon any to do what he willed and commanded, because the natures of things do not depend upon will, being not things that are arbitrarily made, but things that are. To conclude therefore, even in positive laws and commands it is not mere will that obligeth, but the natures of good and evil, just and unjust, really existing in the world.

4. Wherefore that common distinction betwixt things, things naturally and positively good and evil, or (as others express it) betwixt things that are therefore commanded because they are good and just, and things that are therefore good and just, because they are commanded,[11] stands in need of a right explication, that we be not led into a mistake thereby, as if the obligation to do those thetical[12] and positive things did arise wholly from will without nature, whereas it is not the mere will and pleasure of him that commandeth that obligeth to do positive things commanded, but the intellectual nature of him that is commanded. Wherefore the difference of these things lies wholly in this, that there are some things which the intellectual nature obligeth to of itself, and directly, absolutely and perpetually, and these things are called naturally good and evil; other things there are which the same intellectual nature obligeth to by accident only, and hypothetically, upon condition of some voluntary action either of our own or some other persons, by means whereof those things which were in their own nature indifferent, falling under something that is absolutely good or evil and thereby acquiring a new relation to the intellectual nature do for the time become such things as ought to be done or omitted, being made such not by will but by nature. As for example, to keep faith and perform covenants is that which natural justice obligeth to absolutely; therefore upon the supposition that any one maketh a promise, which is a voluntary act of his own, to do something which he was not before obliged to by natural justice, upon the intervention of this voluntary act of his own, that indifferent thing promised falling now under something absolutely good, and becoming the matter of promise and covenant, standeth for the present in a new relation to the rational nature of the promiser, and becometh for the time a thing which ought to be done by him, or which he is obliged to do. Not as if the mere will of words and breath of him that covenanteth had any power to change the moral natures of things, or any ethical virtue of obliging; but because natural justice and equity obligeth to keep faith and perform covenants. In like manner natural justice, that is, the rational or intellectual nature, obligeth not only to obey God, but also civil powers, that have lawful authority of commanding, and to observe political order amongst men; and therefore if God or civil powers command any thing to be done that is not unlawful in itself, upon the intervention of this voluntary act of theirs those things that were before indifferent become by accident for the time obligatory, such things as ought to be done by us, not for their own sakes, but for the sake of that which natural justice absolutely obligeth to.

And these are the things that are commonly called positively good and evil, just or unjust, such as though they are adiaphorous[13] or indifferent in themselves, yet natural justice obligeth to accidentally on supposition of the voluntary action of some other person rightly qualified in commanding, whereby they fall into something absolutely good. Which things are not made good or due by the mere will or pleasure of the commander, but by that natural justice which gives him right and authority of commanding, and obligeth others to obey him; without which natural justice, neither covenants nor commands could possibly oblige any one. For the will of another does no more oblige in commands, than our own will in promises and covenants. To conclude therefore, things called naturally good and due are such things as the intellectual nature obliges to immediately, absolutely and perpetually, and upon no condition of any voluntary action that may be done or omitted intervening; but those things that are called positively good and due are such as natural justice or the intellectual nature obligeth to accidentally and hypothetically, upon condition of some voluntary act of another person invested with lawful authority in commanding.

And that it is not the mere will of the commander that makes these positive things to oblige or become due, but the nature of things, appears evidently from hence, because it is not the volition of everyone that obligeth, but of a person rightly qualified and invested with lawful authority; and because the liberty of commanding is circumscribed within certain bounds and limits, so that if any commander go beyond the sphere and bounds that nature sets him, which are indifferent things, his commands will not at all oblige.

Chapter III

1. But some there are that will still contend that though it should be granted that moral good and evil, just and unjust do not depend upon any created will, yet notwithstanding they must needs depend upon the arbitrary will of God because the natures and essences of all things, and consequently all verities and falsities, depend upon the same. For if the natures and essences of things should not depend upon the will of God, it would follow from hence that something that was not God was independent upon God.

2. And this is plainly asserted by that ingenious philosopher Renatus Des Cartes. . . .[14]

. . . whether Cartesius were in jest or earnest in this business it matters not, for his bare authority ought to be no more valued by us than the authority of Aristotle and other ancient philosophers was by him, whom he so freely dissents from.

4. For though the names of things may be changed by anyone at pleasure, as that a square may be called a circle, or a cube a sphere; yet that the nature of a square should not be necessarily what it is, but be arbitrarily convertible into the nature of a circle, and so the essence of a circle into the essence of a sphere, or that the self-same body, which is perfectly cubical, without any

physical alteration made in it, should by this metaphysical way of transformation of essences by mere will and command be made spherical or cylindrical;
this doth most plainly imply a contradiction, and the compossibility of contra-
dictions destroys all knowledge and the definite natures or notions of things.
Nay, that which implies a contradiction is a non-entity and therefore cannot be
the object of divine power. And the reason is the same for all other things, as
just and unjust; for everything is what it is immutably by the necessity of its
own nature; neither is it any derogation at all from the power of God to say
that he cannot make a thing to be that which it is not. Then there might be no
such thing as knowledge in God himself. God might will that there should be
no such thing as knowledge.

5. And as to the being or not being of particular essences, as that God might
if he pleased have willed that there should be no such thing as a triangle or
circle and therefore nothing demonstrable or knowable of either of them,
which is likewise asserted by Cartesius, and those that make the essences of
things dependent upon an arbitrary will in God: This is all one as if one should
say that God could have willed, if he had pleased, that neither his own power
nor knowledge should be infinite.

6. Now it is certain that if the natures and essences of all things, as to their
being such or such, do depend upon a will of God that is essentially arbitrary,
there can be no such thing as science or demonstration nor the truth of any
mathematical or metaphysical proposition be known any otherwise than by
some revelation of the will of God concerning it, and by a certain enthusiastic
or fanatic faith and persuasion thereupon that God would have such a thing to
be true or false at such a time or for so long. And so nothing would be true or
false naturally but positively only, all truth and science being mere arbitrary
things. Truth and falsehood would be only names. Neither would there be any
more certainty in the knowledge of God himself, since it must wholly depend
upon the mutability of a will in him essentially indifferent and undetermined;
and if we would speak properly according to this hypothesis, God himself
would not know or be wise by knowledge or by wisdom, but by will.

7. Wherefore as for that argument that unless the essences of things and all
verities and falsities depend upon the arbitrary will of God, there would be
something that was not God, independent upon God; if it be well considered,
it will prove a mere bugbear, and nothing so terrible and formidable as
Cartesius seemed to think it. For there is no other genuine consequence
deducible from this assertion that the essences and verities of things are
independent upon the will of God, but that there is an eternal and immutable
wisdom in the mind of God, and thence participated by created beings independent upon the will of God. Now the Wisdom of God is as much God as the
Will of God; and whether of these two things in God, that is, will or wisdom,
should depend upon the other, will be best determined from the several
natures of them. For wisdom in itself hath the nature of a rule and measure, it
being a most determinate and inflexible thing; but will being not only a blind
and dark thing, as considered in itself, but also indefinite and indeterminate,

hath therefore the nature of a thing regulable and measurable. Wherefore it is the perfection of will, as such, to be guided and determined by wisdom and truth; but to make wisdom, knowledge and truth to be arbitrarily determined by will and to be regulated by such a plumbean[15] and flexible rule as that is, is quite to destroy the nature of it; for science or knowledge is the comprehension of that which necessarily is, and there can be nothing more contradictory than truth and falsehood arbitrary. Now all the knowledge and wisdom that is in creatures, whether angels or men, is nothing else but a participation of that one eternal, immutable and increased wisdom of God, or several signatures of that one archetypal seal, or like so many multiplied reflections of one and the same face, made in several glasses, whereof some are clearer, some obscurer, some standing nearer, some further off.

8. Moreover, it was the opinion of the wisest of the philosophers (as we shall show afterward) that there is also in the scale of being a nature of goodness superior to wisdom, which therefore measures and determines the wisdom of God, as his wisdom measures and determines his will. . . . Wherefore although some novelists[16] make a contracted idea of God consisting of nothing else but will and power, yet his nature is better expressed by some in this mystical or enigmatical representation of an infinite circle, whose inmost center is simple goodness, the rays and expanded plat[17] thereof, all comprehending and immutable wisdom, the exterior periphery or interminate circumference, omnipotent will or activity, by which everything without God is brought forth into existence. Wherefore the will and power of God have no command inwardly either upon the wisdom and knowledge of God, or upon the ethical and moral disposition of his nature, which is his essential goodness; but the sphere of its activity is without God, where it hath an absolute command upon the existences of things; and is always free, though not always indifferent, since it is its greatest perfection to be determined by infinite wisdom and infinite goodness. But this is to anticipate what according to the laws of method should follow afterward in another place.

Book IV

Chapter I

7. Wherefore it is evident from what we have declared that there are two kinds of perceptive cogitations in the soul, the one passive, when the soul perceives by suffering from its body, and the objects without; the other active, when it perceives by exerting its own native vigour from within itself. The passive perceptions of the soul have two several names given unto them; for when the soul, by sympathizing with the body, seems to perceive corporeal things as present and really existing without it, then they are called sensations. But when the passive affections of the soul are looked upon not as things really existing without the mind, but only as pictures of sensible things in the mind, or more crass or corporeal cogitations, then they are called phantasms

or imaginations. But these phantasms and sensations being really the same things, as we said before, both of them being passions or affections in the soul, caused by some local motions in the body, and the difference between them being only accidental, insomuch that phantasms may be changed into sensations, and sometimes also sensations into phantasms, therefore all these passive perceptions of the soul may be called in general phantasms. But the active perceptions which rise from the mind itself without the body are commonly called conceptions of the mind; and so we have the two species of perceptive cogitations; the one phantasms, and the other conceptions of the mind.

8. Now that all our perceptive cogitations are not phantasms, as many contend, but that there is another species of perceptive cogitations distinct from them, arising from the active vigour of the mind itself, which we therefore call conceptions of the mind, is demonstrably evident from hence; because phantasms are nothing else but sensible ideas, images or pictures of outward objects, such as are caused in the soul by sense; whence it follows that nothing is the object of fancy but what is also the object of sense, nothing can be fancied by the soul but what is perceptible by sense. But there are many objects of our mind which we can neither see, hear, feel, smell nor taste, and which did never enter into it by any sense; and therefore we can have no sensible pictures or ideas of them, drawn by the pencil of that inward limner or painter which borrows all his colours from sense, which we call fancy; and if we reflect on our own cogitations of these things we shall sensibly perceive that they are not phantastical, but noematical.[18] As, for example, justice, equity, duty and obligation, cogitation, opinion, intellection, volition, memory, verity, falsity, cause, effect, genus, species, nullity, contingency, possibility, impossibility, and innumerable more such there are that will occur to any one that shall turn over the vocabularies of any language, none of which can have any sensible picture drawn by the pencil of the fancy. And there are many whole propositions likewise in which there is not any one work or notion that we can have any genuine phantasm of, much less can fancy reach to an apprehension of the necessity of the connexion of the terms. As for example, nothing can be and not be at the same time. What proper and genuine phantasms can any perceive in his mind either of *nothing,* or *can,* or *be,* or *and,* or *not be,* or *at the same,* or *time.* . . .

Chapter II

10. There are many other such ideas of the mind, of certain wholes made up of several corporeal parts, which, though sometimes locally discontinued, yet are joined together by relations, and habitudes to one another (founded in some actions of them, as they are cogitative beings) and by order all conspiring into one thing; which, though they are altogether imperceptible by sense, and therefore were never stamped or impressed upon the mind from the objects without; yet, notwithstanding, are not mere figments or beings of reason but things of the greatest reality, founded in certain actions of thinking

and cogitative beings; which are altogether imperceptible by sense and therefore could not possibly be outwardly stamped upon the mind; as for example, a polity or commonwealth, called an artificial man, which is a company of many united together by consent or contract under one government, to be regulated by some certain laws as it were by one will for the good of the whole; where, though the eye may see the particular persons (or at least their outsides) that are the respective members thereof, yet it can neither see the bond which unites them together, which is nothing but relation, nor comprehend the whole that is made up of them, that is, a polity or commonwealth according to the formal nature of it, which is an idea that proceeds merely from the unitive power and activity of the mind itself. . . .

13. Just in the same manner it happens many times in the contemplation of that great self-mover of the material universe which is the artifice of God, the artifice of the best mechanist, though there be no more passively impressed upon us from it than there is upon the diaphanous air or liquid ether contiguous to all solid bodies by local motion, of which only sensitive beings have conscious perception; yet there is a wonderful scene of various thoughts and motions raised in the mind thereupon, which are only occasionally invited by those stamps and impressions made from the material fabric and its various furniture without, but owe their true original and efficiency to nothing else but the innate vigour and activity of the mind itself. Some of which we have already instanced in the ideas of those relative considerations of corporeal things themselves and their parts to one another, by means of which the intellect rises up to that comprehensive view of the natures of particular corporeal things and the universal mundane system within itself all at once; which sense perceiving only by little and little, and taking in as it were point after point, cannot sum up its partial perceptions into the entire idea of any one whole. But the intellect doth not rest here, but upon occasion of those corporeal things thus comprehended in themselves naturally rises higher to the framing and exciting of certain ideas from within itself of other things not existing in those sensible objects but absolutely incorporeal. For being ravished with the contemplation of this admirable mechanism and artificial contrivance of the material universe, forthwith it naturally conceives it to be nothing else but the passive stamp, print and signature of some living art and wisdom as the pattern, archetype and seal of it, and so excites from within itself an idea of that divine art and wisdom. Nay, considering further how all things in this great mundane machine or animal (as the ancients would have it) are contrived not only for the beauty of the whole but also for the good of every part of it that is endued with life and sense, it exerts another idea, viz. of goodness and benignity from within itself, besides that of art and wisdom, as the queen regent and empress of art whereby art is employed, regulated and determined; now both these things, whereof the first is art, wisdom and knowledge; the second, goodness, benignity and morality, being looked upon as modes of some intellectual being or mind in which they exist, it from hence presently makes up an idea of God, as the author or architect of this great and

boundless machine; a mind infinitely good and wise; and so as it were re-sounds and re-echoes back the great creator's name, which from those visible characters impressed upon the material universe had pierced loudly into its ears, but in such an indiscernible manner, that sense listening never so atten-tively could not perceive the least murmur or whisper of it. And this is the most natural scale by which the intellectual mind in the contemplation of corporeal things ascends to God; from the passive prints and signatures of that one art and wisdom that appears in the universe, by taking notice from thence of the exemplary or archetypal cause, one infinite and eternal mind setting his seal upon all. For as he that hears a consort of musicians playing a lesson consisting of six or eight several parts, all conspiring to make up one harmony, will immediately conclude that there was some other cause of that harmony besides those several particular efficients[19] that struck the several instruments; for every one of them could be but a cause of his own part which he played. But the unity of the whole harmony into which all the several parts conspire must needs proceed from the art and musical skill of some one mind, the exemplary and archetypal cause of that vocal harmony which was but a pas-sive print or stamp of it. So though the atheist might possibly persuade himself that every particular creature was the first author or efficient of that part which it played in the universe by a certain innate power of its own; yet all the parts of the mundane system conspiring into one perfect harmony, there must of necessity be some one universal mind, the archetypal and exemplary cause thereof, containing the plot of the whole mundane music as one entire thing made up of so many several parts within himself. . . .

Chapter V

5. But probably it may be here demanded how a man shall know when his conceptions are conformed to the absolute and immutable natures of essences of things and their unchangeable relations to one another? Since the immedi-ate objects of intellection exist in the mind itself, we must not go about to look for the criterion of truth without ourselves by consulting individual sensibles as the exemplars of our ideas and measuring our conceptions by them. And how is it possible to know by measuring of sensible squares that the diameter of every square is incommensurable with the sides? Nay, as was observed before, the necessary truth of no geometrical theorem can ever be examined, proved, or determined by sensible things mechanically. And though the eter-nal divine intellect be the archetypal rule of truth, we cannot consult that, neither, to see whether our conceptions be commensurate with it. I answer therefore, that the criterion of true knowledge is not to be looked for any-where abroad without our own minds, neither in the heighth above nor in the depth beneath, but only in our knowledge and conceptions themselves. For the entity of all theoretical truth is nothing else but clear intelligibility, and whatever is clearly conceived is an entity and a truth; but that which is false, divine power itself cannot make it to be clearly and distinctly understood,

because falsehood is a non-entity, and a clear conception is an entity: and omnipotence itself cannot make a non-entity to be an entity.

Wherefore no man ever was or can be deceived in taking that for an epistemonical[20] truth which he clearly and distinctly apprehends, but only in assenting to things not clearly apprehended by him, which is the only true original of all error. . . .

11. It is a fond imagination for any to suppose that it is derogatory to the glory of God to bestow or import any such gift upon his creatures as knowledge is, which hath an intrinsical evidence within itself, or that creatures should have a certainty of the first principles which all men are conscious that they do so clearly understand that they cannot doubt of them, as that *Nihili nulla est affectio. Aequalia addita aequalibus efficient aequalia;*[21] without which they can know nothing at all; though they be notwithstanding ignorant, doubting, and erring in many things, and slowly proceed in their ratiocinations from one thing to another; whereas on the contrary it is plainly derogatory to it[22] to suppose that God cannot make any creature that can possibly have any certain knowledge of God's own existence or anything more than a bare credulity of the same.

12. Wherefore since it cannot be denied but every clear apprehension is an entity and the essence of truth is nothing but clear intelligibility, those philosophers must lay the stress of their cause here, that intellectual faculties may be so made as that men can never certainly tell when they have clear apprehensions, but may think they have them when they have not.

And it cannot be denied but that men are oftentimes deceived and think they clearly comprehend what they do not. But it does not follow from hence, because men sometimes think that they clearly comprehend what they do not, that therefore they can never be certain that they do clearly comprehend anything; which is just as if we should argue that because in our dreams we think we have clear sensations, we cannot therefore be ever sure when we are awake that we see things that really are. . . .

Chapter VI

1. We have now abundantly consumed the Protagorean philosophy[23] which, that it might be sure to destroy the immutable natures of just and unjust, would destroy all science or knowledge and make it relative and phantastical. Having shewed that this tenet is not only most absurd and contradictory in itself but also manifestly repugnant to that very atomical physiology on which Protagoras endeavored to found it, and than which nothing can more effectually confute and destroy it; and also largely demonstrated that though sense be indeed a mere relative and phantastical perception, as Protagoras thus far rightly supposed; yet notwithstanding there is a superior power of intellection and knowledge of a different nature from sense, which is not terminated in mere seeming and appearance only, but in the truth and reality of things, and reaches to the comprehension of that which really and absolutely is, whose

objects are the eternal and immutable essences and natures of things, and their unchangeable relations to one another. . . .

4. But I have not taken all this pain only to confute scepticism or phantasticism, or merely to defend and corroborate our argument for the immutable natures of just and unjust, but also for some other weighty purposes that are very much conducing to the business that we have in hand. And first of all, that the soul is not a mere *rasa tabula*,[24] a naked and passive thing which has no innate furniture of activity of its own nor anything at all in it but what was impressed upon it without; for if it were so then there could not possibly be any such thing as moral good and evil, just and unjust; forasmuch as these differences do not arise merely from the outward objects or from the impresses which they make upon us by sense, there being no such thing in them; in which sense it is truly affirmed by the author of the Leviathan, page 24, that "there is no common rule of good and evil to be taken from the nature of the objects themselves,"[25] that is, either considered absolutely in themselves or relatively to external sense only, but according to some other interior analogy which things have to a certain inward determination in the soul itself, from whence the foundation of all this difference must need raise, as I shall shew afterwards; not that the anticipations of morality spring merely from intellectual forms and notional ideas of the mind or from certain rules or propositions, arbitrarily printed upon the soul as upon a book, but from some other more inward and vital principle in intellectual beings as such, whereby they have a natural determination in them to do some things and to avoid others, which could not be if they were mere naked passive things. . . .

5. Again, I have the rather insisted upon this argument also because that which makes men so inclinable to think that justice, honesty and morality are but thin, airy and phantastical things that have little or no entity or reality in them besides sensuality is a certain opinion in philosophy which does usually accompany it, that matter and body are the first original and source of all things; that there is no incorporeal substance superior to matter and independent upon it; and therefore that sensible things are the only real and substantial things in nature; but souls and minds springing secondarily out of body, that intellectuality and morality which belong unto them are but thin and evanid[26] shadows of sensible and corporeal things and not natural but artificial and factitious things that do as it were border upon the confines of non-entity. . . .

13. Lastly, I have insisted the rather so largely upon this argument for this further reason also, because it is not possible that there should be any such thing as morality unless there be a God, that is, an infinite eternal mind that is the first original and source of all things, whose nature is the first rule and exemplar of morality; for otherwise it is not conceivable whence any such thing should be derived to particular intellectual beings. Now there can be no such thing as God if stupid and senseless matter be the first original of all things; and if all being and perfection that is found in the world, may spring up and arise out of the dark womb of unthinking matter; but if knowledge and understanding, if soul, mind and wisdom may result and emerge out of it, then

doubtless everything that appears in the world may; and so night, matter and chaos must needs be the first and only original of all things.

15. Wherefore we have not only shewed that all intellection and knowledge does not emerge or emane[27] out of sense, but also that sense itself is not a mere passion or reception of corporeal impresses without, but that it is an active energy and vigour, though sympathetical in the sentient. And it is no more possible that this should arise out of senseless matter and atoms by reason of any peculiar contemperation or contexture of them in respect of figure, site, and motion, than that which all atheists stoutly deny, that something should arise out of nothing.

And here we can never sufficiently applaud that ancient atomical philosophy so successfully revived of late by Cartesius, in that it shews distinctly what matter is and what it can amount unto, namely nothing else but what may be produced from mere magnitude, figure, site, local motion, and rest; from whence it is demonstrably evident and mathematically certain that no cogitation can possibly arise out of the power of matter; whereas that other philosophy which brings in a dark unintelligible matter that is nothing and everything, out of whose potentiality not only innumerable qualities, but also substantial forms and sensitive souls (and therefore why not rational also, since all reason emerges out of sense) may be educed, must of necessity perpetually brood and hatch atheism. Whereas we cannot but extremely admire that monstrous dotage and sottishness of Epicurus, and some other spurious pretenders to this atomical philosophy, that notwithstanding they acknowledge nothing else in matter besides magnitude, figure, site, and motion, yet would make not only the power of sensation, but also of intellection and ratiocination and therefore all human souls to arise from the mere contexture of corporeal atoms and utterly explode all incorporeal substances; than which two assertions nothing can be more contradictious. And this is far more absurd, to make reason and intellection to arise from magnitude, figure and motion, than to attribute those unintelligible qualities to matter which they explode.

Editor's Notes

1. Hobbes: Cudworth was citing both *De cive* and *Leviathan*, without giving references and without quoting them exactly.
2. William of Ockham (1285–1349), the best known of the medieval voluntarists.
3. Among the medieval voluntarists it was a matter of debate whether God could command creatures to hate him.
4. Here Cudworth was aiming at the Lutheran and Calvinist teaching about the functions of the moral law. See the section "Luther and Calvin" in the Introduction to this anthology.
5. The target here is the doctrine of predestination: God chooses to give some people grace and so to save them but does not give it to others equally undeserving. Of course, the Calvinist reply would be that all are undeserving, rather than innocent, because of Adam's sinfulness which we have inherited.
6. Not their cleverness – the modern sense – but their ingenuousness, candor, or freedom from reserve.

7. That is, by positive enactment that institutes them.
8. Cudworth was contrasting the older Aristotelian view of perception with the modern Lockean theory.
9. Cudworth elsewhere treated *debita* as meaning "obligatory or just" and *illicita* as meaning "unjust."
10. Although he himself was favorably inclined toward Cartesian science, Cudworth here used the Aristotelian scholastic terminology to say that although God can cause something to come into existence (be the efficient cause), he cannot cause a formal set of properties to have the content and structure they do (be the cause of a form or essence, what makes a thing the kind of thing it is).
11. A common distinction in natural law theory: things commanded because they are good and just are the subjects of natural law; things good and just because commanded are the subjects of God's positive laws, such as those given to the Jews concerning diet or to the Christians concerning worship.
12. Laid down by arbitrary institution.
13. Neither required nor forbidden.
14. Cudworth here was citing a passage from the "Replies" to the Sixth Set of Objections, given in the Descartes selections.
15. Made of lead and therefore malleable.
16. Innovators.
17. Area.
18. Pertaining not to the power of one's ability to fantasize or imagine but to the power to think.
19. Efficient causes, that is, the players.
20. Capable of becoming an object of knowledge. The Oxford English Dictionary cites only this passage as an example of the use of the term.
21. Nothing is caused by nothing; equals added to equals make equals.
22. That is, God's glory.
23. Cudworth was referring to Protagoras of Abdera (490?–421? B.C.E.), the Sophist who held that "man is the measure of all things," a relativism that Cudworth used as a prototype of everything to which he objected.
24. Blank tablet.
25. Hobbes, *Leviathan*, chap. 6; in Oakeshott's edition, p. 32.
26. Evanescent, vanishing.
27. Emanate.

Further Reading

Two excellent anthologies of the Cambridge Platonists' writings, both with good bibliographies, provide source material supplementing the Cudworth selections given here: C. A. Patrides, ed., *The Cambridge Platonists* (Cambridge, England: Cambridge University Press, 1980), and Gerald R. Cragg, ed., *The Cambridge Platonists* (New York: Oxford University Press, 1968). Both of them contain selections from Whichcote's "Aphorisms" and Cudworth's "Sermon to the House of Commons." There is no modern edition of Cudworth's works.

The second volume of John Tulloch, *Rational Theology and Christian Philosophy in England in the Seventeenth Century*, 2nd ed. (Edinburgh: William Blackwood, 1874), is still one of the best general studies of the Cambridge Platonists; chapter 4 is on Cudworth. See also J. H. Muirhead, *The Platonic Tradition in Anglo-Saxon Philosophy* (London: Allen & Unwin, 1931), of which pp. 33–71 discuss Cudworth; Ernst Cassirer, *The Platonic Renaissance in England*, trans. James P. Pettegrove (Austin:

University of Texas Press, 1953); and Gordon R. Cragg, *From Puritanism to the Age of Reason: A Study of Religious Thought in the Church of England 1660–1770* (Cambridge, England: Cambridge University Press, 1950). John Redwood, *Reason, Ridicule and Religion* (London: Thames & Hudson, 1976), chap. 2, discusses Cudworth's attack on atheism.

Cudworth is usually discussed in connection with the Cambridge Platonists, but there are some special studies of him. Of these, by far the best is J. A. Passmore, *Ralph Cudworth: An Interpretation* (Cambridge, England: Cambridge University Press, 1951). Lydia Gysi, *Platonism and Cartesianism in the Philosophy of Ralph Cudworth* (Bern: H. Lang, 1962), is less reliable. James Martineau, *Types of Ethical Theory*, 3rd ed. (Oxford: Clarendon Press, 1891), discusses Cudworth's ethics in vol. 2, pp. 427–59. Arthur N. Prior examines Cudworth in *Logic and the Basis of Ethics* (Oxford: Clarendon Press, 1949), chap. 2.

Finally, Cudworth's opposition to Hobbes's materialism and determinism is considered in Samuel Mintz, *The Hunting of Leviathan* (Cambridge, England: Cambridge University Press, 1962), chaps. 5 and 6.

Samuel Clarke

Introduction

Samuel Clarke was not only a moral philosopher, he was also a theologian, a defender and popularizer of Newton, and a successful Anglican minister whose sermons were much admired. Born in 1675, he studied at Cambridge, where he had to learn Newton's *Principia* by himself because no one on the faculty understood it well enough to help him. Clarke translated a textbook of Cartesian physics into Latin, inserting Newtonian doctrines into the footnotes to contradict the author he was translating. This textbook was used at Cambridge as late as 1730. When he graduated, Clarke entered the Church of England and eventually became chaplain to Queen Anne, who appointed him to a prosperous London church, where he remained until his death in 1729. Clarke was suspected of Unitarian leanings, however, and this lack of orthodoxy regarding the doctrine of the Trinity lost him his chaplaincy and kept him from further advancement.

Clarke's most enduring works were the lectures he gave in the series established by the scientist Robert Boyle, who was eager to encourage up-to-date defenses of the truth of Christianity. Clarke's Boyle lectures, *A Discourse Concerning the Being and Attributes of God* (1704) and *A Discourse Concerning the Unchangeable Obligations of Natural Religion* (1705), made him one of the most influential and frequently reprinted philosophers of the early eighteenth century. A decade after giving these lectures, Clarke began a correspondence with Leibniz, answering Leibniz's criticisms of Newton's views of space, time, and gravity. He and Leibniz each wrote five letters, which were published in 1717.

The first set of Boyle lectures was intended to confute atheism. An atheist, Clarke thought, must be one of three things: stupid, debauched, or misled by bad philosophy. He attempted to cope with the third source of atheism, bad philosophy, by proving that God not only exists but exists necessarily. He also argued that although we do not comprehend God's substance, we can understand some of his attributes. Having shown that the necessary being is eternal, infinite, and omnipresent, Clarke then tried to show that God is intelligent, infinitely powerful, wise, and good and that he acts freely. Clarke proved the necessity of God's existence a priori and the truth about God's other attributes a posteriori from our experience of the causal order in which we live and from the many perfections we find in it.

Clarke ended with a point that led to his views of morality. He argued that although God necessarily always chooses what he sees to be eternally best and most fitting, his freedom of action is in no way impaired. There is a moral necessity that he do what is most fitting, but this is not a "necessity of fate." Moral necessity is consistent with perfect liberty; to think otherwise is to confuse moral motives with efficient causes, such as those treated in Newton's physics. Because God freely chooses to make it his rule to comply with the eternal fitnesses of things, he expects us to do so as well. Hence if we act differently, Clarke asserted, we not only flout the eternal fitnesses of things that reason reveals to us, we also affront God directly.

In the second set of lectures, Clarke defended the assumption that there are eternal fitnesses of things that should guide our actions. He also claimed that we can be moved, by being aware of these fitnesses, to do as they direct. These views, which Clarke put forward in the first three of the fifteen propositions defended in these lectures, are at the core of his ethics. He thus presented a theory asserting the independence of morality from God's will. In so doing, his purpose was not to argue for human autonomy but, rather, to provide the basis for his arguments in support of Christianity. Assuming that he had refuted atheism, Clarke in these lectures attacked the deists, those who admit there is an intelligent creator but who either deny that he concerns himself with the world he made or believe that only what reason can show about him need be accepted. His aim was to lead the deists beyond deism to Christianity. The argument Clarke used to bring the deists to this point rested on an appeal to our moral knowledge, which is independent of anything we think about Christianity.

The argument, briefly, is as follows: We know that to act virtuously is to act piously, justly, benevolently, and prudently. But ordinary experience shows that even if we are virtuous, we may nevertheless not be happy. It is evident, however, that the virtuous deserve to be happy, and because God acts according to the principles we see to be eternally true, we have reason to believe that the virtuous will get what they deserve. Thus we have reason to believe in a future life. Most people cannot come to believe in a future life by means of reasoning, and even the philosophers among the heathens cannot obtain a full and clear grasp of the eternal moral truths. Without such knowledge, however, it is not reasonable to expect people to be virtuous; yet they are required to be so. This shows that a revelation is needed, and because God is benevolent, it follows that there is reason to suppose that there has been a revelation. Furthermore, only the Christian revelation has the features we could reasonably expect in a revelation from a just and benevolent God, and Christian doctrine also has the features one would expect in a divinely revealed truth. It teaches a morality consonant with natural reason and human happiness, and its specifically religious tenets are reasonable and lead to improved morals. In addition, it has the support of miracles. Anyone not convinced by these evidences of Christianity would not, Clarke concluded, be convinced of its truth by any evidence whatsoever, and so it is no use talking with such people.

Clarke's ethics must be understood, then, within this larger religious framework. He was trying to show how we can reject voluntarism while keeping God indispensable to morality. Indeed, to show that disregarding morality is offensive to God and will be punished was as important to Clarke as it was to demonstrate that morality is not constituted by God's will alone. Clarke's main innovation was to propose a model of the laws of nature that the natural lawyers never used, by comparing moral laws with laws of geometry or arithmetic. It plainly makes sense to talk of such laws, and just as plainly, these laws do not seem, as a sovereign's laws do, to need a legislator. At the same time Clarke tried to avoid the Platonism of his rationalist predecessors. Without using any metaphysical doctrine or appealing to innate ideas, he presented principles that he thought his readers would see as so evidently true that no one could deny them. He also attempted to explain how the knowledge of these principles generates a motive for acting as they direct, thus making ambitious claims for the powers of reason in practical matters. These claims were widely debated during the following decades; the present-day reader may find it profitable to engage in this debate as well.

The following selections are from the tenth edition of *A Discourse Concerning the Unchangeable Obligations of Natural Religion*. I have somewhat modernized the spelling and the use of capitals and italics and simplified some of the punctuation.

A Discourse Concerning the Unchangeable Obligations of Natural Religion

I. The same necessary and eternal different relations that different things bear one to another and the same consequent fitness or unfitness of the application of different things or different relations one to another, with regard to which the will of God always and necessarily does determine itself to choose to act only what is agreeable to justice, equity, goodness and truth, in order to the welfare of the whole universe; ought likewise constantly to determine the wills of all subordinate rational beings to govern all their actions by the same rules, for the good of the public, in their respective stations.

That is; these eternal and necessary differences of things make it fit and reasonable for creatures so to act; they cause it to be their duty or lay an obligation upon them so to do, even separate from the consideration of these rules being the positive will or command of God; and also antecedent to any respect or regard, expectation or apprehension, of any particular private and personal advantage or disadvantage, reward or punishment, either present or future; annexed either by natural consequence or by positive appointment to the practicing or neglecting of those rules.

The several parts of this proposition may be proved distinctly in the following manner.

1. That there are differences of things, and different relations, respects or proportions, of some things towards others, is as evident and undeniable as that one magnitude or number is greater, equal to, or smaller than another. That from these different relations of different things there necessarily arises an agreement or disagreement of some things with others, or a fitness or unfitness of the application of different things or different relations one to another, is likewise as plain as that there is any such thing as proportion or disproportion in geometry and arithmetic, or uniformity or disformity in comparing together the respective figures of bodies.

Further, that there is a fitness or suitableness of certain circumstances to certain persons, and an unsuitableness of others founded in the nature of things and the qualifications of persons, antecedent to all positive appointment whatsoever; also that from the different relations of different persons one to another there necessarily arises a fitness or unfitness of certain manners of behaviour of some persons towards others, is as manifest as that the properties which flow from the essences of different mathematical figures have different congruities or incongruities between themselves; or that in mechanics certain weights or powers have very different forces and different effects one upon another, according to their different distances or different positions and situations in respect of each other.

For instance: that God is infinitely superior to men is as clear as that infinity is larger than a point, or eternity longer than a moment. And 'tis as certainly fit that men should honour and worship, obey and imitate God, rather than on the contrary in all their actions endeavour to dishonour and disobey him, as 'tis certainly true, that they have an entire dependence on him, and he on the contrary can in no respect receive any advantage from them; and not only so, but also that his will is as certainly and unalterably just and equitable in giving his commands as his power is irresistible in requiring submission to it. Again, 'tis a thing absolutely and necessarily fitter in itself that the supreme author and creator of the universe should govern, order and direct all things to certain and constant regular ends, than that every thing should be permitted to go on at adventures and produce uncertain effects merely by chance and in the utmost confusion, without any determinate view or design at all. 'Tis a thing manifestly fitter in itself, that the all-powerful governour of the world should do always what is best in the whole and what tends most to the universal good of the whole creation, than that he should make the whole continually miserable or that, to satisfy the unreasonable desires of any particular depraved natures, he should at any time suffer the order of the whole to be altered and perverted. Lastly, 'tis a thing evidently and infinitely more fit that any one particular innocent and good being should by the supreme ruler and disposer of all things be placed and preserved in an easy and happy estate, than that, without any fault or demerit of its own, it should be made extremely, remedilessly, and endlessly miserable.

In like manner, in men's dealing and conversing one with another 'tis undeniably more fit, absolutely and in the nature of the thing itself, that all men should endeavour to promote the universal good and welfare of all, than that all men should be continually contriving the ruin and destruction of all. 'Tis evidently more fit, even before all positive bargains and compacts, that men should deal one with another according to the known rules of justice and equity than that every man for his own present advantage should without scruple disappoint the most reasonable and equitable expectations of his neighbours, and cheat and defraud or spoil by violence all others without restraint. Lastly, 'tis without dispute more fit and reasonable in itself that I should preserve the life of an innocent man that happens at any time to be in my power, or deliver him from any imminent danger, though I have never made any promise so to do, than that I should suffer him to perish or take away his life without any reason or provocation at all.

These things are so notoriously plain and self-evident that nothing but the extremest stupidity of mind, corruption of manners, or perverseness of spirit can possibly make any man entertain the least doubt concerning them. For a man endued with reason to deny the truth of these things is the very same thing as if a man that has the use of his sight should at the same time that he

beholds the sun deny that there is any such thing as light in the world. . . .
Any man of ordinary capacity and unbiased judgment, plainness and simplicity who had never read and had never been told that there were men and
philosophers who had in earnest asserted and attempted to prove that there is
no natural and unalterable difference between good and evil would at the first
hearing be as hardly persuaded to believe that it could ever really enter into
the heart of any intelligent man to deny all natural difference between right
and wrong, as he would be to believe that ever there could be any geometer
who would seriously and in good earnest lay it down as a first principle that a
crooked line is as straight as a right one.

So that indeed it might justly seem altogether a needless undertaking to
attempt to prove and establish the eternal difference of good and evil, had
there not appeared certain men, as Mr. Hobbes and some few others, who
have presumed, contrary to the plainest and most obvious reason of mankind,
to assert, and not without some subtlety endeavoured to prove that there is no
such real difference originally, necessarily, and absolutely in the nature of
things; but that all obligation of duty to God arises merely from his absolute
irresistible power; and all duty towards men merely from positive compact:[1]
And have founded their whole scheme of politics upon that opinion.

Wherein as they have contradicted the judgment of all the wisest and sober-
est part of mankind, so they have not been able to avoid contradicting themselves also. For (not to mention now, that they have no way to show how
compacts themselves come to be obligatory, but by inconsistently owning an
eternal original fitness in the thing itself . . .) if there be naturally and absolutely in things themselves no difference between good and evil, just and
unjust; then in the state of nature, before any compact be made, 'tis equally as
good, just and reasonable, for one man to destroy the life of another, not only
when 'tis necessary for his own preservation, but also arbitrarily and without
any provocation at all, or any appearance of advantage to himself; as to
preserve or have another man's life when he may do it without any hazard of
his own. The consequence of which is that not only the first and most obvious
way for every particular man to secure himself effectually would be (as Mr.
Hobbes teaches) to endeavour to prevent and cut off all others, but also that
men might destroy one another upon every foolish and peevish or arbitrary
humour, even when they did not think any such thing necessary for their own
preservation. And the effect of this practice must needs be, that it would
terminate in the destruction of all mankind. Which being undeniably a great
and unsufferable evil, Mr. Hobbes himself confesses it reasonable that, to
prevent this evil, men should enter into certain compacts to preserve one
another.

Now if the destruction of mankind by each other's hands, be such an evil
that, to prevent it, it was fit and reasonable that men should enter into
compacts to preserve each other, then before any such compacts it was manifestly a thing unfit and unreasonable in itself that mankind should all destroy
one another. And if so, then for the same reason it was also unfit and unrea-

sonable, antecedent to all compacts, that any one man should destroy another arbitrarily and without any provocation, or at any time when it was not absolutely and immediately necessary for the preservation of himself. Which is directly contradictory to Mr. Hobbes's first supposition, of there being no natural and absolute difference between good and evil, just and unjust, antecedent to positive compact. . . .

The true state therefore of this case is plainly this. Some things are in their own nature good and reasonable and fit to be done, such as keeping faith and performing equitable compacts, and the like; and these receive not their obligatory power from any law or authority, but are only declared, confirmed, and enforced by penalties, upon such as would not perhaps be governed by right reason only. Other things are in their own nature absolutely evil, such as breaking faith, refusing to perform equitable compacts, cruelly destroying those who have neither directly nor indirectly given any occasion for any such treatment, and the like; and these cannot by any law or authority whatsoever be made fit and reasonable or excusable to be practiced. Lastly, other things are in their own nature indifferent. . . .

The principal thing that can, with any colour of reason, seem to countenance the opinion of those who deny the natural and eternal difference of good and evil . . . is the difficulty there may sometimes be to define exactly the bounds of right and wrong: the variety of opinions that have obtained even among understanding and learned men concerning certain questions of just and unjust, especially in political matters: and the many contrary laws that have been made in diverse ages and in different countries concerning these matters. . . . it may perhaps be very difficult in some nice and perplexed cases (which yet are very far from occurring frequently) to define exactly the bounds of right and wrong, just and unjust; and there may be some latitude in the judgment of different men, and the laws of diverse nations; yet right and wrong are nevertheless in themselves totally and essentially different; even altogether as much as white and black, light and darkness. . . .

Now if in the flagrant cases the natural and essential difference between good and evil, right and wrong cannot but be confessed to be plainly and undeniably evident, the difference between them must be also essential and unalterable in all even the smallest and nicest and most intricate cases, though it be not so easy to be discerned and accurately distinguished. For if from the difficulty of determining exactly the bounds of right and wrong in many perplexed cases it could truly be concluded that just and unjust were not essentially different by nature but only by positive constitution and custom; it would follow equally, that they were not really, essentially, and unalterably different, even in the most flagrant cases that can be supposed. Which is an assertion so very absurd, that Mr. Hobbes himself could hardly vent it without blushing, and discovering plainly, by his shifting expressions, his secret self-condemnation.

There are therefore certain necessary and eternal differences of things, and certain consequent fitnesses or unfitnesses of the application of different things or different relations one to another; not depending on any positive constitutions, but founded unchangeably in the nature and reason of things and unavoidably arising from the differences of the things themselves. Which is the first branch of the general proposition I proposed to prove.

2. Now what these eternal and unalterable relations, respects, or proportions of things, with their consequent agreements or disagreements, fitnesses or unfitnesses, absolutely and necessarily are in themselves; that also they appear to be, to the understandings of all intelligent beings, except those only who understand things to be what they are not, that is, whose understandings are either very imperfect or very much depraved. And by this understanding or knowledge of the natural and necessary relations, fitnesses, and proportions of things, the wills likewise of all intelligent beings are constantly directed and must needs be determined to act accordingly, excepting those only who will things to be what they are not and cannot be; that is, whose wills are corrupted by particular interest or affection, or swayed by some unreasonable and prevailing passion. Wherefore since the natural attributes of God, his infinite knowledge, wisdom and power, set him infinitely above all possibility of being deceived by any errour or of being influenced by any wrong affection, 'tis manifest his divine will cannot but always and necessarily determine itself to choose to do what in the whole is absolutely best and fittest to be done; that is, to act constantly according to the eternal rules of infinite goodness, justice, and truth. . . .

3. And now, that the same reason of things, with regard to which the will of God always and necessarily does determine itself to act in constant conformity to the eternal rules of justice, equity, goodness, and truth, ought also constantly to determine the wills of all subordinate rational beings, to govern all their actions by the same rules, is very evident. For, as 'tis absolutely impossible in nature that God should be deceived by any errour or influenced by any wrong affection: So 'tis very unreasonable and blameworthy in practice that any intelligent creatures, whom God has made so far like unto himself as to endow them with those excellent faculties of reason and will whereby they are enabled to distinguish good from evil, and to choose the one and refuse the other; should either negligently suffer themselves to be imposed upon and deceived in matters of good and evil, right and wrong; or wilfully and perversely allow themselves to be over-ruled by absurd passions, and corrupt or partial affections, to act contrary to what they know is fit to be done.

Which two things, viz. negligent misunderstanding and wilful passions or lusts, are, as I said, the only causes which can make a reasonable creature act contrary to reason, that is, contrary to the eternal rules of justice, equity, righteousness and truth. For was it not for these inexcusable corruptions and depravations, 'tis impossible but the same proportions and fitnesses of things which have so much weight and so much excellency and beauty in them, that the all-powerful creator and governour of the universe, . . . thinks it no diminution of his power to make this reason of things the unalterable rule and law of his own actions in the government of the world, and does nothing by mere will and arbitrariness; . . . must much more have weight enough to determine constantly the wills and actions of all subordinate, finite, dependent and accountable beings.

For originally and in reality, 'tis as natural and (morally speaking) necessary that the will should be determined in every action by the reason of the thing and the right of the case as 'tis natural and (absolutely speaking) necessary that the understanding should submit to a demonstrated truth. And 'tis as absurd and blameworthy to mistake negligently plain right and wrong, that is, to understand the proportions of things in morality to be what they are not; or wilfully to act contrary to known justice and equity, that is, to will things to be what they are not; or wilfully to act contrary to known justice and equity, that is, to will things to be what they are not and cannot be; as it would be absurd and ridiculous for a man in arithmetical matters, ignorantly to believe that twice two is not equal to four; or wilfully and obstinately to contend, against his own clear knowledge, that the whole is not equal to all its parts.

The only difference is, that assent to a plain speculative truth is not in a man's power to withhold; but to act according to the plain right and reason of things, this he may, by the natural liberty of his will, forbear. But the one he ought to do and 'tis as much his plain and indispensable duty, as the other he cannot but do, and 'tis the necessity of his nature to do it.

He that wilfully refuses to honour and obey God, from whom he received his being, and to whom he continually owes his preservation is really guilty of an equal absurdity and inconsistency in practice as he that in speculation denies the effect to owe any thing to its cause, or the whole to be bigger than its part. He that refuses to deal with all men equitably, and with every man as he desires they should deal with him is guilty of the very same unreasonableness and contradiction in one case as he that in another case should affirm one number or quantity to be equal to another, and yet that other at the same time not to be equal to the first. . . .

In a word; all wilful wickedness and perversion of right is the very same insolence and absurdity in moral matters as it would be in natural things for a man to pretend to alter the certain proportions of numbers, to take away the demonstrable relations and properties of mathematical figures, to make light darkness, and darkness light, or to call sweet bitter, and bitter sweet.

Further: As it appears thus from the abstract and absolute reason and nature of things that all rational creatures ought, that is, are obliged to take care that their wills and actions be constantly determined and governed by the eternal rule of right and equity: So the certainty and universality of that obligation is plainly confirmed and the force of it particularly discovered and applied to every man by this, that in like manner as no one who is instructed in mathematics can forbear giving his assent to every geometrical demonstration, of which he understands the terms, either by his own study or by having had them explained to him by others; so no man who either has patience and opportunities to examine and consider things himself or has the means of being taught and instructed in any tolerable manner by others, concerning the necessary relations and dependencies of things; can avoid giving his assent to the fitness and reasonableness of his governing all his actions by the law or rule before mentioned, even though his practice, through the prevalence of brutish lusts, be most absurdly contradictory to that assent.

That is to say: by the reason of his mind, he cannot but be compelled to own and acknowledge that there is really such an obligation indispensably incumbent upon him; even at the same time that in the actions of his life he is endeavouring to throw it off and despise it. For the judgment and conscience of a man's own mind concerning the reasonableness and fitness of the thing, that his actions should be conformed to such or such a rule or law, is the truest and formallest obligation; even more properly and strictly so than any opinion whatsoever of the authority of the giver of a law, or any regard he may have to its sanction by rewards and punishments. For whoever acts contrary to this sense and conscience of his own mind, is necessarily self-condemned; and the greatest and strongest of all obligations is that, which a man cannot break through without condemning himself.

The dread of superiour power and authority, and the sanction of rewards and punishments, however indeed absolutely necessary to the government of frail and fallible creatures, and truly the most effectual means of keeping them in their duty, is yet really in itself only a secondary and additional obligation or enforcement of the first. The original obligation of all (the ambiguous use of which word as a term of art has caused some perplexity and confusion in this matter) is the eternal reason of things; that reason, which God himself who has no superiour to direct him, and to whose happiness nothing can be added nor anything diminished from it, yet constantly obliges himself to govern the world by. And the more excellent and perfect (or the freer from corruption and depravation) any creatures are, the more cheerfully and steadily are their wills always determined by this supreme obligation, in conformity to the nature and in imitation of the most perfect will of God.

So far therefore as men are conscious of what is right and wrong, so far they are under an obligation to act accordingly; and consequently that eternal rule of right, which I have been hitherto describing, 'tis evident ought as indispensably to govern men's actions, as it cannot but necessarily determine their assent.

Now that the case is truly thus; that the eternal differences of good and evil, the unalterable rule of right and equity, do necessarily and unavoidably determine the judgment and force the assent of all men that use any consideration, is undeniably manifest from the universal experience of mankind. For no man willingly and deliberately transgresses this rule in any great and considerable instance, but he acts contrary to the judgment and reason of his own mind, and secretly reproaches himself for so doing. And no man observes and obeys it steadily, especially in cases of difficulty and temptation, when it interferes with any present interest, pleasure or passion, but his own mind commends and applauds him for him for his resolution, in executing what his conscience could not forbear giving its assent to, as just and right. And this is what Saint Paul means when he says (Rom. 2: 14, 15) that "when the Gentiles which have not the law do by nature the things contained in the law, these having not the law, are a law unto themselves; which shew the work of the law written in their hearts, their conscience also bearing witness, and their thoughts the mean while accusing, or else excusing one another." . . .

Some men indeed, who, by means of a very evil and vicious education, or through a long habit of wickedness and debauchery, have extremely corrupted the principles of their nature, and have long accustomed themselves to bear down their own reason by the force of prejudice, lust, and passion; that they may not be forced to confess themselves self-condemned, will confidently and absolutely contend that they do not really see any natural and necessary difference between what we call right and wrong, just and unjust; that the reason and judgment of their own mind does not tell them they are under any such indispensable obligations as we would endeavour to persuade them; and that they are not sensible they ought to be governed by any other rule than their own will and pleasure.

But even these men, the most abandoned of all mankind, however industriously they endeavour to conceal and deny their self-condemnation, yet they cannot avoid making a discovery of it sometimes when they are not aware of it. For example, there is no man so vile and desperate, who commits at any time a murder and robbery with the most unrelenting mind, but would choose, if such a thing could be proposed to him, to obtain all the same profit or advantage, whatsoever it be that he aims at, without committing the crime, rather than with it; even though he was sure to go unpunished for committing the crime. . . .

But the truth of this, that the mind of man naturally and necessarily assents to the eternal law of righteousness, may still better and more clearly and more universally appear from the judgment that men pass upon each other's actions than from what we can discern concerning their consciousness of their own. For men may dissemble and conceal from the world the judgment of their own conscience; nay, by a strange partiality, they may even impose upon and deceive themselves; . . . But men's judgments concerning the actions of others, especially where they have no relation to themselves or repugnance to their interest, are commonly impartial; and from this we may judge what sense men naturally have of the unalterable difference of right and wrong.

Now the observation which everyone cannot but make in this matter, is this: that virtue and true goodness, righteousness and equity, are things so truly noble and excellent, so lovely and venerable in themselves, and do so necessarily approve themselves to the reason and consciences of men, that even those very persons who by the prevailing power of some interest or lust, are themselves drawn aside out of the paths of virtue, can yet hardly ever forbear to give it its true character and commendation in others. . . .

There is but one thing that I am sensible of which can here with any colour be objected against what has been hitherto said concerning the necessity of the mind's giving its assent to the eternal law of righteousness; and that is the total ignorance, which some whole nations are reported to lie under, of the nature and force of these moral obligations. I am not satisfied the matter of fact is true. But if it was, yet mere ignorance affords no just objection against the certainty of any truth. Were there upon earth a nation of rational and considerate persons, whose notions concerning moral obligations and concerning the nature and force of them, were universally and directly contrary to what I have hitherto represented, this would be indeed a weighty objection. But ignorance and stupidity are no arguments against the certainty of anything. There are many nations and people almost totally ignorant of the plainest mathematical truths; as of the proportion, for example, of a square to a triangle of the same base and height. And yet these truths are such, to which the mind cannot but give its assent necessarily and unavoidably as soon as they are distinctly proposed to it. All that this objection proves therefore . . . [is] that men have great need to be taught and instructed in some very plain and easy as well as certain truths; and, if they be important truths, that then men have need also to have them frequently inculcated and strongly enforced upon them. Which is very true, and is . . . one good argument for the reasonableness of expecting a revelation.

4. Thus it appears in general that the mind of man cannot avoid giving its assent to the eternal law of righteousness; that is, cannot but acknowledge the reasonableness and fitness of men's governing all their actions by the rule of right or equity: And also that this assent is a formal obligation upon every man, actually and constantly to conform himself to that rule. I might now from hence deduce in particular all the several duties of morality or natural religion. But because this would take up too large a portion of my intended discourse and may easily be supplied abundantly out of several late excellent writers, I shall only mention the three great and principal branches from which all the other and smaller instances of duty do naturally flow or may without difficulty be derived.

First then, in respect of God, the rule of righteousness is that we keep up constantly in our minds, the highest possible honour, esteem, and veneration for him, which must express itself in proper and respective influences upon all our passions, and in the suitable direction of all our actions. . . .

Secondly. In respect of our fellow-creatures, the rule of righteousness is that in particular we deal with every man as in like circumstances we could reasonably expect he should deal with us; and that in general we endeavour, by an universal benevolence, to promote the welfare and happiness of all men. The former branch of this rule, is equity; the latter, is love.

As to the former, viz. equity: the reason which obliges every man in practice so to deal always with another as he would reasonably expect that others should in like circumstances deal with him, is the very same as that which forces him in speculation to affirm that if one line or number be equal to another, that other is reciprocally equal to it. Iniquity is the very same in action as falsity or contradiction in theory; and the same cause which makes the one absurd makes the other unreasonable. Whatever relation or proportion one man in any case bears to another, the same that other, when put in like circumstances, bears to him. Whatever I judge reasonable or unreasonable for another to do for me, that, by the same judgment, I declare reasonable or unreasonable, that I in the like case should do for him. And to deny this either in work or action is as if a man should contend that, though two and three are equal to five, yet five are not equal to two and three. Wherefore were not men strangely and most unnaturally corrupted by perverse and unaccountably false opinions, and monstrous evil customs and habits prevailing against the clearest and plainest reason in the world, it would be impossible that universal equity should not be practiced by all mankind; and especially among equals, where the proportion of equity is simple and obvious, and every man's own case is already the same with all others, without any nice comparing or transposing of circumstances. . . .

In considering indeed the duties of superiours and inferiours in various relations, the proportion of equity is somewhat more complex; but still it may always be deduced from the same rule of doing as we would be done by, if careful regard be had at the same time to the difference of relation. That is, if in considering what is fit for you to do to another, you always take into the account, not only every circumstance of the action, but also every circumstance wherein the person differs from you; and in judging what you would desire that another, if your circumstances were transposed, should do to you, you always consider not what any unreasonable passion or private interest would prompt you, but what impartial reason would dictate to you to desire. For example: A magistrate, in order to deal equitably with a criminal, is not to consider what fear or self-love could cause him, in the criminal's case, to desire; but what reason and the public good would oblige him to acknowledge was fit and just for him to expect. And the same proportion is to be observed in deducing the duties of parents and children, of matters and servants, of governours and subjects, of citizens and foreigners. . . . In the regular and uniform practice of all which duties among all mankind, in their several and respective relations, through the whole earth, consists that universal justice which is the top and perfection of all virtues: . . .

The second branch of the rule of righteousness with respect to our fellow-creatures, I said, was universal love or benevolence; that is, not only the doing barely what is just and right, in our dealings with every man; but also a constant endeavouring to promote in general, to the utmost of our power, the welfare and happiness of all men.

The obligation to which duty also may easily be deduced from what has been already laid down. For if (as has been before proved) there be a natural and necessary difference between good and evil, and that which is good is fit and reasonable, and that which is evil is unreasonable to be done; and that which is the greatest good, is always the most fit and reasonable to be chosen: then, as the goodness of God extends itself universally over all works through the whole creation, by doing always what is absolutely best in the whole, so every rational creature ought in its sphere and station, according to its respective powers and faculties, to do all the good it can to all its fellow-creatures. To which end universal love and benevolence is as plainly the most direct, certain, and effectual means; as in mathematics the flowing of a point is, to produce a line; or in arithmetic, the addition of numbers to produce a sum; or in physics, certain kinds of motions to preserve certain bodies, which other kinds of motions tend to corrupt.

Of all which the mind of man is so naturally sensible that, except in such men whose affections are prodigiously corrupted by most unnatural and habitual vicious practices, there is no duty whatsoever, the performance whereof affords a man so ample pleasure and satisfaction, and fills his mind with so comfortable a sense of his having done the greatest good he was capable to do, of his having best answered the ends of his creation and nearliest imitated the perfections of his creator, and consequently of his having fully complied with the highest and principal obligations of his nature; as the performance of this one duty, of universal love and benevolence, naturally affords.

But further: the obligation to this great duty may also otherwise be deduced from the nature of man in the following manner. Next to that natural self-love or care of his own preservation, which everyone necessarily has in the first place for himself, there is in all men a certain natural affection for their children and posterity, who have a dependence upon them; and for their near relations and friends, who have an intimacy with them. And because the nature of man is such that they cannot live comfortably in independent families, without still further society and commerce with each other; therefore they naturally desire to increase their dependencies by multiplying affinities, and to enlarge their friendships by mutual good offices, and to establish societies by a communication of arts and labour; till by degrees the affection of single persons becomes a friendship of families; and this enlarges itself to society of towns and cities and nations; and terminates in the agreeing community of all mankind. The foundation, preservation, and perfection of which universal friendship or society, is mutual love and benevolence. And nothing hinders the world from being actually put into so happy a state, but perverse iniquity, and unreasonable want of mutual charity.

Wherefore since men are plainly so constituted by nature, that they stand in need of each other's assistance to make themselves easy in the world, and are fitted to live in communities, and society is absolutely necessary for them; and mutual love and benevolence is the only possible means to establish this society in any tolerable and durable manner; and in this respect all men stand upon the same level, and have the same natural wants and desires, and are in the same need of each other's help, and are equally capable of enjoying the benefit and advantage of society: 'Tis evident every man is bound by the law of his nature, as he is also prompted by the inclination of his uncorrupted affections, to look upon himself as a part and member of that one universal body or community, which is made up of all mankind; to think himself born to promote the public good and welfare of all his fellow-creatures; and consequently obliged, as the necessary and only effectual means to that end, to embrace them all with universal love and benevolence. . . .

Thirdly, with respect to ourselves, the rule of righteousness is that every man preserve his own being, as long as he is able, and take care to keep himself at all times in such temper and disposition both of body and mind as may best fit and enable him to perform his duty in all other instances. That is: he ought to bridle his appetites, with temperance; to govern his passions, with moderation; and to apply himself to the business of his present station in the world, whatsoever it be, with attention and contentment. That every man ought to preserve his own being as long as he is able, is evident; because what he is not himself the author and giver of, he can never of himself have just power or authority to take away. He that sent us into the world, and alone knows for how long time he appointed us our station here, and when we have finished all the business he intended we should do, can alone judge when 'tis fit for us to be taken hence and has alone authority to dismiss and discharge us. . . . Lastly: For the same reason that a man is obliged not to depart wilfully out of this life, which is the general station that God has appointed him, he is obliged likewise to attend the duties of that particular station or condition of life, whatsoever it be, wherein providence has at present placed him, with diligence and contentment, without being uneasy and discontented, that others are placed by providence in different and superiour stations in the world; or so extremely and unreasonably solicitous to change his state for the future as thereby to neglect his present duty.

From these three great and general branches, all the smaller and more particular instances of moral obligations, may (as I said) easily be deduced.

5. And now this (this eternal rule of equity, which I have been hitherto describing) is that right reason which makes the principal distinction between man and beasts. This is the law of nature. . . .

6. Further yet: as this law of nature is infinitely superiour to all authority of men and independent upon it; so its obligation, primarily and originally, is antecedent also even to this consideration, of its being the positive will or command of God himself. For as the addition of certain numbers necessarily produces a certain sum, and certain geometrical or mechanical operations give a constant and unalterable solution of certain problems or propositions: So in moral matters, there are certain necessary and unalterable respects or relations of things, which have not their original from arbitrary and positive constitution, but are of eternal necessity in their own nature. . . .

The existence indeed of the things themselves, whose proportions and relations we consider, depends entirely on the mere arbitrary will and good pleasure of God; who can create things when he pleases, and destroy them again whenever he thinks fit. But when things are created, and so long as it pleases God to continue them in being, their proportions, which are abstractly of eternal necessity, are also in the things themselves absolutely unalterable. Hence God himself, though he has no superiour from whose will to receive any law of his actions yet disdains not to observe the rule of equity and goodness, as the law of all his actions in the government of the world; and condescends to appeal even to men for the equity and righteousness of his judgments. To this law, the infinite perfections of his divine nature make it necessary for him (as has been before proved) to have constant regard. And . . . not barely his infinite power, but the rules of this eternal law, are the true foundation and the measure of his dominion over his creatures. (For if infinite power was the rule and measure of right, 'tis evident that goodness and mercy and all other divine perfections would be empty words without any signification at all.) . . .

7. Lastly, this law of nature has its full obligatory power, antecedent to all consideration of any particular private and personal reward or punishment, annexed either by natural consequence or by positive appointment to the observance or neglect of it. This also is very evident, because, if good and evil, right and wrong, fitness and unfitness of being practiced, be (as has been shown originally) eternally and necessarily in the nature of the things themselves, 'tis plain that the view of particular rewards or punishments, which is only an after-consideration and does not at all alter the nature of things, cannot be the original cause of the obligation of the law, but is only an additional weight to enforce the practice of what men were before obliged to by right reason. There is no man who has any just sense of the difference between good and evil but must needs acknowledge that virtue and goodness are truly amiable, and to be chosen for their own sakes and intrinsic worth; though a man had no prospect of gaining any particular advantage to himself, by the practice of them; and that, on the contrary, cruelty, violence and oppression, fraud, injustice, and all manner of wickedness are of themselves hateful and by all means to be avoided, even though a man had absolute assurance that he should bring no manner of inconvenience upon himself by the commission of any or all of these crimes. . . .

Thus far is clear. But now from hence it does not at all follow either that a good man ought to have no respect to rewards and punishments or that rewards and punishments are not absolutely necessary to maintain the practice of virtue and righteousness in this present world. 'Tis certain indeed, that virtue and vice are eternally and necessarily different, and that the one truly deserves to be chosen for its own sake, and the other ought by all means to be avoided, though a man was sure for his own particular neither to gain nor lose anything by the practice of either. And if this was truly the state of things in the world, certainly that man must have a very corrupt mind indeed who could in the least doubt, or so much as once deliberate with himself, which he would choose. But the case does not stand thus. The question now in the general practice of the world, supposing all expectation of rewards and punishments set aside, will not be whether a man would choose virtue for its own sake, and avoid vice; but the practice of vice is accompanied with great temptations and allurements of pleasure and profit; and the practice of virtue is often threatened with great calamities, losses, and sometimes even with death itself. And this alters the question and destroys the practice of that which appears so reasonable in the whole speculation, and introduces a necessity of rewards and punishments. For though virtue is unquestionably worthy to be chosen for its own sake, even without any expectation of reward; yet it does not follow that it is therefore entirely self-sufficient and able to support a man under all kinds of sufferings, and even death itself, for its sake, without any prospect of future recompence. Here therefore began the error of the Stoics, who taught that the bare practice of virtue was itself the chief good and able of itself to make a man happy, under all the calamities in the world.[2] Their defence indeed of the cause of virtue was very brave. They saw well that its excellency was intrinsic and founded in the nature of things themselves, and could not be altered by any outward circumstances; that therefore virtue must needs be desirable for its own sake and not merely for the advantage it might bring along with it; and if so, then consequently neither could any external disadvantage which it might happen to be attended with change the intrinsic worth of the thing itself, or ever make it cease to be truly desirable. Wherefore, in the case of sufferings and death for the sake of virtue, not having any certain knowledge of a future state of reward . . . they were forced, that they might be consistent with their own principles, to suppose the practice of virtue a sufficient reward to itself in all cases, and a full compensation for all the sufferings in the world. And accordingly they very bravely indeed taught that the practice of virtue was not only infinitely to be preferred before all the sinful pleasures in the world, but also that a man ought without scruple to choose, if the case was proposed to him, rather to undergo all possible sufferings with virtue, than to obtain all possible worldly happiness by sin. . . .

But yet, after all this, 'tis plain that the general practice of virtue in the world can never be supported upon this foot. The discourse is admirable, but it seldom goes further than mere words. And the practice of those few who have acted accordingly has not been imitated by the rest of the world. Men never will generally, and indeed 'tis not very reasonably to be expected they should, part with all the comforts of life and even life itself without expectation of any future recompence. So that if we suppose no future state of rewards, it will follow that God has endowed men with such faculties as put them under a necessity of approving and choosing virtue in the judgment of their own minds; and yet has not given them wherewith to support themselves in the suitable and constant practice of it. The consideration of which inexplicable difficulty ought to have led the philosophers to a firm belief and expectation of a future state of rewards and punishments, without which their whole scheme of morality cannot be supported. . . .

Thus have I endeavoured to deduce the original obligations of morality from the necessary and eternal reason and proportions of things. Some have chosen to found all difference of good and evil in the mere positive will and power of God. But the absurdity of this, I have shown elsewhere. Others have contended that all difference of good and evil and all obligations of morality ought to be founded originally upon considerations of public utility. And true indeed it is, in the whole, that the good of the universal creation does always coincide with the necessary truth and reason of things. But otherwise (and separate from this consideration that God will certainly cause truth and right to terminate in happiness) what is for the good of the whole creation, in very many cases, none but an infinite understanding can possibly judge. Public utility is one thing to one nation, and the contrary to another: And the governours of every nation will and must be judges of the public good. And by public good they will generally mean the private good of that particular nation. But truth and right (whether public or private) founded in the eternal and necessary reason of things is what every man can judge of, when laid before him. 'Tis necessarily one and the same, to every man's understanding; just as light is the same, to every man's eyes. . . .

And now, from what has been said upon this head, 'tis easy to see the falsity and weakness of Mr. Hobbes's doctrines that there is no such thing as just and unjust, right and wrong, originally in the nature of things; that men in their natural state, antecedent to all compacts, are not obliged to universal benevolence, nor to any moral duty whatsoever; but are in a state of war, and have every one a right to do whatever he has power to do; and that, in civil societies, it depends wholly upon positive laws or the will of governours to define what shall be just or unjust. The contrary to all which, having been already fully demonstrated, there is no need of being large in further disproving and confuting particularly these assertions themselves. . . .

II. Though these eternal moral obligations are indeed of themselves incumbent on all rational beings, even antecedent to the consideration of their being the positive will and command of God, yet that which most strongly confirms and in practice most effectually and indispensably enforces them upon us, is this: that both from the perfections of God and the nature of things, and from several other collateral considerations, it appears that as God is himself necessarily just and good in the exercise of his infinite power in the government of the whole world, so he cannot but likewise positively require that all his rational creatures should in their proportion be so too, in the exercise of each of their powers in their several and respective spheres. . . .

This proposition is very evident, and has little need of being particularly proved.

For first, the same reasons which prove to us that God must of necessity be himself infinitely holy, and just, and good manifestly prove, that it must also be his will that all his creatures should be so likewise, according to the proportions and capacities of their several natures. . . .

3. The same thing may likewise further appear from the following consideration. Whatever tends directly and certainly to promote the good and happiness of the whole and (as far as is consistent with that chief end) to promote also the good and welfare of every particular part of the creation must needs be agreeable to the will of God; . . .

Now that the exact observance of all those moral obligations which have before been proved to arise necessarily from the nature and relations of things . . . is the certainest and directest means to promote the welfare and happiness as well of every man in particular, both in body and mind, as of all men in general considered with respect to society, is so very manifest, that even the greatest enemies of all religion, who suppose it to be nothing more than a worldly or state policy, do yet by that very supposition confess thus much concerning it. . . .

III. Though the fore-mentioned eternal moral obligations are incumbent indeed on all rational creatures, antecedent to any respect of particular reward or punishment, yet they must certainly and necessarily be attended with rewards and punishments. Because the same reasons which prove God himself to be necessarily just and good, and the rules of justice, equity, and goodness, to be his unalterable will, law, and command, to all created beings, prove also that he cannot but be pleased with and approve such creatures as imitate and obey him by observing those rules, and be displeased with such as act contrary thereto; and consequently that he cannot but some way or other, make a suitable difference in his dealings with them. . . .

This proposition also is in a manner self-evident.

[VII. On the need for a revelation]

1. There was plainly wanting a divine revelation to recover mankind out of their universal corruption and degeneracy; and without such a revelation, it was not possible that the world should ever be effectually reformed. For

if (as has been before particularly shown) the gross and stupid ignorance, the innumerable prejudices and vain opinions, the strong passions and appetites of sense, and the many vicious customs and habits which the generality of mankind continually labour under make it undeniably too difficult a work for men of all capacities to discover every one for himself, by the bare light of nature, all the particular branches of their duty; but most men, in the present state of things, have manifestly need of much teaching and particular instruction;

if those who were best able to discover the truth and instruct others therein, namely the wisest and best of the philosophers, were themselves unavoidably altogether ignorant of some doctrines, and very doubtful and uncertain of others, absolutely necessary to the bringing about that great end, the reformation of mankind;

if those truths which they were themselves very certain of they were not yet able to prove and explain clearly enough to vulgar understandings;

if even those things which they proved sufficiently and explained with all clearness, they had not yet authority enough to enforce and inculcate upon men's minds with so strong an impression as to influence and govern the general practice of the world, nor pretended to afford men any supernatural assistance, which yet was very necessary to so great a work; and

if, after all, in the discovery of such matters as are the great motives of religion, men are apt to be more easily worked upon and more strongly affected by good testimony, than by the strictest abstract argument, so that, upon the whole, 'tis plain the philosophers were never by any means well qualified to reform mankind with any considerable success;

Then there was evidently wanting some particular revelation, which might supply all these defects. . . .

It may here perhaps be pretended by modern deists that the great ignorance and undeniable corruptness of the whole heathen world has always been owing, not to any absolute insufficiency of the light of nature itself, but merely to the fault of the several particular persons in not sufficiently improving that light; and that deists now, in places where learning and right reason are cultivated, are well able to discover and explain all the obligations and motives of morality without believing anything of revelation. But this, even though it were true . . . that all the obligations and motives of morality could possibly be discovered and explained clearly by the mere light of nature alone, yet even this would not at all prove that there is no need of revelation.

For whatever the bare natural possibility was, 'tis certain in fact the wisest philosophers of old never were able to do it to any effectual purpose, but always willingly acknowledged that they still wanted some higher assistance. . . . the clearness of moral reasonings was much improved, and the regard to a future state very much increased, even in heathen writers, after the coming of Christ. And almost all the things that are said wisely and truly by modern deists, are plainly borrowed from that revelation which they refuse to embrace; and without which they could never have been able to have said the same things.

Now, indeed, when our whole duty with its true motives is clearly revealed to us, its precepts appear plainly agreeable to reason; and conscience readily approves what is good, as it condemns what is evil. Nay, after our duty is thus made known to us, 'tis easy not only to see its agreement with reason, but also to begin and deduce its obligation from reason. But had we been utterly destitute of all revealed light, then to have discovered our duty in all points, with the true motives of it, merely by the help of natural reason, would have been a work of nicety, pains and labour; like groping for an unknown way in the obscure twilight. . . .

'Tis one thing to see that those rules of life which are beforehand plainly and particularly laid before us are perfectly agreeable to reason; and another thing to find out those rules merely by the light of reason, without their having first been any otherwise made known. We see that even many of those who profess to govern their lives by the plain written rule of an instituted and revealed religion are yet most miserably ignorant of their duty; and how can any man be sure he should have made so good improvement of his reason as to have understood it perfectly in all its parts, without any such help?

Editor's Notes

1. In *Leviathan*, chap. 31, Hobbes said, "The right of nature, whereby God reigneth over men . . . is to be derived, not from his creating them, as if he required obedience as of gratitude for his benefits, but from his *irresistible power*." The reader will be able to see Hobbes's view of duties toward men in the selections from Hobbes in Part I.
2. See the section on "Stoicism and Epicureanism" in the introduction to this anthology.

Further Reading

There is no modern edition of Clarke's complete works or of the lectures containing his moral philosophy. His exchange with Leibniz is available in H. G. Alexander, ed., *The Leibniz–Clarke Correspondence* (Manchester, England: Manchester University Press, 1956). On this topic, also see A. Rupert Hall, *Philosophers at War: The Quarrel Between Newton and Leibniz* (Cambridge, England: Cambridge University Press, 1980). Relatively little has been written about Clarke, and even less about his ethics. James P. Ferguson, *Dr. Samuel Clarke: An Eighteenth Century Heretic* (Kineton, England: Roundwood Press, 1976), is a general study of Clarke's life and religious controversies. Ferguson also wrote *The Philosophy of Dr. Samuel Clarke and Its Critics* (New York: Vantage, 1974). John H. Gay, "Matter and Freedom in the Thought of Samuel Clarke," *Journal of the History of Ideas* 24 (1963), bears on Clarke's ethics indirectly. Howard M. Ducharme, "Personal Identity in Samuel Clarke," *Journal of the History of Philosophy* 24 (1986): 359–83, examines some of Clarke's less widely read works that pertain to his ethics. Clarke is discussed briefly at several points in Norman Fiering, *Jonathan Edwards's Moral Thought and Its British Context* (Chapel Hill: University of North Carolina Press, 1981); consult the index. There also is an attack on Clarke's moral philosophy in John Finnis, *Natural Law and Natural Rights* (Oxford: Clarendon Press, 1980), pp. 36–42. Otherwise, despite his considerable importance in his own time and despite Sidgwick's admiration of him, Clarke remains well known but little discussed.

Gottfried Wilhelm Leibniz

Introduction

Leibniz, born in 1646 in Leipzig, was a child of an academic family. During his early years he read widely, and although he studied law, he never confined his interests to any single subject. After finishing his formal education, he spent some time carrying out diplomatic and legal functions for a minor German prince. Leibniz then spent four years in Paris and in 1676 attached himself to the ruling family of Hanover. He spent the rest of his life in the service of successive Hanoverian rulers. The last one he served, Georg Ludwig, became the king of England in 1714. Leibniz, deeply interested in European unity and harmony, saw the reunification of Protestant and Catholic confessions as necessary for that accomplishment. He hoped his own philosophical work might help, by producing a generally acceptable religious view. He carried out extensive historical research for his masters, worked on increasing cooperation of scientists of all nations, kept up with advances in technology, and, in addition to all this, did fundamentally important work in mathematics, logic, and metaphysics. Leibniz published a variety of papers but only one book, the *Theodicy* (1710), which was an attempt to resolve the problem of evil. When he died in 1716, he left behind a vast mass of manuscripts from which selections have gradually been published and of which no complete edition yet exists.

A man of astonishing versatility, intellectual power, and originality, Leibniz was also in many respects quite conservative. His desire to harmonize and unify the warring nations and sects of Europe found a counterpart in his philosophy, which aimed to show that the new science was not at odds with religion, that explanations involving mechanical or efficient causes did not exclude explanations involving purposes or final causes, and that a better understanding of physics would lead to a better understanding of God. To achieve all this, Leibniz propounded an ingenious metaphysical theory.

The created world, Leibniz held, consists of indivisible substances that are essentially centers of force or activity. Each of the indefinitely large number of these centers, which Leibniz called *monads*, is created by God and has built into its nature all its properties, including what we think of as its relations to others. Hence, whatever occurs during the history of a monad is always present in it. It follows that monads do not really interact. What looks like interaction to us is the correlation that God has set up among the unfolding inner natures of each monad. Leibniz called this correlation the "preestablished harmony of the monads." When I am programmed to shove, you are programmed to fall; so it will look as if my shove made you fall, when in fact God had arranged from the very beginning that at the time of my shove you would topple.

Leibniz opposed materialism and held that all monads perceive. But perception occurs on a continuum, from the extremely obscure and confused to the very clear and distinct. Inanimate objects are composed of monads with the most confused perceptions; animals have clearer perceptions; and humans, who have perceptions ranging from the most obscure to the very clear, also have perceptions of themselves as having perceptions; hence we are self-conscious. The perceptions of each monad contain counterparts of the perceptions of every other, Leibniz claimed, so that a change anywhere in the universe has its echo, however obscure, in every other part. We all thus are parts of a single community ruled by its creator, God.

When God created the universe, he was faced, so to speak, with a choice. He could see, before anything was actual, what combinations of what kinds of beings were possible. Some possible combinations would contain more kinds of things, some fewer; some would organize them by simple laws, some by complex laws. God created the world as an expression of himself, and so he chose to make real the possible world that best expressed his nature. It contains the largest possible variety of kinds of being organized in the simplest way and (because God is good) enjoying their existence as much as possible. It is – in the phrase Voltaire made famous with his satire on it in *Candide* – the best of all possible worlds. An all-powerful, perfectly just, all-knowing, and benevolent God could choose no other.

In action, on Leibniz's view, we strive for perfection, and our feeling pleasure is a sign to us of the attainment of some perfection, which we may not clearly and distinctly understand. Each of us is necessarily moved to strive for his or her own perfection, and in that sense voluntary action is always self-interested. For Leibniz, however, self-interest did not entail selfishness. Through love we can find pleasure in increasing the perfection of others. Because we obtain pleasure for ourselves in this way, the more perfection we can bring to others, the more we ourselves will benefit.

What virtuous Leibnizian agents must know, then, is the various amounts of perfection that might be brought about by the actions among which they must choose. Choosing what is more perfect is choosing in accordance with the degree of perfection that God built into the universe. And to know what those degrees of perfection are, the agents should, ideally, understand not only the details of the laws of physics and psychology and their implications but also their metaphysical presuppositions. A perfectly virtuous agent would know Leibniz's system and see all of its entailments.

Leibniz did not tell us much about how everyone is to attain this knowledge or how those who lack it are to be guided. He was more interested in explaining the basic concepts of morality, particularly those needed to develop a system of law. These thoughts he presented in various manuscript notes and in a number of published papers. Leibniz's own reputation among the learned added weight to his often acute criticisms of other theorists, and enough of his own theory was known to enable those who found it attractive to develop it further. It was mainly through a systematic development of his various suggestions – worked out by the German philosopher Christian Wolff – that Leibnizian ideas on morality came to be widely known.

The following selections come from several different sources. The first is from "The Principles of Nature and of Grace," written in 1714 for a prince who wanted a general introduction to Leibniz's metaphysical views. Next comes a paper, "On Wisdom," probably written in the last decade of the seventeenth century. Both selections are from Leroy E. Loemker, ed. and trans., *Leibniz: Philosophical Papers and Letters* (Dordrecht: Reidel, 1969), copyright © 1969, D. Reidel Co, Dordrecht, The Netherlands. Reproduced by permission of Kluwer Academic Publishers. The short paper "Felicity" was written in the early 1690s, and the "Meditation on the Common Concept of Justice" was written later, in 1702–3. The next excerpt is from the preface Leibniz wrote for a large collection of medieval legal documents pertaining to contemporary politics, published in 1693. Finally, Leibniz's criticism of Pufendorf, originally written in 1706 as a letter, was translated into French by Barbeyrac and appended in 1718 to an edition of his translation of Pufendorf's short handbook *The Duty of Man and Citizen*. All of these selections are from Patrick Riley, trans. and ed., *The Political Writings of Leibniz* (Cambridge, England: Cambridge University Press, 1988), reprinted by permission of the Cambridge University Press.

The Principles of Nature and of Grace, Based on Reason

7. So far we have been speaking simply as *natural scientists;* now we must rise to *metaphysics* and make use of the great, but not commonly used, *principle* that *nothing takes place without a sufficient reason;* in other words, that nothing occurs for which it would be impossible for someone who has enough knowledge of things to give a reason adequate to determine why the thing is as it is and not otherwise. This principle having been stated, the first question which we have a right to ask will be, "Why is there something rather than nothing?" For nothing is simpler and easier than something. Further, assuming that things must exist, it must be possible to give a reason *why they should exist as they do* and not otherwise.

8. Now this sufficient reason for the existence of the universe cannot be found in the series of contingent things, that is to say, of bodies and their representations in souls. For since matter is in itself indifferent to motion or rest, and to one motion rather than to another, one cannot find in it a reason for motion and still less for some particular motion. Although the present motion in matter arises from preceding motion, and that in turn from motion which preceded it, we do not get further however far we may go, for the same question always remains. The sufficient reason, therefore, which needs no further reason, must be outside of this series of contingent things and is found in a substance which is the cause of this series or which is a necessary being bearing the reason for its existence within itself; otherwise we should not yet have a sufficient reason with which to stop. This final reason for things is called *God.*

9. This simple primary substance must include eminently[1] the perfections contained in the derivative substances which are its effects. Thus it will have perfect power, knowledge, and will; that is to say, it will have omnipotence, omniscience, and sovereign goodness. And since justice, taken in its most general sense is nothing but goodness conforming with wisdom, there is also necessarily a sovereign justice in God. The reason which has made things exist through him has also made them depend on him for their existence and operation, and they are continually receiving from him that which causes them to have some perfection. But whatever imperfection remains with them comes from the essential and original limitation of the created beings.

10. It follows from the supreme perfection of God that he has chosen the

best possible plan in producing the universe, a plan which combines the greatest variety together with the greatest order; with situation, place, and time arranged in the best way possible; with the greatest effect produced by the simplest means; with the most power, the most knowledge, the greatest happiness and goodness in created things which the universe could allow. For as all possible things have a claim to existence in God's understanding in proportion to their perfections, the result of all these claims must be the most perfect actual world which is possible. Without this it would be impossible to give a reason why things have gone as they have rather than otherwise.

11. The supreme wisdom of God has made him choose especially those *laws of motion* which are best adjusted and most fitted to abstract or metaphysical reasons. There is conserved the same quantity of total and absolute force or of action, also the same quantity of relative force or of reaction, and finally, the same quantity of directive force. Furthermore, action is always equal to reaction, and the entire effect is always equal to its full cause. It is surprising that no reason can be given for the laws of motion which have been discovered in our own time, and part of which I myself have discovered,[2] by a consideration of *efficient causes* or of matter alone. For I have found that we must have recourse to *final causes* and that these laws do not depend upon the *principle of necessity* as do the truths of logic, arithmetic, and geometry, but upon the *principle of fitness,* that is to say, upon the choice of wisdom. This is one of the most effective and obvious proofs of the existence of God for those who can probe into these matters thoroughly.

12. It follows also from the perfection of the supreme Author, not only that the order of the entire universe is the most perfect possible, but also that each living mirror which represents the universe according to its own point of view, that is, each *monad* or each substantial center, must have its perceptions and its appetites regulated in the best way compatible with all the rest. From this it also follows that souls, that is to say, the most dominant monads, or rather animals themselves, cannot fail to awake from the state of stupor into which death or some other accident may place them.

13. For everything has been regulated in things, once for all, with as much order and agreement as possible; the supreme wisdom and goodness cannot act except with perfect harmony. The present is great with the future; the future could be read in the past; the distant is expressed in the near. One could learn the beauty of the universe in each soul if one could unravel all that is rolled up in it but that develops perceptibly only with time. But since each distant perception of the soul includes an infinity of confused perceptions which envelop the entire universe, the soul itself does not know the things which it perceives until it has perceptions which are distinct and heightened. And it has perfection in proportion to the distinctness of its perceptions.

Each soul knows the infinite, knows everything, but confusedly. Thus when I walk along the seashore and hear the great noise of the sea, I hear the separate sounds of each wave but do not distinguish them; our confused perceptions are the result of the impressions made on us by the whole universe. It is the same with each monad. Only God has a distinct knowledge of everything, for he is the source of everything. It has been very well said that he is everywhere as a center but that his circumference is nowhere, since everything is immediately present to him without being withdrawn at all from this center.

14. As for the reasonable soul or *spirit,* there is something more in it than in monads or even in simple souls. It is not only a mirror of the universe of creatures but also an image of divinity. The spirit not only has a perception of the works of God but is even capable of producing something which resembles them, though in miniature. For not to mention the wonders of dreams in which we invent, without effort but also without will, things which we should have to think a long time to discover when awake, our soul is architectonic also in its voluntary actions and in discovering the sciences according to which God has regulated things (by weight, measure, number, etc.). In its own realm and in the small world in which it is allowed to act, the soul imitates what God performs in the great world.

15. For this reason all spirits, whether of men or of higher beings [*genies*], enter by virtue of reason and the eternal truths into a kind of society with God and are members of the City of God, that is to say, the most perfect state, formed and governed by the greatest and best of monarchs. Here there is no crime without punishment, no good action without a proportionate reward, and finally, as much virtue and happiness as is possible. And this takes place, not by a dislocation of nature, as if what God has planned for souls could disturb the laws of bodies, but by the very order of natural things itself, by virtue of the harmony pre-established from all time between the realms of nature and of grace, between God as architect and God as monarch, in such a way that nature leads to grace, and grace perfects nature by using it.

16. Thus, though reason cannot teach us the details of the great future, these being reserved for revelation, we can be assured by this same reason that things are arranged in a way which surpasses our desires. God being also the most perfect, the happiest, and therefore the most lovable of substances, and *true pure love* consisting in the state which causes pleasure to be taken in the perfections and the felicity of the beloved, this love must give us the greatest pleasure of which one is capable, since God is its object.

17. And it is easy to love him as we ought if we know him as I have said. For though God is not visible to our external senses, he is nonetheless most love-worthy and gives very great pleasure. We see how much pleasure honors give to men, although they do not consist of qualities which appear to the external senses. Martyrs and fanatics, though the affection of the latter is not well ordered, show what power the pleasure of the spirit has. What is more, even the pleasures of sense are reducible to intellectual pleasures, known confusedly. Music charms us, although its beauty consists only in the agreement of numbers and in the counting, which we do not perceive but which the soul nevertheless continues to carry out, of the beats or vibrations of sounding bodies which coincide at certain intervals. The pleasures which the eye finds

in proportions are of the same nature, and those caused by other senses amount to something similar, although we may not be able to explain them so distinctly.

18. It may even be said that the love of God already gives us, here and now, a foretaste of future felicity. And although it is disinterested, by itself it constitutes our greatest good and interest, even when we do not seek these in it and when we consider only the pleasure it gives and disregard the utility it produces. For it gives us a perfect confidence in the goodness of our Author and Master, and this produces a true tranquillity of spirit, not such as the Stoics have who resolutely force themselves to be patient, but by a present contentment which itself assures us of future happiness. And apart from the present pleasure, nothing could be more useful for the future, for the love of God also fulfils our hopes and leads us in the way of supreme happiness, since, by virtue of the perfect order established in the universe, everything is done in the best possible way, as much for the general good as for the greatest particular good of those who are convinced of it and are satisfied by the divine government. This cannot fail to be true of those who know how to love the source of all good. It is true that the supreme happiness (with whatever *beatific vision* or knowledge of God it may be accompanied) cannot ever be full, because God, being infinite, cannot ever be known entirely. Thus our happiness will never consist, and ought never to consist, in complete joy, which leaves nothing to be desired and which would stupefy our spirit, but in a perpetual progress to new pleasures and new perfections.

On Wisdom

Wisdom is merely the science of happiness or that science which teaches us to achieve happiness.

Happiness is a state of permanent joy. The happy man does not, it is true, feel this joy at every instant, for he sometimes rests from his contemplation, and usually also turns his thoughts to practical affairs. But it is enough that he is in a *state* to feel joy whenever he wishes to think of it and that at other times there is a joyousness in his actions and his nature which arises from this.

Present joy does not make happy if it has no *permanence;* indeed, he is rather unhappy who falls into a long wretchedness for the sake of a brief joy.

Joy is a pleasure which the soul feels in itself. *Pleasure* is the feeling of a perfection or an excellence, whether in ourselves or in something else. For the perfection of other beings also is agreeable, such as understanding, courage, and especially beauty in another human being, or in an animal or even in a lifeless creation, a painting or a work of craftsmanship, as well. For the image of such perfection in others, impressed upon us, causes some of this perfection to be implanted and aroused within ourselves. Thus there is no doubt that he who consorts much with excellent people or things becomes himself more excellent.

Although the perfections of others sometimes displease us – as for example, the understanding or the courage of any enemy, the beauty of a rival, or the luster of another's virtue which overshadows or shames us – this is not because of the perfection itself but because of the circumstance which makes it inopportune for us, so that the sweetness of our first perception of this perfection in someone else is exceeded and spoiled by the consequent bitterness of our afterthoughts.

We do not always observe wherein the perfection of pleasing things consists, or what kind of perfection within ourselves they serve, yet our feelings [*Gemüth*] perceive it, even though our understanding does not. We commonly say, "There is something, I know not what, that pleases me in the matter." This we call "sympathy." But those who seek the causes of things will usually find a ground for this and understand that there is something at the bottom of the matter which, though unnoticed, really appeals to us.

Music is a beautiful example of this. Everything that emits a sound contains a vibration or a transverse motion such as we see in strings; thus everything that emits sounds gives off invisible impulses. When these are not confused, but proceed together in order but with a certain variation, they are pleasing; in the same way, we also notice certain changes from long to short syllables, and a coincidence of rhymes in poetry, which contain a silent music, as it were, and when correctly constructed are pleasant even without being sung. Drum beats, the beat and cadence of the dance, and other motions of this kind in measure and rule derive their pleasurableness from their order, for all order is an aid to the emotions. And a regular though invisible order is found also in the artfully created beats and motions of vibrating strings, pipes, bells, and indeed, even of the air itself, which these bring into uniform motion. Through our hearing, this creates a sympathetic echo in us, to which our animal spirits respond. This is why music is so well adapted to move our minds, even though this main purpose is not usually sufficiently noticed or sought after.

There can be no doubt that even in touch, taste, and smell, sweetness consists in a definite though insensible order and perfection or a fitness, which nature has put there to stimulate us and the animals to that which is otherwise needed, so that the right use of all pleasurable things is really brought about in us, even though these things may give rise to a far greater harm through abuse and intemperance.

I call any elevation of being a *perfection*. Just as illness is a debasement, as it were, and a decline from health, so perfection is something which rises above health. But health itself stands balanced in the middle and lays the foundation for perfection. Now illness comes from an injury to action, as medical men rightly observe. Just so perfection shows itself in great freedom and power of action; since all being consists in a kind of power; and the greater the power, the higher and freer the being.

The greater any power is, moreover, the more there is found in it the many revealed through the one and in the one, in that the one rules many outside of itself and represents them in itself. Now unity in plurality is nothing but harmony [*Übereinstimmung*], and since any particular being agrees with one rather than another being, there flows from this harmony the order from which beauty arises, and beauty awakens love.

Thus we see that happiness, pleasure, love, perfection, being, power, freedom, harmony, order, and beauty are all tied to each other, a truth which is rightly perceived by few.

Now when the soul feels within itself a great harmony, order, freedom, power, or perfection, and hence feels pleasure in this, the result is joy, as these explanations show. Such joy is permanent and cannot deceive, nor can it cause a future unhappiness if it arises from knowledge and is accompanied by a light which kindles an inclination to the good in the will, that is, virtue. But when pleasure and joy are directed toward satisfying the senses rather than the understanding, they can as easily lead us to unhappiness as to bliss, just as a food which tastes good can be unwholesome. So the enjoyment of the senses must be used according to the rules of reason, like a food, medicine, or exercise. But the pleasure which the soul finds in itself through understanding is a present joy such as can conserve our joy for the future as well.

It follows from this that nothing serves our happiness better than the illumination of our understanding and the exercise of our will to act always according to our understanding, and that this illumination is to be sought especially in the knowledge of such things as can bring our understanding ever further into a higher light. For there springs from such knowledge an enduring progress in wisdom and virtue, and therefore also in perfection and joy, the advantage of which remains with the soul even after this life. . . .

Felicity

1. Virtue is the habit of acting according to wisdom. It is necessary that practice accompany knowledge.

2. Wisdom is the science of felicity, [and] is what must be studied above all other things.

3. Felicity is a lasting state of pleasure. Thus it is good to abandon or moderate pleasures which can be injurious by causing misfortunes or by blocking [the attainment of] better and more lasting pleasures.

4. Pleasure is a knowledge or feeling of perfection, not only in ourselves, but also in others, for in this way some further perfection is aroused in us.

5. To love is to find pleasure in the perfection of another.

6. Justice is charity or a habit of loving conformed to wisdom. Thus when one is inclined to justice, one tries to procure good for everybody, so far as one can, reasonably, but in proportion to the needs and merits of each: and even if one is obliged sometimes to punish evil persons, it is for the general good.

6*a*. Now it is necessary to explain the feeling or the knowledge of perfection. The confused perception of some perfection constitutes the pleasure of sense, but this pleasure can be [productive] of greater imperfections which are born of it, as a fruit with a good taste and a good odor can conceal a poison.

This is why one must shun the pleasures of sense, as one shuns a stranger, or, sooner, a flattering enemy.

7. Knowledge is of two kinds, that of facts and that of reasons. That of facts is perception, that of reasons is intelligence.

8. Knowledge of reasons perfects us because it teaches us universal and eternal truths, which are manifested in the perfect Being. But knowledge of facts is like that of the streets of a town, which serves us while we stay there, [but] after [leaving] which we don't wish to burden our memory any longer.

8*a*. The pleasures of sense which most closely approach pleasures of the mind, and are the most pure and the most certain, are that of music and that of symmetry, the former [being pleasure] of the ears, the latter of the eyes; for it is easy to understand the principles [*raisons*] of harmony, this perfection which gives us pleasure. The sole thing to be feared in this respect is to use it too often.

9. One need not shun at all pleasures which are born of intelligence or of reasons, as one penetrates the reason of the reason of perfections, that is to say as one sees them flow from their source, which is the absolutely perfect Being.

10. The perfect Being is called God. He is the ultimate reason of things, and the cause of causes. Being the sovereign wisdom and the sovereign power, he has always chosen the best and acts always in an orderly way.

11. One is happy when he loves God, and God, who has done everything perfectly, cannot fail to arrange everything thus, to elevate created beings to the perfection of which they are capable through union with him, which can subsist only through the spirit.

12. But one cannot love God without knowing his perfections, or his beauty. And since we can know him only in his emanations, these are two means of seeing his beauty, namely in the knowledge of eternal truths (which explain [their own] reasons in themselves), and in the knowledge of the Harmony of the Universe (in applying reasons to facts). That is to say, one must know the marvels of reason and the marvels of nature.

13. The marvels of reason and of eternal truths which our mind discovers in itself [are essential] in the sciences of reasoning about numbers, about figures, about good and evil, about justice and injustice.

14. The marvels of physical nature are the system of the universe, the structure of the bodies of animals, the causes of the rainbow, of magnetism, of the ebb and flow [of the tides], and a thousand other similar things.

15. One must hold as certain that the more a mind desires to know order, reason, the beauty of things which God has produced, and the more he is moved to imitate this order in the things which God has left to his direction, the happier he will be.

16. It is most true, as a result, that one cannot know God without loving one's brother, that one cannot have wisdom without having charity (which is the real touchstone of virtue), and that one even advances one's own good in

working for that of others: for it is an eternal law of reason and of the harmony of things that the works of each [person] will follow it. Thus the sovereign wisdom has so well regulated all things that our duty must also be our happiness, that all virtue produces its [own] reward, and that all crime punishes itself, sooner or later.

Meditation on the Common Concept of Justice

I

It is agreed that whatever God wills is good and just. But there remains the question whether it is good and just because God wills it or whether God wills it because it is good and just: in other words, whether justice and goodness are arbitrary or whether they belong to the necessary and eternal truths about the nature of things, as do numbers and proportions. The former opinion has been followed by some philosophers, and by some Roman [Catholic] and Reformed theologians: but present-day Reformed [theologians] usually reject this doctrine, as do all of our theologians and most of those of the Roman Church.

Indeed it [this view] would destroy the justice of God. For why praise him because he acts according to justice, if the notion of justice, in his case, adds nothing to that of action? And to say *stat pro ratione voluntas*, my will takes the place of reason, is properly the motto of a tyrant. Moreover this opinion would not sufficiently distinguish God from the devil. For if the devil, that is to say an intelligent, invisible, very great and very evil power, were the master of the world, this devil or this God would still be evil, even if it were necessary to honor him by force, as some peoples honor such imaginary gods in the hope of bringing them thereby to do less evil. . . .

It is a question, then, of determining the formal reason of justice and the measure by which we should measure actions to know whether they are just or not. After what has been said one can already foresee what this will be. Justice is nothing else than that which conforms to wisdom and goodness joined together: the end of goodness is the greatest good, but to recognize it wisdom is needed, which is nothing else than knowledge of the good. Goodness is simply the inclination to do good to everyone, and to arrest evil, at least when it is not necessary for a greater good or to arrest a greater evil. Thus wisdom is in the understanding and goodness in the will. And justice, as a consequence, is in both. Power is a different matter, but if it is used it makes right become fact, and makes what ought to be also really exist, in so far as the nature of things permits. And this is what God does in the world.

But since justice tends to the good, and [since] wisdom and goodness, which together form justice, relate to the good, one may ask what the true good is. I answer that it is nothing else than that which serves in the perfection of intelligent substances: from which it is clear that order, contentment, joy, wisdom, goodness and virtue are good things essentially and can never be evil; that power is naturally a good, that is to say in itself, because, everything being equal, it is better to have it than not to have it: but it does not become a certain good until it is joined with wisdom and goodness: for the power of an evil person serves only to plunge him farther into unhappiness sooner or later, because it gives him the means to be more evil, and to merit a greater punishment, from which he will not escape, since there is a perfectly just monarch of the universe whose infinite penetration and sovereign power one cannot avoid.

And since experience shows us that God permits, for reasons unknown to us but doubtless very wise, and founded in a greater good, that there be many evil [persons who are] happy in this life, and many good [persons who are] unhappy, which would not conform to the rules of a perfect government such as God's if it were not redressed, it follows necessarily that there will be another life, and that souls do not perish at all with the visible body; otherwise there would be unpunished crimes, and good actions without recompense, which is contrary to order.

There are, besides, demonstrative proofs of the immortality of the soul, because the principle of action and of consciousness could not come from a purely passive extended thing indifferent to all movement, such as matter is: thus action and consciousness must come from something simple or immaterial [and] without extension and without parts; which is called soul: now everything which is simple or without parts, is not subject to dissolution, and as a consequence cannot be destroyed. There are people who imagine that we are too small a thing in the sight of an infinite God, for him to be concerned with us; it is conceived that we are to God that which worms, which we crush without thinking, are in relation to us. But this is to imagine that God is like a man, and cannot think of everything. God, by the very fact that he is infinite, does things without working by a species of result of his will, as it results from my will and that of my friend, that we are in agreement, without needing a new action to produce the accord after our resolutions are made. But if the human race were not well governed, the universe would not be either, for the whole consists of its parts. . . . the beauty and the justice of the divine government have been partly concealed from our eyes, not only because it could not be otherwise, without changing the whole harmony of the world, but also because it is proper in order that there be more exercise of free virtue, of wisdom and of a nonmercenary love of God, since rewards and punishments are still outwardly invisible and appear only to the eyes of our reason or faith: which I take here for the same thing, since true faith is founded in reason. And since the marvels of nature make us find that the operations of God are admirably beautiful, whenever we can envisage a whole in its natural context, though this beauty is not apparent in looking at things detached or torn from their wholes, we must conclude that everything which we cannot yet disentangle or envisage as a whole with all its parts must have no less of justice and of beauty. . . .

Codex iuris gentium (Praefatio)

XI. . . . The doctrine of law, taken from nature's strict confines, presents an immense field for human study. But the notions of law and of justice, even after having been treated by so many illustrious authors, have not been made sufficiently clear. Right is a kind of moral possibility, and obligation a moral necessity. By moral I mean that which is equivalent to "natural" for a good man: for as a Roman jurisconsult has well said, we ought to believe that we are incapable of doing things which are contrary to good morals.[3] A good man is one who loves everybody, in so far as reason permits. Justice, then, which is the virtue [that] regulates that affection which the Greeks call φιλανθρωπία [philanthropy], will be most conveniently defined, if I am not in error, as the charity of the wise man, that is, charity which follows the dictates of wisdom. So that assertion which is attributed to Carneades, that justice is supreme folly, because it commands us to consider the interests of others while we neglect our own, is born of ignorance of the definition of justice.[4]

Charity is a universal benevolence, and benevolence the habit of loving or of willing the good. Love then signifies rejoicing in the happiness of another, or, what is the same thing, converting the happiness of another into one's own. With this is resolved a difficult question, of great moment in theology as well: in what way disinterested love is possible, independent of hope, of fear, and of regard for any question of utility.[5] In truth, the happiness of those whose happiness pleases us turns into our own happiness, since things which please us are desired for their own sake. And since the contemplation of the beautiful is pleasant in itself, and a painting of Raphael affects a sensitive person who understands it, although it brings him no [material] gain, so that he keeps it in his [mind's] eye, as the image of a thing which is loved; when the beautiful thing is itself capable of happiness, this affection passes over into pure love. But the divine love excels all other loves, because God can be loved with the greatest result [*Deus cum maximo successu amari potest*], since nothing is happier than God, and nothing more beautiful or more worthy of happiness can be conceived. And since he possesses supreme power and supreme wisdom, his happiness does not simply become ours (if we are wise: that is, if we love him), but even creates ours. But since wisdom ought to guide charity, it will be necessary to define it [wisdom]. I believe that we can best render the concept that men have of it, if we say that wisdom is nothing but the science of happiness itself. Once again we return to the concept of happiness, which this is not the place to explain.

XII. Now from this source flows natural right [*ius naturae*], of which there are three degrees: strict right [*ius strictum*] in commutative justice; equity (or, in the narrower sense of the term, charity) in distributive justice; and, finally, piety (or probity) in universal justice: hence come the most general and commonly accepted principles of right – to injure no one, to give to each his due, and to live honestly (or rather piously); . . . The precept of mere or strict right is that no one is to be injured, so that he will not be given a motive for a legal action within the state, nor outside the state a right of war. From this arises the justice which philosophers call commutative,[6] and the right which Grotius calls a legal claim [*facultas*].[7] The higher degree I call equity or, if you prefer, charity (that is, in the narrower sense), and this I extend beyond the rigor of strict right to [include] those obligations which give to those whom they affect no ground for [legal] action in compelling us to fulfill them, such as gratitude and alms-giving – to which, as Grotius says, we have a moral claim [*aptitudo*], not a legal claim [*facultas*]. And as [the principle of] the lowest degree of right is to harm no one, so [that of] the middle degree is to do good to everybody; but only so far as befits each one or as much as he deserves; for it is impossible to favor everyone. It is, then, here that distributive justice belongs, and the precept of the law which commands us to give to each his due. And it is here that the political laws of a state belong, which assure the happiness of its subjects and make it possible that those who had a merely moral claim acquire a legal claim; that is, that they become able to demand what it is equitable for others to perform. In the lowest degree of right, one does not take account of differences among men, except those which arise from each particular case, and all men are considered equal; but now on the higher level merits are weighed, and thus privileges, rewards and punishment have their place. This difference between the two degrees of right was nicely suggested by Xenophon,[8] in his example of the boy Cyrus, who was chosen to judge between two boys, the stronger of whom had forcibly exchanged garments with the other because he found that the other's coat fitted him and his own fitted the other better. Cyrus pronounced in favor of the robber; but he was admonished by his teacher that in this case it was not a question of deciding whom the coat fitted better, but only to whom it belonged, and that the other manner of judging might more properly be used only when he himself had coats to distribute. Equity itself demands strict right, or the equality of men, in our dealings, except when an important consideration of a greater good makes us depart from it. What is called respect of persons, however, has its place, not in exchanging goods with others, but in distributing our own or the public goods.

XIII. The highest degree of right I have called probity, or rather piety. What I have said thus far can be interpreted as limited to the relations within mortal life. Simple or strict right is born of the principle of the conservation of peace; equity or charity strives for something higher – [namely] that while each benefits others as much as he can, he may increase his own happiness in that of the other. And, to say it in a word, strict right avoids misery, while the higher right tends toward happiness, but only such as is possible in this life. But that we ought to hold this life itself and everything that makes it desirable inferior to the great advantage of others, and that we should bear the greatest pains for the sake of those near us: all this is [merely] taught with noble words by philosophers, rather than proved by solid demonstration. For the dignity and glory, and our mind's sense of joy on account of virtue, to which they appeal under the name of honor [*honestas*], are certainly goods of thought or of the mind and are, indeed, great ones, but not such as to prevail with all [men], nor to overcome all the bitterness of evils, since not all men are equally moved by the imagination; especially those who have not become accustomed to the thought of virtue or to the appreciation of the goods of the mind, whether through a liberal education or a noble way of living, or the discipline of life or of a sect. In order really to establish by a universal demonstration that everything honorable is useful and everything base is damned, one must assume the immortality of the soul, and God as ruler of the universe. In this way we can think of all men as living in the most perfect state, under a monarch who can neither be deceived in his wisdom nor eluded in his power; and who is also so worthy of love that it is happiness [itself] to serve such a master. Thus whoever expends his soul in the service of Christ will regain it.[9] The divine providence and power cause all right to become fact, and [assure that] no one is injured except by himself, that no good action goes unrewarded, and no sin unpunished. Because, as we are divinely taught by Christ, all our hairs are numbered,[10] and not even a drink of water is given to the thirsty in vain;[11] nothing is neglected in the state of the universe. It is on this ground that justice is called universal, and includes all the other virtues; for duties that do not seem to concern others, as, for example, not to abuse our own bodies or our own property, though they are beyond [the power of] human laws, are still prohibited by natural law, that is, by the eternal laws of the divine monarchy, since we owe ourselves and everything we have to God. Now, if it is of interest to the state, of how much more interest is it to the universe that no one use badly what is his? So it is from this that the highest precept of the law receives its force, which commands us to live honorably (that is, piously). It is in this sense that learned men have rightly held, among things to be desired, that the law of nature and of the nations [*ius naturae et gentium*] should follow the teachings of Christianity, that is, the sublime things, the divine things of the wise, according to the teaching of Christ. Thus I think that I have interpreted the three precepts of the [Roman] law,[12] or the three degrees of justice, in the most fitting way, and have indicated the sources of the natural law.

　　XIV. Besides the eternal right [or law] of rational nature, flowing from the divine source, there is also held to be voluntary right, derived from custom or made by a superior. And in the state the civil law [*ius civile*] indeed receives its force from him who has the supreme power; outside of the state, or among those who participate in the supreme power (of whom there may be more than one, even in the same state), is the sphere of the voluntary law of nations, originating in the tacit consent of peoples. It is not necessary that this be the agreement of all peoples or for all times; for there have been many cases in which one thing was considered right in India and another in Europe, and even among us it has changed with the passage of centuries, as this very work will show. . . .

　　XV. But Christians have yet another common tie, the divine positive law contained in the sacred Scriptures. To these can be added the sacred canons accepted in the whole Church and, later, in the West, the pontifical legislation, to which kings and peoples submit themselves. And in general before the schism of the last century, it seems to have been accepted for a long time (and not without reason) that a kind of common republic of Christian nations must be thought of, the heads of which were the Pope in sacred matters, and the Emperor in temporal matters, who preserved as much of the power of the ancient Roman emperors as was necessary for the common good of Christendom, saving [without prejudicing] the rights of kings and the liberty of princes. . . .

The Principles of Pufendorf

IV

So much for what regards the end and the object [of natural law]; it remains now to treat the efficient cause of this law, which our author does not correctly establish. He, indeed, does not find it in the nature of things and in the precepts of right reason which conform to it, which emanate from the divine understanding, but (what will appear to be strange and contradictory) in the command of a superior. Indeed, Book I, chapter I, part I, defines duty as "the human action exactly conforming to the prescriptions of the laws in virtue of an obligation." And soon chapter II, part 2, defines law as "a command by which the superior obliges the subject to conform his actions to what the law itself prescribes."[13] If we admit this, no one will do his duty spontaneously; also, there will be no duty when there is no superior to compel its observance; nor will there be any duties for those who do not have a superior. And since, according to the author, duty and acts prescribed by justice coincide (because his whole natural jurisprudence is contained in the doctrine of duty), it follows that all law is prescribed by a superior. This paradox, brought out by Hobbes above all, who seemed to deny to the state of nature, that is [a condition] in which there are no superiors, all binding justice whatsoever (although even he is inconsistent), is a view to which I am astonished that anyone could have adhered. Now, then, will he who is invested with the supreme power do nothing against justice if he proceeds tyrannically against his subjects; who arbitrarily despoils his subjects, torments them, and kills them under torture; who makes war on others without cause? . . .

It is without doubt most true, that God is by nature superior to all; all the same the doctrine itself, which makes all law derivative from the command of a superior, is not freed of scandal and errors, however one justifies it. Indeed, not to mention that which Grotius justly observed, namely that there would be a natural obligation even on the hypothesis – which is impossible – that God does not exist,[14] or if one but left the divine existence out of consideration; since care for one's own preservation and well-being certainly lays on men many requirements about taking care of others, as even Hobbes perceives in part (and this obligatory tie bands of brigands confirm by their example, who, while they are enemies of others, are obliged to respect certain duties among themselves – although, as I have observed, a natural law based on this source alone would be very imperfect); to pass over all this, one must pay attention to this fact: that God is praised because he is just. There must be, then, a certain justice – or rather a supreme justice – in God, even though no one is superior to him, and he, by the spontaneity of his excellent nature, accomplishes all things well, such that no one can reasonably complain of him. Neither the norm of conduct itself, nor the essence of the just, depends on his free decision, but rather on eternal truths, objects of the divine intellect, which constitute, so to speak, the essence of divinity itself; and it is right that our author is reproached by theologians when he maintains the contrary; because, I believe, he had not seen the wicked consequences which arise from it. Justice, indeed, would not be an essential attribute of God, if he himself established justice and law by his free will. And, indeed, justice follows certain rules of equality and of proportion [which are] no less founded in the immutable nature of things, and in the divine ideas, than are the principles of arithmetic and of geometry. So that no one will maintain that justice and goodness originate in the divine will, without at the same time maintaining that truth originates in it as well: an unheard-of paradox by which Descartes[15] showed how great can be the errors of great men. . . .

V

. . . Nor do I see how the author, acute as he is, could easily be absolved of the contradiction into which he falls, when he makes all juridical obligations derivative from the command of a superior (which we have shown through citations of him), while afterwards in Book I, chapter II, part 5, he states that in order that one have a superior it is necessary that they [superiors] possess not only the force [necessary] to exercise coercion, but also that they have a just cause to justify their power over my person. Consequently the justice of the cause is antecedent to this same superior, contrary to what had been asserted. Well, then, if the source of law is the will of a superior and, inversely a justifying cause of law is necessary in order to have a superior, a circle is created, than which none was ever more manifest. From what will the justice of the cause derive, if there is not yet a superior, from whom, supposedly, the law may emanate? And it would be strange that so acute a person could take such measures against himself, if we did not know that to those who undertake to maintain paradoxes it happens easily that, when good sense prevails in them, they forget their own doctrines. . . .

But whoever examines carefully what he says, will not fail to notice that he is neither consistent, nor resolves the difficulty. Indeed, if neither coercion without reasons, nor the latter without force is sufficient, why – I ask – when force ceases and reason alone remains, shall I not return to that liberty which it is said I had when, before the application of force, reason alone was present? What the author says, in fact – that, failing fear, no one can stop me from behaving according to my own will rather than according to someone else's –

would be valid even if reasons existed. On the other hand, if reasons restrain even by themselves, why did they not already restrain by themselves, before fear arose? And what force, I pray you, can fear give to reasons, except itself – which it would not itself provide even without reasons? Or will this not very durable sentiment impress some indelible character on unwilling minds? Suppose that a man who owes obedience to another solely in virtue of reasons, is afterwards also constrained by force on the part of the other, and that he persists nonetheless in his soul's original disposition, by which he does not want to obey any more than he is constrained [to do]; I do not see why, once constrained, he ought to remain in submission in perpetuity. Supposing, for example, that a Christian who is ill falls into the power of a Turkish doctor, by whom he is made to practice hygienic precepts that he already knew [to be efficacious] for some time, but which are now imposed on him coercively; when, afterwards, he is offered an occasion to escape, would he be obliged to [observe] temperance more than he had before his imprisonment? One or the other, then: either reasons oblige prior to force, or they do not obligate any longer when force fails.

The things [which I have indicated] show sufficiently that the author is lacking sound principles on which to found the true reasons for laws, about which he himself has arbitrarily supposed principles which cannot be maintained. For the rest, the foundations of jurisprudence, whether common to all law (even to that which is derived solely from equity), or proper to law in a narrow sense (which involves a superior), have been indicated by us elsewhere. To summarize, we shall say in general that: the end of natural law is the good of those who observe it; its object, all that which concerns others and is in our power; finally, its efficient cause in us is the light of eternal reason, kindled in our minds by the divinity.

Editor's Notes

1. What is contained "eminently" in God is analogous to what is contained "formally" in created beings, but it exists in a fuller and more perfect way.
2. Leibniz and Newton were rivals for the honor of discovering the infinitesimal calculus. Leibniz was also critical of various aspects of Newton's physics. For an account of their controversies, see A. Rupert Hall, *Philosophers at War* (Cambridge, England: Cambridge University Press, 1980).
3. Leibniz was referring to the Roman jurist Papinian.
4. Grotius attacked Carneades (c. 213–128 B.C.E.), a leader of the Platonic Academy and a major skeptical thinker, on the same point. See the "Prolegomena," §5, in the Grotius selections in Part I of this anthology.
5. The possibility of totally disinterested love was a topic of heated theological debate in France during the late seventeenth century.
6. Aristotle, *Nicomachean Ethics*, 1130b.
7. Or perfect right. See Grotius, *Law of War and Peace*, I.i.4, in the selections in Part I of this anthology.
8. The story is told in Xenophon, *Cyropaedia*, I.3. 17; Grotius used it to illustrate the difference between perfect and imperfect rights.
9. Matt. 10:39.

10. Luke 12:7.
11. Matt. 10:42.
12. That is, to injure no one, to give each his due, and to live honestly (or piously) – precepts summarizing justice as given at the beginning of Justinian's *Institutes*.
13. For these views of Pufendorf and those to which Leibniz later referred, see the selections from Pufendorf's *Law of Nature and of Nations* in Part I of this anthology.
14. See the selections from Grotius in Part I of this anthology. Leibniz was referring to the "Prolegomena" to the *Law of War and Peace*, §11.
15. For Descartes's voluntarism, see the selections from the "Replies to Objections" in Part II of this anthology.

Further Reading

More of Leibniz's work on moral and political issues is contained in the two volumes from which the selections given here were taken. The reader may also wish to consult Leibniz's chapter-by-chapter commentary on John Locke, *New Essays on Human Understanding*, trans. and ed. Peter Remnant and Jonathan Bennett (Cambridge, England: Cambridge University Press, 1982). For every passage in which Locke said something about ethics, there is a corresponding passage in Leibniz, and in some but not all of them he developed positive views of his own.

G. MacDonald Ross, *Leibniz* (Oxford: Oxford University Press, 1984), is a brief introduction to Leibniz's thought, with a helpful bibliography. Other general studies of Leibniz are H. W. B. Joseph, *Lectures on the Philosophy of Leibniz*, ed. J. L. Austin (Oxford: Oxford University Press, 1947); Nicholas Rescher, *Leibniz: An Introduction to His Philosophy* (Oxford: Oxford University Press, 1979); and Stuart Brown, *Leibniz* (Minneapolis: University of Minnesota Press, 1984).

There is one book in English on Leibniz's ethics: John Hostler, *Leibniz's Moral Philosophy* (London: Duckworth, 1975). G. H. R. Parkinson's monograph *Leibniz on Human Freedom* (Wiesbaden, West Germany: Franz Steiner Verlag, 1970) (*Studia Leibnitiana* Sonderheft 2) is a helpful analysis of a topic important to his ethics.

For a general study of Leibniz in the context of seventeenth-century thought, see Leroy E. Loemker, *Struggle for Synthesis: The Seventeenth Century Background of Leibniz's Synthesis of Order and Freedom* (Cambridge, Mass.: Harvard University Press, 1972), which examines the moral issues of that time. R. W. Meyer, *Leibnitz and the Seventeenth Century Revolution*, trans. J. P. Stern (Cambridge, England: Bowes & Bowes, 1952), also relates Leibniz's thought to the general problems of his era.

Christian Wolff

Introduction

Christian Wolff was born in Breslau, Germany, in 1679. He studied theology and mathematics and in 1706 was appointed professor of mathematics and natural science at the University of Halle. An early essay of his on the application of mathematical method to practical philosophy won Leibniz's admiration. Leibniz thereafter corresponded with him and sponsored him for various positions, and the philosophy Wolff developed became known as the "Leibniz–Wolff" philosophy. In 1713, while Latin was still the dominant language of the learned world, Wolff began to publish philosophical works in German. The first concerned the powers of the human understanding; it was followed by volumes explaining metaphysics, ethics, politics, cosmology, and teleology (the study of the ends or reasons for the existence of different kinds of things).

With these early German works, Wolff established his reputation as an important systematic thinker, and he also introduced into the German language many philosophical terms that are still in use. Having developed his system in German, Wolff then proceeded to expand and refine it, publishing Latin expositions six or seven volumes long on each of the subjects that he had covered in German in only one volume. He wrote on many other subjects as well. Even in his own lifetime Wolff was reproached for his verbosity, but his Latin works were nonetheless widely read and gave Wolff an international reputation. Indeed, the fact that a long French summary of his work was written especially for women suggests that it was important in fashionable circles, and not only at the universities, to know something about his views.

In 1721 as rector of the University of Halle, Wolff gave an address in which he argued that Chinese morals and European morals were so similar that it could be concluded that morality can be learned from reason alone and, consequently, that religion is not necessary for happiness and decent living. He had already aroused a good deal of opposition among the Pietistic members of the university faculty, who were less rationalistic and more orthodox than he was. Wolff's speech led to a movement that resulted in the Prussian king's ordering him in 1723 to leave Halle within forty-eight hours. One account states that the king was finally moved to give this order by the claim that, according to Wolff, soldiers who ran away from battle could not help themselves and therefore could not be held responsible. When Frederick the Great came to the throne in 1740, he recalled Wolff, who from then until his death in 1754 continued to teach and write in Halle.

The aim of philosophy, Wolff held, is to give a definitive account of the abstract possibilities of things. What is actual must be learned from experience, but whatever is actual must be possible, and the philosopher's task is to explain why there are the possibilities there are and no others. The philosopher must do this for all subjects. Wolff started with the basic concept of being and worked through the concepts involved in the constitution of the natural world and human psychology to the most detailed expositions of the proper arrangement of political and personal life, showing how the concepts needed to structure these fields arise from or are made possible by the principle of sufficient reason and the principle of identity. God is the sole being whose existence is necessary, but although the existence of every other kind of entity is contingent, the essences that those entities exemplify are necessarily connected through an intricate web of possibilities and impossibilities.

Wolff divided philosophy into two parts. Theoretical philosophy relates to our capacity for knowledge as such. Practical philosophy relates to our appetitive faculty, giving scientific direction to our capacity for choosing good and avoiding evil. Practical philosophy itself has three main parts. Ethics deals with people before the existence of any political organization. It considers people as they live in the company of others but not under any political superior. Economics explains the management of life in small societies or groups in which there is some authority, such as the family, regarding which Wolff demonstrated that the father is naturally the head. Politics refers to the direction of life in political society, which has a supreme authority all must obey. Although there are principles for each of these subdivisions, there also are universal principles of practical philosophy. These universal principles direct all free action in pursuit of good (or avoidance of evil, as Wolff always insisted on adding), and the principles within each of the more specialized realms only exemplify the universal directives.

Although Wolff's basic ideas about the essence of humanity and about human action are Leibnizian, their elaboration into a full and coherent system is his own. On a number of important matters, such as the nature of obligation, Wolff gave more detail than Leibniz did, thereby raising the question of whether Leibniz would have agreed with him on all these points. And in other respects, the social and political aims that provided some of Wolff's motivation led him to positions that we cannot clearly identify in Leibniz.

Wolff was eager to spread the Enlightenment to the general population, and it was no accident that he believed the human good to lie in the constant increase of knowledge. To enable people to be happier and better, he held, we must educate them. He approved of the many German magazines that imitated the English *Spectator* of the early eighteenth century and that were extremely popular in Wolff's Germany. The "middle brow" culture and the models of politeness they were spreading were an improvement over what merchants and shopkeepers and wealthier artisans had previously had available. They made known an alternative to the style of the courtier, which had been the dominant pattern of manners for those who had enough money and leisure to improve themselves. Wolff believed that the systematic knowledge contained in his universal practical philosophy would do more to help people become cultivated, polite, and thoughtful than would unsystematic moral instruction. As he demonstrated, he felt that he owed it to his fellows to help them improve themselves; and if we bear in mind the generally backward state of culture and economy in Germany at that time, we can see past the elitism of his remarks to a genuine concern for human betterment.

Evident in Wolff's work, moreover, is a strong interest in human self-direction. In his view, we can learn what to do by reason alone, without revelation; God himself cannot order us to do anything except what the rational laws of nature bid us do; we do not need to be bribed or coerced into obedience by threats of punishment or offers of reward. We are, in short, autonomous moral agents – or we can be if we are sufficiently educated. The difficulty Wolff faced was that it did not seem obvious that everyone could be sufficiently educated to reach the stage of perceiving clearly and distinctly that happiness is to be attained only through virtue. And those who did not see this could be brought to a decent course of behavior only by the threat of punishment. Wolff's intellectualist theory of the good did not allow him to underwrite the kind of universal ascription of self-directive capacities that he wanted to support. If he showed us how far a Leibnizian view can go in this direction, he also made clear just where it must stop.

I have translated the following selections from Wolff's *Vernünftige Gedancken von der Menschen Tun und Lassen zu Beförderung ihrer Glückseeligkeit,* first published in 1720. I have used the text of the Olms reprint of the fourth edition of 1733. In the notes I have added some passages from the "German metaphysics," *Vernünftige Gedancken von Gott, der Welt, und der Seele des Menschen* (Reasonable thoughts about God, the world, and the human soul), also first published in 1720, to help explain some of the terms Wolff used in his ethics.

Reasonable Thoughts About the Actions of Men, for the Promotion of Their Happiness

Foreword to Second Edition

. . . I treat here a part of philosophy,[1] namely, that which explains the acts and omissions of man. Whoever does not want these words to mean other than what the subject calls for must, in such an endeavor, show what is possible through man's will and how it is possible that a man can determine himself to do certain actions and omit others. A philosopher shows the reason from which one can see that something is possible rather than impossible and explains accordingly in any given case why one determines oneself to this rather than that act. . . . I have accordingly investigated for all cases how actions must be constituted so that one can will them and how they must be if one is averse to them, once one fully sees their constitution. And thereby I have shown conceptually that human actions are in themselves necessarily good or evil and that in no way do they become good or evil only through the command or prohibition of a superior. . . .

I have further shown how it is possible to obligate a man to do or omit something, and especially I have placed natural obligation in an unexpected light, which previously could more easily be named than explained. And precisely from this it follows that virtue can exist with natural obligation alone; everything beyond that works simply as an outer compulsion. Because in ethics [*in der Moral*] it should be shown how man arrives at virtue, what matters most is to show how to begin to satisfy one's natural obligations. In this kind of obligation, man remains wholly free in his actions, and he is never freer than when he acts in accordance with it. In all other obligation, on the contrary, a sort of force is encountered, which is necessary for those who are not able to see correctly the properties of their actions. Men of understanding and reason need no obligation beyond the natural. But dull and unreasonable men are in need of another. The servile fear of the force and might of a superior must restrain them from doing what they would like to do.

Accordingly, if one wishes to guide man, one can do it in two ways: one guides him either through compulsion, like a beast, or through the aid of reason, like a reasonable creature. With the former I have, in ethics, nothing to do; for through it no one is brought to virtue but only to an outer habit of goodness, or even to a sham being in which there is no truth. Only the other is my work, as I have allowed myself to take on the task of making virtue more acceptable among men. . . .

Part I: Of Human Action and Omission in General

Chapter 1: Of the Universal Rule of Human Action and the Law of Nature

1. We find from experience that some thoughts of the soul as well as movements of the body are originated by the will of the soul; others, however, are not subordinated to it. . . . Now because what our will originates has its ground in the will, and therefore in ourself[2] – whereas the movements of the body that are subordinated to the will have their ground in the condition of the body – both the thoughts of the mind and the movements of the body that depend on the will belong to our actions. And because the will is free to choose from among the possible things the one that pleases us most, this action of man is free and [so] is called free action.[3]

2. . . . The inner and outer conditions of the soul and the body, which are sustained with the aid of our free actions, either agree with the essence of the soul and the body and with their previous condition or are contrary to them. Because the proof of this goes too deeply into the most subtle truths . . . I will here content myself by merely calling on experience and a few examples to explain the proposition.

Man is suited by nature to know truth.[4] The more truth he recognizes, the more fit he is to know it. So the condition of soul in which it is kept aware of truth through its free actions, that is, its manifold strivings for knowledge, agrees with its natural condition and in no way opposes it. Suppose there is a man in good bodily condition without pain: if he eats and drinks a great deal, he will find himself dull and have pains in his head and perhaps in other parts of his body. The present condition of his body is contrary to the previous one; even his soul is at odds with the previous condition. For although his soul was previously capable of thinking over a subject with pleasure and contemplating what it chose, now it is vexed and cannot keep its thoughts together for long. Earlier it was peaceful and joyful; now through pain and other disagreeable feelings it is restless and disturbed. . . .

Now, if the present condition agrees with the previous and the following conditions, and all of them together agree with the essence and nature of man, then the condition of man is perfect; and the greater the agreement is, the more perfect the condition will be.[5] By contrast, if the past condition disagrees with the present, or the present with the future . . . then the condition of man is imperfect. In this way, man's free actions promote either the perfection or the imperfection of his inner and outer condition.

3. What makes our inner and outer conditions perfect is good; by contrast, what makes them less perfect is bad. Hence man's free actions are either good or bad.

5. Man's free actions become good or bad through their consequences . . . and what follows from them must necessarily follow and cannot remain unrealized. They are therefore in and of themselves good or bad and are not first made so by God's will. Thus if it were possible that there were no God and the present connection of things still subsisted, the free acts of man would remain good or bad. . . .

6. The knowledge of good is a motive [*Bewegungsgrund*] of the will.[6] Whoever distinctly conceives[7] those free acts of man that are good in and of themselves will recognize that they are good. And therefore the good we perceive in them is a motive for us to will them. Now, because it is not possible for something to be a motive both to will and not to will, it cannot happen that one does not will an inherently good act if one distinctly conceives it. . . . So if we do not will [such acts], there is no other cause than that we do not recognize them [as good]. To have an aversion to them we must represent them as different from what they are.

7. In the same way, the knowledge of evil is a motive for not willing or for aversion from a thing. . . .

8. To obligate [*verbinden*] someone to do or omit something is only to connect a motive of willing or not willing to it.[8] For example, the magistrate obligates a subordinate to omit thievery through the penalty of the noose attached to it. Because through his power and force this punishment is attached to thievery and it will certainly follow that whoever is caught stealing will hang, anyone who wants to steal will know that stealing is bad because it brings the gallows, and from this he will acquire an aversion to theft. . . . Whatever gives a motive to will or not to will an act obligates us to do or not do it.

How from this concept all obligation in all cases can be shown, and how fruitful it is for the derivation of other truths, will be explained fully not only in this book but also in the next, on the social life of man.

9. Now, because whatever follows from human actions and makes them either good or bad arises from their essence and from nature and because the good and bad that we meet in actions are the ground of willing or not willing them, it follows that nature has connected motives with men's inherently good and bad actions. And in this way the nature of things and of ourselves obligates us to do the inherently good and omit the inherently bad.

12. . . . Because good actions make our inner and outer conditions more

perfect, and wicked ones make them less perfect, nature obligates us to do what makes us and our condition, or (what is the same thing) our inner and outer conditions, more perfect. . . . And therefore we have a rule by which we should direct the free actions that we have in our power, namely, *Do what makes you and your condition, or that of others, more perfect; omit what makes it less perfect.*

16. A rule according to which we are obligated to direct our free actions is called a law. Hence, because we are obligated to act according to the universal rule of free action, this rule is a law.

17. A rule is specifically called a law of nature if nature obligates us to direct our free actions according to it, just as we call a divine law a rule according to which God obligates us to direct our free actions, and again, a human law is a rule according to which men obligate us to direct our actions.

19. Because nature obligates us to do what makes us and our condition more perfect . . . the rule "Do what makes you and your condition more perfect, and omit what makes you and your condition less perfect" is a law of nature. Because this rule covers all free human actions, there is no need of any other law of nature, but all special laws must be derived from it. . . . So this rule is the entire ground of all natural laws.

20. Again, because this rule is a law because it obligates, and the obligation comes from nature, the law of nature is validated by nature itself and would hold even if man had no superior who could obligate him to it. In fact it would hold even if there were no God.

21. And so those are in error who imagine that an atheist may live as he will . . . this holds only if the atheist is uncomprehending and does not rightly see the properties of actions. . . .

23. Because our free actions are good or bad because of what necessarily follows from them, either simply or under certain conditions, to judge them we need insight into the connections of things. Now, insight into the connections of things is reason. So good and bad are known through reason. Accordingly, reason teaches us what we should and should not do; that is, reason is the schoolmistress of the law of nature.

24. He who directs his action according to reason, that is, acts reasonably, lives according to the law of nature, and insofar as he is reasonable, he cannot act against the law of nature. Because we know through reason what the law of nature requires, a reasonable man needs no further law, for because of his reason he is a law unto himself.[9]

25. Because inherently good acts are necessarily good and inherently bad ones are necessarily bad, neither can be altered. The law of nature requires that we do the one and do not do the other, and therefore it is unalterable.

26. Moreover, what is necessary is eternal; because the law of nature is necessary, it is also an eternal law.

27. This eternal law extends to all actions of man in all cases. . . .

29. Because the divine understanding makes all things possible and through

[God's] will brings the possible to reality, so it has also become possible through the understanding of God that the free actions of men can affect the perfection or imperfection of themselves and their condition, and through [God's] counsel it is so in reality. Because the representation of this perfection is the motive for doing the acts . . . it follows that God has connected the motives with the actions, and accordingly he obligates men to do what the law of nature requires. . . . In this way simultaneously, natural obligation is divine obligation, and the law of nature is a divine law. It follows at once from this that God can give men no other law than the law of nature, and never a law that conflicts with the law of nature.

34. Because God obligates men to just what nature obligates them to . . . whoever directs his life according to the law of nature directs it also according to God's will and lives according to his will. . . .

38. Because a reasonable man is a law unto himself and, besides natural obligation, needs no other, neither rewards nor punishments are, for him, motives to do good acts and avoid bad ones. So the reasonable man does good acts because they are good and does not do wicked ones because they are wicked. In this case he becomes like God, who has no superior who can obligate him to do what is good or not do what is wicked, but does the one and not the other simply because of the perfection of his nature.

39. An unreasonable man, on the other hand, will need, besides natural obligation, another if he is to live according to the law of nature. For him, rewards and punishments are motives for doing good actions. . . . Hence the unreasonable man does the good and omits the evil out of fear of punishment and hope of reward; in this he is like a child. . . .

40. Because through our actions we preserve the perfection of ourselves and our condition, the perfection of ourselves and our condition is the aim of our action, or the actions are the means through which we achieve our aims. Hence, because all free acts are directed at this aim, it is the final aim of all our free acts and the main aim of our whole life.

42. I shall not here explain that the perfection of our nature and our own condition is radically different from self-interest (*Eigen-nutz*], but I shall recall only this, which will be made clear as the sun in what follows, that included in the perfection of our nature are the honoring of God and the service of the common good. . . .

43. And therefore we do not approve the opinions of those who make self-interest the basis of the law of nature. Whoever is selfish looks only to himself and seeks his own benefit, even at the expense of others . . . by contrast, whoever seeks to make himself as perfect as possible seeks also what others seek and desires nothing at their expense. . . .

44. Because the greatest perfection is really God and no creature can partake of it, it is also not possible that a man, even if he daily uses all his strength, should ever attain it. He can therefore achieve no more than to progress from one perfection to another and, increasingly, to avoid imperfec-

tion. And this is the highest good he can attain, so that the highest good of man or his blessedness is rightly explained as an unhindered progress to greater perfections.

45. Because man will progress to always greater perfection if he directs his acts according to the law of nature, it is through observation of the law of nature that the highest good or blessedness is attained; hence its observation is the means through which we attain the highest good or blessedness of which we are capable on earth.

49. He who progresses unhampered from one perfection to another and avoids imperfection, and is aware of this, has an intuitive awareness of perfection. Intuitive knowledge of perfection affords pleasure or enjoyment; so he has a continuous pleasure. So the highest good or blessedness of man is connected with continuous pleasure.

52. The condition of continuous pleasure constitutes happiness. Now, because the highest good or blessedness is connected with continuous pleasure, the man who possesses it is in the condition of continuous pleasure. And therefore the highest good is connected with happiness.

56. It is certainly true that a man can be displeased by a true good, just as he can be pleased by a specious good, if he does not recognize either of them or harbors some other error about them. . . . But because both the displeasure and the pleasure come from our error, I cannot say that the true good displeases me and the specious good pleases me, so that the one makes me unhappy and the other makes me happy. For I cannot attribute to things that I do not recognize and about which I harbor errors what comes from my ignorance and error. . . .

57. Because true goods rest on a true perfection in man or his condition but specious goods do not, only that can make man happy that rests on a true perfection. . . . Hence because we preserve the perfection of ourselves and our outer condition through observation of the law of nature, the law of nature is the means to preserve our happiness.

64. Readiness to direct one's actions according to the law of nature is what we usually call virtue. . . . Human weakness is the natural inability to act in accordance with the law of nature. I say: natural inability. For whoever owes the inability to himself cannot attribute his failings to natural weakness. . . .

65. Because the law of nature is required for the perfection of ourselves and others, virtue is a readiness to perfect oneself and others as much as possible.

66. The observation of the law of nature is what makes man happy. Because readiness to live in accordance with the law of nature is virtue, virtue makes man happy. And accordingly, one cannot call happy anyone without virtue.

Chapter 2: Of Conscience

73. The judgment of whether our actions are good or bad is called conscience. Insofar as man is capable of judging the consequences of his actions

as to whether his inner or outer condition or the inner or outer condition of another is more perfect, so far he has a conscience.

77. The judgment of an action made before it is done is called the antecedent conscience, and that made when it has been done is called the consequent conscience.

78. If we judge an action before it is done or omitted, then we judge only whether it is good or bad or whether we ought to do it or not. . . . In the first case I call the conscience a "theoretical conscience"; in the second, a "practical conscience."[10] For in the first case, conscience merely gives us information about the constitution of the action. In the second, however, it moves us to do the action.

81. The pleasure and pain that we anticipate or receive from something usually mix in with motives, as do the feelings that either affect us or will affect us because of it.[11] If we do not rely on clear knowledge, we will become accustomed to distinguish the good through the pleasure it offers us. . . . But then man is in the condition of slavery, and so he is not really free.[12] Therefore one must distinguish whether the last judgment on which one relies occurs in the condition of complete freedom or, instead, in a condition of slavery. In the first case we call the conscience free, in the second, hampered.

83. If we note an action without the particular circumstances that can occur in special cases in which there is an opportunity to do or omit it, the consequences of the act can not only seem but also be different from what they would be if these circumstances did not have to be taken into account. Because we have to judge from the consequences whether acts are good or bad, better or worse, it can happen that under certain circumstances we have to recognize an act as bad that otherwise we would see to be good. . . . Now in such a case the practical conscience differs from the theoretical conscience, but we act according to the practical conscience. Then we act against the theoretical conscience.

And so it is clear that and when one can act against the theoretical conscience. We recognize the good, but when the opportunity comes to do it, we fail to do it. . . . Cause: because of special circumstances, we take the good for bad.[13]

90. Conscience is man's judgment of whether acts are good or bad. Whether acts are good or bad is judged by what consequences they bring concerning what is changeable in our or another's inner or outer circumstances. To know this, we need insight into the connection of truths. Because reason consists of insight into the connection of truths, it follows that conscience comes from reason. Man has a conscience because he has reason.

94. If we wish to be certain that our judgment agrees with other truths, nothing more will be needed than our putting the proof into rational form and earnestly investigating whether the matter and the form are correct. And in case some propositions are accepted from experience, when reason is not competent, we must assure ourselves of the experience. So demonstration is the means to decide whether or not conscience is right.

96. Thus it is possible to settle the question as to whose conscience is right, although this is difficult, as it is not an easy thing to obtain facility in demonstration. One can see immediately that this will not work for all people. For whoever cannot understand demonstrations will not be convinced by them. One can see also how necessary it is that those who should judge matters of conscience attain facility in demonstration. . . . If one reflects on the misery that erring consciences cause today, one will find what I say confirmed by experience.

97. Admittedly it is true that no one can get so far as to be able to judge good and bad in all cases, particularly under special circumstances; so occasionally probability will have to be enough. Only now do we recognize that up to this time no one has a right conscience in these matters. So as long as we cannot determine the degree of probability more precisely, without having a rational art of the probable, we must leave each to his own conscience. And because it is often a question of probability when we have to judge human actions, particularly under special circumstances, we can see how important it is to peace of conscience that the rational art of probability be brought into good condition.

112. Pangs of conscience are the unease that the consequent conscience gives us. The consequent conscience cannot make us uneasy except when it contradicts the antecedent conscience. But it cannot contradict except when the antecedent conscience is erroneous and uncertain. To avoid pangs of conscience, therefore, we must strive to act according to a right and certain conscience, or at least to one so attentive to probability that conscience excuses us.

136. Because conscience gives us considerable pain when we have done something bad and gives us pleasure and peace when we have done something good, and because pleasure and pain are among the motives, our conscience connects motives to good and bad actions. Consequently, it obliges us to do good acts and omit bad ones, that is, to do what makes us and our condition more perfect.

137. Now, because the law of nature also demands that we do what makes us and our condition more perfect, our conscience obligates us to direct our actions according to the law of nature. And so we can call the law of nature a law of conscience. But because conscience comes from reason, this law of conscience – and consequently the law of nature – is what our reason teaches. Hence the law of nature is called an expression of reason.

*Chapter 3: Of the Way in Which Man Can Attain the Highest Good or
His Blessedness on Earth*

139. The law of nature is the means by which man attains the happiness of which he is capable through his natural powers in this life. Now, because the law of nature requires the perfection of us and our condition and because this perfection is the final goal of all free action, man, wanting the happiness he

can achieve through his natural powers in this life, must set as the final goal of all his free actions the perfection of his inner and outer conditions. Hence he must not undertake anything but what leads immediately or mediately to this end, that is, what is a means to this goal.

140. In order not to undertake anything but what leads immediately or mediately to his final goal, he not only must have a certain goal in all his actions but must also connect all his special goals so that one is always a means to another and all together are a means to the main goal.

141. Because this knowledge is wisdom,[14] the man who connects his goals in the way described, plans wisely. . . .

146. Now, because man must direct his action so that everything can be seen as a means serving the perfection of his inner and outer conditions, he must be able to judge in every case whether or not his action serves this perfection. To be fit for this, it is necessary that he put all the perfections of man, that is, of soul and body, including his outer condition, into orderly classes, dividing them into genera and species. Similarly, all free actions, whether thoughts of the soul or motions of the body, and all outer things that man needs must be classified into genera and species. Moreover, he must investigate – from clear concepts of perfections and of acts and things for which he strives – those acts and things that forward the perfection of man. And finally, he must commit to memory the rules arising from this. . . .

148. If one is to derive rules from these grounds, one must have an aptitude for drawing unknown truths from known ones. The art of discovery is needed to do this, and because that art cannot operate without wit and understanding and especially ability at inference, all these also are needed.

150. Perhaps someone will wonder how it will go with the pursuit of good and the omission of bad if so much is required in order to distinguish good from bad. Here it will do to respond that we are now speaking only of those who are to generate from their own reflections the rules according to which men are to judge their free actions in the different conditions of life, that is, of the discoverers of the truths that belong to a doctrine of morals. But it is not necessary that all men be discoverers. It is enough if some among the learned devote themselves to discovery, whose findings the others can afterward learn, which is much easier.

The ingenuity necessary for discovery need not be all in one man but can be divided among different discoverers who live in quite different ages. This happens in all sorts of discoveries. In fact, if we in our time discover something new, it does not happen only through our ingenuity. Rather, the ingenuity of those who preceded us and discovered other things, on which our discoveries are based, also has a part in our discoveries and often a larger part than we ourselves have.

We shall, however, to the extent the present circumstances allow, permit ourselves to be directed to this work.

164. . . . The highest good is attained through observation of the law of nature. Consequently, whoever wants to attain it must have a powerful

desire to do nothing but what is in accordance with the law of nature and to do nothing contrary to it. He who wants to reach the goal must use the means.[15]

Chapter 4: On Recognizing Some General Rules of the Human Mind

190. We know that man can neither will nor refrain from willing, and therefore can neither act nor refrain from acting, without a motive. Now, because the motive of the will as well as that of the sensible desires is the representation of the good . . . and because if we are to judge whether something is good or bad a maxim[16] is required, man must have certain maxims or general rules according to which he directs his action, even if he himself does not clearly recognize this. Our present enterprise is to see how we uncover the maxims according to which we are accustomed to judge good and bad.

192. All pleasant feelings arise from unclear representations of good. . . . Accordingly, if man is affected by a feeling from some thing or situation, he must represent it as either good or bad. For this representation, however, a maxim is required, by which he is used to judging the good and bad. Experience shows him the constitution of the thing or situation; imagination brings the maxim to mind, according to which we judge whether something is good or bad; memory reassures us of it; and thereupon we represent the present thing or situation as good or bad. So, if we want to explain clearly what happens in the soul, we will find here a complete rational argument. The minor is the experience we have of the present thing or situation; the major, the general maxim according to which we judge; and the conclusion, the representation through which the feeling is aroused.

Part II: Of the Duties of Man Toward Himself

Chapter 1: Of the Duties of Man Toward Himself in General

221. By duty we understand an action that is in accordance with the law. Because there is no law without obligation, duties are actions that we are obligated to perform. And so we usually say "It is my duty to do this" when we mean that we are obligated to do it. . . .

222. The distinction of duties comes, accordingly, from the distinction of laws. And so "natural duty" means an action that is in accordance with the law of nature, or to which we as men are obligated through the law of nature. And now we shall discuss these.

223. Duties toward ourselves are those actions that man, because of the law . . . must undertake in relation to his own person. . . .

224. Because the law of nature requires that man do what will make him and his condition more perfect and not do what makes him and it less perfect, as long as man consists of soul and body, he must care for his soul as well as for his body and his outer condition. Hence we have three sorts of actions to

undertake for our own sake – some serving the perfection of our soul; some, the perfection of our body; the third, the perfection of our outer condition.

228. Man must promote the perfection of his soul, his body, and his outer condition. . . . so he must learn to know his soul and his body as well as his outer condition.

230. Because man is obligated to know himself, and a means to this is to be concerned about others, he is obligated to concern himself about others, that is, to pay close attention to them and their actions, so as to know what good is missing and what bad is being suffered.

233. Because not everyone is skilled at discovery and because one is not to live for oneself alone but to care also for others, those to whom God has lent the strength and opportunity to carry out this work better than others are obligated to share in books for the others what they have learned about the soul. From this urge there came what I have written in my *Reasonable Thoughts About God, the World, and the Human Soul* and what else I shall put in this book. . . .

242. With the three sorts of duties, the three sorts of good agree. Those things through which the condition of our soul is made more perfect are the goods of mind; those perfecting our body, the goods of body; [and] those perfecting our outer condition, the goods of fortune. . . .

243. . . . we are obligated to pursue the goods of fortune as well as those of mind and body.

Chapter 2: Of Duties Toward the Understanding

253. Now we come to the special duties of man and consider first the duties toward the soul. . . . In the soul we find understanding and will. So we must look at . . . duties toward the understanding and also duties toward the will. . . .

254. The understanding is the ability of the soul to represent clearly what is possible. Because the more perfect it is, the more things it can represent clearly and the more it will be capable of representing clearly what is in one thing, we are therefore obligated to do everything that promotes the number and clarity of representations and to omit what hinders this.

255. . . . so we must let no opportunity slip to acquire a concept of something or learn something and must seek as much knowledge as it is possible for us to get.

313. We can show quite generally that man is obligated to acuteness, facility in inference, the art of discovery, wit, the art of experiment, comprehension of language, and whatever else belongs to these perfections. For he is obligated to practice the good, that is, to do nothing but what makes his condition more perfect. Now, I have shown that if he is to be skillful in all cases in judging the properties of his action, he must possess acuteness, facility in inference, and the like. Who can doubt, then, that man is obligated to strive for these?

314. In the same way, it can be shown that each is obligated to strive for wisdom. . . .

315. . . . because we are obligated to wisdom, it follows in a new way that we also are obligated to knowledge.

Chapter 3: Of Duties Toward the Will

372. Perfection of the will is this: that man uses for motives the better among the goods he recognizes. Because he is obligated to make himself and his condition as perfect as possible, he must also strive to do nothing but the good and, among good things, the one that is better, and, consequently, to reject nothing but the bad and the less good.

373. Because the understanding must judge what is good and what among the good is better, the will is made more perfect or improved when man is led to a lively knowledge of the good. So the will can be improved only through the understanding. . . .

374. Perhaps some will think that experience shows daily how one can control the will in another way. . . . For we keep children from evil by taking away the opportunity to be bad, or we make them good by beatings if they cannot be won over by words. But although this means in its proper place has its uses – as many have shown – it still is certain that through it the will is not improved. . . . For the will is an inclination to a certain action. . . . It is not enough that we prevent man from following his inclinations. For if the inclination remains as it is, the will will not be improved. . . .

375. He who does the good out of clear knowledge, and out of clear knowledge omits the bad, does the good and omits the bad in complete freedom. Thus one does the good voluntarily when the will has been improved through the understanding. By contrast, when one needs other means to control the will . . . then one acts only out of fear of punishment or out of hope of a good . . . and so does the good . . . out of slavery as a servant of men. Out of need or out of an interest, one subordinates one's will to that of others and so becomes the others' servant. . . .

Part III: Of Duties of Man Toward God

Chapter 1: Of Duties Toward God in General

650. By duties toward God I understand the actions that man must undertake because of the law (and as we are speaking only of natural duties, because of the law of nature) in relation to God.

651. God is immutable and needs no external assistance to be what he is. So man cannot undertake anything through which God's perfection is promoted. Hence there remains nothing else but that he should recognize the perfections of God and make them the motives of his actions. Acts whose motive is the divine perfections are duties toward God.

652. He who acts and refrains so that his awareness of the perfections of God is his motive honors God. Because in relation to God we can do nothing else but act on the motive of his perfection, all duties to God consist in honoring him. Hence the main rule by which to judge duties to God is to honor God.

653. If man honors God, he uses the divine perfections as his motives. Then he must direct his actions so that from them it can be seen that he holds God to be as perfect a being as God is. For because men's actions are determined by their motives, one can come to see what the motives are by considering the actions. . . .

654. Man is also obligated by God to comply with the law of nature. Through this obligation God, like a good and loving father, shows his goodness and love to us. He who uses this knowledge as an additional motive to perform actions to which he is obligated by the law of nature honors God in all his actions and promotes his honor through all of them. From this one can see how man can eat, drink, work, and sleep for the honor of God.

671. He who wishes to be blessed [*gottseelig*] must direct all his acts to God's honor. . . . So a man who wishes to be blessed must think of God in all his actions. . . .

673. Blessedness is not a special virtue but constitutes a special degree of all virtues. Moderation, for example, is a virtue, but it reaches a higher degree when blessedness is added, so that one does not eat and drink moderately simply because of one's health and one's means but also to honor God. . . .

PART IV: OF THE DUTIES OF MAN TOWARD OTHERS

Chapter 1: Of the Duties of Man Toward Others in General

767. Man is obligated to make as perfect as his powers allow not only himself and his condition but also other men and their condition. And therefore he is obligated to undertake all acts through which he can promote the perfection of others and their condition. These acts consist of the observance of the law of nature, which is a means to happiness, and so man is obligated to do as much as he can for the happiness of others.

768. Duties toward others are those acts that man, because of the law, . . . must undertake toward others. Man must undertake for himself as well as for others such acts as make more perfect the inner condition of soul and body as well as the outer condition. Hence duties toward others are the same as duties toward self. What we owe to ourselves, we owe to others. I have shown in a previous part what man owes himself, and so we can immediately tell from that what we owe others. . . .

769. Whatever a man can do by his own powers, he does not need done for him by others. So we are not obligated to help him here. . . .

770. Only when a man does not have it in his power to do something to

which the law of nature obligates him, when it is in our power, are we bound to help him. . . .

772. The utility of these rules is great and extensive. For through them we can judge in all cases whether or not we are obligated to help someone. For example, we see that a man on the road has been attacked by a robber, who is robbing him and trying to kill him. We are by nature fearful and weak and, consequently, unfit to protect anyone. We must therefore be aware that [if we intervened] we would not save the victim but would be [put] in danger with him. Because we as well as the other are obligated to avoid all danger to life, and it is not in our power to run to his aid, we are not obligated to do so. One obligation cannot be opposed to another. By contrast, if we are hearty and strong, hence fit to protect ourselves against another, and are also provided with weapons . . . then it is in our power to help the other, and so we are obligated to do so. It is true that there is still some danger of being wounded, but because the danger to life for the other is greater than the danger of a wound, one must choose the lesser danger to avert the greater. . . .

774. Because man can will only the good, and the good is what makes us and our condition more perfect and consequently brings pleasure, man wills only what brings pleasure. Hence if he should will another's happiness, he must be prepared to receive pleasure from it and accordingly to love the other.[17] Now he is obligated to will the happiness of others; hence he is also obligated to love others.

775. Because we should derive as much pleasure out of another's happiness as out of our own, we are obligated to love others as ourselves. . . .

796. Man is obligated to love others as himself. He who loves another as himself . . . sees the other's happiness as his own and the other as himself. So we are obligated to see others as if they were one person with us. Therefore one should not set oneself above others.

Chapter 2: Of Duties Toward Friends and Enemies

834. Friends love us and are led by this to care for our well-being as much as they can. Works of love are called benefits, and accordingly friends strive to benefit us. Because we are obligated to love all men as ourselves, we owe the most love to those who benefit us. . . . The love of the benefactor is called gratitude, and so we should be grateful to our benefactor.

863. I must here remind everyone that in this book we consider man outside civic society, insofar as each lives freely for himself without being subordinated to any other, that is, in natural freedom. By natural freedom we understand a condition in which man in his actions depends on no one else or in which no one is justified in limiting the freedom of others through his will. In this condition, various things can be right that in civic life or in the commonwealth would be wrong. Although we do not now live in natural freedom, it is not idle to consider what is right in natural freedom. For one thing, it is certain that great lords live among themselves in natural freedom, and so in

their actions toward one another they must be judged accordingly. Second, the commonwealth does not cancel natural freedom but only limits it. I cannot understand the limitation, however, if I do not first know what things have what properties in the condition of natural freedom. Even the limitations do not cancel natural freedom, and hence many acts remain as before in the natural condition. Through the limitation, things are not altered, but more comfortable ways arise for acquiring them, whereas in natural freedom this is done only with difficulty. . . . Natural freedom is the standard of the commonwealth. If one wants to judge in it what is good or bad, one must always seek the grounds in natural freedom. In this small point there is contained a great insight into the commonwealth and the whole of statecraft.

Chapter 4: Of the Duties of Men in Speech and in Contracts

1003. An expression with which one affirms to another that one will do something is called a promise. Because man is obligated to perform certain actions, namely, to do what is good in itself, he may not promise to do anything except what is good. . . .

1004. If we promised to do what is bad, our promise is wrong, and because the law of nature cannot be altered, we still have after our promise the obligation we had before we made it. Because we must then violate either the law of nature or the promise, it is clear that we must violate the latter. . . .

1005. If we promise to do something good, we must keep our promise, because in any case we should do it, even if we had not promised.[18]

1006. Sometimes it happens that we promised something that we later find unprofitable and that we therefore should not have promised. In such a case, if we should fail to keep the promise, the other would suffer harm and annoyance, which by the law of nature we should not cause him. But because one of two things has to happen – either we keep our promise or we violate it – there must be an exception to one of these rules. The exception should be such that the greatest agreement with the law of nature is maintained in the action. So one has to inquire what will follow in both cases, if one keeps the promise or one breaks it. If the outcome is less against the law of nature, that is what should be done; but if the outcome is more at odds with that law, then it should not be done.

1022. Man is obligated to show everyone as much good as possible and so to evince as much goodness as he can. He is also obligated to [show] wisdom, and therefore his conduct should be orderly, so that each of his actions contains in itself the ground of the next. Therefore, he must not do anything that he does not find a sufficient reason to do in his preceding action. This must also be observed when one does good for another. One's goodness therefore must be directed by the rules of wisdom. And goodness directed by the rules of wisdom, or goodness agreeing with wisdom, is what we customarily call justice, and accordingly, it is clear that we should be just.

1023. Consequently, as often as we have dealings with others, and so in the agreements and contracts we make with them, we must be just and also show ourselves to be good and wise. And thus it will no longer be hard, as it may appear to be if we consider goodness alone. Goodness also will not mislead us so that we deny someone something that belongs to him. This is because love, from which goodness comes, makes us bestow all good on each person, but wisdom makes us give good to those to whom it belongs and forget neither ourselves for others nor others for ourselves. Thus justice gives to each what is his and is his due, regardless of the person. From this one can see that justice is nothing but goodness directing itself according to wisdom. For everyone recognizes that it is proper to justice that each should keep his own.[19] But this cannot occur through man's free will without external force, including the fear of punishment, except when man is good with wisdom, as I have shown.

1024. We see, accordingly, that he who wants to be just must act not only according to upright love but also according to wisdom and so according to knowledge. The more that love and wisdom come together, the greater will be the justice. The two must exist together. When love exists alone, much often happens that is unjust. Those we love obtain good and also what is properly others'. Love also leads us to do what is not proper and to omit what should be done. When wisdom is added, we no longer act through the mere drive of love, but we attend to the grounds for each act. We look at the constitution of things and not elsewhere for the grounds for our having this or that attitude toward people. Because I have shown throughout this work what sorts of grounds the actions of man have, and have thereby pointed toward an upright love, I do not doubt that through it one may achieve justice, which I wish to everyone from my heart!

Editor's Notes

1. Wolff's term is *Weltweisheit* ("worldly wisdom"), which he usually contrasts with *Gottesgelehrtheit* ("learning about God," or "theology"). Wolff's work appeals only to natural reason, not to revelation. It is for theologians to show how this treatment of morality is to be interpreted by Christians.
2. In the *Metaphysics* §197 Wolff explained that whatever belongs to thought belongs to the self and that nothing else does. For Wolff, thought includes confused as well as clear ideas, and perceptions and feelings are confused ideas.
3. Wolff explained freedom in the *Metaphysics*. Several conditions combine to make an action free: "§514 . . . 1. that we understand or distinctly conceive the constitution of the action. . . . §515. . . . 2. that the actions that we call free are not simply necessary, because what is contrary to them is equally possible. . . . §518 . . . 3. that the soul has within itself the ground of actions that we usually called voluntary. For the representations that it needs as motives are contained in it and come from it, and it inclines itself through its own power toward the thing that pleases it. . . . §519. If we take all this together, it will be clear that freedom is nothing but the power of the soul through its will to choose what most pleases it, from two equally possible things, to neither of which it is determined by either its own nature or by something external." Wolff added in §521 that "it is not to be denied that a man who recognizes something as better cannot possibly prefer the worse;

so it necessarily occurs that he chooses the better. But this necessity does not oppose freedom. For the man is not forced by it to choose the better, because he could choose the worse if he wished, as both are possible in themselves. . . . And from my *Thoughts About the Actions of Men* . . . it can be seen that without this sort of necessity (which has been called moral necessity) there would be no hope for certainty in morality."

4. What lies behind this claim is Wolff's Leibnizian belief that all of the contents of the mind are ideas, of varying degrees of clarity and distinctness. Even feelings and desires are ideas; they are indistinct representations of good and bad. The will is also ideational. Because the soul or mind is what is distinctive about man, and the soul can do nothing but know – more or less clearly – a teleological argument assuming that our distinctive features show us what God meant us to do leads to the conclusion that our function is to know.

5. In *Metaphysics* §157 Wolff defined perfection: "The agreement of the manifold constitutes perfection. For example, we judge the perfection of a watch by its ability to show correctly the hour and its divisions. It [the watch] is made of many parts assembled together, and these as well as the assembly are aimed at enabling the hands to tell correctly the hour and its divisions. Thus in a watch we find a multitude of things all of which agree with one another. . . . The conduct of man consists of many actions, and if these all agree with one another, so that they all are finally grounded in one general goal, then the conduct of man will be perfect."

6. In *Metaphysics* §496 Wolff observed that there must be a sufficient reason for anything to occur or fail to occur. In the case of an act of will the reason, or ground, is the perception of good or evil. Hence such perceptions are what move the will.

7. A technical notion. Wolff explained it in the *Metaphysics* §206 ff.: We have a distinct idea of something when we can distinguish its parts, so that if asked we can explain them to another. The more parts within parts that we discover, the higher the degree of distinctness our idea will have.

8. One could also say that a motive binds someone to do something or that through a motive one is bound to do it, but for consistency I use the word "obligate" throughout this translation.

9. Wolff here refers to Rom. 2:14–15.

10. In German, these would be a "teaching" and a "moving" conscience, but Wolff gives Latin equivalents for his German in an appendix, and I have followed the Latin.

11. Pleasure, pain, and feelings are confused ideas. Wolff here is showing how confused ideas come into our motivation, along with clear ideas of the constitution of an action.

12. In the *Metaphysics* §491 Wolff stated: "In emotion man does not think what he is doing, and so he does not have his actions in his control. He is, as it were, forced to do what he otherwise would not do. Because the emotions come from the senses and imagination, the mastery of the senses, imagination, and emotions is the slavery of man. And one calls slaves those who let their emotions rule and who remain with the unclear knowledge of the senses and imagination."

13. Wolff went on to spell out several other ways in which one can act against conscience in its various aspects.

14. Wolff is referring us to his *Metaphysics,* §914, where he defined wisdom as the knowledge of how to connect goals so that one serves as means to another, and of how to choose means so that they lead to our ends.

15. Having earlier discussed the difficulties of obtaining precise rules that will cover widely varying circumstances, in the rest of this chapter Wolff talks about ways of keeping one's desire clear and strong for the ultimate goal.

16. Wolff is referring us to the *Metaphysics* §337, where he explained that we form rules about classes of cases, by generalizing from one case and then seeing that we can apply the generalization to another.
17. Love is defined in the *Metaphysics* §449 as "readiness to receive pleasure from another's happiness."
18. Wolff is referring here to §9: his thought is that because we should bring about good, we should do so regardless of our promise to bring about the good.
19. Wolff gives here his account of the commonplace that justice is the constant will to give each his own (*suum cuique tribuere*), a formula derived from Roman law.

Further Reading

To the best of my knowledge there is nothing in English on Wolff's practical philosophy or his ethics. There is, indeed, relatively little in English about any of Wolff's thought. The best general review of his philosophy is that by Lewis White Beck, *Early German Philosophy* (Cambridge, Mass.: Harvard University Press, 1969), which contains a bibliography of secondary material. Wolff is treated briefly in John Herman Randall, *The Career of Philosophy,* vol. 2 (New York: Columbia University Press, 1965), and in Frederick Coplestone S.J., *A History of Philosophy,* vol. 6 (New York: Doubleday, 1964). Richard J. Blackwell translated Wolff's *Preliminary Discourse on Philosophy in General* (Indianapolis: Bobbs-Merrill, 1963), which will give the reader a good idea of Wolff's vision of the way in which philosophy should be systematic and of the place in his system for practical philosophy. Blackwell also wrote a useful article on this subject: "The Structure of Wolffian Philosophy," *The Modern Schoolman,* 38 (1961): 203–18.